"There is so mucl

- Joan Peters, "From Time Immei.

Arab-Jewish Conflict Over Palestine." [1]

"Philistine-To-Palestine"

Copyright © Joseph D. Shellim 2014.

Immense appreciation for permissions granted for limited usage of the copyright works, images & services of:

• Ambassador Alan Baker; 'The Legal Basis of Israel's Rights, JCPA.

• American-Israeli Cooperative Enterprise.

• Bob Siegel; 'The Historical truths behind the Israel-Palestine conflict' [Commdiginews].

• CAMERA [Committee for Accuracy in Middle-East Reporting in America].

• Frantz Kantor Productions [Illustrations; Art].

• Greenger, Nurit. [Translation].

• Jewish Virtual Library.

• Mechon Mamre Org. The English-Hebrew Bible.

• Steven Shamrak ['Food For Thought'/History].

• Cover Image Andrea Vaccaro, Italian [LACMA].

Disclaimer. The portrayals in this manuscript are not representative of any theological or national sectors, groups or persons and are derived from independent personal research and interpretations of historical archives by the author.

Also From Shhhh! Studios

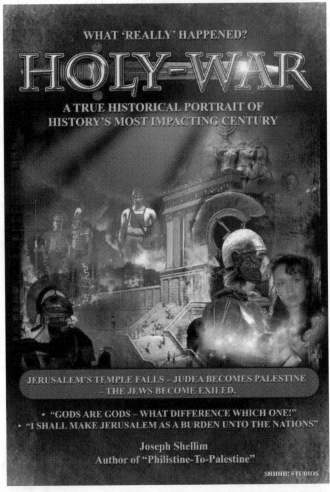

WHAT 'REALLY' HAPPENED?

HOLY-WAR

A TRUE HISTORICAL PORTRAIT OF
HISTORY'S MOST IMPACTING CENTURY

JERUSALEM'S TEMPLE FALLS – JUDEA BECOMES PALESTINE
– THE JEWS BECOME EXILED.

- "GODS ARE GODS – WHAT DIFFERENCE WHICH ONE!"
- "I SHALL MAKE JERUSALEM AS A BURDEN UNTO THE NATIONS"

Joseph Shellim
Author of "Philistine-To-Palestine"

SHHHH! STUDIOS

> "No Library is complete without this book - every page astounds. I never wanted it to end." - [Stanley Joseph - Director, Producer, Composer].

> "I could not put it down to take a breath" - [K. Solo - Middle East History].

> "I literally felt I was experiencing the events that have influenced our world to this day. Exhilarating!" - [Gregory James Green - Writer/Director].

> "I'm proud of the people of Israel who in the moment of truth knew what was important" - [Benjamin Netanyahu, Prime Minister of Israel, Chairman of the Likud Party. [Twitter Quote]

- "Gods Are Gods – What Difference Which One?" Vespasian to the Jews.
  [Selected For Best Loglines/Festival for Drama in Film Screenplays]

PHILISTINE
-TO-
PALESTINE

- A 4,000 Year Historical Treatise.

Israel has never occupied another people's land in all her 4,000 year recorded history; Israel is the world's most accused country of illegally occupying another peoples' land.

Flinders Petrie

"This stele will be better known in the world than anything else I have found." - Flinders Petrie; Archaeologist; discoverer of The Merneptah Israel Stele, 1896.

• <u>Left</u>. The first time the name <u>Israel</u> (Yisrael) is found outside of the Bible; "The Merneptah Stele" [aka Israel Stele], dated Early 13th Century BCE (1213 to 1203 BCE).

• <u>Centre</u>. The first time the name <u>Hebrew</u> (Hibiru) is found outside the Bible; "The Amarna Letters", 14th Century BCE (1350s - 1330s BCE).

• <u>Right</u>. The first time the name <u>David</u> is found outside of the Bible; "Tel Dan Stele", late 9th Century BCE, mentions "House of David" (*bytdwd/Beth David*).[2]

[Tel Dan inscription. דן תל כתובת in the Israel Museum in Jerusalem/GNU FDL "Samuel and Saidye Bronfman Archaeology Wing DSCN5105" by Yoav Dothan - self made. Licensed under GFDL/ Merneptah-Israel Stele, licensed under the Creative Commons Attribution-Share Alike 3.0 Unported]

Table of Contents

Foreword

"What if I told you Israel has never occupied another people's land in all her 3,000 year recorded history?"

Britain is one of history's greatest nations. In 1917 Britannia Ruled. Both conqueror and elevator of many distant lands, triumphant in two World Wars, Britain was duly handed the Mandate Caretaker role of the Middle East. Thereby, Britain inherits foremost merit. But also foremost onus; the 20th Century was the 'baddest' one in all recorded human history.

There was a World War, the Armenian Genocide, a Holocaust, India lost 1/3rd of her lands, Palestine lost 80% of the land originally allocated for 'one only state for the Jews'. How do the deeds and miss-deeds of the previous century impact the world's future politics, history and theologies, and continuing in that path?

The Middle-East conflicts began early. In 1920, large deposits of oil reserves were discovered in Arabia; Britain's PM accounted Britain's follow-up deeds thus:
• "What a heinous, collective crime of history! An act of national perfidy which will dishonor the name of Britain" - (Lloyd George, the Prime Minister of Great Britain; national radio speech.)

Causes and Effects must apply for the 21st Century's extended worldly chaos and mayhem. Great nations can perform both Positive and Negative deeds:

In 1920, Britain 'altered' the Balfour Declaration texts to include a "Historic 2-State Compromise in Palestine" and removed 80% of its landmass that became Jordan. This land's division was regarded both heinous and illegal; Balfour did not envisage partitions. It became the first cause of today's irresolvable and extending global issue - even after it was accepted by the overwhelmed Jews.

In 1939, Britain issued two White Papers - one with Hitler for Europe and one with Hajj Amin al-Husseini for Arabia. Both targeted the Jews.

In 1950, Britain supported a 3-State in Palestine west of the river that was illegally annexed by Jordan. The 3,000 year names of Hebrew towns like Bethlehem and Nazareth of Judea became Arabic; the land was also given a new name as the West Bank. This became the '3-State' in Palestine, now accounted as a '2-state'.

In 1964, Britain promoted the name 'Palestinian' – after first rejecting a demand by the Arab peoples not to use this name. It was a name exclusively held by the Jews for 2,000 years, and was transferred to the Arab people in 1947; it overturned all of Britain's previous treaties and pledges. It can stand as the loudest and most blatant historical falsehood in the modern world today.

In 2015, Britain promoted a new region called East Jerusalem as not part of Israel; it contradicted the history and scriptures of three belief systems.

• **"Occupied Palestinian Territories**. This oft-used term is totally inaccurate and false. The territories are neither occupied nor Palestinian. Claims by the UN, European capitals, organizations and individuals that Israeli settlement activity is in violation of international law therefore have no legal basis whatsoever." - [Courtesy of Israel's Ambassador to Canada and Negotiator in Peace Agreements with Egypt, Jordan and Lebanon, Alan Baker; 'The Legal Basis of Israel's Rights; courtesy JCPA Org].

How much don't you know of the world's most controversial issue? These are examples of the suppressed and de-classified archives you will find in this book:

• **"The original text of the [1917] Balfour Declaration** had read "Palestine should be reconstituted as the National Home of the Jewish people." The text was changed to read "the establishment in Palestine of a Home for the Jewish people." The single word "in" was used subsequently to justify removing all of Transjordan from the British

Mandate that resulted from the Balfour Declaration. - [President of Israel, Chaim Weizmann, Trial and Error, 1949, p 257]

• **The British-Hitler-Hajj Amin Deal**: "Germany will destroy the entire Jewish people from Europe till the Southern end of Caucasia; then the fuehrer will give Al-Husseini, appointed as Grand Mufti of Jerusalem by Britain, the sole authority to destroy all Jews in the Middle-East." - [Minutes of the meeting; Memorandum of an official of the FM Secretariat in the presence of Reich Minister Grobba in Berlin [fuh 57a.g.Rs; Berlin, Nov 30, 1941].

• **"A Division of Destroyers** was being employed to ascertain that those who had escaped Hitler did not escape the British capture as they approached Palestine. - [Mr. Malcolm Mac-Donald, the Colonial Secretary, PRO House of Commons Debates, July 20, 1939].

• "The oft-used term "occupied Palestinian territories" is totally inaccurate and false. The territories are neither occupied nor Palestinian. Claims by the UN, European capitals, organizations and individuals that Israeli settlement activity is in violation of international law therefore have no legal basis whatsoever." - [Courtesy of Israel's Ambassador to Canada and Negotiator in Peace Agreements with Egypt, Jordan and Lebanon, Alan Baker; 'The Legal Basis of Israel's Rights; courtesy JCPA Org.]

"Philistine-To-Palestine" is not a politically correct or a fundamentalist presentation. It accounts the modern world's most controversial and shrouded issue, one that has extended globally across the nations. That Palestine was never a local issue of land occupation has become manifest today; the trajectories that stem from Israel have widespread impacts on humanity's history, theologies and politics. There was a disruptive underlying agenda here that Britain either failed to foresee, or had adverse designs; it is time these are confronted for the benefit of all.

The historical imposition of the name Palestine and its derivative adjective Palestinian have not worked, and there is much to learn by its errors. Here, even when the ground talked none hearkened; the omen of the Dead Sea Scrolls was hidden away, its message flaunted. Thereby did the greatest deceptions of the modern world become covered and shrouded. Yet its effects grew and extended; its intended impacts backfired on all sectors. Perhaps the world is driving on the wrong lane of this highway?

Now, long suppressed and de-classified archives, secret British and Middle East files, revealing interviews and 3,000 year population surveys, will arouse reconsideration. Whatever your views, this book can arm you with the issues that have been shrouded and deflected. A 4,000 journey unfolds the historical, theological and political encumbrances the world has accumulated from past errors; these have been placed on the shoulders of new generations left without adequate information. It requires un-covering.

Now, the message is made accessible to all via a clickable E-book read; and should it be seen as compelling, a printed book edition will act as an armory of information in your library - for keepsake. More than half of its pages act as an almanac of 100's of quotes - from Presidents, Kings, Sultans, Emirs, Scholars, Theologians, Clerics, Prime Ministers, Ambassadors, Authors, Talk Show Hosts, Human Rights Advocates and Bloggers. It will cause debate; it may even change one's views. Also included are 40 compelling historical images.

In the new age of mass communication all is open; the history of the world's most controversial conflict can untangle us. Only when this history is fully opened to all and confronted; un-covered and un-shrouded. This is one such endeavour.

About. As a documentary film writer for 25 years I produced a diverse range of subjects such as Making Movies, Trial At Nuremberg, Deep Space Encounters, and biographical films of The Beatles and James Dean. In 2014, I published "Holy-War" [Alternate title "Ben Hur II - Exile"], a historical depiction what really happened following the crucifixion of Jesus in history's most impacting century. Un-Published: I wrote the screenplay for "Staying Alive! The Brigitte Gabriel Story". I am currently working on 'Emanation" and "Yulla!"

Thank you,
Joseph Shellim.

"How has Bethlehem my birthplace become as West Bank - have you not read the Gospels!"

- **The Gospels**. "But you, Bethlehem, in the land of Judah, are by no means least among the rulers of Judah; for out of you will come a ruler who will shepherd my people Israel." [Matthew 2:6]

- **The Quran**. "Allah assigned Israel to the Jews (Sura 5 Verse 21); Jews are the inheritors of Israel (Sura 26 Verse 59).

Act 1.
The Power of a Name.

1. WHAT'S IN A NAME?

Have you considered it?

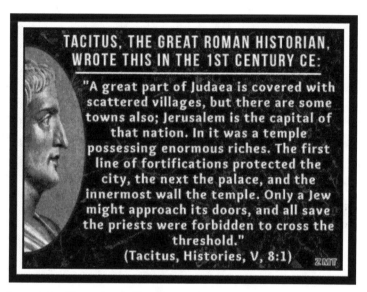

TACITUS, THE GREAT ROMAN HISTORIAN, WROTE THIS IN THE 1ST CENTURY CE:

"A great part of Judaea is covered with scattered villages, but there are some towns also; Jerusalem is the capital of that nation. In it was a temple possessing enormous riches. The first line of fortifications protected the city, the next the palace, and the innermost wall the temple. Only a Jew might approach its doors, and all save the priests were forbidden to cross the threshold."
(Tacitus, Histories, V, 8:1)

'**Judea**' was the Roman name for 'Land of Judah'; one previously called as 'Land of Israel'. These names are recorded in a host of archives, including those of the ancient Egyptians, the Hebrew Bible, the Gospels, the writings of the Greeks and the Romans, and the Dead Sea Scrolls. They are also seen in a vast array of archaeological relics and coins, and acknowledged in the Quran as the land of the Jews. (1 Samuel 13:19; Matt.2:20; Qur'an 5:21; "The Merneptah Stele" dated 13th Century BCE) [3]

'**Palestine**' is the name the Roman Empire applied to Judea in the 2nd Century (135 AD/CE). Thereafter, both the names Palestine and its derivative Palestinian became the symbols referred exclusively to the Jews and their historical connection to their homeland. It is seen in the

British, French, American and Arab documents, including by the previous Ottomans and the Arab Chieftain Emir Faisal in 1917.[4]

Question: How then did this name come to represent the antithesis of the 'Land of Israel' 2,000 years later in the 1960's?

It is not a provocative or controversial question; it is an incumbent one today and the examination premise of this book. The question raised is perhaps the modern world's singularly most impacting and perplexing historical conundrums incurred by a name. Its trajectories have extended globally, across humanity, history, theologies, ideologies and politics. The hallowed offices and thinkers are left entangled in their lands and not knowing where to turn. All are rendered overwhelmed and inadequate; all can see it. Here, the 'WHY?' factor becomes the most compelling.

The underlying factors of the world's # 1 reported issue are also the most shrouded. The name Palestine's focus has shifted to its extended outgrowth across the nations. Embedded in this name's underbelly are manifold layers of controversy and past errors that none have been able to resolve. It won't be resolved in this presentation. The price was always seen as too high. What was not seen was the rejection of its resolving was even higher; and the modern world is now entrapped in its global warp.

The indications are that we have clearly been driving on the wrong side of this highway. There are anticipations of a crash scene on the horizon, of end of days scenarios, even of world wars. More accurately, there has never been a time of greater chaos and mayhem in the modern world, including with our foremost ruling quarters of power and our most esteemed pundits.

Now, perhaps it is time to offer some bold re-considerations; there have been errors that have been shrouded too long. Such is not an exposure for contention, for there is enough of that engulfing the modern world today. Ultimately, it is a long due and required re-consideration for the benefit of all people and nations everywhere. Humanity's inter-contentious groupings envisage a negative future, one resigned to unquestionably.

Palestine, an isolated, barren notch of a land, became a global monstrosity by events and deeds incurred in the 20th Century, resulting in the world's most volatile and irresolvable hotspot. Yet there is no credible reasoning for such a diabolical result; what price a few cubits

14

of land that cannot be seen on a map; or maybe land has nothing to do with this conflict's unappeasable angst?

Thereby, this investigative journey will thread with due caution, yet without withholding historically credible manifestations. A means to un-shroud the shrouded in the new age of communication that is irrepressible. It will begin by unraveling and deciphering the original basis of this issue via its historical veracity, both ancient and modern, via the utilization of a 'name'. Because a name matters; it is an identification mark uniquely attached to humans. A name has much to tell who we are and of our history; we are each accounted by our names. In our new lexicon a name holds our metadata. The same applies for nations.

Palestine is a complicated and compelling name. In rendering this presentation more than opinions, a host of quotes, scholarly opinions and legal archives merit their due consideration; these are culled from a diverse array of sources that are historical, theological and judicial; of both ancient and recent vintage, and from the vox populi opinions and popular blogs of our pedestrian sources. The factors appear more intriguing than they are complicated, because they impact one and all, here and there; the stats presented can act as collectables and an armory of knowledge how to proceed. Because the subject matter is controversial and open to intense debate, the historical references can also facilitate any chapter's individual dissection without re-reading the entire book again. Thereby, some of these archives may be necessarily repeatable where multiple contexts apply; these have been reduced to limited occurrences by its focused re-editing.

This assessment will minimize the aligning of gratuitous theological and political impartations by utilizing factors supplemented by their historical veracity throughout; its aim to rationalize this conflict by an empirically validated and affirmable accounting. Here, any applicable religiosity factors, a most impacting consideration of this region, will be presented as 'theological'. As well, long suppressed and de-classified archives will be included; they manifest new, variant dispositions than the held. Thereby the reader may draw their own conclusions based on independent and personal investigations of the factors presented herein; some are controversial.

It is unavoidable that certain factors in this presentation will be presented as 'deceptions' where the historical misappropriation appears blatant. However, to see such a term as focusing on any peoples or any beliefs will be a miss-representation of its application. The term 'deception' is rather a focus on the underlying paradigms they arose from and of measuring their veracity against validated, empirical history. This is especially so when a belief infringes on historical validity, ancestry, nativity and heritage name marks; they become as existential issues based on manipulations and distortions of the truth known or held by many. Thereby, historical veracity will be measured as the most appropriate truths; it necessarily has to transcend all our mutually exclusive beliefs.

'Palestinian' is an adjective derived from the name Palestine; yet the twain do not meet anymore. While Palestine was allotted only as a stateless 'region' for 2,000 years, Palestinian became a people in the 20th Century. In the modern world a name is afforded legal protection, its abuse can lead to charges of slander and identity theft. Today, the name Palestine has outlived its statutory period of protection. Now, only its historical, moral and political applications remain for our investigative consideration. Also, as will be seen later, its future impacts are applicable far away from Palestine per se.

Names can also act as a mighty weapon of war; it can turn humanity's paradigms without the use of a single shot being fired. Inevitably, the name Palestinian became a powerful political implement. Today, the name Palestinian bestows for one what it negates for another; factors of heritage, nativity and land occupation are its attachments; also much commercial impacts. Then there is the inescapable phenomenon of 'belief', the ruling implement crouched and hidden behind all other factors.

Names Matter.

Thereby, the *when, how* and *why* did the name Palestinian become transferred from one group to another in the 20th Century, and assumed upon itself the name that was applied to another group for 2,000 years, becomes a compelling historical journey. It says either a heritage transfer occurred from one people to another, or else its reverse phenomenon occurred, whereby a lost one was restored back to its original people. But whose; and how did such a phenomenon occur; why; and what difference does it make? These become critically impacting investigative factors in the pursuit of historical truth and its impacts in the extending chaos and mayhem of the current and future times. Causes and effects apply.

16

Historically, the change of name phenomenon is not unusual. It occurred 2,000 years ago when the Romans changed the name of Judea to Palestine; and 4,000 years ago when Abram was changed to Abraham; and again when Jacob's name was changed to Israel. Then Jesus became the anglicized Latin name of the Hebrew Yeshua. Those names were history-turning game changers. It happened again last century. Palestine, which was Judea, the Roman name for the 'Land of the Jews' became the Modern State of Israel, as was its name 3,000 years ago. It caused a dire upheaval. Israel's return became an affront. Such is the power of a name.

In the ancient realm name changes acted as blessings and curses, war and peace treaties, protection and extermination provisions. Certainly, this name's history is not attended in most school history lessons, its past connection with the Home of the Jews never mentioned in mainstream media, allowing the new generation and most of the population limited to politically driven news stories. These are not always representative of real history. One thing the Jews did not steal or illegally occupy from another people is the name 'Palestine' or its derivate adjective Palestinian.

Two thousand years after Rome changed the name of Judea to Palestine, its reverse syndrome happened in the Mid-20th Century - it became the antithesis of itself. Those Jews who were enlisted in the British forces of WW2 and named as the 'Jewish Palestinian Brigade', ceased being called as Palestinians after the 1960's. Another people became the Palestinians and it ushered a controversy in the modern world.

Yet prior to 1960, both the names Palestine and Palestinian were held exclusively by the Jews and their historical national home; one even detested in the scorched environment of Arabia. Fifty years ago, the name Palestinian was akin to Zionist, one not embraced in the Middle East realms. Yet it turned full circle thereafter; suddenly; within a mere thirty years.

Thereby, how much does a name matter is nowhere more impacting for consideration. How about, it resulted in the world's most irresolvable conflict, and its chaos has only just begun to unfold before the nations, underlying the omens of its future consequences. Or how about, it is related to a minuscule patch of land and people in the Middle East, but its impact crosses all borders today. How about, No-Go Zones are a mode of West Banks and 2-state claims for peace, as paradigms that can travel globally across all nations' borders. It has. Now it does matter; now that is interesting. Even alarming.

Thus, measuring this name's historical impacts is not a hypothetical phenomenon anymore; it has become the world's # 1 issue and a legitimate examination of the times. Names matter when used as weapons of war. It proved as Mighty Rome's greatest attack on the Jews when Judea was named as Palestine; it was more destructive than all other weapons of Rome. It happened again 2,000 years later. And it's not limited to one people or nation anymore.

Consider the impacts on Christianity, the world's largest religious group. Is Jesus of Nazareth from Judea or a Palestinian from the West Bank? And what of the true heritage of the Arab people now laden with the names West Bank and Palestinian; what historical disruptions do they incur of their history? Like an ecosystem, altering historical names in one sector has extending trajectories elsewhere; there is no immunity any place. Mighty Rome well understood it and used it as a weapon that proved mightier than all her legions.

Today, the impacts of ancient historical name changes allow both the Christian and the Arab peoples' history to become re-appraised in its sweep. Here, changing the reference of the name Palestine will require all historical and biblical archives to be altered, or at the very least qualified with new additional footnotes; prayer chants and psalms will also need poetic adjustments; maps will require re-drafting. It is a process well underway.

Clearly, the transfer of the name Palestinian from Jews to Arabs alters the world's history; its impacts are extensive and global. If past history can be changed by a name, John Doe can cease to be John Doe and the Eifel Tower not wholly French anymore; these icons are recent relative to Palestine. It works as a paradigm altering syndrome brewing under humanity's feet. What seemed as circumstantial and as political maneuvers in the 20th Century hid a stratagem missed by all, including by the Jews who saw no issue in discarding the name Rome applied as a mark of disdain and annihilation of both the Hebrew and the emerging Christian infrastructures. But Rome's re-enactment in the 20th Century is not a strategy limited to the Jews anymore; it is impacting all in the Middle East and the nations globally. In the big picture the usurping of the name Palestinian disrupts Christianity and the Arab sectors more so than it does the Jews or Israel; certainly, it has crossed borders afar.

18

So why were these name changes implemented and what were its larger motives, becomes incumbent to all. Although having enormous impacts, it is the least debated factor in the discourse, rendered irrelevant, a throw away vexation and deemed as inconsequential. Yet let's just take a walk down this history to see how inconsequential it is not. This conflict is not about a notch of land. Never was. 'What's in a name' has never been more impacting in the modern world than that of Palestine and its derivative adjective Palestinian.

A Global Chaos.

Today, one name marks as the most pivotal issue of an unfolding globalized conflict of chaos and mayhem, to the extent the conflict almost disappears without this name's acceptance. A thread connects all of today's global upheavals arising from one source point. One ancient name impacted history 2,000 years ago and it has again emerged; this time piercing the nations across the seas. It is not the first time this name turned history and it is not inconsequential, nor can its global impacts quell unless attended. The matter is hinged on a fulcrum point expanding both ways, to our past and our future histories.

In The Beginning.

This iconic name's unraveling and future impacts involve a 4,000 year journey of exploration. It will be accounted by a concise division of ancient and modern history, its transitory impacts between those two phases, and its infiltration syndrome into today's prevailing chaos. Thereby, this name's veracity and its original source is the first step of an investigative thread. A host of icons will be confronted in its pathways and some controversies will arise. Much will be arousing, some un-covered for the first time and thus far missing from the discourse of the world's most reported issue. Prepare yea; it is a jolting, bumpy ride on history's most turbulent pathway, one that turned humanity as no other. It is best begun with 'In the beginning' - back to the ancient history-turning name *Palestine.*

An Ancient Name Returns.

In the early 20th Century the Arabs convinced the British that the name of this land should be Palestina, from the Arabic version of the name Filastin and the Greek Syria-Palestina, and not from the Roman Judea ('Land of the Jews'/Latin). The Jews insisted on the traditional Hebrew name Eretz Israel (Land of Israel); arguing the term Filastin is a later copy of a name introduced in the Hebrew Bible. Thereby, in the modern world this land became anglicized as Palestine, one re-enacted by the British, and as Eretz Israel for the Jews. The impacts of this name became a controversy as no other in history, asking, does historical veracity depend on a name, or the other way round. Here, the 'when' factor of this ancient name's origin is well established.

Palestine is the name of an ancient people introduced in the Hebrew Bible and called as the Philistines; it is today the name attached to the Arab peoples in the regions called as Israel, West Bank and Jordan. Palestine is a small landmass in the Middle East, yet its impacts belie its size. Here, a new paradigm occurred in the 1960's; the Arabs in Palestine self anointed themselves as Palestinians, claiming a time-immemorial history. It assumed an antithetical or counter employ of the Jews who previously held this name since the Roman reign some 2,000 years ago.

Thereby, what was the reasoning behind this recent name transfer that it hovers so large, one supported by the world's nations, including leading figures of Christianity and Islam in contradiction of their own scriptures and historical positions. Equally, why do a few figureheads of high prominence of the world's two largest religions reject the premise altogether?

If the Jews were called by this name previously, and it was once disdained by the Arabs, the enigma is only further compounded. Here, there appears a fastidious refraining from any reference to the origins of this name in the discourse. Politicians, kings, queens, political and religious groups and the media refrain from mentioning this name's previous employ; as if it has no relevance anymore. The term Palestinian has become an evocative emblem of rage, hovering as a dark cloud always on the verge of an erupting tsunami. Thereby, tracking this name's origins and history is essential of its global reasoning. Wherein did it all begin?

The Source.

Both the names Philistine and Arab were introduced in the Hebrew Scriptures; both names were later spread by the Greeks, as were a host of other historical and biblical names that became anglicized to the English via the Greeks. The Hebrew Bible was first translated by the Greeks in 300 BCE ('The Greek Septuagint Bible'), then into the Latin, then the English. The Hebrew Scriptures spread to the nations via the Greek Empire and Christianity and it became history's most widely impacting writings.

The ancient Egyptian writings as well as the Hebrew mentioning the Philistines, both without associating Arabs with this name, affirms it emerged later; in the recent 20th Century, with no Arab Palestinians seen prior. The term Arab does not appear alongside a vast array of the names of ancient nations and ethnic groups by any source of the period when the ancient Egyptians and Hebrews interacted. The Egyptian writings mention Hebrews, Israel and Jerusalem, even a war with Israel over 3,000 years ago. The absence of a record of any group in this time that may be associated or likened to the Arabs is an anomaly and will be catered to as a separate chapter ('Who Are Arabs?').

Today, there is a historical conundrum in the modern world concerning this name's recent transfer away from the Jews and Judea, formerly Israel. In the latter half of the first century there was a name change from one people to another, and it has assumed a threshold in our vocabulary with a vast multitude as a historical given. History per se was over-turned in the latter 20th Century.

Yet this name's historicity and significance is the essential background factors that must be confronted if the chaos is to be cleared.

It is a name usurping that will affect many sectors globally; it is a name transfer that never anticipated its trajectory impacts or that it was not limited to one nation in the Middle-East. Dislodging one brick can topple a wall; if past history is to be altered, the same will apply to subsequent future history. Israel's history has trajectories that are inter-dependent. It is far from being an inconsequential factor; if an antidote to today's chaos and mayhem is sought there may be no other means to restore historical sanity to the modern world than restoring historical reasoning. Changing one sector of past history has consequences.

One name has become a formidable issue to contend in it's un-raveling. It consumes more than 50% of the UN workload and the political portfolios of the nations; it is the media's most favored reporting. Today, the Palestinian adjective is chanted in more processions of protests and more loudly than any other. Palestinian and land occupation disputes have become synonymous and inter-dependent. The historical record will show that clearly a held name and heritage transfer has occurred; but whose, how and why is not in the discourse. None appear to know quite what's happening anymore; all reasoning of this conflict have resulted in inaccurate conclusions by the world's most prominent mindsets. Confronting was replaced by deflecting. It didn't work out as anticipated.

Consider the global paradigm if the name Palestinian is again re-transferred back to the people of Judea, which is Israel today. Consider whether the Palestinian Jews, as they were always referred to, could still be charged with occupying another peoples' land without the name transfer. Namely, can the Palestinian Jews be accounted as illegally or disputably occupying another peoples' land called Palestine; or else occupying Arab lands with their original 3,000 year Hebrew town names instead of West Bank. Would 2,000 year Palestinian Jews or the 20th Century Palestinian Arabs then be illegally occupying Palestine, for this name was indeed held exclusively by the Jews for 2,000 years till the 1960's? The answer is 'yes' when one considers such is not hypothetical; it is precisely what happened. The 'why' factor then becomes a considerable factor.

In the chaos of the times, Hebron, Bethlehem and Nazareth are accepted as 'West Bank' and a new region called as 'East' Jerusalem has emerged. The Jerusalem Temple is presented as a myth in the Arab world; the same Temple destroyed by the Arabs who are recorded as the most prominent members in the Roman legions destroying that temple 2,000 years ago (Josephus Wars, Book V, Ch 13, 4). Here, the deflection of Palestine as the historical homeland of the Jews is in contradiction of the previous Ottoman Empire's determination of this history, the Gospels and the Quran. Yet it remains inadequately confronted with no impact of decisions that flow on unperturbed. Here, even the Dead Sea Scrolls revelation of this history did not impact. Today, the chaos made of history displays a global phenomenon of two widely impacting contradictions. Compare them with two examples of the times:

• "This is the Al-Aqsa Mosque that Adam, peace be upon him, or during his time, the angels built. It was never anything other than a

22

mosque, dating all the way back to the beginning of the world." - (Sheikh Muhammad Ahmad Hussein, Muslim cleric in charge of the Al-Aqsa Mosque in Jerusalem, speaking of the 8th century mosque built by Caliph Abd al-Malik ibn Marwan; Israel's *Channel 2* interview.)

And this, the immediately previous reign of Palestine's Ottoman rulers:

"Who can challenge the rights of the Jews in Palestine? Good Lord, historically it is really your country" - Ottoman Mayor and scholar Yusuf Diya al-Khalidi; Jerusalem, 1899.

Britain, who's original Mandate treaty declared all of Palestine, including Trans-Jordan, as the 'national home of the Jews' now claims East Jerusalem is not part of Israel - contradicting its own mandate and the Ottomans. A Roman Pope calls Arabs as Palestinians, defying the Gospel writ of 'Land of Israel' (Matt.2:20). The Muslim people re-interpret their own Quran that acknowledges Jerusalem as the holy city of the Jews. And the UN grants the 3,000 year Jerusalem Temple wall as Islamic heritage. Chaos?

Here, West Bank, East Jerusalem and Arab Palestinians are new name entities fostered by Britain and Hajj Amin in the 20th Century; both emerging after the discovery of oil and the transfer of history's most validated historical names occurring in the 20th Century.

Thereby, these name changes, although in contradiction of historical and theological archives and a vast collection of archaeological relics, are vigorously disputed, pursued and held steadfastly as a prized asset, even as a weapon of war. History per se has been changed, or at least how the west considered it 100 years ago. History's dislodging is not the same as that of geographical lands; the latter can be altered while the former cannot.

Significantly, such depictions are not the imaginative views of any writer or of targeting any group or ideology; this presentation wholly relies on validated historical archives. This makes the chaos engulfing humanity ever more considerable and confounding. Here, history and beliefs do not see eye to eye. Here, the only error may be the absence of recognizing the reasoning behind the name changes of Israel's historical symbols and its most reasonably anticipated consequences. Whether these changes are about a meagre patch of land, heritage, nativity and ancestry factors, or something else, something deemed outside the discourse make this an incumbent and required consideration.

The Judeo-Christian history and belief is in contradiction of an equally held opposing one. It is one that is self-declared numerously as a Caliphate doctrine, proclaiming its own theologically based transcendence that has an extending global portfolio. Thereby this is more than a localized conflict of one minuscule land and people that is presented as its central feature; such is perhaps the primal revelation of the times. History says that the faculty of belief is the most effective means of exploitation, and its most powerful weapon is via a 'name'. Mighty Rome understood this power in the first century and it was most successfully employed again in the 20th Century.

Yet there are consequences that are not limited to the Middle East anymore. Chaos and mayhem has become a global syndrome unrelated to one patch of land. Otherwise, how can past and present history and its theologies become reconciled if negated; do they become dramatically altered by name changes and displacements if many accept it? It appears so by the acceptance of a vast multitude; but not so without wider consequences erupting. Such wider consequences have now erupted with global impacts; the discourse has shifted. We are in it; and it was never limited to a few cubits of barren land in Palestine.

Clearly, this is the new reality's reasoning; it now appears the Israel-Arab conflict was exploited and used as a springboard to a grander conflict.

This issue looms larger and there may be no resolving without addressing the 'what's in a name' phenomenon. Many have tried other methods by its skirting and have failed. Vexing it may be, yet both past and future history depend on it. Try saying: 'The Palestinian Jews are illegally occupying Palestine'. Or else, when 'End the occupation of the Palestinians' or 'Free Palestine' is chanted in protest marches, ask if we can produce an Arab Palestinian prior to the 20th Century. Why not?

Examining this history, the name usurping and changes occurred as a new phenomenon that emerged after the discovery of oil, perhaps a coincidence. Also, it emerged following the appointing of the wrong man as the mayor of Jerusalem instead of a Jewish mayor that would accord with the Balfour treaty. Britain gave the world Hajj Amin who formed the Brotherhood, legitimizing a declared Caliphate intended against the Jewish state. Was Britain, handed the caretaker role of Mandates, one pertaining to the Jews before her appointment that she accepted, confused in the turbulence of the region; if so it coincided with the discovery of oil and Hajj Amin's appointment as Jerusalem's mayor. It produced global impacts thereafter. Prior to this action by the British, the Arabs acknowledged all of Palestine as a state for the Jews with no division of its landmass contemplated (Faisal-Weizmann Agreement of 1919).

• "The 1919 Faisal-Weizmann treaty provided a firm foundation for League of Nations ratification of the Balfour Declaration at the San Remo Conference in 1920. The proposals covered Palestine - from the Mediterranean through the entire Galilee, up to the Litany River, hundreds of miles east of the Jordan River through all of current day Jordan, and into part of the Sinai. The League assigned Palestine Mandate administration to Britain, entrusting it to establish the National Home for the Jews." (*"Battleground: Fact & Fantasy in Palestine" by Samuel Katz; EretzIsraelOrg*)

• "This site is one of the oldest in the world. Its sanctity dates from the earliest times. Its identity with the site of Solomon's Temple is beyond dispute. - (A Guide to Al-Haram Al-Sharif Jerusalem, booklet published by the Supreme Muslim Council, 1924)

• "The attacks on the Jewish community in 1920, 1921, 1929, were instigated by a call of the mufti of Jerusalem, Hajj Amin al-Husseini, who was later sought for war crimes in the Nuremberg trials because he had a central role in fomenting the final solution," (Mr. Benjamin Netanyahu, Prime Minister of Israel, in a speech to delegates at the 37th World Zionist Congress in Jerusalem; JPost.)

• "The Mufti Hajj Amin el Husseini - was involved in Military Jihad against the Jews of Israel but was also actively involved in the annihilation of a half million Hungarian Jews in 1944. Europe will be the next objective of that very same Jihad, which is already in the midst of exporting itself to Europe by means of massive Muslim immigration to the aging and deteriorating continent." - ("It's Jihad, Stupid" By Dr. Mordechai Kedar, Senior Lecturer in the Department of Arabic Studies, Bar-Ilan University.)

The issue of Hajj Amin being an accessory in the Holocaust merits a separate chapter ("Britain, Hajj Amin and the Holocaust") and presented with evidence of this controversial and shrouded issue. It does not mean that Hitler and the Nazis become exonerated in any way; nor can Britain. This history is thereby also expressed with remorse if it invokes offense to many sectors concerned. Yet it has to be told and accorded its rightful place in the chaos witnessed in the modern world. Here, even the nation wearing the prefix of 'Great' must be confronted; perhaps more so than any other by virtue of being among the greatest in modern history. Here, the primal feature to be impressed is the elicit flaunting of history by the usurping of names. It is not a gratuitous addendum or a divergence from the theme of this history; it merits to be given the primal preamble in the discourse when merited.

It does mean that an array of forces worked in unison of what was held as their Jewish problem and their final solution. Thereby the return of a Jewish state, far from being an occupation of another peoples' lands, always was and remains as an affront; any surprise of it lacks historical credibility. Israel has never occupied another peoples' land in all her 4,000 year recorded history. Israel is theologically commanded not to do so and has well adhered to this edict in the Hebrew Bible.

Anomalies.

Tracing the history of this name's origins begins with a stark anomaly, one not seen among all other native peoples: the absence of any historical imprints of a non-Jewish Palestinian before the 20th Century. The anomaly is further extended by a new group of prominent Arab figures that call themselves as Palestinians and claim a 7,000 year native habitation in Canaan, the land which became Israel and claimed by the Jews as their historical homeland established 3,000 years ago. Namely, the 7,000 year native people claim they never encountered a 3,000 year native people of a sovereign nation called as Israel or Judea, one recorded in the archives of a host of nations and in a vast collection of historical relics. It is an anomaly of historical and biblical proportions, in contradiction of both the Quran and the Gospels, yet its provision was accepted with a total absence of historical credence. Equally anomalous, the claim is not based on an acknowledgement Israel was once the homeland of the Jews and later lost by a Roman invasion. The 7,000 year nativity claim resolutely negates any ancient homeland of the Jews; that Judea and Israel have no past attachments to this land and that Jews were never its sovereign inhabitants. A Jerusalem Temple is declared as a myth, even that today's Jews are not Jews. Even more chaotic, while the world at large condones the Arab Palestinian narratives, prominent Islamic theologians and scholars reject it, negating any past or modern association of the Arab claims and stand in alignment of the Jewish claims; not so the western world; not so Roman Popes; not so Britain. The nations hail at the UN the past seventy years with no indications of retreating amidst manifold anomalies reigning.

Impacting again is another view by some sectors and a more subdued one. That the Jews have been absent for 2,000 years, with the Arabs achieving a heritage attribute within this period and thus have acquired such nativity rights. Otherwise, it is claimed, all other lands can merit the same right of nativity as do the Jews and an unrealistic, unacceptable worldly upheaval will ensue. Thereby, any previous right of Israel to exist is also negated.

However, this view also does not vindicate such claims when examined. Aside from it being rejected by the Arabs themselves, there was never a time in history when the Jews were not inhabitants of this land or absent from it. The historical record says the Jews were in fact the people who did have sovereignty of this land and were exiled forcefully by invading forces; yet that portions of the Jews remained continuously in Jerusalem and its surrounding towns, even during harsh periods under various invading forces. No other nation or peoples can make an equivalent claim.

Numerous invasions by the Crusaders till the 12th Century, and many other forces thereafter up to the Ottoman period evidence a consistent and continuous Jewish presence; these were Jews who remained in Palestine, prayed in Jerusalem and did not disperse to the Middle East or to Europe by the Roman and Babylonian exiles. Thereby, although the major population of the Jews was forcefully dispersed, some always remained holding ownership keys and the deeds and title to their house. This presentation evidences the un-broken habitation of Jews in this land with 3,000 years of historical surveys.

Another significant anomaly is that unlike the 3,000 year Jewish claimants, the 7,000 year Arab people have not offered any historical validations to substantiate its claims. The first mention of the name Arab, from the Hebrew book of Nehemiah and dated as 450 BCE is of an Arab soldier that appeared in the land when the Jews were returning from a 70 year Babylonian exile to build the Second Jerusalem Temple; this narrative says the Jews were the previous inhabitants of their homeland. Today, the Arabs are rejecting the return of the Jews from the Roman exile; ironically, both the Arabs and the Britons were in the Roman legions as witness of this land's inhabitants.

The Persian writings of Cyrus the Great granting the Jews a return to their homeland, and the remains of a re-built second Jerusalem Temple validate it; the archives of the Romans who destroyed that temple also do so.

Thus, either Palestine was Judea, the historical homeland of the Jews, or else the homeland of the Arabs. Arab Palestinians are either the true native peoples of this land or the Jews. Yet both claim nativity in the same landmass by a mutually exclusive mode of each other and overlapping the same space-time. Both cannot be correct. Its deflection instead of its confronting manifests the chaos that the world is immersed in today.

One may claim that past history is not the issue, erroneously, only when it appears as a negation of the charges made on Israel. Yet history remains the only factor that caters to land occupation, nativity, return and of heritage and refugee displacement claims; to the extent these can only be denied when their charges do not possess such evidential historical factors, yet claim them based solely on the recent usurping of names.

Thereby, there are a host of anomalies arisen as monoliths in our midst; they stand as astonishing contradictions confronting all held in its global trajectories as a force of its own and despite every means to avoid them. Arabs presented as Palestinians has seeped into the lexicon of a vast worldly multitude as natives to Palestine; and the Jews made as occupiers in their ancestral land they were legally returned to. This premise has become akin to a religious belief. It is a deception disputed by the Jews and a smaller minority of impressive scholars, historians and theologians. Such anomalies leave only one safe and correct path to examine the modern world's biggest controversy.

What Does History Say?

One census report held in 1864 by the British Embassy found twice as many Jews than Arabs in Jerusalem as inhabitants under the previous Ottoman Empire. And, significantly, that these Jews were then referred to as the Jews of Palestine. The name and the land represented the counter of Arabs and Arab land; especially when directed at Jerusalem. The British documentation also referred the name Palestine and Palestinian exclusively to the Jews, as did America and the French; now there was no region called East Jerusalem. The entire four centuries of census counts in the Ottoman reign evidence a most prominent sector of Jews in Jerusalem and numerous towns of Palestine. Namely, the Ottoman history says the Jews were at no time absent from this land for the last 400 years prior to WW1. The previous historical records dating to the Roman reign also say the same for 2,000 years thereafter. These historical stats have been ousted from the discourse; even reversed against the Jews by a time immemorial claim by the Arabs.

When the land was invaded by periodical swarms of the crusades and the Jews were slaughtered and expelled from Jerusalem, the crusaders kept confronting the returned Jews each time. Ironically, it was the invading Islamic forces that secured the Jews to be safely returned. Here, the negation and rejection of the Jews in the modern state of

Israel is a recent phenomenon that sprouted under the watch of Britain.

Thereby, that the Arabs have acquired a nativity by virtue of an earlier habitation while the Jews were exiled and absent, requires a historically evidenced examination to defend this falsehood entirely, both via modern and ancient periods, even of the past 3,000 years up to the present. The Arabs and Britons should acknowledge this truth; both were in the Roman legions when the Jews defended Jerusalem against history's mightiest super power, braving the destruction of their holy temple and a holocaust in the first century incurred under the Roman destruction.

The Jews were indeed inhabitants of Palestine under the previous Ottoman Empire and the treaties enacted in the 20th Century. Thereafter, two separate peoples claimed nativity in Palestine; of these only one is based on historical credibility. The other stated via a self declared theological right, one that pays no mind to any historical value and inculcated and unleashed humanity's darkest epochs, both in Europe and Arabia. The parallels of diatribe are not avoidable, nor should it be seen as limited to one minuscule land and people.

• "I swear on the Quran not a single Jew will remain in Palestine. If the enemies do not understand this they are stupid." - (Palestinian Cleric & TV Host Sheik Uyad Abu Funun, Al Aqsa Hamas-Gaza TV)

Right of Return.

The basis of a Caliphate doctrine can have numerous avenues of achieving its ends. The claim of a right of return is such an example. Based on the evidence that the Jews were this land's consistent inhabitants, the right of return should be allocated to the people who were the land's original inhabitants, more so than those who accumulated here by invasion and immigration under Britain's watch, and based on 'we shall dominate' doctrines. Historically, there was never an Arab state called Palestine; it is the name applied to Judea, the Roman name for Judah, the homeland of the Jews. Thereby, the right of return should have no association with any people other than the land's ancestral and continuous habitants.

The 'right of return' is perhaps best exposed by the UN's hitherto new heritage designation of a mere two year habitation, and applying it to only one region and people, and using the right of return as its basis to thereby obfuscate an underlying Caliphate design. Its negation of a non-Arab ancient nation with a 3,000 year ancestry, one that was legally returned via the UN, becomes questionable of its underlying premise. Namely, why would an alleged native people require such a demeaning two year facility as its mark of heritage, and how can it dislodge a precedent nativity when two years is a lesser heritage than a 3,000 year period.

Thereby the UN has corrupted the premise of a heritage right, as is also seen by its focus on Arab refugees instead of the Jewish refugees, greater in number, and unlike the Arabs, with no place to retreat and facing genocide in Arabia and worse in Europe. It is not an exaggeration; it is history.

Additionally, how does the UN's new heritage accounting impact on those Jews who were inhabitants of Arab ruled lands of the Middle East for 2,500 years; will they also be accounted as returnees to the lands they returned from and meriting equal consideration as accorded the Arabs. Will the Jews have states in Iraq, Egypt, Syria, Yemen and Lebanon by merit they were inhabitants of these lands prior to the emergence of the Arab peoples? Such modes of chaos are pervasively disingenuous of this conflict; they conform to theological doctrines that flaunt the law via political manipulations. Here, those nations who had voting power at the UN cannot claim non-complicity when these extend across all barriers. It is the chaos engulfing the nations today by the error of assuming Israel was its only targeting.

The 'right of return' to Palestine was applied exclusively to Jews in the legal treaties of the Balfour Mandate. Although most of the Jews arrived after the 19th Century from Russia, Europe and the surrounding regions, such an in-flow would apply more with the recent Arab migration than the Jews. This land was barren before the Jews began returning in large numbers, while the Arab migration was not of the lands natives, thus not of a returning native people. In the Ottoman reign and till the 20th Century the only Palestinians were the Jews.

In 1920 the International Community recognized the unique historical connection of the Jews to Palestine and deemed as international law in the San Remo Resolutions; all nations participated in this conclusion. Britain was appointed the Mandatory power charged with facilitating and encouraging the return of the Jewish People to their homeland, and prevented - in law - from ceding any land to any foreign powers.

Britain entered her caretaker role after accepting the Balfour treaty; it contained no right of return of the Arabs. Britain reversed the core essentials of the Mandate entrusted to her.

Here, aside from the flaunting of legal pledges, the return factor was equally flaunted; it should have applied to the Jews not the Arabs. It was the Jews, not the Arabs, given the legal right of return. It was the Arabs, not the Jews, who immigrated illegally under Britain's watch and assisted to do so. The land was never absent of Jews at any time the past 2,000 years; and more so the prior 1,000 years when King David established Jerusalem as Israel's capital city. Thereby, the issue of 'return' and 'nativity' mark a variant conclusion when accorded to the Arabs via transferring the name held by the Jews; such is also in contradiction of the Balfour Mandate and history itself.

The historical population archives are fully known to the UN and the British; so who owns the house when many of its occupants are away, yet some remained home is a critical factor. Perhaps this issue is more complicated than its given reasoning; otherwise, why would this syndrome extend globally where there is no issue of a nativity premise and land occupation. Perhaps more than history and international laws apply in this conflict, one declared by the Arabs themselves as a theological premise:

• "If one wants to get to know the program of the Islamic State, its politics, and its legal opinions, one ought to consult its leaders, its statements, its public addresses, its own sources" - (Abu Muhammad al-Adnani, official spokesman of the Islamic State, May 21, 2012; The Brookings Project on U.S. Relations with the Islamic World Analysis Paper | No. 19.)

Thereby, if the Jews alone have ancestry validation and were at no time absent from this land, even after invasions and their ousting by the Babylonians, the Romans and the Crusaders; and the previous Muslim invasions who granted the Jews their return and stay, then the term 'return' ought not to effect the Jews. The last occupiers of this land, the Ottomans, who were not Arab, housed a widespread Jewish community in Palestine. This says that aside from enforced displacements by stronger military forces of most of the population, sizeable portions of Jews at all times remained and never abandoned their homeland. Such is affirmed by the Crusader and Islamic invasions of Jerusalem, and the historical census accountings of this region.

A 3,000 Year Census Chart.

The previous Ottoman phase significantly impacts in determining which people were 'returning' to their ancestral homeland in Palestine, and which people were not; which people were immigrating freely with no inherent historical right to do so and which people had the right to do so. Clearly, both cannot hold the same provision. Clearly, a native people would not partake on the name of another and will not rest on a two year period of habitation as its veracity; especially where 3,000 and 7,000 year claims are proposed by the parties.

Thus, did Rome invade an Arab sovereign nation or a Jewish one called as Judea 2,000 years ago, which name was changed to Palestine; and did that people become absent from this land in that period. Such factors become impacting on all nations globally and on a future history that will attend them; one that appears has now arrived.

Were the British in error of the Balfour Declaration that described a historical connection of the Jews to Palestine; or Churchill who accounted their 3,000 year connection with this land - by right and not by sufferance? These are well known issues by scholars, yet they have been largely absent from the discourse and should be re-enacted as essential. The historical records say the Jews are the only people that possess the 'right of return' because they were never absent from their ancestral land; the Arabs do not possess a 'right of return' because they were not this land's ancestral inhabitants.

• "A common misperception is that the Jews were forced into the Diaspora by the Romans after the destruction of the Second Temple in Jerusalem in the year 70 A.D. and then, 1,800 years later, suddenly returned to Palestine demanding their country back. In reality, the Jewish people have maintained ties to their historic homeland for more than 3,700 years. A national language and a distinct civilization have been maintained." - ("Pre-State Israel: Jewish Claim to the Land Of Israel" by Mitchell Bard; Jewish Virtual Libr.)

Here, a historical census chart is a key factor. There can be no confusion of this region's history by the UN who created an exclusive recognition of the Arab refugees instead of the Jewish refugees from Arab lands. Israel's history is among the most known of all nations, especially so by Britain and the Arabs in this region. A population census chart of Jerusalem (below) shows that the Jews were the only consistent habitants of this land at all times; that they were never absent for 3,000 years, despite of their numerous invasions and enforced exiles:

Jerusalem Population Surveys.

- **1 AD/CE Pre-Roman War:** 80,000. [Josephus; Magen Broshi, Bar 4:02]
- **70; Roman War:** 1.1 M. [Josephus Wars; Book VI Ch 9 Sec 3; 600,000 Est. by Roman Historian Tacitus who was not a contemporary of the period]
- **After 2nd Century AD/CE:** Jewish population was meagre under Rome and Christianity; it began to increase in 1,500 AD/CE; and again after the Islamic invasion.
- **1500:** Jews 1194; Muslims: 3704; Christians: 714. [Ottoman Taxation Est; Amnon Cohen and Bernard Lewis (1978).
- **1824:** Jews 6,000; Muslims 10,000; Christians 4,000. [Fisk and King, 'Description of Jerusalem,' in *The Christian Magazine*, July 1824, page 220]
- **1844:** Jews 7,120. Muslims: 5,000. Christians: 3,390. [Jerusalem, Eine Vorlesung, pages 33-34]
- **1853:** Jews 8,000. Muslims: 4,000. Christians: 3,490 [César Famin, French diplomat]
- **1864:** Jews 8,000. Muslims 4,000. Christians 2,500. [British Embassy; "The Fight for Jerusalem", Dore Gold, Regnery publishing. p. 120.]
- **1869:** Jews 9,000. Muslims 5,000. Christians 4,000. [Hebrew Christian Mutual Aid Society. Almanack of 1869]
- **1876:** Jews 4,000. Muslims 13,000. Christians 3,560. [Kark, Ruth; Oren-Nordheim, Michal (2001).Jerusalem and its environs; Wayne State University Press, p.28]
- **1882:** Jews 9,000. Muslims 7,000. Christians 5,000. [Wayne State University Press. p. 28.]
- **1885:** Jews 15,000. Muslims 6,000. Christians 14,000. [Wayne State University Press. p. 28]
- **1896:** Jews 28,112. Muslims 8,560. Christians 8,748. [Harrel and Stendel, 1974]
- **1905:** Jews 13,300. Muslims 11,000. Christians 8,100. [Usiel Oskar Schmelz, in Ottoman Palestine, 1800-1914: studies in economic and social history, p. 35, Gad G. Gilbar, Brill Archive, 1990]
- **1922:** Jews 13,971. Muslims 13,413. Christians 14,669. [Census of Palestine (British)]
- **1931:** Jews 51,200. Muslims 19,900. Christians 19,300. [Census of Palestine (British)]
- **1944:** Jews 97,000. Muslims 30,600. Christians 29,400. [Harrel and Stendel, 1974]
- **1967:** Jews 195,000. Muslims 54,963. Christians 12,646. [Harrel, 1974]
- **1987:** Jews 340,000. Muslims 121,000. Christians 14,000. [Jerusalem Municipality]
- **1995:** Jews 417,100. Muslims 182,700. Christians 14,100. [Jerusalem Municipality]
- **2011:** Jews 497,000. Muslims 281,000. Christians 14,000. [Israel Central Bureau of Statistics]
- **2006:** Jews 724,000. About 10% of the total population of Israel; of which 65.0% were Jews. [Israel Central Bureau of Statistics]
- **2011:** Jews 497,000 (62%); Muslims 281,000 (35%); Christians 14,000 (about 2%) – [World Zionist Org]

Theological Census. [Based on Hebrew Scriptures]

- **Circa 2000 BCE:** The Patriarch Abraham, revered figure of three religions, began with one Hebrew in Ur (Babylon; Iraq); who then settled in Canaan. [Encyclopaedia of World Biography | 2004 COPYRIGHT 2004 The Gale Group Inc.]

- **Circa 1400 BCE:** 3 Million Israelites are accounted in one of the earliest recorded scientific census accounts, with age, gender and family tribes sub-totals. The total is based on an estimated aggregate of 600,000 men and the anticipated number of women, children and elders. [Book of Numbers, Ch.1.]

The chart's first century account says the Jewish populations prior to the Roman war were widespread in the Middle East region and in North Africa and Europe (mainly in Greece and Rome), so that its numbers in Judea refer only to those in the land at this time (80,000). Those who later returned to participate in the Roman war with the Jews of 70 AD/CE during the Passover period show a ten-fold increase; in this pre-exilic and pre-synagogue period the temple was the only place the holy festivals could be observed; 1.1 Million represents only those that perished in the Roman destruction of 70 AD/CE (Josephus). The chart then says the land was invaded by Christians; then by the Islamic invasion in the 7th Century; both confronted the Jews as inhabitants who remained in the land. The Arab populations that began with the Islamic invasion depleted, then increased again from the year 1824 of a mixed people that included Christians and a diverse assembly of non-Arab Muslims made of Turks, Bosnians, Persians, Greeks and Phoenicians; as well as Arabs from the Middle East. The chart confirms both the Ottoman period Jews in Palestine and the British survey as being twice the population of Jews to Muslims in the 19th Century.

In 1517 under the Ottomans, Jews lived in Jerusalem, Hebron, Gaza, Shechem (now, Nablus) and Safed, comprising those Jews who had never left the land since the Roman invasion. In the Mid-16th century the Jewish population was 10,000 according to other estimates, with Safed a thriving textual centre ('Pre-State Israel'; Virtual Jewish Libr.).

Prior to the Roman war, this was the sovereign homeland of the Jews, accounted by numerous scriptures and relics including the Dead Sea Scrolls. Thereby, the Jews were always native inhabitants of Palestine. In 1840, the Sultan Abdulmecid denounced the European blood libel, inviting the Jews back to their homeland, marking it as a Jewish nation and welcoming the Jews to return as subjects of Palestine, the post-Judea name. Thereby, the Sultan was declaring Palestine as the ancestral land of the Jews and referring to their enforced Roman exile and the persecution of enforced conversion demands in Spain:

• "For the love we bear to our subjects, we cannot permit the Jewish nation, whose innocence against the crime alleged against them is evident, to be worried and tormented as a consequence of accusations which have not the least foundations of truth."

36

Thereby a wave of Jews returned from the Spanish expulsion to join the Jews in Palestine. These Jews, exiled by the Romans, are the only returnees to their ancestral land. It is also an auspicious time in history when a ship laden with Jewish sea faring maps departs Spain and went astray; they will encounter the lands of The Americas.

Other population trend estimates give smaller Muslim population accounts in Palestine and identify these to be non-natives; the lesser accounts are vouched by numerous prominent travelers from the west who reported a barren and isolated land in the 18th and 19th centuries:

• "Most Muslims living in Palestine in 1948 when the State of Israel was created had been living there for fewer than 60 years: 1890: Arab Population 432,000.1947: Arab Population 1,181,000. Growth in Arab population from 1890 to 1947: 800,000. - ("Demography in Israel/Palestine Trends Populations & Policy Institutions"; Sergio Della Pergola, Hebrew University of Jerusalem)

• Non-Arab Immigration: "By the early 1800s the Arab population in Palestine was very little, just 246,000. It was in the late 1800s and early 1900s that most Muslim Colonists settled in Palestine because of events such as the Austro-Hungarian Occupation of Bosnia-Herzegovina, the Crimean War and World War 1. Those events created a great quantity of Muslim Refugees"

Non-Arab Immigration: "There were about five million Muslims displaced due to the Austro-Hungarian occupation of Bosnia-Herzegovina, the Crimean War, Balkan wars, the Turkish war of independence and World War I. In 1878 an Ottoman law granted lands in Palestine to Muslim colonists from Crimea and the Balkans who settled in Anatolia, Armenia, Lebanon, Syria and Palestine." - ("Forced Migration & Mortality in the Ottoman Empire" by Professor of History, Justin McCarthy, University of Louisville)

The lands given the Arab immigrants by the Ottomans were as landlord status titles. These landlord positions will account for the British granting of vast countries to the Arabs via secretive arrangements for military assistance against the Ottomans. The creation of numerous new regime states resulted in the 20th Century that, unlike Israel, never existed before. Like Christianity in Europe, when Islam emerged in the 7th Century it conquered and ruled over all independent states and kingdoms, converting them with little choice applying. It is one reason the return of an independent Jewish state that refused conversion became an affront both in Europe and Arabia; it also accounts for the negative support merited to Israel.

The new state allocations in the Middle East emerged following WW1 and the provision given Britain to establish mandates for the region. The Balfour Mandate, decided by the world powers at San Remo which Britain accepted, was corrupted with the discovery of oil. Thus began the elimination process of the Jewish state with the first division of Palestine that created Trans-Jordan; it was followed by a continuing history of destructive measures against the Jews. The land issue was the placebo that shrouded an underlying Caliphate premise and Britain's commercial arrangements.

It is also why no other non-Arab state was allocated for other groups in the Middle East and why no conditions of rule were placed on the regime states, arguably the primal reason for the human rights abusive reign suffered by all people in this region. The total absence of any conditions of rule on the regime states is an error by Britain that has come to haunt the modern world; it spurred a Caliphate by default. The Copts, the Lebanese and other groups of the region paid a high price for the absence of their rights to be protected and safe guarded.

• "Jerusalem's Jewish connection dates back more than 3,000 years. Even after Jews lost control of the city in 70 CE, a Jewish spiritual and physical bond with Jerusalem remained unbroken, despite 2,000 years of dispersion." ('Jerusalem in a Nutshell' by Eli E. Hertz.)

It is reasonable to surmise the continuous and numerous corruptions of the mandate pledges and the absence of ruling conditions on the regime states resulted from a theological doctrine demanded of Britain, and to conclude the applicable currency for Britain was commercial oil agreements; that the charges on Israel also stem from such a cause. No other reasons are equally logical as applying. Israel did not occupy another peoples' land; nor can it be credible that the Arabs are the native Palestinians.

Britain won the war that felled the Ottomans, and although much credence was given to the participation of the Arab assistance it was not the deciding factor; the Jews also assisted in the war. The war acumen of the Arab armies and their war abilities was limited, and Britain was well aware of the theological premises in the region when it preferred to incline with acquiring oil arrangements; these are the disclosures in suppressed archives of Britain's own war time ministers. Britain exploited against the Jews un-proportionately, both in Arabia and Europe to formidable extents that will extend to WW2 and beyond.

Thereby, soon after the discovery of oil Britain initiated a host of land divisions and name changes within the heart-line of the minuscule state allocated for the Jews. With the first 2-state division Britain will define the removal of 80% of Palestine as a historic compromise, a resoundingly radical and disingenuous definition that stunned world Jewry. A host of international law professors conclude the British actions of dividing Palestine were illegal. Britain will continue focused on the Jews as the softest target to exploit.

Hereafter, the names West Bank and Arab Palestinians will emerge for the first time in history, with claims effectively negating and opposing the historical connection and ancestry of the Jews with this land. Jerusalem's Jewish history will be denied via a theological premise and it will be supported and pursued by Britain for commercial gains.

A New History.

With Britain's appointing of Hajj Amin as Jerusalem's mayor, a new history will be declared and a conflict with no end in sight will emerge that should never have been allowed to initiate. It is the early 20th Century; herein began the chaos of history's over-turning and the denial syndromes seen in slogans and posters in global Arab protests of Israel occupying Israel. Herein will also evolve as the 'No-Go-Zones' of the nations. It is reasonable, if not utterly logical that the onslaught of lands of other nations outside of the Middle East is not about illegal occupation but the legitimizing of history's denials in Palestine. Britain targeted an independent state for Jews to satisfy a Caliphate demand in gaining Arab allies; it was not about illegal occupation by the Jews or the displacement of Arabs. It was the Jews that became displaced from their lands.

A Caliphate is not limited to Israel; in the following 21st Century radical groups emerged in the Middle East; they battle each other in securing a dominant role in extending the Caliphate across the nations, one that was legitimized by default. It evolved via infiltration into the core sanctums of the nations in the west. The flaunting of Israel's rights thereby also ushered an over-turning of history:

• "The claim of the Jews to the right over [Jerusalem] is false, and we recognize nothing but an entirely Islamic Jerusalem under Islamic supervision…" - (The Chief Moslem cleric of the Palestinian Authority, Mufti Ikrama Sabri)

Are Arabs Native to Palestine?

Generally, true natives are not known to usurp the names of the original or previous natives of a land. In 1947, Britain rejected an Arab demand that the land should not be called as 'Palestine'. In 1960, the Arabs will form a new stratagem via Egyptian born Arafat as its front man, to become the original 'Palestinians'. Its dark underlying significance negates Israel's history and right to exist, a doctrine aligned in numerous terror group charters. It was infamously accepted by Britain, to become perhaps the most blatant mendacity in the modern world.

Native Palestinians?

ARAFAT – Born in Cairo Egypt.

Jordan's Queen Rania
- Born in Kuwait.

Saeb Erakat
- Saudi Arabian Family Descent.

Mahmoud Abbas
- Iranian Family Descent.

Images [5]

41

A nativity term can be utilized inappropriately, even inverted against the true natives via manipulation, propaganda and age-old historical and theological animosities. Namely, being born in a land via invasion or immigration differs from an ancestral provision; the latter does not equal the former. The Jews alone possess an ancestral nativity in Palestine continuously for 3,000 years; they alone trace their original emergence and inception as a people and nation via historical and archaeological imprints, cross-nation archives, a unique language and acknowledged so in legal treaties of the 20th Century. The Arabs or any other group do not share such a history with Palestine. Thereby, the Jews are the only people who can be classified as returning to their ancestral land, one varied from an invasion or immigration.

That this is correct despite their smaller numbers remaining in the land, and the larger portions dispersed via invasions and enforcements, becomes the stronger witness of the Jews' ancestry rights than by an inappropriately utilized claim by another group. The Jews displayed the essential criteria to defend their claim to their homeland in the face of immense forces. Palestine, which was Judea, was not the ancestral land of Arab Palestinians; it is of the Palestinian Jews, as they were called till the 1960's. Namely, the allocation of the term native Arab Palestinian is thereby a manipulation of history. Such factors are borne out by a reversal of the history records.

Following the Roman war with the Jews and Judea being re-named Palestine, the emerging Christianity controlled this land till the 7th Century. Thereafter, it was later followed by other non-Arab Islamic invasions, extending up to the previous Ottoman period; all of these forces were foreign to this land. Thus, while Arabs lived in Palestine for many centuries, as did numerous other non-Arab peoples including Greeks, Christians, Turks (Ottomans), Persians (Iranians), Bosnians, and with the Arabs as one of the groups, none of these were the original native inhabitants of Palestine other than the Jews when the land's name was Judea. A vast collection of archaeological discoveries and the Dead Sea Scrolls that cover a period over 600 years affirm the Jewish history of Palestine. Israel was not occupying another peoples' land; the Arabs were doing so and it was based on theological doctrines, namely a Caliphate, and not on historical factors. (Carbon-Dating the Scrolls; DSS, 408 BCE-203 CE; Wadi-Daliyeh Deed, p. 467)

Contrastingly of the 7th Century Arab invasion, the Jews at all times inhabited Palestine, constituting a historical thread extending over 3,000 years. The world is not accusing the native ancestral American Indians of illegally occupying America, or the Aboriginal natives of occupying lands of Australians. Usually, such a premise is explained by citing that the natives of America and Australia did not become dispersed as with the Jews and thereby they never vacated or abandoned their land. Such a given reason is false; the Jews did not vacate their land at any time and such is fully evidenced by all invading nations, from the crusaders and the Islamic invasion of the 7th Century leading up to the previous Ottoman period.

The more credible reason points to an invasive theological doctrine than land occupation; numerous people in the Middle East who predate the Arabs also never abandoned their lands, yet the Copts who are the original inhabitants of Egypt are not afforded their own state or even an autonomous region.

Almost the entire Arab population of today's Palestine are made of immigrants from other lands, including from outside of Arabia; the name Palestine was referred exclusively to the Jews and their ancestral homeland prior to the reversal of history in the 1960's.

A host of prominent Arab figures of today who account themselves as native Palestinians have two or three generations of habitation in the land, yet claim a 7,000 year ancestry. A perusal of history says they are recent arrivals. Of note, the reference of Joshua ben Nun, cited here incorrectly by the PA's Saeb Erekat, could have only derived from the Hebrew Bible wherein it was introduced; aside from making such a claim there is no historical imprint of its validation. The Canaanites were not Arab:

• "I am the proud son of the Canaanites who were there 5,500 years before Joshua bin Nun burned down the town of Jericho." According to his family tree posted on Facebook, his clan descends from Arabia, not Canaan, and is part of the Huwaitat tribe who migrated from Medina, then coming to Israel many decades ago, but not centuries nor millennia. Also inaccurate was Erekat's reference to the Biblical prophet Joshua, who lived some 3,300 years ago, not 5,500 years ago. - (PA Negotiator Saeb Erekat Claims Family was Canaanite, in Israel for 9,000 Years; Algemeiner)

• "The great majority of the Arab population in recent decades was comparative newcomers - either late immigrants or descendants of persons who had immigrated into Palestine in the previous seventy years. The Arab population of Palestine was small and limited until Jewish resettlement restored the barren lands and drew to it Arabs from neighboring countries." - (Carl Hermann Voss, Chairman of the American Christian Palestine Committee; recorded 1953)

The late Arafat was born, raised and educated in Cairo. The Jordanians are also Arabs and not Palestinians. Palestine has the same historical ancestral value as Judea. Namely, Palestine is the name referred to as 'Land of the Jews' in the Hebrew and Christian Scriptures, the Roman archives and the Dead Sea Scrolls. Jordan is a new country created in the 20th Century and was equally barren as was Palestine in the previous centuries. Many Jordanians are originally from the surrounding regions outside of Palestine, including the present Queen Rania who was born in Kuwait; King Abdullah II bin Al-Hussein of the Hashemites are from the royal family of the Hejaz (1916-1925), Iraq (1921-1958), and Jordan (1921-present). Mahmoud Abbas, the P.A. President, regardless of his birth, also has an outside ancestry that is not of Palestine.

Unlike the Jews, the Arabs are not returning to their ancestral home; the reverse is the case. Namely, this was the land of the Jews. The claim by members of the Palestinian Authority is based on un-historical and newly manipulated interpretations of theological factors that seek to undermine another peoples' ancestry. The historical records say the Jews, not the Arabs, hold the authority of the name Palestinian.

Are Jews Native to Palestine?

The most fundamental question of the world's most reported issue is not being addressed. Whether it is the native land of the Jews or that of the Arabs should be the foremost issue. The associating of Arabs as native to Palestine, with the absence of listing the nativity of the Jews to this land renders a selective and false reporting of this history; especially so when the Jews, not the Arabs, were called as Palestinians for 2,000 years up to the Mid-20th Century. While the term 'Palestinian' consumes more energy than the environment, the economy and a host of other serious issues confronting humanity, comparatively, Arabs as Palestinians is a new phenomenon that

44

emerged less than 100 years ago. [See, 'Who Are Palestinians?']. The usurping of this name is saying that Jews are not of Judea that was named as Palestine, that the Jews have no nativity in this land, that Arabs are the real Palestinians and that Israel is occupying Arab land; namely it denies and over-turns history.

• "Why Are Palestinians Called Palestinians? This word morphed into the name of an altogether different people (Arabs) thousands of years later." - (By Elon Gilad, Haaretz)

The question is best answered by another: has the world's most invaded and dispersed nation ever illegally occupied another nation's sovereignty the past 3,000 years of recorded history? What about those making such a charge? The issue of 'clean hands' is a legally accepted provision and thereby a historically validated answer that does impact the charge that has been made as international law. That the charge is unrelated to occupation of land is self declared by its plaintiff claimant as a theological and political charter, and thereby it is not a historical premise.

Equally, the issue of nativity of the Jews concerning Palestine is more defensible than that of any other nation by the world's historical archives. The Arabs were not the natives of Judea 2,000 years ago, nor previously when this land was called Israel.

The only attachment of Arabs with Palestine is by way of an invasion in the 7th Century, and the name usurped in the 20th Century. Spain, among other lands, is also similarly subscribed by way of an invasion, its changed name made as Andalus, also known as Muslim Spain or Islamic Iberia. It does not alter the nativity status of the people of Spain, while the Jews possess a longer nativity in Palestine than the people of Spain. Such manipulations of history have evolved with extending consequences impacting globally.

While the Jews in Israel have become overwhelmed and succumbed to the transfer of the term Palestinian, which was one of their national symbols and thereby its aligned occupation libel, it is not an Israeli issue. The Caliphate doctrine is focused on the entire Middle East with an extending goal of dominion across all national barriers.

The new names imposed on Israel's historical lands belie the issue of nativity; the newly enacted term of West Bank should correctly be seen as one of the 1,000's of 'No-Go-Zones' that have overwhelmed the native inhabitants of other nations globally and become as enclaves seeking variant rule of law than the host nations. The immigrants are not the natives of those lands, and likewise not the ancestral natives of Palestine, except via a name usurped as a political weapon. Thereby, the parallels concerning Israel and other nations rest upon the same doctrines.

To recount this history, the Arabs who were embedded in the Roman legions were engaged in the displacing of the native Jews from their ancestral land of Judea; not the Jews displacing the Arabs. The historical record says there was at no time an Arab Palestinian country in Palestine, nor an Arab people called by that name. Thereby, no other people can apply as a dislodging of the ancient nativity of the Jews. The reluctant acceptance by Israel of the term Arab Palestinian is a result of an overwhelming imposition thrust by British and Arab promotions and via modes of corruption. It is difficult to list a greater falsehood impacting the modern world than the allocation of such a historical name rendered as its own antithesis.

• "There was no such thing as Palestinians. It was not as though there was any people in Palestine considering themselves as a Palestinian people and we came and threw them out and took their country away from them. They did not exist." (Golda Meir, Prime Minister of Israel; Quoted in *Sunday Times* 15 June 1969)

• "Half of the Palestinians are Egyptians and the other Half are Saudis" - (Hamas Minister of the Interior and of National Security Fathi Hammad)

3,000 Year Jewish Nativity.

Whereas the Arab nativity claim is predominantly derived from the name usurping of another people in the late 20th Century, its validation should be evidenced without the usage of this name; other independent means should be employed. Palestine is the name that was attached to the Jews and their homeland of Judea; it was the Jews, not the Arabs, who were the natives of Judea. Such a requirement is essential because no Arabs used the term Palestinian prior to the 20th Century, and no previous Arab state or nation existed by the name of Palestine. In contrast, Palestine is the name referred to Jews and their homeland for 2,000 years.

There is historical evidence that the Jews have a 3,000 year continuous history in Palestine with smaller populations remaining

46

throughout, with their substantial populations always returning to re-establish their sovereignty. Such is historically evidenced with ancient Egypt, Babylon, the Greek and Roman Empires and with Christianity and Islam; these are recorded in both historical and theological archives and affirmed in archaeological relics.

The abuse of the rights of this small land of the Jews by theological premises can extend elsewhere; especially so with the nations of the west who do not possess an equal evidential history as does Israel.

No-Go Zones.

The British and Arab groups have emulated Mighty Rome, both being witnessing participants in Rome's destructions and the changing of the name of Judea to Palestine. It has been resurrected again via corruptions of treaties and commercial preferences. It is where the modern world is stationed today and increasingly questioned by the vox populi in the new internet age of mass communication and search facilities; it is marching to the streets and town squares of many nations in foreboding and chaos of the people. New terms such as 'No-Go Zones' have no alliances with land ownership or nativity factors; these are hinged on declared theological agendas.

Thereby, the chaos and bewilderment that is now a global syndrome has no connectivity with the Jews or Israel as has been promoted, except that the errors condoned in one sector can today cross all borders. This then is a self declared Caliphate doctrine that is not limited to one minuscule sector in Palestine; its reverse applies:

• "We place our hope that our triumph will not be restricted to Palestine, but to the banner of the caliphate over the Vatican, the Rome of today" - (Dr. Subhi Al-Yaziji, Dean of Koranic Studies, Islamic University of Haza; Al-Aqsa TV, Hamas-Gaza)

• The government of Yemen recently issued a proclamation that all Jews in the country must leave or convert to Islam, Israeli Deputy Minister of Regional Cooperation, Likud MK Ayoob Kara told *The Algemeiner* on Sunday. Yemen's Jewish community numbered around 50,000 in the 1940s, but the vast majority fled to Israel shortly after the founding of the Jewish state in 1948. - ('Jews Told to Leave or Convert'; Algemeiner)

Who are the Returnees?

When Judea was invaded by Rome and its name changed to Palestine, the Arabs were embedded in the invading Roman legions (Josephus Wars, Book V, Ch 13:4). Thus the Arabs cannot be portrayed as both the invaders and the native 'returnees' of Palestine. It is not a bygone ancient history because such was also declared in the treaties of the 20th Century (The Balfour Mandate and The Palestine Mandate).

In the modern world invasions with declared goals of annihilation on a UN established state are deemed illegal; the Arabs committed numerous such multi-state attacks on Israel and cannot charge the Jews of invasions when this is their own declared doctrine of dominion. When the invasions failed to achieve its stated result, name usurping of Israel's ancient historical symbols and mass immigration replaced the military premise.

That the name West Bank was used to cover 3,000 year Hebrew town names and the 2,000 year Jewish symbol of Palestinian, both names used as a mark of native replacement, it reflects the history turning measures underlying a religious premise of dominion and land occupation. Israel's plight was worsened by the encouragement and assisting by Britain of a mass immigration of Arabs west of the river and by imposing restrictive quotas on Jewish immigration. Thereby, the extending affects of these errors can only be corrected by attending their original causes.

The name corruptions of Israel's historical symbols and their restoration are both the cause and its resolving factors. These corrections will always remain as the prerequisites of resolving this conflict and thereby it's underlying theological basis that is assuming a global enterprise.

With the restoration of Israel's heritage symbols, its concluding provisions will validate the nativity of the Jews with the historical connection to their homeland. Such measures can also correct the unrestrained immigrants from the surrounding regions that created a region called as West Bank, and the negation of another state west of the river, namely a 3-state that has been deceptively presented as a 2-state. The absence of such measures will hinder any means of stemming this process globally.

Here, the provisions of the Oslo Agreement and the UN Resolutions must conform to the corrected history of this region's ancient and modern periods. This onus rests on those who control the UN Security Council votes and have exploited the minuscule state of Israel for their commercial interests and age-old animosities that have inspired their motivations the last 70 years. Its default factor is the underlying Caliphate premise of dominion that rejects the state of the Jews. Thereby, if Israel was legally established and declared as the natives of Palestine with a 3,000 year connection to this land, and cannot be tolerated, then no other nations can assume immunity; certainly not one that cannot validate is history as does Israel.

Correcting the Refugee Crisis.

• "The country is facing a refugee catastrophe, which will lead to the country collapsing." - (Foreign Minister Margot Wallstrom, Stockholm)

• "Up to five million refugees will come to Germany this year." - (Former Berlin major, SPD party)

In the new worldly scenario of Middle East refugees, even the might of super powers cannot stop the in-flow of immigrants seeking new pastures when terrorized by fear. Here, correcting the errors of Israel's names and land usurping, and applying credible ruling conditions on the states created by Britain that safe-guards all peoples in the region regardless of their beliefs, is thereby the only means of negating an underlying theological doctrine of dominion and ending its globally extending phenomenon. The new refugee crises happened to Israel and it has enlarged across the Middle East borders; in the process the real refugees have been forgotten or disregarded.

The thrust of unrestricted immigration has successfully covered the plight of the Jewish refugees from Arab lands and of the true returnees of Palestine; yet it is not an Israel issue but a worldly one. The Arab refugees have more facilities, options, lands and resources than any other refugees in all recorded history. As was done with Israel, a refugee crises that is fostered and encouraged by rogue regimes can act as invasions elsewhere with no immunity to any sector.

Who are the Immigrants?

It is an essential question because Israel is accused of occupying another peoples' land. Thereby, who are the immigrants in Palestine, the Jews or the Arabs, is an incumbent examination; such a question is hardly raised. History says the Arab populations grew after the 7th Century invasion at which time the Christians ruled; at this time the land's ancestral people, the Jews, were present in the land. The incoming Mohammedans did not oust the Jews or call them as invading immigrants of Palestine, even offering them facilities and welcoming them back to their land. Thereby, the Jews inhabited Palestine from the 7th Century invasion and numerous other invasions that followed, up to the last Ottoman period which ended in WW1. Thereafter the Jews again became as the majority inhabitants, although their population ratios were relative to their historically constant limitations. The Jews always accounted for a small land and a small population.

History says at no time in the last 2,000 years, between the Roman war and the Ottoman period, was Palestine un-inhabited by Jews. Thus the issue of immigrants cannot apply to Jews but to those forces that were invaders. The Jews were the ancestral natives of Palestine and at all times maintained a presence in the land.

The invading forces did not maintain the land; its previous renown and glory was not seen again till its sovereign control was returned to the Jews. The historical imprints say Palestine was a neglected and undeveloped region in the Ottoman reign and that the Arabs were the substantial new immigrants arriving from the surrounding regions in direct proportion of the land's development by the Jews. Thus the present Arabs are not native returnee immigrants of Palestine despite that the name Palestinians being adopted in the 1960's; prior to the usurping of this name the Jews were the only people referred to as Palestinians.

Thereby, both people cannot be accounted as native returnees of the same land and overlapping the same time-span; one of these are immigrants as is seen in all historical surveys. Thus the nativity status of the Jews cannot be undermined as secondary to any other people based solely on recent name transfers and immigration when the land was unprotected. Nor does the moral premise apply when the immigrating side has no dearth of landmass at its disposal.

The British documents expose its later acceptance of the name Palestinian that was transferred away from the Jews as a tragic error. The onus of its correction lies with the British people's honour and duty in compelling their leaders to confront this aberration. The Jews

50

trusted Britain and her solemn pledges and this was failed them; it remains as a mark of dishonor that is un-worthy of such a great nation.

Jews and Christians of Arabia.

To recount this history, after the Roman destruction and the name change of Judea the Arabs were one among a host of other non-Arab peoples in Palestine that was largely un-protected. These included Greeks, Christians, Mongols, Armenians, Persians, Turks, Lebanese (Phoenicians), Britons, Romans, Arabs and Jews. Thereby, many diverse invading nations battled in this land the past 2,000 years and many groups of peoples became its residual cosmopolitan inhabitants, including in the Ottoman period (The British survey of 1860). All throughout, the Jews were a consistent and constant group of inhabitants in Palestine since the 7th Century Islamic invasion, and along with the Christians, constitute one of two groups that retained their independent beliefs.

In the 18th and 19th centuries of the Ottoman rule the land was substantially barren, unattended and isolated. The Arabs were the immigrants from the surrounding regions, not from Judea-Palestine, their numbers meager, then heavily compounded by Jewish development which began when Herzl began promoting the return of the Jews to their homeland. The last Ottoman Sultan granted the Jews the right of worship in Jerusalem.

• "There was of course a small Arab population in Palestine that could trace its roots back for centuries. But overall, the Arab population began to blossom only after the beginning of Jewish immigration and the subsequent improvements in economic conditions, infrastructure, and agricultural techniques. The idea of "uninterrupted settlement…rooted in its soil," is thus inconsistent with history. It was put forward primarily in an attempt to delegitimize Jewish history." ("The Myth of Jewish "Colonialism": Demographics and Development in Palestine" By David Wollenberg; Harvard Israel Review).

MARK TWAIN WROTE AFTER VISITING "PALESTINE" IN 1867

"A desolate country whose soil is rich enough, but is given over wholly to weeds.

A silent mournful expanse.

A desolation is here that not even imagination can grace with the pomp of life and action. We never saw a human being on the whole route.

There was hardly a tree or a shrub anywhere.

Even the olive and the cactus, those fast friends of the worthless soil, had almost deserted the country."

Who are the Displaced People?

The larger displacement was of the Jews by Arabs prior to the advent of any land disputes, yet promoted adversely by the UN:

• "Hundreds of thousands of Jews were torn cruelly from their Homes. Whole communities of Jews, who had always resided in the heart of the Arab-Muslim world, underwent expulsion, persecution and malicious liquidation and it has been denied for a lengthy period."

52

(The Inconvenient truth about Jews from Arab Lands"; Nathan Weinstock)

The Jews were in Middle-East lands that were later controlled by the Arabs, dating since the Babylon exile of the 6th Century BCE; these constitute those Jews who did not get exiled to Europe under Rome. Of the period of 2,600 years the Arabs ruled these lands for 1,400 years; thereby the Jews inhabited countries in the region 1,200 years prior to the Arab control and by reason of enforced displacement, not by invasions, as was seen by the Arabs since the 7th Century. The Jews were not recent immigrants in those lands but lived there for 2,600 years; these were Jews inhabiting regions of Arabia that predated the emergence of the Arab group. Yet the Jews at no time made attempts to declare those lands as their own, as is seen in Palestine.

In the 20th Century the Jews were displaced from Arab controlled lands and have been miss-represented of displacing Arabs from Palestine. Instead, it was the declared goals of the Arabs to exterminate and displace the Jews from their homeland that was legally re-established at the UN. When numerous military attacks failed to dislodge the Jews, the Arabs usurped the name Palestinian, a falsified means of heritage replacement.

The Babylonians were a pre-Arab empire; the first mention of a group named as Arab emerged in the following Persian Empire in the reign of Cyrus the Great (See "Who Are Arabs?"). Thereby, the Jews held an older habitation in those lands than the Arabs, yet were displaced by the Arabs in the 20th Century. The Jews left without claiming displacement rights, while the Arabs in Palestine employ the reverse premise.

Thereby, there cannot be an ancestral claim by Arabs to the land of the Jews as uniquely applying, as has been erroneously supported by the British and the UN. That this error was a fully realized corruption and is unrelated to the displacement or occupation of any Arab lands by the Jews will be illustrated separately in extended detail.

The transfer of a historical name should not grant a nativity position of itself; it can more reduce the credibility of such a claim when seen as newly usurped from another people. Without the relatively recent adapted names of Palestine and Palestinian by the Arabs, the nativity and ancestral credibility of the land of Israel and the West Bank are vested with the Jews. This includes the names Palestine and

Palestinian that were directed at the Jews by the Ottomans, the Arab chieftains (Emir Faisal) and all documentation of the nations of the west. Notably, all research fails to produce an Arab Palestinian referred to by this name prior to the 20th Century.

The heritage of the Jews as defined by the UN's two year period of Arab habitation in Palestine also bears a lack of credibility. A two year period does not define a peoples' heritage, and as portrayed in centuries of surveys, cannot dislodge a 3,000 year history of the Jews. More than a copyright or trademark issue of a name or the requirement of land, it denies Israel's validated heritage and thereby the state of Israel's right to exist, identifying itself with a declared theological doctrine of rejection focused on all other ethnicities.

• A report from the United Kingdom-based Catholic charity group Aid to the Church in Need (ACN) has found that Middle East Christians are "on course for extinction" within a generation or sooner. The report blames "religio-ethnic cleansing" that is being powered by the "well-publicized threat of genocide" as the main factor behind the persecution of Christians. - (Issuu 2015 Executive Summary; ACN)

While this conflict may appear as a theological issue, it is also newly interpreted with a modern political stratagem, largely promoted by Britain and her appointing of Hajj Amin as the mayor of Jerusalem. It is seen by the emergence of terror groups that overturned the positive agreements executed with the Arab Representatives and the Jews in early 20th Century. It was followed by the corruption of the Balfour, the White Paper Policy and creating new implements of West Bank and Arab Palestinians that were initiated from the British-Hajj Amin alliance.

The new claims and charges made on Israel are in contradiction of this region's Biblical Scriptures, including in the Quran which tells of a return of the Jews to their homeland and attributes this land's sovereignty as vested with the Jews.

The historical imprints do not condone both peoples as returning to their ancestral land because both cannot be viewed as equally possessing a 3,000 year nativity or nationhood. Thus the status of this name has extensive impacts for both past and future history, deemed and declared to extend on numerous other nations far from Israel.

The name weapon has never been a more imperative issue to attend for the modern world that is reluctant to confront such errors. The chaos it derived has thus far resisted the efforts of the greatest powers and minds to resolve this conflict. 'No-Go Zones' across the west can be seen as extensions of the 'West Bank' syndrome thrust upon Israel. Such name titles are based on immigration in-flow, followed by enclaves of variant law applications and the barring of the host country's legislation. Thereafter, as is seen in Palestine, autonomy and independent 2-state demands will result via corruptions of international laws secured via the UN. The West Bank and Pakistan are syndromes of where the No-Go Zones culminate when they combine to form regions within states.

Thereby, such name dislodgement impacts are not hypothetical; consider how the British people would react to enclaves in London being called as Londonistan, or regions in France as Paristan, and its equivalence of subjecting Israel to such a situation. It says the restoration of Israel's historical names is the prerequisite in correcting ancient theological forms of dominion extending globally, and that Britain's people should be in the forefront of such corrections incurred by their leaders, whether made intentionally or otherwise.

A declared Caliphate doctrine is not limited to Israel which is barely half of 1% of Arabia. Here, the reasoning why names changes are condoned and promoted, despite being contradictions of history and by the Christian and Islamic scriptures, is perhaps the most difficult task for the modern world to confront and rectify anymore. The issue is the condoning and promoting of an identity theft as was seen in the Roman mode of a heritage erasing; in the 20th Century the name Palestinian was used in a reverse mode of the same parallel stratagem of Rome, evoked by declared goals of an ancient nation having no right to exist.

The Name Weapon.

An Arab Summit conference in 1964 led by Egyptian President Nasser inaugurated the usurping of the name Palestinian as a new policy, ushering the name weapon in a new kind of war. Arafat will soon emerge from this assembly as the President of the Palestinian Authority. It should have failed, with the world dismissing the premise as a historical absurdity and devoid of a past. Despite that it made Arabs as new Palestinians as dated from the 1960's and thereby not historically validated natives, it succeeded beyond all anticipations. The Christian community fully accepted it; astonishingly.

Implementing Arabs as Palestinians.

The Arab League Summit of 1964.

Admittedly, the correcting of decades of accumulated portfolios of Arabs called as Palestinians is a difficult task anymore. Like the infamous Blood Libel and the Protocols of Zion, this notorious falsehood has successfully seeped into the world community, even within Israel. Yet it is incumbent to consider the consequences if there is no correction of this name's corruption and its true designs. Thereby, its underlying agenda merits a thorough examination what lies ahead for the world community.

The term Palestinian applied to the Arabs will ensure Israel will forever be charged with illegally occupying Arab Palestinian lands; it applies not only to certain sectors but all of Palestine. The usurping of the name Palestinian was not a naive implement; it was a strategic plan undertaken when wars of extermination failed to achieve its result. While such is the declared goal enshrined in the charters of numerous Arab groups, its application is not limited to Israel; it applies to any state or independent enclave for the Copts, Christian Lebanon, the Baha'i, the Armenians and irrespective of any group having a more ancient history in the region. It is also not limited to the Middle East. Aside from the subsequent upheaval of the Christian and Islamic histories and scriptures, it legitimizes a Caliphate doctrine with a self declared agenda across all borders.

Whether Britain understood the reasoning behind the names West Bank and Arab Palestinians or not, as the appointed caretaker of this region she holds the responsibility for the corruption of the Balfour and as the first nation to accept the fictitious name of West Bank that covered Israel's 3,000 year Hebrew town names. As well, its follow-up implementation of Arab Palestinians soon emerged; it fully contradicted the Balfour and Palestine Mandates that occurred under Britain's watch. Both these implements will incur enormous impacts on Christians as it did with the Jews. Its correction must lie with the honorable British people who have unwittingly inherited the corruption of history as a legacy.

The given reasons for changing the land's historical names are avoided in all sectors, including by Governments, politicians, media and theologians. However, the name distortions that are directed at Israel are a placebo of its underlying premise of a theologically based dominion that is not related to land occupation. Instead, Israel is rejected because it contradicts a theological premise. There is a partially emerging phenomenon in the recent times of a growing sector beginning to raise these issues, primarily because of its extensions across the borders of Palestine and the Mediterranean Seas.

An extensive search why the name Palestinian, once fully disdained by the Arabs, was usurped from the Jews, offers one reason by supporters of this bewildering chaos of history. Namely, that because both Jews and Arabs are living in the land called as Palestine it allows both peoples to use the name 'Palestinians'; both may have passports as citizens of Palestine. Thereby, both Arabs and Israelis are Palestinians of one land. However, this can harbor an adverse underlying application when further examined, appearing as a denial and rejection rather than an enjoined assembly of two peoples as citizens of one country. One side rejects the other's history and existence, using the issue differently than so defined.

Today, both Israelis and Arabs are not equally referred to as Palestinians; they are rival displacement premises of the Arabs against the original people who were referred to as Palestinians prior to 1960.

The usurping of the name held by the Jews for 2,000 years displays a deception and intent of displacement of the Jews; it is accompanied by denial of the Jews' attachment to this land and a claim of a separate state, aligned with formidable incitement. In the West Bank example, the Arabs were not called by the name Palestinian in the 1940's or prior; this emerged after an illegal annexation and the changing of this land's name by Jordan in 1948. The land's previous name was Judah and Samaria and its changing marked a negation of Israel's history.

Both the names West Bank and Arab Palestinians are a successive outcome of Jordan's illegal annexation of Israel's historical and legally allocated territory, whereby Arabs as Palestinians occurred soon after the West Bank name emerged. If this was not intended to dislodge the Jews from their land, then Israel's ancient Hebrew names would not be changed to West Bank, and the Arabs would call themselves as Israeli Arabs instead of Palestinians. Instead, the Jews are barred from their most sacred portion of lands west of the river, as well from the new state of Jordan.

West Bank is a fictional name with no heritage or historical veracity and applied illegally. Otherwise, this land would not be made as an Arab Palestinian land with claims for another separate state, a 3-state that is deceptively presented as a 2-state and also seen in the Oslo Accords. The western nations that promoted West Bank, Arab Palestinians and a 3-state also approve of Jerusalem's capital being split. Where a 3,000 year Capital can be denied, those like Britain and Paris, far younger, can more easily be denied, allowing no means of stopping such a phenomenon that will use the same criteria as was done to Israel. It is not a hypothetical issue anymore.

One can see that No-Go Zones across the nations represent, sadly and not stated wantonly, as omens of West Bank implements. No country is immune from the same syndrome, assuredly not so Britain and France whose heritage is far less evidential than that of Israel. Here there is also the declared rejection of Israel's existence in the Arab charters, affronted with the name held exclusively by the Jews as a rejection of a Jewish state via the name used as a weapon, indicating its underlying designs:

• "Before local Jews began calling themselves Israelis in 1948, the term "Palestine" applied almost exclusively to Jews." - (Eli E. Hertz; Myths and Facts)

• "Palestine' is alien to us. It is the Zionists who introduced it." - (Local Arab leader to the British Peel Commission, 1937).

• "There is no such thing as 'Palestine' in history, absolutely not." - (Arab-American historian and Princeton University Professor, Philip Hitti, testifying before the Anglo-American Committee in 1946)

The Arabs rejected the 2,000 year Jewish held name Palestinian prior to 1948, and then used it as a weapon to reject Israel after 1960. Thus, both the names West Bank and Arab Palestinian are not heritage marks of two peoples in the same land as is presented. All indicators say these newly improvised name usurping has been utilized as a weapon against Israel's heritage instead; it is a rejection, not a shared provision. Now the Jews of Israel are no more called as Palestinians as they were for 2,000 years; Palestine is no more referred to as Israel or Judea; it is presented as a negation of the Jewish homeland. Its impacts in other countries are also seen; today, prominent authors have published books with titles that portray western countries with take-over titles, including "Londonistan" and "Eurabia".

Pre-Dating Islam.

History says the disdain and rejection of Israel by the Arabs predated the advent of the Islamic Scriptures which fully identifies this land as of the Jews. It infers a paradigm that pre-dates the belief and as one later used as a political provision in the 20th Century. The Pre-Islamic Arabs that were fully embedded in the Roman legions that destroyed Jerusalem predate the religion by six centuries; thereby it cannot appear only as a theological premise.

Equally, it is implausible that the Christian community would contradict their own scriptures and history, yet they are altogether aligning with its antithetical paradigms. Today, the temple which is recorded in the Roman archives, the Gospels, the Quran and the Dead Sea Scrolls, is presented as a Zionist myth; its denial is not responded to by Christian states that control the UN Security Council votes.

Such positions of silence become a legitimizing of historical corruptions and difficult to rectify later; it is seen with the difficulty in rectifying the term Palestinian as a Jewish symbol. The same is seen in the Middle East with long admitted false charges parading the Arab world such as the Blood Libels and the Protocols of Zion; these too get no attention by Christian states despite being their own liabilities and seen as best-selling books reprinted annually and made as TV Mini-Series. Like the silence of Christian leaders of Arab Palestinians, the denial of the Temple and the Holocaust must also be accounted as condoning of these falsehoods. Its error is of not recognizing that such measures can backfire on the Christian communities, both in the Middle East and beyond those borders, as in a manifest reality.

The understanding of this region's history and why it has taken such a sharp turn in the last century requires its accounting to determine its altered positions. Absent in the discourse is whether there is any legitimacy in attaching the name Palestinian, a historical symbolic mark of the homeland of the Jews for 2,000 years, to the Arabs, and its further aims.

The future consequences of history must thereby rely on the merit of more forthright people than their representatives ruling them. Here, a growing number of ordinary people from all sectors are beginning to voice their concerns with their peers; it is an evolving paradigm that has little to do with Israel. Thereby, the new generation - the future inheritors of humanity - should be informed of the history of the Palestinian premise which has been portrayed by their leaders antithetically against Israel, and why the modern world is in chaos today. The new Arab Palestinian phenomenon is not confusing or complicated, and its history requires its thorough knowledge and unfolding. Here, the truth can only set free those who embrace it.

Historical Origins.

Today's Arabs are not historically connected with the name Palestinian. It is the name anointed by the Romans 2,000 years ago on Judea. The Arabs adopted this name recently in the 1960's, as a rejection of Israel, spurred by Hajj Amin and Arafat. Here, Arafat claimed that there was no temple in Jerusalem, Arabs are the Canaanites and that Jesus was a Palestinian; none in the Christian community challenged him. Thereby it is clear what accepting Arabs as Palestinians represent.

The condoning of one historical falsehood will have impacts on a host of other falsehoods by an uncontrollable thread of extensions. The origin of the Arab Palestinian error and its condoning is thereby an incumbent exposure of its consequences thus far and where it can lead.

Its unraveling must track the first historically validated recording of the names Palestine and Palestinian, and in its sweep, any other known imprints of its associated nativity claimants, including the thread of names from their originally recorded source points to the 20th Century. It must track the source points wherein did the names Palestine emerge, and when did Arabs become as Palestinians, and why it was condoned by the Christian states. Such a journey will include tracking the following entities:

Canaan; Egypt; Babylon; Hebrew; Israel; Abraham; Ishmael; Philistine; Jew; Arab; Judea; Modern Israel; the West Bank; Palestine; Palestinian; Britain; the Vatican and the UN.

That this conflict evolved with the usurping of a historical name, and is thereby also negated by the absence of this name's illicit transfer, must be considered as a difficult yet indispensible solution; that the name weapon may be seen as frontage of an underlying doctrine that is not aligned with the given reasons of this conflict should be accordingly appraised.

The 'Name' Factor.

The phenomenon of a name transfer acts as both the primal cause and the relief of this issue. It presented an un-historical premise as an historical one and thereby an unfolding historical chaos. It is demonstrably the modern world's foremost falsehood and is accepted by a large multitude; why then did it succeed so overwhelmingly is a pivotal issue that must be confronted and corrected before its extensions can be stemmed. Namely, was this name's transferring from Jews to Arabs a circumstantial outcome or a stratagem of destruction; a benign advent of the times or an intentional design directed only to the Jews or to many; and what great upheaval if all peoples living in Palestine are called as Palestinians, a premise seen in all other countries and granted to people by their birth and legal immigration.

The modern world measures us by our name's merit; a life's worth can depend on it, and thereby we are our names and not so without it. In the first century one name has been utilized in the world's lexicons by a reverse application than all its past recorded history. It is one pursued with a determined zeal as a historically valid fact; to the extent questioning its veracity is now a surge against the tide. Yet it is a path not without its negative impacts for humanity at large and one growing and de-stabilizing.

That the Middle East conflict is not related to Israel or the charges of occupation, and that the same situation will extend upon the nations, is told us by doctrines embedded in the region that is deemed outside of the requirements of the faith; thereby, how much more concerning other minorities of different faiths is self evident. In a letter to Mr. Leon Blum, PM of France, Suleiman Assad, the grandfather of Syria's embattled Dictator Bashir al Assad warns France of the dangers in 1936 and predicts slaughter of minorities and praises the Zionists:

• "Dear Mr. Leon Blum, Prime Minister of France.

• The spirit of fanaticism and narrow-mindedness, whose roots are deep in the heart of the Arabs toward all those who are not Muslim, and therefore there is no hope that the situation will change. Why, even today the situation of the Jews in Palestine is the strongest and most concrete proof of the importance of the religious problem among the Arabs toward anyone who does not belong to Islam. Those good Jews, who have brought to the Muslim Arabs civilization and peace, have not hurt anyone and have not taken anything by force, and nevertheless the Muslims have declared holy war against them and have not hesitated to slaughter their children and their women despite the fact that England is in Palestine. Therefore a black future awaits the Jews and the other minorities."

One only needs to see through the fog whose path is impacted negatively, and how many historical accounts relied upon will be over-turned in its sweep. Here, the world's validated history is altered by a name change to create the false claim of occupation and thereby procure its underlying doctrine, giving no immunity to any sector. And allowed to pass a certain point, it becomes akin to a belief and not retractable anymore.

The Judeo-Christian history and its scriptures will be conquered by the power of a name change; and it will impact equally on the Arabs and the Islamic Scriptures and extend beyond. Thereby, a name's original source point is essential in determining its historical evolution, and what provisions are implied of its future impacts.

If the 3,000 year names of Judea and Samaria are made as West Bank, and 2,000 year Palestinian Jews are made as Palestinian Arabs within a mere 30 years following the equally un-historical name of West Bank, what names will be altered of enclaves in Britain, which are less old and less historical than Israel; and after such a precedence been set and legitimized? Arab Palestinian is a name that has impacts on many sectors; if it affects Israel's heritage, then it also does of the two largest belief groups by extension.

An Ancient Name.

Palestine is a name derived from a Hebrew word, one in alignment with the ancient Egyptian archives and the Dead Sea Scrolls as its historical veracity; a name's historical validation does not get better. [6]

Arguably, Israel is the lesser affected because the name Palestine is of a post-Hebrew Biblical period and its impact limited; not so for the Gospel's dependence of King David's genealogy and its encumbrances of Jesus Christ as born in Bethlehem of Judea. In a sense Israel should view losing a name applied to it as a mark of Roman disdain and extermination as better discarded. Yet not so when this name is usurped and used as a weapon of avowed destruction; then it becomes an existential issue and should be viewed as the primal premise of this name's utilizing. This was declared as Mighty Rome's agenda following the destruction of Jerusalem, its people exiled and the Hebrew belief and language forbidden. All was enacted with a name change and the issue of Rome's "Judea Capta" coins. Similar agendas are aligned with the usurping of this name in the modern world; it is declared and enshrined in charters as a means of destruction, allowing none to appear confused why this name transfer was initiated and confuse it as a land issue. The Jews of Palestine have not occupied the land of Palestinian Arabs; the reverse is the case. Here, the doctrine is based on any land invaded will forever remain as the land of the invader; it also applies to Spain and India.

The Name Impacts.

Names have a mysterious impact for humanity and can be made akin to a propaganda stratagem that can be used as a formidable weapon. A name can incur tremendous impacts for the future stability of peoples and nations, including wars, castigation and conflict, and can succeed even in the absence of any validation when it is enforced and not responded to by reason of induced corruptions. It is the fundamental reason why Britain corrupted the Balfour Declaration and created Jordan in Palestine; Britain had to over-turn a host of other paradigms to cover her deeds, including her approval of the name West Bank and Arabs as Palestinians.

In ancient times a name change denoted a historical extermination of a people or nation, aligning with the modern term of genocide. Following the destruction of Jerusalem, a change of name was used by Rome as her ultimate weapon against the Hebrew belief which

63

rejected Rome's divine king status; it marks a syndrome for the Jews across their history, beginning with the first Hebrew in Babylon some 4,000 years ago. Abraham had to flee to neighboring Canaan to escape a death sentence by the divine King Nimrod. It happened again with Mighty Rome's emperors who changed Judea's name to Palestine; the Jews rejected Caligula's demands to be worshiped. Here, those using a name as a weapon can also be seen as inclined with a genocide premise, including by those accepting and supporting its historically false employ.

The name premise is a credible factor to deliberate upon; it was Mighty Rome's most powerful weapon upon the Jews. The claim of the land of Israel as being Arab land, not only of recent time, but from time immemorial, thereby also negating any Jewish history, will subsequently do the same of other histories, and inevitably so. It is indicative why it was usurped when once disdained by the Arabs.

Today, the UN and a multitude of nations, historians and theologians use the name Palestinian as referring to the Arab peoples. Yet Britain, who resurrected the name Palestine in the early 20th Century following the conquest of the Ottoman Empire, referred this name to the 'national home of the Jews' and the term Arabs as the counterpart of the Jews. The same applied with the League of Nations, the previous name of the United Nations, as well by the early Presidents of America and France till the 1960's. What really happened here to over-turn this history has long been outside the discourse of one of the most reported issues; why such a prominent name corruption was so successful is an incumbent enquiry.

The anomalies were stark and blatant, yet it succeeded beyond measure. The former part of the first century's narratives and documentation contradicts the latter part of that century. The name Palestine in legally recognized agreements prior to 1950 had their applications reversed thereafter. The Palestinians of the W.W.2 battalion, who were called as the Jewish Palestinian Brigade, became Arab Palestinians thirty years later. It is a phenomenon that is especially arousing because the two paradigms are not equally validated by either ancient or modern history. Arabs as Palestinians is in contradiction of three scriptures and the world's history; its future affects an unknown quantity. Thereby, more than the history of the Jews is being over-turned; history per se as we knew it was changed.

64

Its consequences have not yet fully arisen, yet there is no avoiding it. All historical archives left by the Greek and Roman writers, the Gospels and the Quran can be reconsidered or qualified. The UN Resolutions that contain the terms Palestine and Arabs will also require re-stating with footnotes and editing. Such depictions are not meant to trivialize, as they represent the future global impacts that will have to be confronted.

A new history will have to accommodate the Arabs who battled Rome to defend their homeland, while the Gospel says this was 'the land of the Jews' and 'the land of Israel'; both scenarios cannot subsist as history. Clearly, a new version of past history cannot stand without far reaching impacts to numerous nations and belief structures; yet they are accepted as a stark anomaly of the modern world that confronts all nations and societies in shrouded dismay.

The coming conundrums will require adjusting. Certainly, the name 'West Bank' does not represent any land presented as from time immemorial; the state of Jordan changed the 3,000 year Hebrew names of Israel's towns in 1950. Thereby a heritage transfer occurred via the usurping of names from one people to another, and the UN soon changed its heritage criteria to two years.

Instead of confronting the illegal action of Jordan and returning this land, Israel became charged with illegally occupying her most historical and revered portion of land, and the name Palestinian transferred from Jews to Arabs soon thereafter for the first time in the 1960's. When all military weapons and numerous wars failed to annihilate Israel, a new weapon was employed by a summit of Arab nations in 1964; it was a war strategy of declared extermination via a name as its weapon.

• "We first hear of Arabs referred to as "Palestinians" when Egypt's President Nasser, with help from the Russians, established the "Palestine Liberation Organization" in 1964. It was only during the 1970s that the newly minted "Palestinians" began to promote their narrative." - (Debunking the claim that "Palestinians" are the indigenous people of Israel; Daniel Grynglas. *JPOST 5-12-15)*.

• "Egypt's Gamel Abdel Nasser launched a new revolutionary group in 1964 — the Palestine Liberation Organization (PLO). - (Livingstone, N.C. and Halevy, D., *Inside the PLO*, William Morrow & Co., New York, 1990, pp. 68-70).

65

• "Many of those who now consider themselves Palestinian refugees were either immigrants themselves before 1948 or the children of immigrants. This historical fact reduces their claim to the land of Israel; it also reinforces the point that the real problem in the Middle East has little to do with Palestinian-Arab rights. - (Middle-East Forum, 'From Time Immemorial' Reviewed by Daniel Pipes, July 1984)

A Historical Template.

Thereby, how much of history is impacted by name changes the world now accepts is not a benign issue; it can be considered as a covert mark of genocide. Israel's return, minuscule as the land she holds (0.5% in Arabia), is yet a significant factor by virtue of its pivotal role in this history, and, tragically, it is seen as an affront to two of the largest belief structures, themselves mutually exclusive of each other, instead of an advocate for both.

Israel is made as a generic premise of rejection in this warp, yet not so outside this realm. The plight of the Jews is an enigma that looms large and continues as one that is older than the current players of this conflict. The extent of the historical miss-representation of Israel's iconic names and its widespread potential impacts for history are noteworthy.

Here, some significant dates, names and icons are appropriate as a template of this history's bigger picture view; it is one which past is not subject to change, yet it is contested and ever challenged. Consider the historical platform that is being negated.

Prior to the 20th Century none of these entities existed:

Iraq; Saudi Arabia; United Arab Emirates; Jordan; Tel Aviv; West Bank; A 2-State Solution; Illegal Occupation; 1967 Borders; Disputed Territory; East Jerusalem; The UN; A sovereign country called Palestine; The Palestinian Authority; Arab People called as Palestinian, A Palestinian Nation, Language, Writing, King, War, or archaeological relic denoting an Arab Palestinian heritage in the pre-20TH Century period.

Prior to the 20th Century these did exist:

Canaan; The Hebrews; The Israelites; Ancient recorded interactions of the Israelites with Egypt; Relics over 3,000 years old with the terms 'Hebrew' and 'Israel'; a war between the Israelites and the ancient Philistines; 3,000 year ancient Hebrew language and writings; Proof of King David as a confirmed 3,000 year historical figure; the sovereign State of Israel with Jerusalem as the Capital established in 1002 BCE; The Jerusalem Temple; a line of Hebrew Kings; Hebrew coins of sovereignty; A War with the Assyrians and the exile of The Ten Lost Tribes of Israel; A War with Babylon and the exile of the Jews to the Arabian region; The Second Jerusalem Herodian Temple; A War with the Greek Empire and a partial exile to Greece; The Septuagint Bible - the first translation of the Hebrew Bible to another language in 300 BCE; Judea - the Roman name for Judah; A War with the Roman Empire - an exile of the Jews to the European continent; Palestine - a name applied to Judea by Rome in 135 CE.

A Lineage of a People's Names.

Abram was the first recorded Hebrew who arrived in Canaan from neighboring Ur in the Land of the Chaldee's /Babylon/Modern Iraq. (Gen. 11:27) **Abraham.** Abram's name is changed to Abraham as recorded in the Hebrew Bible [Gen. 17:5]. **Tribes of Jacob.** The twelve sons of Jacob, grandson of Abraham, were called as the Tribes and Sons of Jacob ['House of Jacob']. The Hebrew tribes constituted one of the groups of Canaan.

The Hebrews. The name of a people used in the Hebrew Bible and by the ancient Egyptians [The Amarna Letters].

The Israelites. The Patriarch Jacob has his name changed to Israel. (Gen. 32:28). **Jew.** The term 'Jew' comes from the name Judah, one of the sons of Jacob. It became the Greek Ioudaios, then the Latinized Iudaeus, then Judea, from which the Old French 'giu' was derived after dropping the letter "d"; it developed into the English word "Jew."

Palestinian. It is a controversial term introduced in the 20th Century and applied for the first time to a people other than the Jews.

A Lineage of a Land's Names.

Canaan - Land of Israel. The opening historical record affirms the previous name of the Land of Israel was called as Canaan 4,000 years ago. The Canaanites, which included the Hebrew Canaanite group,

67

were not an Arab people.[7] Canaan is where the ancestors of the Jews were born and incepted as a nation, a land referred in ancient times as:

Land of the Canaanites [Pre-Abraham Egyptian name/Egyptian Amarna Letters]. **United Kingdom of Israel** The name of Canaan was thereafter changed to 'Israel' with Jerusalem established as its capital under the reign of King David; circa 1002 BCE - [1002-970 BCE 1 Sam 13:9; Carr, David M & Conway / Matt. 2:20-21/N.T / The Annals, XII:54/ Roman Archives). **Land of Judah & Samaria.** The Kingdom was divided into two ruling states following the reign of King Solomon. [Southern & Northern States/9th & 8th Century BCE; 1Kings 16:24] **Land of the Jews** From the Greek 'Ioudas'. [derived from Ἰούδας, α, ὁ /from Yehudah Heb/Ptolemaic Reign/319 BCE/ Baskin, Judith R.; Seeskin, Kenneth (2010); The Cambridge Guide to Jewish History, Religion and Culture, Cambridge University Press, p.3] **Judah** became the name of the southern breakaway state of Israel in the 8TH Century BCE, 200 years after King David's reign. **Judea** Judah was as Judea by its Roman name. [Roman Latin/64 BCE/ From 'Land of the Jews'; Yehudah-Heb.] **Palestine**. In 135 AD/CE, following the destruction of Jerusalem and the Bar Kokhba revolt [132-135 CE], the Roman Emperor Hadrian applied the name Palestrina to the land of the Jews, which Rome previously called as Judea, from the land's Hebrew name Judah. The first official usage of the name Palestrina was by the church historian Eusebius in the 4TH Century; and later anglicized as Palestine. Eusebius' reference applied to the Land of Israel; it remained as a reference to the homeland of the Jews for 2,000 years.[8] **The State of Israel.** Palestine again became The State of Israel ('Medinat Yisrael'); and the Kingdom of Jordan in 1948. (It followed the British Balfour Declaration and Mandate.]

While history and archaeology substantially affirm such a historical template, it is yet made as the most contested issue of the modern world, its stated reasoning also the most contradicting. The charges of occupation and Arab nativity of Judea, which became Palestine, is one even the Romans would balk on; yet not so by a Roman Pope whose ancestors would never have anticipated such a turn. To determine how extensively history has been overturned, and thus perhaps the underlying reasoning of this conflict, requires a contrast ratio of names between ancient history and the 20th Century.

A Denial of History.

Panel A2 is of a Black Obelisk relic located in the British Museum as reference ME 118885. Discovered by archaeologist Sir Austen Layardin in 1846, it verifies a historical event three thousand years ago of the then earliest ancient depiction of a Hebrew biblical figure, that of Jehu, King of the northern state of Israel, invaded by the Assyrian King Shalmaneser who reigned 858-824 BCE. It is 200 years after King David's kingship.

In the reign of King David, the State of Israel battled with the Philistines, a foreign people from across the Mediterranean Sea that occupied Gaza and prevailed as a province called as Philistia for a short period; these were not Canaanites, Hebrews or Arabs, but represent Europe's first invasion of the Middle East. The Philistines are a people also mentioned in the ancient Egyptian writings as a cross reference of this history. Two hundred years after King David's reign Israel battled with the Assyrian invasion and the Northern state of Israel fell, while the southern state of Judah prevailed. Here, in the 9th Century BCE, no imprints of the term 'Arab' are found as a people or nation state from any source. Ancient Egypt was not Arab; it became as an Arab country 1,600 years later, after the 7th Century emergence of Islam. A map contains the name Israel appearing, as well of the Philistines in the land they occupied and called as Philistia; and of Judah which became Latinized as Judea; and numerous towns with Hebrew names which are recognizable today. These are the cities and the land which names were changed as being part of a new region called as the West Bank and as Arab Palestinian native land from time immemorial; that it is illegally occupied by Israel. Significantly, the term 'Arab' is absent in this map of regions and towns.

West Bank is Israel Territory.

The historical picture fully contradicts the 7,000 year Arab nativity claim of this land. Today's West Bank was part of the sovereign territory of Judah (Judea), the homeland of the Jews (see Map below). The Hebrew towns, their names strewn across the Hebrew Bible include Shiloh, Jericho, Bethlehem, Hebron, En Gedi and Beersheba; Gaza, which was captured by the Philistines for a short period, was returned to Judea after King David's battle.

The name Palestine and its derivative Palestinian became the reference allocated to the Jews and their homeland following the Roman Emperor Hadrian naming Judea as Palestine in the 2nd

Century. The ironic factor here is that although the Romans used this name as relating to the ancient enemies of the Jews, namely the Philistines, and denoting the end of Israel, they were fully unaware the Philistines converted and enjoined themselves with the nation of Israel (See, Philistines Became Hebrews').

West Bank is today defined as occupied territory of Arab Palestinians and marks the overturning of Israel's history, as well as of Christianity by subsequence. A map affirms the ancient names of Samaria and Judea's towns, which became as West Bank in 1948 via Jordan's illegal annexation west of the river.

MAP OF JUDEA AND SOUTHERN ISRAEL

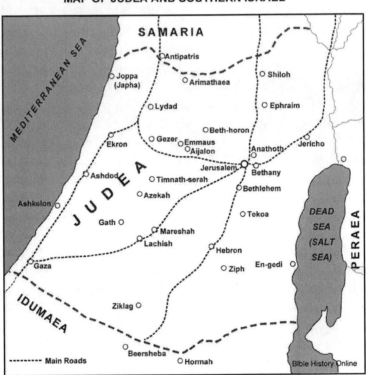

Kingdoms of Samaria and Judah.

Thereby, how much of modern history is impacted by name changes is not vindicated by an occupation charge; history contradicts such a charge. A theological doctrine has been accepted by the UN and presented as a historical premise.

"All anyone can do is to state the truth, as we actually see it and not as we're supposed to see it. The Arabs don't hate Jews because of Israel;

70

they hate Israel because of Jews. The situation in the West Bank and Gaza exists because 45 years ago several Arab countries attacked Israel, unprovoked, with overwhelming odds, because it was a Jewish state. And they attacked with an intention of wiping it from the map and committing genocide." - ("The Great Palestinian Lie"; Pat Condell, English Writer, Secularist)

A NWO.

In the New World Order deceptions are compulsory implements in the political realm; we all do so on some level. Sometimes it becomes an existential threat and its understanding is vital. The held paradigms of the 20th Century contradict many previously held historical positions without presenting a valid counter claim, even presenting them in its reverse historical position. Palestine and Palestinian are names exclusively referring to the homeland of the Jews for 2,000 years, yet it has an antithetical meaning today.

Here, a miss-appropriation of one peoples' history in one sector has impacts in other areas. Today, even Biblical figures as Moses, David and Jesus are denied their historical heritage. While these are genuinely held beliefs, they are also negations of history and the precedent beliefs of others, incurring dire impacts related to the charges on Israel that will extend further afield via similar manipulations of history:

• "**Moses** becomes Muslim because the word Muslim means "one who submits to the will of God (Allah)"

• "**Jesus** using the word "Muslim" in Luke 6:40: Let us look at Luke 6:40 from my N.I.V. Bible". A student is not above his teacher, but everyone who is fully <u>trained</u> will be like his teacher." - (Answering-Christianity)

Recognizing Deceptions.

A deception unchecked can become akin to a belief, one that is inculcated via corruption or enforcement. This presentation posits the case for consideration the allocation of the name Palestinian as an Arab group's title is more than a benign error or limited deception; it can be seen as a covert genocide premise against another people and nation, and numerously declared so. Today, such un-checked manipulations of history affords the reader ready access to investigate them and decide their veracity; these are not presented as absolutes but as challenging of the held dispositions.

Validated ancient history of this controversial name of Palestinian is thereby an indispensible examination, to the extent it is a prerequisite study for those not given its access or presented with a falsified history by manipulation. The term of deception is derived via resurrecting validated history and the premises of faith that are enshrined in both the world's judiciaries and theologies:

• "Thou Shall Not Bear False Witness" [Ex. 20: 16]

• "Not to violate an oath or swear falsely" (Lev. 19:12)

• "That one who possesses evidence shall testify in Court" (Lev. 5:1)

• "You shall surely rebuke" (Lev. 19:7)

• "The Truth Shall Set You Free" [John. 8:22]

• "Acquire knowledge, it enables its professor to distinguish right from wrong" [Hadith/SAV]

2. Resurrecting the Philistines.

A historical conundrum emerged in the 20th Century. One view says that ethnic Arab Palestinians were not heard of prior to the 1960's; another that the Arabs always existed in Canaan and prior to Israel. It is seen in two contrasting views of this issue:

• "The use of the term "Palestinian" for an Arab ethnic group is a modern political creation which has no basis in fact and had never had any international or academic credibility before 1967." - (Joseph E. Katz, Middle-East History analyst). [9]

• "The Palestinian people have been present for thousands of years in Canaan; they [the Palestinians] gathered in the area before anyone else, centuries before the Jewish religion. An Israeli engineer and an archaeologist brought Israeli coins - shekels and agoras - and threw them on the ground in order to prove the Israelis were present here." - (Salwa Hadib, Fatah's Revolutionary Council, Palestinian Authority TV, May 24, 2015)

It is a strange phenomenon that such historical contradictions can subsist in the modern world and be both supported and denied with strong convictions. However, to understand the underlying reasoning of such contradictions, its past history has to be examined, even back to its known origins.

Origins of the Name Palestine.

'Palestinians' - a derivate of Philistine, evolved from a foreign people who arrived in Arabia via the Mediterranean Sea and settled in Canaan. Such is aligned with cross-nation Egyptian verification of the Hebrew Scriptures. There is no historical validation or records from any source of a people called as Arabs having any connectivity with ancient Canaan. Namely, there are no records of a known ancient Arab group or Arab cities, nations, kingdoms, kings, wars or monuments as existing 3,000 years ago by either of those names. Nor were the Philistines, the Canaanites or the Hebrews an Arab people. In contrast to the widespread belief of Arabs and the Hebrews as aligned genealogically or theologically, there is no historical evidence of such a held premise or that the Arabs existed in this time. The name Arab was coined by the Greeks in 300 BCE and adapted from the Hebrew Book of Nehemiah dated as 450 BCE; it is 1,500 years away. [See "Who Are Arabs"]

Contrastingly, we do have writings and relics of the terms Hebrew, Israel, Jerusalem, Canaan, House of David and of numerous wars, kings and monuments, in successive periods 100 years apart of the last 3,000 years, that are recorded in the Hebrew Bible and these are substantially validated via archaeology. It is an impressive contrast.

There are no records of Arabs battling the ancient Philistines 3,000 years ago. Rome applied the name Palestine to a Jewish land 2,000 years ago. Neither did Britain or the Arab people refer the name Palestinian to the Arab people in the 20th Century. Till the 1950's all of Israel's institutions were prefixed with the term Palestinian. The Palestinian Post was Israel's leading newspaper. Therefore, how did this name's attribution become so reversed after 2,000 years in a sudden stroke of the mid-20th Century; and why?

Here, we are left with no alternatives in the tracing of this name's origins than the Hebrew writings that introduced it and the archaeological discoveries of this region as its evidential factors. The archaeological discoveries were not all made by Jews; many are from the British and Arab people themselves prior to Israel's re-establishment. The Hebrew narrative refers to a 3,500 year setting in the land of Canaan, its data the only source available of this name's origins. Numerous surprises become evident with its renewed retrospective examination.

Canaanites were not Arabs.

The Hebrews is the name of this people prior to being called as Israelites, and are accounted as one of the ancient Canaanite groups. They confronted their first invasion of the Philistines as a people from across the seas, namely from the Crete Islands off Greece. The ancient Hebrew and Egyptian records introduced the name 'Peleshet' that became anglicized as Palestine. It is appropriate that unless a contradicting or counter historical archive or archaeological relic emerges, the UN and the nations ought to qualify its description of the term Palestinian by including its association with Israel and the Jews; at the very least the UN and all educational institutions should include such a notice in all places that mention the names Palestine and Palestinian in its archives. The absence of such a connection can be seen as a deception or even a lie-by-omission. Of an estimated one million relics uncovered of Israel's connection with Canaan, there has not been a single equivalent one relating to an Arab ancestry in pre-Israel Canaan.

The reason we have no record of the Philistine people after the 9th Century is because the Philistines became Israelites following a war with King David in 1002 BCE ["Who Are the Philistines"). Thereby, the absence of this name's connection with Israel and the Jews, even rendering it as antithetical of its original recipient, can correctly be seen as among history's great deceptions. It says a strong propaganda strategy can turn a vast multitude with a reversing of a held paradigm and use it as a powerful political weapon. Thereby, one antidote is to fully explore the extent of such a corruption.

First Mention of Philistines.

A biblical verse marks the first interaction of the Hebrews with the Philistines in the time of Abraham, recorded early in the Book of

Genesis, given with credible contemporaneous names of this land's towns and inhabitants:

• "So they made a covenant at Beersheba. Then Abimelech and Phicol the commander of his army rose up and returned to the land of the **Peleshet** [Philistines]." (Gen. 21:32)

"Peleshet" is Palestine.

Thereby, the term 'Philistine' that became as Palestine comes from the Hebrew word '**Peleshet**' (P-L-S-H-T); it means 'invader; Migrant' (Heb.). Namely, this was a group of foreign invaders that migrated from across the seas into Arabia; significantly, that this was a foreign people in the Middle-East. The Hebrew narratives describe the Philistines as the invaders of this land, a reversal of the modern day premise of the Jews occupying the Palestinian peoples' land.

The Philistines are nowhere better described than in the Hebrew Bible; the term Peleshet (Palestine) appears more than 250 times in its Scriptures, in Genesis, and in the later Prophetic writings that include the Books of Judges, Jeremiah, Isaiah, Ezekiel, Joel and the Book of Kings. Thus there was an extensive interaction between the Hebrews and Philistines more than 3,000 years ago and co-referenced in ancient Egyptian relics. Canaan's southern coastline was invaded and occupied by the Philistines in the time of Abraham, including of Gaza, Ashkelon, Ashdod and Gath. Philistia was the name subscribed to sections of the coastline of Canaan that the Philistines invaded and controlled.

Philistines Were Not Arabs.

These historical writings that mention the Philistines are not referring to any indigenous Middle-Eastern group, including the Hebrews and Canaanites, but to pirate sea vessels invading Canaan from 'the other side of the Mediterranean Sea' - the Egyptian description of those who came from the lands today called as Europe. Namely, that these were a foreign non-Semitic invading people. The Philistines ceased to exist 3,000 years ago after a 200 year battle that culminated with King David. Thereby, the Hebrew Bible also marks the earliest recorded interaction of the Canaanites, Egyptians and Hebrews with the Europeans, over a thousand years prior to the Greek Empire's invasion.

The Philistines were a Greek associated people from the Island of Crete who settled in the coastal region of Canaan, establishing their base in a well fortified underground city of tunnels in Gaza; many of these tunnels still subsist, their goal the conquering of new lands, a generic syndrome in human history. A map depicts the region of Canaan invaded and occupied by the Philistines, lands which later became as Israel, then split as two north and south sovereign Hebrew states called as Israel and Judah:

Map of Philistia

Coastal Regions Occupied by the Philistines.

Philistine Origins.

While the Noah story is not historically validated, it remains the only archives mentioning the origins of the Philistines; they are first recorded as stemming from Noah in the genealogy thread of names listed in the Book of Genesis:

• "And Pathrusim, and Casluhim—whence went forth the Philistines—and the **Caphtorim**. [Gen. 10:14].

Thereby, this people came from **Caphtor** (Crete); Caphtorim is the pluralized term for this people that invaded Canaan in circa 12th - 15th Century BCE; they became called as **Peleshet** (Invaders; Migrants) by their invasion of Canaan's coastline. Their superior new iron weaponry soon conquered and destroyed several towns, with authentic

76

geographical period names as is seen with 'Gaza' being far south of Canaan. Of note, the term 'Avvim' is not related to Arabs or a people who emerged from Arabia, but are the invaders:

• "And the Avvim, that dwelt in villages as far as Gaza, the **Caphtorim**, that came forth out of Caphtor, destroyed many towns. (Duet 2:23; Jer. 47:4).

The later Hebrew Prophetic writings recall the Philistine invasions of the towns by names again, also illustrating Gaza and Ashkelon as part of the land of Judah, which the Romans called as Judea. These names correspond with the names of towns in the 20th Century as a mark of their credibility:

• "Because of the day that cometh to spoil all the Caphtorim (Philistines), to cut off from Tyre and Zidon every helper that remaineth; for the LORD will spoil the Philistines, the remnant of the isle of Caphtor. Baldness is come upon Gaza, Ashkelon is brought to naught, the remnant of their valley; how long wilt thou cut thyself? [Jere. 47:4]

Ancient Minoans.

Further archives conform to the Philistines as foreign ship-pirating enemy combatants, originally from the largest Greek island of Crete and of Asia Minor, a mixed people of non-Arabian refugee tribes that included the Danauna, Tzakara, Masa, Shardana and Akhaiusha peoples. Thus by their means of robbery and ransom demands comes the name "Peleshet" (invader; migrants/Heb). Their plight appears subsequent to being a displaced people when the ancient Minoan civilization disintegrated and was taken over by the Greeks. Thereby, Goliath is an indicative non-Arabian Philistine name, as is Delilah; such name recordings cast a positive indicator of the Hebrew writing as both contemporaneous and credible.

The Iron Age.

The land the Philistines occupied in Gaza was referred to as 'Philistia' after the Hebrew 'Peleshet', which the Greeks used to derive the name Philistine, expressing a Greek conquered land in Judea which never came to fruition. The Philistines were a warring and invading people who caused great fear with the introduction of their new 'iron' weaponry; it is the advent of the Iron Age. They incurred many battles with the Israelites and the Egyptians. This people also showcased a refinement of skills in crafts, building of religious monuments and weapons artistry; they would have served good knowledge in Arabia had they ceased resorting to war and mayhem. They worshipped a lesser known deity known as Dagon and erected huge fire-belching subterranean monuments of worship. Thereby, this was a people who occupied the land of the Canaanites and conducted attacks on the Egyptian and Canaanite peoples, by invasion and usurping of lands, and by demanding ransoms for kidnapped hostages. Not even the great Egyptian power could conquer the Philistine war hardy people. Thus the Jews and Arab peoples, despite being called by this name, are not Philistines from the other side of the sea, but natives of the Middle East.

• "Art exhibiting Aegean characteristics has been uncovered at recent excavations at the Canaanite palace of Tel Kabri in Israel." - (Minoan Frescoes at Tel Kabri; Biblical Archaeological Society)

Theologically, it is believed the Israelites returning to Canaan in the Exodus under Moses took the long circuitous desert paths rather than the shorter 200 mile distance from Goshen via the coastal King's Highway; they appear to have done so to avoid a confrontation with the 'path of the Philistines' who prepared an ambush for them. The Israelites are told by the Hebrew God, via Moses, to 'turn back; turn around'; it is also by divine providence that Moses was commanded to bring the Israelites to Mount Sinai in the heart of the Arabian Desert, as is recorded in the Hebrew narratives in the Book of Exodus:

• "When thou hast brought forth the people out of Egypt, ye shall serve God upon this mountain." [Ex.12:3]

The Philistine Departure.

Samson, from the Hebrew tribe of Dan, battled with the Philistines. (Book of Judges; Ch.13). But none in the region could conquer this iron-clad war hardy pirate people till King David finally vanquished the Philistines in their underground bases in Gaza, thereby marking the end of this group's historical thread and its invasion attempts of the Hebrew and Egyptian lands.

Sheppard lad and Poetic Harpist David smites Goliath

Philistines Became Israelites.

After the invading Philistines were conquered as an enemy force they held prominent positions in King David's army. Namely, Israel's ancient enemy ceased being as enemies, becoming followers of the Hebrew belief and were absorbed within the Hebrew nation. As with the Jebusites and other non-Hebrew Canaanite groups, the Philistines became fully embedded with the Ten Tribes of Israel and were exiled along with the Jews when the Northern Kingdom of Israel was invaded by Assyria in 722 BCE. Hereafter, the Philistine people will cease to exist other than their absorption into the Northern tribes of Israelite nation; we do not hear of them again. [10]

The Philistine name will become resurrected again 2,000 years later.

3. Rome-To-Palestine.

The Roman Empire conquered the Greek Empire, entering Arabia in 64 BCE, with Judea falling under the Roman reign. Monotheism, a Hebrew law based on the belief in one God became a dire issue for the Jews in the divine emperor realm. Six years after Jesus of Nazareth is killed under the reign of Tiberius, a new king ascended the throne in 37. Rome's most notorious emperor soon proclaimed himself as divine, issuing a heresy decree that would ensure great calamity for the Jews. Caligula demanded a statue of his likeness, made of fine gold, which he decreed must be worshipped by the Jews in their Holy Temple with daily sacrifice, as they did of their Hebrew God:

• "So you are the only people who reject my divinity!" (Caligula; Roman Emperor; 37 AD/CE)

The Hebrew laws forbade the Jews of accepting Rome's edict despite its dire consequences; it is a primal law of the Hebrew Monotheism, one that contested the Jews with the nations they interacted throughout their history. The law of Monotheism is the most wordy and elaborated of all laws commanded to the Jews by their Hebrew God:

• "Thou shalt have no other gods before Me. Thou shalt not make unto thee a graven image, or any manner of likeness, of anything that is in heaven above, or that is in the earth beneath, or that is in the water under the earth; thou shalt not bow down unto them, nor serve them. [Ex. 20:1]

The Jews sought to negotiate with Rome for their freedom of belief and as an exception of such an edict, but they were rebuffed for seeking special privileges. Caligula threatened the destruction of Jerusalem and its temple monument of its refusal. A temporary respite for the Jews came when Caligula and his family were assassinated by his own people. Thereby, the Jews became the only people in the empire who rejected the Roman Emperors' self-appointed divinity commands, and became Rome's greatest enemies. The same syndrome was seen of the Jews with the Greek, Babylonian and Egyptian Empires. The Monotheism belief threatened the status quo and became the substantial cause in the felling of the ancient divine king realm, a law that later prevailed upon the Roman Empire with the advent of Christianity, one that upheld the monotheistic belief as a global phenomenon.

The Birth of Palestine.

Monotheism was thereby the chief reason for the woes of the Jews with the Romans. Otherwise, the Jews enjoyed distinguished positions in the institutions of the nations. The first century was a period of decline of the Roman beliefs; it had been evolving since the first translation of the Hebrew Bible (The Septuagint) by the Greeks in 300 BCE. The Hebrew belief spread around the Greco-Roman empires with estimates of over 10% of the population inclined with the Hebrew monotheism that aligned with Aristotle's 'First Cause' philosophy. Many Roman senators and emperors, including Nero, had Jewish wives; monotheism became the source point of the tottering of the divine king belief.

Thereby, the Roman emperors' fury against the Jews who rejected worshipping them had no bounds. Rome went to war with the Jews in 70 CE, destroying Jerusalem and its temple and killing over a million Jews. When this failed to convince the Jews to forgo their monotheism, Rome decided to eliminate all memory of the Hebrew belief in 135 CE by changing the name of Judea, the Roman name of the Land of Judah, to Palestine, resurrecting the name of Israel's ancient enemy. Rome's name change stratagem will impact history and the modern world 2,000 years later; it became a weapon via a name that measured more destructible upon the Jews than all other weapons of Mighty Rome.

Palestine is Judea.

The premise of changing and forbidding of names is an ancient one, usually as a means of exterminating the victim from all historical memory. The name Peleshet, one later Anglicized as Palestine, was thus applied to the Jewish homeland of Judea 2,000 years ago by Rome in the second century by the Emperor Hadrian. The Hebrew language was also forbidden. A study of the Roman archives says Mighty Rome was not only a military power but also a mighty force of guile and propaganda. Rome had a strategic agenda for changing the name of the land of the Jews.

The Jews were seen as an anti-establishment rebellious people that threatened to de-stabilize the prevailing order of the empire's divine emperor structures. Rome had good cause to worry; monotheism was a new kind of foe, a counter theological premise that will eventually fell the worldly realm of divine emperors. When some 10% of Romans and Greeks, estimated as over a million, held secret conversions or attraction to the Hebrew belief, it ignited the wrath of the emperors and their enormous propaganda machine against the Jews.

• "The issues came to a head over the large number of Gentiles who became converts, or who wanted to become converts, to Judaism" - (Baron, 1983, vol. 1, p. 181).

• "Propaganda is considered to be a modern political art, but the Romans were masters of 'spin'. It is how Rome's leaders communicated their power and policies to a massive and diverse empire." - ("The Official Truth: Propaganda in the Roman Empire" *By Dr Neil Faulkner, Ancient Roman Propaganda, BBC.*)

A Clash of Beliefs.

Rome's war with the Jews varied from all other wars. In the first century, half of humanity's future belief system hung in the balance. Monotheism, more than the miniscule province of Jews, held a latent weapon shrouded within, and Rome correctly erupted with a wrath upon the Jews not seen with any other nation. The historian Flavius Josephus states Rome's emperors never spared anyone for anti-Roman activities, that all writings were scrutinized and had to be approved; many bold Roman philosophers who spoke against the emperors were killed. [111] Huge marble statues of Roman Emperors and Roman Gods dominated all town squares, their images embossed on coins that the people faced daily wherever they turned. Inevitably, the Jews inherited a legacy of disdain from the Roman inculcation that became embedded within the history that impacted the western and Arabian realms; the Britons and the Arabs were both embedded in the Roman legions from the destruction of Jerusalem, to the name changing of Judea to Palestine and up to the last stand of the Jews at Masada.

The Jews, via their stiff-neck allegiance of their monotheist faith, achieved a legacy as the greatest foe of the nations and a counter of the prevailing status quo, impacting both the Arabian and the Greco-Roman world of divine kings. Since the Hebrew Bible's first translation into Greek, monotheism's impact grew in the new Roman reign, whereby a nation's future credibility had to have this new belief discipline as foundational.

With the advent of Christianity, monotheism marked the demise of the divine emperor realm, yet holding in its wake much residual Roman negativity toward the Jews; such was the power of the inculcated Roman propaganda. Arguably, Rome's enormous propaganda inculcations throughout the empire's nations was the forerunner of anti-Semitism and the rejection of Israel as its residual imprints, infiltrating the theological and political structures that followed.

The minuscule Hebrew nation should not have survived among the theological forces that arose out of the Roman war with the Jews; inexplicably, it did. The Jews remained as Jews and their belief continued in a state of exile and bondage, despite their stiff-neck opposition to the two new monotheistic belief systems that evolved, each pursuing the dominant role in the emerging new monotheist realm. Ironically, the Jews became the faithless and the un-believers by the very belief systems that sprang from the Hebrew belief; the bondage assured them as a surety will continue unabated.

Hereafter, Rome's "Judea Capta" made the ousting of the Hebrew belief as manifest to the new religions, accounting it as divine punishment instead of attributing their situation to the Romans. Contrastingly, the Jews saw the Roman war as a battle for their freedom of belief. For the nations, the changing of Judea's name to Palestine and the utter Roman destruction of Jerusalem said there is no return of this nation; 'Judea Capta' was the held paradigm. Thus did the Jews inherit the legacy whereby the modern state of Israel's return was accounted as an affront.

Thereby, in a certain sense the usurping of a name in the 20th Century is a historical drama that symbolizes the upholding of Rome as a dismissing of Israel. Thus did the first century mark history's greatest clash of beliefs; the divine king realm fell and three monotheistic beliefs prevailed, yet with inherently self contradicting and mutually exclusive values of the same space-time they refer to. In the modern world it is represented by the historical chaos of the term Palestinian as its legacy and marked by the reversing of the Palestinian attribution from the Jews to the Arabs, one condoned and supported by the leaders of the Christian nations. History was overturned via a name reversal.

A New History is Born.

For the Jews Mighty Rome is always lurking. The past 2,000 years of history made the name Palestine referred exclusively to the Jews as a reminder of their vanquished homeland. It became a name aligned with a mark of the "Judea Capta" symbol - it signified the fallen, with a disdain, empathy, wonder and reductionism, extending in Europe and Arabia, within Christianity and Islam, with the British and into the 20th Century. The chaos is seen with the Jews first referred to as Palestinians, a people from their historical homeland of Palestine, then it reversed upon itself the same century.

All British and American archives referred the name Palestine to the historical land of the Jews, including legal treaties such as the San Remo Resolutions and the Palestine Mandate; the Jews remained as the Palestinians till the 1960's. Then history turned and a new people and history are born by the name held by the Jews for 2,000 years.

A Theological Affront.

It is difficult to remove the theological factor from this chaos; it appears to rule all else. It is an unavoidable factor and arguably transcends all other reasoning in this theological hotbed. In the 20th Century a new paradigm will emerge, as if a delayed realization occurred; Israel's return will become an affront and a hate fest. The world will reject their own enactments and scriptures that Palestine is Judea, as well their previously declared mandates that proclaimed Palestine as the historical national home of the Jews, altogether reversing the Roman anointing of this land. Humanity's most advanced phase became its most chaotic.

The notion of a minuscule Israel's return, instead of being seen as a welcome historical premise, erupted as a delayed rejection of the Balfour Declaration of 1917, indenting on both the British and Arab determinations, the Christian and Islamic beliefs and subsequently worldly politics. Here, even the enormous richness of oil wells and granting the Arabs more than 95% of the region will not stem the forces arrayed. The Vatican will call Arabs, not Jews, as Palestinians, in contradiction of its own scriptures; the Arabs will deny the existence of the Jerusalem temple in contradiction of both the Christian and Islamic Scriptures; and both will support each other in this quest. They will enact abounding UN Resolutions of international laws against Israel, demanding 2-state divisions in minuscule Palestine every 50 years.

Here, carving off 80% of Palestine for a 2-state compromise, the White Paper Policy, the West Bank, the transfer of the name Palestinian and the demand of half of Israel's capital will not suffice. Israel will be called as an apartheid state and Zionism, derived from a 3,000 year religious symbol, will be declared as racism. A great multitude will follow the new paradigm and the bondage assured to the first Hebrew, Abraham, will stay unceasing. Thereby this name became as a weapon and used against the Jews in the latter 20th Century akin to Mighty Rome's stratagem 2,000 years ago. Israel's return will be presented by a host of politically improvised mechanizations, with the name usurping of Palestine acting as its pivotal weapon. Judea, which became Palestine, will be presented as the historical home of the Arabs. A new history will be embraced; the Jewish Palestinians will be charged with illegally occupying the land of a new group of Arab Palestinians in the same 20th Century that returned the Jews. The world's media, dictionaries, encyclopedias, clerics and priests, and the UN will follow suit. Israel will be overwhelmed.

A great chaos will unfold; it will contradict both the Gospel and the Quran that refers to Palestine as the Land of the Jews and the Land of Israel, as they do of Jerusalem being a Jewish holy city, as do all of Rome's historians and the Dead Sea Scrolls. When Christianity and Islam ascended as powerful new religions, their doctrines of belief did not cater to the return of the Jews to their homeland; these engaged in numerous battles to each claim this land. With the enforced Roman exile of the Jews, their homeland was invaded by the Crusaders and the Mohammedans; these battled each other without any relevance of its Jewish association. 'The Kingdom of Heaven' will showcase the battle of the Crusaders and the Sultan Saladin with not a frame of the Jews and be hailed as an epic historical drama.

"Judea Capta" held sway; a return was not in their radar. Both beliefs said so; thereby God said so. Love and peace their slogans, but not for the Jews, and any notion the Jews paid the price of this rejection would not satisfy. The return of Israel is thereby an unanticipated controversy and an un-welcomed disruption. In Arabia it contradicted a Caliphate doctrine; nor was Israel's resurrection the preferred anticipated result for most of Christianity. In 1964, the Arabs will assume the name Palestinians and claim an attachment of this land from time immemorial and the Christian community will not be moved to counter such a claim; it will be supported. Yet the historical

85

records will yield no references to an Arab state called Palestine, or Jerusalem as the Capital of any other nation than the Jews. For 2,000 years Palestine was referred to as a stateless 'region' that was previously the 'land of the Jews'.

In 1964 Palestine will be promoted as the ancient land of the Arab Palestinians and enter the world's vocabulary as a historical fact, one validated as international law. New regions called as West Bank and East Jerusalem will appear for the first time in recorded history. Chaos will enter the new world order and Israel will be more focused upon at the UN and in the nation's reporting than any other issue. Global protest marches will emerge of the pre-1960 Jewish Palestinians occupying the post-1960 Arab Palestinian lands from time immemorial. All this happened; it is not a mockery or over indulgence of colorful imagery; it is real history. It was initiated by the two prominent players of this history's new world order.

Britons and Arabs in Rome's Armies.

Significant to this history, both the Britons and the Arab people were embedded among the Roman legions as mercenaries in the destruction of the Jerusalem Temple by Titus in 70 CE, and in Hadrian's anointing of Judea as Palestine in 135 CE following the Bar Kokhba war. Such is recorded in the Roman and Hebrew archives, including by Deo Cassius and Flavius Josephus. Here, even the brutal Roman commander Titus who commanded the war with the Jews, the son of the Emperor Vespasian, uses the harshest terms in denouncing the un-restrained hatred of the Arabs towards the slain corpses of the Jews. Titus charges the Arab barbarity against slain Jewish corpses of disgracing the honor of the Romans. It is seven centuries before the advent of Islam emerged, thereby furthering the anomalies by questioning whether this is a theological or pre-dating evolving disdain. Flavius Josephus writes:

• "For there was found among the Syrian deserters caught gathering pieces of gold out of the excrements of the Jews bellies. 5. When Titus came to the knowledge of this wicked practice, he had like to have surrounded those that had been guilty of it, and have shorten them dead; and said to them, "What? Have any of my own soldiers done such things as this, out of the uncertain hope of gain, without regarding their own weapons, which are made of silver and gold? Moreover, do the Arabians and Syrians now out of their barbarity in

86

murdering men; and out of their hatred to the Jews, get it ascribed to the Romans?" [12]

Equally significant in the 20th Century is what the angst against the Jews was all about. As with Mighty Rome, the land allocated for the Jews will be rejected even as they faced potential extermination omens both in Europe and Arabia; barred from leaving their exilic positions and barred from returning to Palestine. Britain's war ships will take time out from a world war to sink refugee boats of Jews fleeing Europe, while the Jews will face chants of genocide in Arabia. Thereby, what really all the fuss was about with the Jews becomes an incumbent issue of its retrospection.

A Barren Swamp.

There were no oil reserves here and hardly any water. In the early 19th and 20th Centuries, Palestine was a neglected swamp-like region under the Ottoman Empire (later, Turkey), one which held a Caliphate doctrine, but fell in WW1 to the Allied forces led by Britain.

Following the demise of the Ottomans, the British resurrected the name Palestine back to this region, referring this land as the 'national home of the Jews' (The Balfour Declaration). The Arab chieftains and the Zionist representatives of the Jews deliberated, then executed positive agreements of the Balfour Declaration of 1917; the Emir Faisal accepted that Palestine, all of it including Jordan, would be assigned as the state for the Jews. The outlook was positive for the Jews in 1919. Then, vast deposits of oil were discovered; Britain will appoint, instead of a Jewish mayor, the notorious anti-Semitic Hajj Amin as Jerusalem's mayor, one who will align with the Nazis that Britain will later go to war with. It is in such a scenario and with Britain and Hajj Amin as the two most prominent players that the Jews' darkest period will emerge in Europe and Palestine's name usurping will occur.

It will awaken a conflict that will become the world's most intractable one of all, even assuming centre stage from all other worldly issues. Britain's handing out 22 new Arab regime states and the carving away of 80% of the land allocated for 'one only Jewish state' in the original Balfour texts, will not suffice to quell this conflict. Britain and all Christian states, the Vatican and the UN will also turn on the barren minuscule state allocated for the Jews.

- "Until the late 60s, to call an Arab a "Palestinian" would mean to insult him because until the late 60's the word "Palestinian" was commonly and unanimously associated in the entire world with Jews. Palestine was just another name for Israel and Judah." - (Palestinians: The Invented People; Cherson and Molschky)

- "Brothers, half of the Palestinians are Egyptians and the other half are Saudis," - (Hamas Minister of the Interior and of National Security, Fathi Hammad; Al-Hekma TV)

While Rome applied the name Palestine as a negation of the Jewish state and the Hebrew belief, the Arabs and Britain will remove this name from Israel for the same reason 2,000 years later. Thereby the name Palestinian, one without any prior association with Arabs, will again become resurrected 2,000 years after its Roman anointing on Judea by a new group other than the Jews. Inexplicably, it will be supported by a host of Christian states and culminate in the greatest historical deception of the modern world. Britain and Europe will support the Arabs with provisions antithetical of both Israel and Christianity's histories.

Britain's Caliphate.

The 21 Islamic states created by Britain were not of land owned by the Arabs previously. Most of the region's land enclaves were allocated by the Ottomans to Arab chieftains as 'landlord' status that collected rents from the occupants. While the region before the Ottomans were once ruled by the Arabs, this was by way of invasion in the 7th Century of other countries; yet the Arabs claimed a return to the lands they invaded which were not theirs previous, and claim Israel has no right of return, despite that Israel was legally re-established in her own land. Thereby there is hypocrisy of such a claim.

The countries that Britain created were not independent states that existed before; Iraq, Saudi Arabia, Jordan and all the Gulf States were new countries. Israel is the only state that previously existed as a sovereign one. The issue does not align with situations and reasoning offered why Israel should not return; Israel's past history is altogether denied. Here, the issue is not whether the Arabs merited states, which they correctly did as inhabitants of the region; the issue is the British mode of settling this region.

While Britain was handed the responsibility of creating mandates for states, this did not mean the entire region to be handed to one group, substantially to one family and bereft of any conditions of rule. Many other groups merited states and their basic human rights protected; Britain can be seen as failing in this regard, exposing a high mode of corruption. In this regard Britain facilitated a Caliphate and further assisted the Arabs against a Jewish state's existence. It is the fundamental reasoning of the charges on Israel that were manipulated as land occupation and Arab displacement in Palestine; the reverse is the fact.

The errors of Britain's facilitating of a Caliphate, whether by default or to serve her own commercial interests, and the absence of any ruling conditions on the regime states, resulted in consequences that extended beyond Israel and the Middle East. The exodus of refugees fleeing Arabia is the result of the regimes appointing clerics to incite groups with radical agendas as a deflection from their dictatorial rule. These issues are not connected with Israel, although such inferences are seen in the British and European media. They were most substantially caused by Britain.

That Britain included highly demanding conditions of governance on Israel with the Balfour Mandate but none on the regimes remains a pivotal cause of the ensuing conflict in the Middle East, including the basis of a Caliphate doctrine that has sprouted. This was a misguided British, not a Zionist, plot.

In the aftermath of W.W.II the situation appeared calamitous for the Jews. Yet Israel's return and re-establishment was not initiated by Britain, Europe or by Herzl as is commonly portrayed, but by another entity that held variant dispositions. It is a nation that had a Constitution varied from both Arabia and Europe and harbouring a different accounting of historical jurisprudence. In the 15th Century, by the turn of a strong easterly wind, the Jews who were expelled from Spain secured a refuge. A ship loaded with Jews, Africans, Spanish and Italians washed ashore, arriving before the British did, and it will abide them, even raising a new found land with a glory not seen in prior history.

4. America-To-Palestine.

Israel's re-establishment was not a consequence of World War II or the Holocaust as is promoted by some sectors. Although the dedication of Theodor Herzl was the true engine of Israel's eventual return up to his death in 1904, the historical record from the early 1800's says it was the early American Presidents who initiated the return of the Jews to their historical homeland, impacting upon Britain toward such a goal before Herzl did. It marks the contrast to many citing W.W.II as the cause of Israel's re-establishment, namely that the Jews illegally occupied someone else's land by using the Holocaust as its reasoning. Contrary to such a view the Jews were in fact hindered from returning prior to W.W.2 by both the British and the Arabs, even with the full awareness of the Holocaust that both had a substantial role in its cause.

Early Presidents.

The historical portrait says the hope of return was a 2,000 quest by the Jews, embodied in their daily prayers of 'next year in Jerusalem'. Of immense historical significance, the early American President's archives use the names 'Judea' and 'Palestine' as both referring to the Jews and their national homeland; they promoted such a quest before Herzl became the successful deliverer of one of the greatest recorded prophesies that became an empirical premise:

• "I believe in the rebuilding of Judea as an independent nation. I will insist the Hebrews have done more to civilize man than any other nation." (John Quincy Adams' letter to Major Mordecai Manuel Noah; 1829)

• "Restoring the Jews to their national home in Palestine is a noble dream. My emancipated hope is the restoring of the Jews to their nation home in Palestine" (President Abraham Lincoln to Canadian Zionist Wentworth Monk; 1863.

• "I think that I, the son of the manse, should be able to restore the Holy Land to its people" - (President Woodrow Wilson, 1913-21)

• "It is impossible for one who has studied at all the services of the Hebrew people to avoid the faith they will one day be restored to their historic national home" - (President Warren Harding, 1921-23)

• America's follow-on Presidents all made similar declarations, including Calvin Coolidge (1923-28), Herbert Hoover (1928-1932), Franklin Roosevelt (1932-44), Harry Truman (1944-60), Dwight D. Eisenhower (1952-60), John Kennedy (1960-63), Lyndon Johnson (1963-68), Richard Nixon (1968-74) and Gerald Ford (1974-76). [13]

Britain followed the American advocating accordingly with her Balfour Pledge:

• "The allied nations with the fullest concurrence of our government and people are agreed that in Palestine shall be the foundations of a Jewish Commonwealth." (Woodrow Wilson response to the Balfour Mandate; 1915)

• "I am strongly wedded to the Zionist policy of which I was one of the authors." - Churchill wrote to President Roosevelt, on August 9, 1942.

"Israel was not created in order to disappear - Israel will endure and flourish. It is the child of hope and home of the brave."

- (John F. Kennedy speech to the Zionists of America Convention, August 26, 1960)

5. A Worldly Multitude.

In W.W.2 both the names Palestine and its derivative adjective still applied exclusively to the Jews, as is seen in the regiment of the Jewish Palestinian Brigade of the 20th Century, one the 26,000 Jewish soldiers wore with the Star of David on their uniforms in the British Army's Jewish Palestinian Battalion.[14]

Jewish Palestinian Brigade under the Union & Jewish Flags

Britain's Balfour Declaration emerged in the early 20th Century. Britain was handed a care-taker role to mandate and settle this region, with the pre-dating commitment of a mandate for the re-establishment of Israel she accepted, one that was initiated by America and Herzl; both of their historical documents listed Palestine as the home of the Jews, as did the previous Ottomans Empire.

Two thousand years after Rome changed Judea's name to Palestine, the British re-introduced this name again in the early 20th century, one previously advocated by the symbols used by America's early

Presidents. Following the defeat of the Ottoman Empire (later, Turkey) by Britain and her allies, the British initiated the re-establishment of Israel as one of many states created in the Middle-East. In its allocation for a National Homeland for the Jews in Palestine in 1917, Britain issued a document known as The Balfour Declaration; a legal treaty the Jews fully depended upon:

- *"His Majesty's government view with favor the establishment in Palestine of a national home for the Jewish people, and will use their best endeavors to facilitate the achievement of this object, it being clearly understood that nothing shall be done which may prejudice the civil and religious rights of existing non-Jewish communities in Palestine, or the rights and political status enjoyed by Jews in any other country."*

Early Corruptions.

This text was varied from the original by Britain's grammatical and textual manipulation that facilitated the division of Palestine ("The Balfour Corruption"). Yet it emerged as the operational treatise, one the overwhelmed Jews had to accept reluctantly. The conflict was fuelled early with Britain appointing, instead of a Jewish mayor, the notoriously anti-Semitic Hajj Amin al-Husseini as the grand mayor of Jerusalem in 1921, an illicit contradiction of both the Balfour Declaration of 1917, and the positive agreements signed between the Zionists and the Emir Faisal in 1919.

It soon thereafter resulted in the turmoil this action endorsed by Britain, with the rejectionist Brotherhood groups aligned with Hajj Amin. Britain's deeds against the Jews will emerge as a conspiracy and lead to one of history's darkest periods.

The conflict intensified with Mr. Lord Balfour, the British Foreign Secretary who earnestly sided with the Jews for a return to their 'historical national home' - the term he used in the text. The Jews saw the term 'national' as signifying all of Palestine, as did Lord Balfour. That this was a correct understanding by the Jews is seen by Britain's later over-turning of this pivotal document with a subsequent newly enacted varied position; it required its renewed legalized status via the UN with a corrected version that will alter the original and become the first cause of this conflict.

Mr. Balfour altogether negated an additional Arab state in Palestine, even disavowing self-determination of some 700,000 Arabs that emigrated here from the surrounding regions; those Arabs who favored living amidst the Jews than under the ruling powers of the countries they came from. In 1917 the Arabs are not called as Palestinians; it is the reference exclusively directed to the Jews. What was Britain's intention that the Jews should have Hajj Amin as their mayor must speak for itself.

Significantly, the original Balfour Declaration pledged '*One Jewish State in Palestine*' as is seen in the statements of Lord Balfour himself; namely, no inferences or indication of more than one state appears, a most essential factor should this have been intended. Here, the reference '*nothing shall be done which may prejudice the civil and religious rights of existing non-Jewish communities*' was also absent, added later, but unseen in the conditions placed on the Arab states. The former texts rejects any political and citizen rights in Palestine for the Arabs, as indicated by Lord Balfour himself; nor is there any mention of a 2-state division.

Mr. Balfour negates an additional Arab state in Palestine.

"For in Palestine we do not propose even to go through the form of consulting the wishes of the present inhabitants of the country [i.e., we do not accept the principle of self-determination for the Arabs of Palestine] ... the four great powers are committed to Zionism. And Zionism, be it right or wrong, good or bad, is rooted in age-long traditions, in present needs, in future hopes, of far profounder import than the desires and prejudices of the 700,000 Arabs who now inhabit that ancient land ..."

-- Lord Balfour – As British Foreign Secretary, he was responsible for the Balfour Declaration in 1917 which promised Zionists a national home in Palestine.

Sabbah Report: www.sabbah.biz

Lord Balfour negates Arab self-determination in Palestine.

Three years after the Balfour Declaration was issued Britain will propel a new global paradigm, one that will foster utter calamity upon the Jews. Here is also a darker phenomenon that will cast a foreboding premise, one that will compel Britain to cause a new reality in direct opposition to that espoused by Lord Balfour and by Britain's own pledges to the Jews; even in opposition of the prominent Islamic figures who welcomed the Zionists in 1919. We learn why a solemn pledge made before a global multitude was corrupted, and why many other peoples of the region that were among the most ancient inhabitants of this region were not handed a state nor their rights protected; and why so many regime states were created and handed substantially to one family, with no conditions attached as was seen in the Balfour Declaration. In the aftermath of the Balfour pledge of 1917 the British Empire will align with a newly created country.

• "In early 20th Century, Saudi Arabia discovers its enormous oil reserve and starts to do business with the Western Countries. Saudi oil becomes central to fuelling the industrial revolution. The Saud family becomes immensely rich overnight." - [Muslim Brotherhood; Tell Children the Truth Org].

Britain's Historic Compromise.

In 1922 the League of Nations (Later the UN) receives a British Memorandum directing a 2-state in Palestine. It will declare that 80% of Palestine is to be edited out of the Balfour Declaration and be made as an Arab state called as Transjordan. Churchill, among others, will define this as a bad, even illegal deed.

• "The field in which the Jewish National Home was to be established was understood at the time of the Balfour Declaration to be the whole of historic Palestine, and the Zionists were seriously disappointed when Trans-Jordan was cut away from that field under Article 25" - [1937 Peel Royal Commission Report on Palestine. Paragraph 42(3)]

• "It was grossly unfair to the Jews… yet another promise broken and a most dishonest act. The Balfour Declaration was being torn up by degrees and that the official policy of His Majesty's Government to establish a Home for the Jews in Biblical Palestine was being sabotaged. - [Colonel Richard Meinertzhagen's book, Middle East Diary: 1917-1956", published by Thomas Yoseloff, New York, (1960), p. 100)]

• "In my considered legal opinion, the State of Israel still has dormant legal rights to Transjordan. These Rights were recognized as inherent when the highest representatives of the Great Powers who had defeated Turkey in WW1 met at the Paris and San Remo Peace Conferences in 1919/20. Under the settlement, the whole of Palestine on both sides of the Jordan was reserved exclusively for the Jewish people as the Jewish National Home, in recognition of their historical connection with that country, dating from the Patriarchal period" - (Howard Grief, renowned author of NATIV Policy Paper 147, 2003)

Now, in the aftermath of the industrial revolution and another world war on the horizon, oil beckoned to turn the world's new age engines, and the world followed. For the Jews the catastrophe of losing 80% of Palestine will not be their direst issue. The Jews' darkest period will begin to unfold; it will be ushered with a propaganda program against the Jews and become widely institutionalized into the modern world's psyche. It will alter the historical trajectory and render an outcome antithetical of the Balfour Declaration's provisions. Henceforth, Britain will turn on the Jews in focused and compounding proportions.

Britannia rules.

Caricature of Cecil Rhodes by Edward Sambourne; Punch Magazine.

The state that Britain pledged for the Jews in the Balfour Declaration of 1917 will be diminished to 20% of the Palestine landmass. It is the first 2-state division of Palestine and called as Trans-Jordan, accounted as east of the river and severed from the Palestine landmass that was allocated for the Jews. This was an over-turning of what the Jews and a host of British Ministers, war Captains and legal experts of its period accounted as illegitimate. It also aligned with the discovery of vast new oil reserves.

From herein will a worldly multitude be promoted by Britain with a propaganda premise to justify the overturning of the treaties made with the Jews. Britain, a worldly superpower, will use all her tether to inculcate such a stratagem when the Jews were at their most precarious situation. Britain also used the full weight of the Arab world to promote an array of negative charges against the Jews.

The success of such a paradigm must rest substantially with Britain who held all governing power. Britain will precipitate the over-turning of numerous agreements, initiating a calamity for the Jews by promoting a falsified historical portrayal to the world community. The history of such a promotion's success is incumbent today; chiefly because this was a corruption that now impacts all nations. With victory in WW1, Britain represented a mighty power. Consider what the Jews confronted of Britain's formidable array of worldly forces and assets:

• "The largest empire in history and the foremost extending global power. By 1922 the British Empire held sway over about 458 million people, one-fifth of the world's population at the time. The empire covered almost a quarter of the Earth's total land area." - (Ferguson, Niall (2004). *Empire, The rise and demise of the British world order and the lessons for global power*. Basic Books; Elkins, Caroline (2005). *Imperial Reckoning: The Untold Story of Britain's Gulag in Kenya*. Owl Books.)

• Accorded control of the Middle East to settle the region and form states via legally binding mandates.

• A global network of War Allies and Colonies.

• Commercial contracts for oil wealth, security protection and weaponry sales.

Such a power would correctly act prudently to protect her status and interests, as would any other. Britain did so with the Jews to the very extremities of possibilities, by choice more so than by a compelling requirement. The Jews became the preferred soft target for Britain to acquire winnings in Arabia as with the Ottoman Empire also accounted as the soft target of choice to win W.W.1. Britain's PM Chamberlain will seal two notorious agreements, one for Europe with Hitler and one for Arabia with Hajj Amin. Britain traded the land allocated to the Jews with the Arabs and promoted a thread of new partition plans, continuing 2-state demands, name transfers and name changes in Palestine, numerously overturning both history and her pledges; it acquired Britain strong alliances with the Arabs.

The question whether Britain miss-appropriated her power and honor, even participating in the direst deeds in history, and promoting them as a legitimate worldly view, is again best answered by another question: what does this history say?

Over-Turning History.

Only an immense power such as Mighty Rome could undertake a propaganda stratagem the likes of which were then hitherto unequalled and able to turn history. Britain emulated this stratagem again. While Rome turned a 2,000 year nation's history with the anointing of the name Palestine, Britain will perform twice as successfully. In the 20th Century, the 4,000 year historical icons of the Jews will lose their titles and be replaced by new ones without a history; it is represented by Britain's creation of a new region called as West Bank, which contains Hebron, the birthplace of Judaism and a host of sacred towns of the Jews. The Hebrew names of 3,000 year towns will be changed in 1951 to West Bank, with Britain being the first nation to approve it. Soon thereafter the Palestinian Jews recruited in Britain's WW2 armies will become the new Arab Palestinians in the 1960s. For the first time in history a region called as East Jerusalem will emerge. A new history will enter the worldly lexicon under Britain's watch.

In W.W.2, both the names Palestine and its derivative adjective still applied exclusively to the Jews, as in the regiment of the Jewish Palestinian Brigade of the 20th Century, one the 26,000 Jewish soldiers

99

wore with the Star of David on their uniforms in the British Army's Jewish Palestinian Battalion. .[14] None will come to the rescue of the Jews. Britain will unleash a pre-internet viral phenomenon across the nations, one that has no basis of historical imprints, exploiting the power of names illicitly against the beleaguered Jews who were now fully dependent on her.

From here did Nazareth, Bethlehem and East Jerusalem become as West Bank; from here emerged the paradigms held by the modern world's multitude of Arabs to be called as Palestinians. Its agenda is not difficult to assess; namely a Caliphate doctrine and a commercial gain became its processor and the Jews the soft target to acquire all blame. Its consequences account for the chaos and mayhem in its aftermath, both for the Jews and the world community at large.

Of Heritage Denial. Britain's deeds against the Jews can be accepted, rejected, qualified or denied, yet none can question the enormity of its impacts or that Britain was not privy to it. Some factors are un-deniable:

1. Of all the new states created by Britain in the 20th Century, Israel is the only one that is known to have previously existed as a sovereign state. The British term 'returned to their historical homeland' cannot apply to any other state Britain created.

2. Israel is the only state that was legally mandated and accepted by Britain prior to her accorded control of the Middle-East; (The San Remo Conference, article 4, obliged Britain "to assist in the establishment of the Jewish National home").

3. The term Palestine and Palestinian were 2,000 year heritage symbols exclusively referring to Jews and their homeland when Britain was handed control of this region; it is a symbol that cannot in any wise be viewed as a nativity conclusion of another people. Britain's own legal documentation said so.

4. West Bank, Palestinians and East Jerusalem are fictional recent icons created and fostered by Britain against the Jewish state and was in dire contradiction of the Balfour Mandate and the known history of the Jews.

Israel became the most compromised and abused state via Britain's inculcation to a vast multitude, one initiated via the nation renown for her educating and re-shaping of the modern world as no other. Over twenty new states that never existed before emerged in this region and India will lose a third of her landmass for the same reason of British corruption of appeasement.

The new lands created will not dent any satisfaction in this region; its turmoil will extend out of control. Britain's carving away 80% of Palestinian to form an Arab 2-state in Palestine, referred to as "Trans-Jordan"; trans being "across and east of the Jordan River" will not satisfy demands for more states in Palestine. It will not produce any semblance of peace.

Britain and Hajj Amin.

It is reasonable to view Britain's actions and inactions, even if by default, as one that accommodated a Caliphate, a theological doctrine that rejects any independent state in the Middle East that is not of the Islamic faith, one with a self declared extending global provision. It is a doctrine held regardless of any nation's predating historical validity in this region, and applying also to any past conquering lands that have been lost again centuries prior in Europe. Thereby it is a doctrine that has no alignment with any causative factors by Israel.

The premise of a Jewish state will soon became the chief focus with Britain's appointing of Hajj Amin of The Brotherhood, a virulent rejecter of the Jews and promoting genocide, now with the power of the Grand Mayor of Jerusalem accorded by Britain. Such an appointment was not a simple error of naivety on Britain's part; ample evidence of its consequences hovered.

Now, the chants of a Caliphate emerged as a reason to reject a Jewish state; Jerusalem will be promoted for the first time as the far mosque and the 3rd most sacred site of Islam; a gold plating of the mosque dome will be undertaken by Hajj Amin in the 1920's by raising funds from the Arab world as an incitement design.

Thereby, under Britain's promotion, the first holiest site of the Jews will be promoted as the third holiest site of another people, and Israel will be seen as invaders of Jerusalem. That Britain supposedly went to war to negate the previous Ottoman Caliphate will create demands of a new Arab Caliphate as the replacement of the one felled in WW1. How unaware or handicapped was Britain to stem such a situation is a

101

subject of retrospection; its trajectories will thereafter impact all nations and peoples globally.

A murderous campaign of terror inevitably erupted upon the Jews, promoted by Hajj Amin, who aligned with the Brotherhood and the Nazis and promoted genocide of the Jews to Hitler. Britain's appointment as the Grand Mufti (Mayor) of Jerusalem denoted control of all of Jerusalem. Britain's declaring East Jerusalem as not a part of Israel emerged from this source point, beginning with the early corruption of the Balfour Declaration when oil was discovered and the appointing of Hajj Amin as Jerusalem's mayor; it legitimized a larger agenda.

Till 1920, the Arabs were not rejecting a state for the Zionists; they were at war between themselves and battling against numerous internal parties and groups emerging. It is a syndrome that will not cease; chiefly because of the British stratagem of creating fictional borders that would stir such ethnic turbulence among the Arab groups; the same strategy was employed with the appointing of an Arab mayor for Jerusalem.

The success of a new Caliphate paradigm that emerged in the early 20th Century and spread globally in the 21st Century must rest with Britain who made no provisions for the Jews, Christians and numerous other inhabitants of the Middle East. When Britain failed to apply any conditions of rule on the regime states she established, it disregarded the basic human rights of all peoples in the Middle East, including the Arab peoples. Israel's right to exist will be expressed as a bad foreign affairs policy to the nations.

The Jews' future woes were being sealed and culminate in history's most terrible consequences. Instead of offering protection from such doctrines, Britain will turn on the Jews with a consistency. A worldly multitude was inculcated to cover the truth of this history by its extending terror and chaos not being confronted, affording Britain an immunity that continues in the modern world.

In the Post-W.W.2 era the Arabs were handed 22 separate new states that never existed before; such an occurrence of new states is not seen anywhere in history. This was the dispensation made by Britain, a democratic nation that made no conditions attached of the states she created, as with bestowing vast countries with enormous resources as a gift to one person forever. Those countries Britain installed need not cater to any form of justice and fairness of its own citizens or any others; there can be no penalties, dislodging or appropriation of rule.

Thereby it disregarded the rights of many groups of ancient habitants of this region, even those more ancient and thereby with greater rights. The 22 states Britain created do not have to abide by the conditions made on Israel. The following represents the scenario that should have been placed on the new Arab states but never did, in line of The Balfour Declaration made with the Jews:

• "It being clearly understood that nothing shall be done which may prejudice the civil and religious rights of existing non-Muslim [as with non-Jewish] communities in Arabia, or the rights and political status enjoyed by non-Arabs [as with non-Jews] in any other country." - (The Balfour Declaration).

"Leave Them Fighting"

To give rationalization why such an anomaly may be undertaken, that countries may rule without conditions, and their borders designed so that inter-ethnic conflicts would be assured, two stand-out factors can be considered. One to foster favorable commercial arrangements for Britain with oil arrangements and weapon sales; the other to cater to a war stratagem of "Leave them fighting."

Here, the notion this region was not conducive to democracy or catering to the basic human rights of other inhabitants does not appear the credible reasons, especially so from Britain, a nation that spread such sacred premises of ethical and law based governing premises globally. India had a population far larger than Arabia, its people of a greater mixture of varied beliefs and far less likely to embrace democracy; otherwise what was the requirement of Britain as an appointed caretaker to settle this reason. India became the largest democracy of all and catered to the rights of other belief systems; the states created by Britain did not.

While all nations became obligated to respect Arab doctrines, the same was not accorded to others; it is one of the consequences impacting the nations of the modern world. The other that it is now apparent is that democracy does not work without reciprocity. Britain legitimized such a status and became the one that got away unscathed. All the states Britain created belonged to one belief system, predominantly to one family, although numerous other beliefs and peoples pre-existed in the Middle East.

Wars emerged which group will prevail as the controller of a Caliphate, fuelled by fictional oil-based borders that infringed the ethnic divisions of the region. It was a strategy of 'leave them fighting', also seen in India. However these war stratagems were employed on nations and peoples that were not war adversaries but those who assisted Britain in two world wars and relied on her pledges.

Why did the minuscule state of Israel's right to exist became an issue, or why Jordan was handed to a figurehead from Saudi Arabia; these are vital questions that align with a Caliphate and oil deposits, and far away from the notion of the Jews illegally occupying their historical homeland, as promoted by Britain upon the worldly multitude. The multi-state Arab attack on the newly established state of Israel in 1948 occurred when all of the disputed lands were in Arab hands.

Thus, by default or corruption, Britain supported a Caliphate doctrine, with the Jews as its most prominent focus. Yet its consequences will not cease with one people of this region. The transfer of names and its use as a weapon is a historically charged issue of the ancient world that has seeped into a modern world's political provision. It culminated in global chaos and disruption.

Britain and Mighty Rome.

The usurping of a name that serves as a means to dislodge another holding that name can be classed as a perversion and an underlying genocide premise. It was the premise when Palestine replaced Judea in the ancient world, and can equally align in the reverting of the term Palestine being again removed from the Jews in the modern world; both exhibit the same premise. Hajj Amin will pursue a genocide goal under Britain's watch.

It is a means of heritage manipulation of the historical record and it will impact Christianity and the Arab people held under the rule of British created governance systems in Arabia. The name changes of the 20th Century held reverse premises when Judea became as Palestine 2,000 years ago; and when Palestine became the land Britain promoted as illegally occupied by the Jews 2,000 years later.

Consider well this anomaly. Britain called Jews as Palestinians; and Arabs as Arabs in the 20th Century. Britain then turned coat with the Jews of that name's ownership in the latter part of that same century. A new group called as the Palestinian Arabs became the antithesis of the Palestinian Jews. Judah and Samaria became as West Bank. Here, history per se was reversed by name replacements as a means to foster charges of illegal land occupation. Such was promoted and absorbed by a vast multitude as a historical paradigm; yet it is one that has no historical imprints of illegal land occupation by the Jews; the reverse is the position.

Who Are Palestine's Natives?

The issue is germane and intrinsic to this conflict; it is also the most commonly known via history and the most challenged. The historical record says there was never an Arab Palestinian state, both in the modern world or any other time in past history. Here, it is incumbent to determine what constitutes nativity and ancestry to a homeland. Namely, who this land's ancestral people are becomes the fundamental issue that impacts what the worldly multitude received and accepted under Britain's watch.

The Reverend James Parkes, an authority on Jewish/non-Jewish relations in the Middle East, assessed the Zionists' "real Title Deeds" in 1949. He states further:

• "They never abandoned the land physically, nor did they renounce their claim to their nation — the only continuous claim that exists. The Jews never submitted to assimilation into the various victorious populations even after successive conquerors had devastated the Jewish organizational structure. But, more important, despite becoming "much enfeebled in numbers and deprived both of political and social leaders and of skilled craftsmen." [15]

A brief history of time is the only trustworthy measure of a nation's ancestral native veracity. By subsequence, such also answers whether any other people can hold possession of the same nativity claims on this land. Consider Israel's history from her inception to the modern period of the 21st Century.

Birth of Israel.

105

History says there were no other people than the Jews that had any input in the creation and formation of Israel and Jerusalem in its inception 3,000 years ago, and likewise of the modern state of Israel. Thereby, Israel is not replacing another nation other than returning to her ancestral homeland, one reinstated via legal protocols that are more pronounced than any other nation in history. The treaties of the early 20th Century that allocated Palestine as the 'historical homeland of the Jews' is disputed today; another people are claiming such a status, asserting their ancestral nativity to the same land from time immemorial.

The claims harbor contradictions. Namely, non-validated claims are also made of other lands, and while a return is demanded for Arabs, such is not given to the Jews who lived 2,600 years in lands now controlled by Arabs:

Muslims discovered America before Columbus, claims Turkey's Erdogan:

• "Contacts between Latin America and Islam date back to the 12th century. Muslims discovered America in 1178, not Christopher Columbus," Erdogan said. "Muslim sailors arrived in America from 1178. Columbus mentioned the existence of a mosque on a hill on the Cuban coast." However, most scholars insist the "mosque" mentioned was a metaphorical allusion to a striking land feature. There have been no archaeological discoveries of Islamic structures pre-dating Columbus's arrival in the New World. (Washington Post)

• Muslim groups are demanding right of return to Spain for potentially millions of descendants of Muslims who were expelled during the Middle Ages. But historians point out that the Jewish presence in Spain predates the arrival of Christianity in the country and that their expulsion was a matter of bigotry. By contrast, the Muslims in Spain were colonial occupiers who called the territory Al-Andalus and imposed Arabic as the official language. Historians say their expulsion was a matter of decolonization. (Muslims Demand "Right of Return" to Spain by Soeren Kern; Gatestone Institute).

Concerning the ancestral claim of Arabs in Palestine as from time immemorial, the first requirement is its veracity of such an ancient inception. It should be illustrated via the known imprints of a historical validation, rather than via a belief or a disregard of another peoples' rights. All groups have beliefs, yet history says the Jews are both native and ancestral to the land they claim as their homeland. History also says no other peoples possess an equivalent claim. Otherwise, such would not be recorded in three scriptures, the archives of many nations and in uncovered relics of this land. The Dead Sea Scrolls, considered among ancient history's greatest discoveries, and the ancient Egyptian letters, affirms the Jews as the ancient 3,000 year inhabitants of Canaan, which became Israel and Judea.

The Hebrew nation was born and formed in the land of Canaan, which became the sovereign state of Israel, with Jerusalem established as its capital under King David in 1002 BCE. The Hebrews had a prominent history in the Egyptian vassal state of Canaan, a land closely adjoining Ur, a city in Mesopotamia (today's Iraq). The Hebrew Israelites constituted one of the numerous Canaan groups. They held assets of land, burial fields, wells, extensive trade relations and communal inter-marriage with other Canaanite groups for many centuries. Abraham was a highly respected figurehead both in Canaan and Egypt.

The Hebrew Canaanites were varied from the other groups by their own unique language no other nation spoke, and an equally variant belief system. The Canaanites would accept the Abrahamic circumcision ritual when they wed a Hebrew maiden; Jacob's daughter Dinah was married to a Canaanite prince who agreed to undertake this Hebrew ritual.

While such details can only be presented by scriptural narratives, they are substantially credible, lacking any overt reason to be dismissed. Circumcision was an ancient tradition in this region, predating the Hebrews, perhaps originating in ancient Babylon and not seen with the other Canaanite groups or the Egyptians; circumcision and anointing of stones with oil were also traditional ancient marks of agreements, oaths and contracts; both are recorded in the Hebrew Scriptures.

Jews are Canaanites.

The Hebrew Israelites did not invade another peoples' land, a notion proposed by some sectors. The Hebrews constituted one of the Canaanite groups, born and incepted in that land. This people knew no other land as their origins, showcasing 3,000 year relics and Hebrew etchings from this region, and cross-nation archives that mention both the Hebrew and Israel names that evidence their historical nativity to this land.

Ancient Canaanite Battles.

As with such groups in all lands, the Hebrew Canaanite group incurred a domestic battle with six of the eight Canaanite groups that were vassal states under Egypt, a super power of its time that fostered human slavery and dominion; slavery was a commonplace form of wealth and industry in the ancient realm. The Hebrews returning to their homeland from a severe bondage of captivity had to do battle with the Canaanite groups that refused them entry.

It is a time when the Philistine invaders were already settled in Gaza, who the Canaanites and Egypt were unable to conquer.

The six Canaanite groups rejected Joshua's peace offers, as he was bound to make by the laws of Moses before deciding on a war (Deut. 20:10-18). The adhering to the Mosaic laws is intriguing by its inference the Hebrew Bible was already in the possession of the Israelites. The six Canaanite groups responded to the Israelite peace offer with an ancient mode of genocide:

• "Come, curse me Israel, and come, execrate Israel." (Num. 23:7).

This past history marks as a strong parallel in today's Middle-East conflict that denies the return of Israel; the Israelites faced an existential issue in their past as they do in the 20th Century. It should not be thereby aligned there was an Arab group in ancient Canaan 3,000 years ago; there are no historical imprints of Arabs in this period and both the remaining Canaanites and Philistines became absorbed in the Hebrew nation (See, "Who Are Arabs?"). Instead, the Jews faced such battles with all nations throughout their history, each time with different forces, always over the same issue of their variant beliefs and customs and chiefly of the strict monotheism laws they followed.

Israel's Canaanite Ancestry.

Israel is thus a Canaanite nation, born, incepted and created in that land by all affirmable historical imprints, and not an illegal occupier in the modern state of Israel. The claim by the PA President Mahmud Abbas is thereby false as is his and the P.A. Minister claims of being of time immemorial Palestinian ancestry. Thereby, today's Jews,

108

despite their numerous invasions, enforced dispersions and mixed inheritances, constitute the only people by a historically validated connectivity to Canaan and possessing the 'Right of Return'.

There is thereby historical cadence in Churchill's '3,000 year unique Jewish connection of right not sufferance' to this land, and its enshrining in the Balfour Mandate of a 'National home of the Jews'; these align with all three scriptures of this region and history per se.

The History accounting thus places the Hebrews as one of the groups of Canaan; then that Canaan became the Jews' sovereign land for 1,400 years since the reign of King David by the name of Israel, and where the Israelites lived for 2,000 years prior to the Roman destruction of the Jerusalem Temple and the Jews' enforced exile across the Middle East, North Africa and Europe. This 2,000 year pre-Roman invasion also included a short 70 year Babylonian exile and that portions of the Jews remained in the land continuously; it is evidenced by the Arab interaction of the Jews in the Book of Nehemiah (2:19), the Roman destruction in the first century and the Islamic invasion of the 7th Century.

Exilic Jews.

The Jews that became exiled by the Roman Empire to Europe and Arabia strived to end the barring of their return for many centuries. Both the Jews and the Arabs achieved approval mandates by the nations following the fall of the Ottomans; the Jews were legally approved with a mandate of return to their historical land, and the Arabs attained similar approval mandates for new states. All of the landmass of Palestine, including the regions now called Jordan and West Bank was declared as one state for the Jews in 1917; it is a time when the Jews were exclusively referred to as Palestinians by the British, American and the Arab Representatives and their legal documentation. The situation turned with the discovery of oil, the British appointing of Haj Amin as the Jerusalem mayor and the corruption of the Balfour Mandate.

Big Lie Claims.

Thereby a false historical portrait was promoted that culminated in a large multitude inheriting the British-Arab propaganda. The charges promoted against Israel are rejected by a growing number of scholars and theologians of this region; they are voicing long held 'big lie' counter charges of the powers arrayed against Israel, especially referring to the illicit Hebrew name changes of towns and the Palestinian identity manipulation under Britain's watch. Such reports and views are also accepted by a host of prominent and respected Arabs, especially that Arabs are not Palestinians, a name anointed by the Romans on Judea, and that Judea is not West Bank:

• "Christian Arab is a fake terminology, one created only 100 years ago by a Pan-Arab theology. We are an Aramaic population who were forced to speak Arabic. We are not Arabs." - (Father Gabriel Nadaf of Nazareth; 'Christians in Israel' CBN).

• "Our latest big lie is that Israel is stealing our land in the West Bank. The reality is that the West Bank is Judea and Samaria for the Jews." - (Fred Maroun, Canadian of Arab origin, writer and essayist.)

Jerusalem is not Arab

Jerusalem is not mentioned in the Quran, accept as the holy city of the Jews. Israel's capital was invaded numerously throughout history, including by Babylon, the Greeks, the Romans, the Crusaders, and lastly by the Mohammedans in the 7th Century; a mosque was erected on the destroyed Jewish temple site in Jerusalem. The reasoning of the acceptance by Britain of West Bank marks a flaunting of Israel's history and the caretaker appointment handed her; it will also foster enormous chaos for Christianity and the nations at large.

The true reasoning of such a name transfer is a corruption of history thrust upon a world multitude, especially a generation that may not be privy to this region's history or have access of examining the legal treaties when this name was usurped; these are suppressed and almost never mentioned in the discourse of this region's accounting. The charges on Israel are instead derived from theological doctrines and corruptions based on oil provisions; they are not based on any historical or judiciary factors that are aligned with land or treaties.

Contrary to the 7,000 year nativity claims by the PA Ministers, there was never a time in the past when the Jews did not inhabit Palestine. The British and Arabs are history's strongest witnesses of this history via their presence in the Roman legions when the Jews battled Rome 2,000 years ago. The ancestry claim of the past 3,000 years, including under the Babylonian, Roman, Crusader and Islamic invasion, and up

110

to the immediately previous Ottoman rule, rests solely with the Jews. Thereby, such a phenomenon renders the premise of a Palestinian title cast upon the Arabs in the 20th Century as an oxymoron; it is especially so when the British and the UN support it so vigorously.

The name changes of West Bank and Palestinians are thereby as genocide premises and a rejection of Israel's right to exist, aside from its evidential historical falsity. Such are not as opinions; aside from self-declared clauses in Arab group charters, they are now exposed in de-classified British and German archives.

The Arabs that claim another state in Palestine initiated numerous wars when the territories now called as West Bank was not held by Israel. Gaza was illegally held by Egypt, and Jordan illegally annexed west of the river; yet Israel was made the recipient of occupation of her ancestral land.

A host of prominent legal scholars have categorized the corruptions relating to Israel's southern region called as disputed territory to be itself illegal, including that the name West Bank was enacted by an illegal annexation by Jordan. Thereby, the impression held by the worldly community requires re-evaluation of the name corruptions of Arab Palestinians, West Bank and East Jerusalem. These three names are recent fictional titles and are devoid of any historicity, even a corruption of history.

Although Jerusalem is revered by many peoples and nations and also merits them this respect, Jerusalem as a capital city is a fully created and developed entity of the Jews. The Arabs had no input in Jerusalem's creation and were not part of the Canaanite peoples; accept by an invasion of the homeland of the Jews in the 7th Century. The historical imprints affirm the Jews were born and incepted in Canaan as a sovereign nation and alone established Jerusalem as their capital city.

• "You ought to let the Jews have Jerusalem; it was they who made it famous" - (Winston Churchill to diplomat Evelyn Shuckburgh, 'Descent to Suez; Diaries 1956, London 1986)

The worldly multitude that examines this history will find that Rome did not go to war with the Arabs in Judea, but with the Jews, and that the devised international laws of illegal occupation and nativity are in contradiction of this land's history. The nativity factor rests solely

111

with the Jews, its condoning can legitimize the flaunting of history all places:

• "Jerusalem's role as 'The Third Holiest Site in Islam' in mainstream Islamic writings does not precede the 1930s. It was created by the Grand Mufti Hajj Amin al Husseini - (Joseph E. Katz, Middle Eastern Political and Religious History Analyst, New York)

• "Mecca is holy to Muslims; Jerusalem is holy to the Jews." - 13th Century Arab biographer Yakut ("The Jews of Islam" by Prof. Bernard Lewis Princeton University Press 1987 & "Whose Jerusalem" by Eliyahu Tal International Forum for a United Jerusalem 1994)

• "There were no mosques in Jerusalem in 632CE when the Prophet Mohammed died." - (Dr. Manfred R. Lehmann)

• "Pray for the peace of Jerusalem; they shall prosper that love thee." (Hebrew Psalms 122:6; part of the Dead Sea Scrolls archives, dating up to 408 BCE or 11 centuries prior to Islam's emergence.)

Seeking a return from exile to one's historical homeland is not an illegal or criminal enterprise, as has been inculcated upon a worldly multitude. Here, those holding 99.5% of this region's landmass are obsessed over the Jews holding a mere 0.5%; it affirms only that this is a theological rejection, and thereby not one limited to the Jews or to Arabia.

Palestinian is not Arab.

If Palestine was a heritage and historical reference to Jews and their homeland for 2,000 years, then its derivative adjective must also likewise correspond to the same attribute. It is as the adjectives British is of Britain; Russian is of Russia, and Indians is of India. There can be no confusion that the name Palestine was applied to no other nation but that of Judea by Rome, or that the Jews were the only people referred to by this name thereafter for 2,000 years. Such is affirmed by this name being a reference to the Jews that was retained as an emblem till 1950 by Israel's currency, banks and a host of her institutions. Today's Jerusalem Post newspaper was called as The Palestinian Post till 1951, issued in Hebrew and English; the 26,000 Jews who enlisted in the British army in W.W.2 were called as 'The Jewish Palestinian Brigade'. Thus, how a new native people can emerge in 1964, less than thirty years after WW2 and be called as Palestinians appears a historical, biblical and political oxymoron.

112

This name issue merits re-appraisal by the world community and marks the pivotal factor of this conflict; that such a task is difficult to overcome anymore should be measured against the consequences of not doing so and it's extending global impacting. Scholars and authors view the Palestinian name employ as 'the biggest hoax' ever perpetrated, and of stealing the name Palestinian in the 20th Century:

• "There has never been a civilization or a nation referred to as "Palestine" and the very notion of a "Palestinian Arab nation" having ancient attachments to the Holy Land going back to time immemorial is one of the biggest hoaxes ever perpetrated upon the world!" - (Rockwell Lazareth, author of the essay "Who are the Palestinians"; News With Views)

• "The current debate on the inevitable future of the "Palestinian Nation" seems to lack one simple fact: Palestine has no past and was never a sovereign nation. The closest thing the Palestinian people have to a history is that there was once a British Colony from which they had stolen their modern name." - ('The True History of Palestine: The Nation-State Fallacy' By William John Hagan)

A 20th Century Hoax.

Thereby the worldly multitude was deceived by a British-Arab conspiracy. A native people should have no need of usurping another peoples' symbol to present their nativity. Historical imprints should be a simpler means to vindicate such claims. This is especially so for the Arabs who, unlike the Jews, are not known to have ever been exiled out of Arabia and thereby be better expected to affirm their historical evidence.

The Historical record affirms there is no imprint from any source of a non-Jewish Palestinian people prior to the 20th century, or any of the emblems and embellishments all nations possess that affirm nativity as evidences, such as a Capital, a flag, a national anthem, a historical habitation, a unique Palestinian language or a writing, as are aligned with any native people. All of these are possessed by the Jews of their homeland in both ancient and modern times.

Thereby, such qualifies as a myth cast on a multitude, one invented in the 20th Century and based on usurping of another peoples' historical heritage via name usurping as its sole implement.

Such means cannot be viewed as limited to any one nation or people. The focus of this myth can thus align credibly with the term 'deception', as an intentionally designed political conspiracy derived via commercial interest and historical corruption. It is a theological claim else another peoples' historical names would not be manipulated by those holding so much of lands. Numerous countries and cities undergo name changes and their existence is not thereby denied; usually the name change reverts to its original status.

Palestine, Judea and Israel are one inseparable historical entity that ought not to be disputable by the usurping of the term Palestinian. Such is a manipulation designed to infer that Arab Palestinians are the native proprietors of Palestine. It is a deception akin to calling Arabs as the more credible Zionists or Israelis than the Jews, for the term Palestinian was equally disdained by the Arabs in the early 20th Century when they deliberated with Britain of this land's naming.

Thereby, upon the re-establishment of Israel, the name Palestine should have been rejected from attaching it to another people, or else its attribution should apply exclusively to the Jews, as it did for 2,000 years; Britain and the UN could have and ought to have done so.

The historical imprints say Palestine is not an Arab associated symbol of ancient or modern history; it is a name fully connected with the Jews, introduced and mentioned in the Hebrew Bible in 250 instances. In the past 2,600 years there were no Arab people called as Palestinian.

History of Middle-East Jews.

Historically, the Jews have been recorded as living in numerous regions of the Middle-East for thousands of years, before the advent of the Greek and Roman Empires arriving in this region. The history of the Jews in Babylon and Egypt predates the names of Arabia and Arab being cast on this region by the Greeks in 300 BCE. The Copts, the Lebanese Phoenicians and the Jews possess older historical imprints and are not an Arab people. xv

A host of claims are made to overturn this history, including that the Jews of today are not true Jews of their recorded past. Such a corruption uses the natural phenomena of any exiled people's adaptation of language, culture and other imprints of the host nations the Jews were exiled to and when the Hebrew language was

114

forbidden, as a means of negating their heritage. When the Arabic was made as an enforced language in the 7th Century, the Jews in the region became proficient in it; a host of the Hebrew writings was made in

The Arabic.

The same was seen in Europe, whereby Yiddish is a combination of German and Hebrew when the Hebrew was forbidden. Such imprints do not mean the Jews exiled to Europe and Arabia were not Jews; it says the reverse, for the older Hebrew writing was 'transcribed' into Arabic of Hebrew words, and the Yiddish language never existed prior to the European exile. These were Jews exiled from their land, not of European or Arab lineage. Nor were the Jews absent from Palestine at these times; smaller numbers remained at all times, even under harsh conditions.

Following invasions and exiles, the historical, biblical and archaeological imprints of Jews are ancient and plentiful as 2,600 year inhabitants in Babylon (Iraq), Yemen, Persia (Iran) and Medina (Saudi Arabia) and its markings imprinted till the 20th Century; the Jews did not claim these as their lands and remained as Jews, nor a return to those lands by their 2,600 year nativity; namely, the Jews in the Middle East have a greater nativity claim in Arab lands than the Arabs in Palestine.

The Jews' presence was ever constant in Palestine, including under the Ottoman Empire rule; namely, not all Jews left Palestine. The situation began to change in the mid-20th century onwards with the rejection of a state for the Jews and is aligned with a period of mass Arab migration of recent years and by the later usurping of names.

Of Popes and Palestinians.

Whether it is an inevitable cultural impact or modern history's mendacity, the premise of this controversy is fuelled not by habitation factors but via name transfers that entered our lexicon recently, condoned by sectors which can be least confused of this history. Otherwise, how can a much respected Roman Pope call Arabs as Palestinians and referring this land to anything else aside from 'The land of Israel' and 'The land of the Jews' - as is explicitly stated in the Gospel and by the Romans. History says the Pope's own Roman ancestors applied this name specifically and exclusively upon the

115

homeland of Judea - the same 'Land of Israel'. In the scriptures of the Gospel there is this historical and biblical entry that contrasts the Pope's description of this land and its correct inhabitants:

• 'And he arose, and took the young child and his mother, and came into *the land of Israel.*' [Matt. 2:21].

So either the Gospel or the Pope is in contradiction of his own ancestors, his holy scriptures and of a 2,000 year history. It is an especially poignant contradiction as it emulates a mark of genocide decreed 2,000 years ago by the Roman Emperor Hadrian with the proclamation, "Judea is destroyed" ('Judea Capta') and never to rise again. Here, any improvisation to justify such a miss-adventure appears inapplicable considering its formidable implications; Israel's return ought not to be held as an affront again. Here, what difference a change of name can make exposes a historical and biblical negation, one recurring and continuing of a people and their known ancient history.

Thereby, the Pope is highlighted because his office marks a bastion to enlighten history's darkness to a worldly multitude, expressing that the truth shall set us free, and to prevent such past errors; because the Vatican is a firsthand witness of the names Palestine and Palestinian history. Indeed, Rome referred to this land as Judea and 'the land of Israel' in numerous historical archives, and printed coins with its 'Judea Capta' insignia. Aside from its historical and biblical distortions, there are also the moral and ethical premises that become violated and questionable; its poignancy is vested in its potential genocide premise as was the aspiration of the Roman Empire.

Thus there is a contradiction of manifold proportions in the world's camps; a great multitude is at variance from of our historical veracity, to the extent an exclusive 2,000 year held name of a people is made as the antithesis of that people, in a mode while they still actively exist. Changing a nation's ancient names is not a cultural or humanitarian effort to safeguard a people; it is a mode of dislodging of a people, a phenomenon that has previously occurred in history by empires of heritage and belief extermination.

Rome's name change resulted in the 2,000 year exile of the Jews from their homeland and two Holocausts - one in 70 CE, another during World War Two; ancient Rome's Emperors and modern Rome's Mussolini were embedded in both scenarios. The agenda of using a name deceptively against a people can act as a deathly weapon, as was seen by Mighty Rome and it, culminated it WW2. Never again must apply:

• It resulted in an estimated 50 to 85 million fatalities; these made World War II the deadliest conflict in human history - (Sommerville 2011, p5.)

The two largest belief groups have engaged in actions that target the smallest belief group, by mutually contradictive belief and historical reasoning. Calling Arabs as Palestinians is, whether by unintended default or otherwise, renders Israel as forever illegally occupying Israel. Illegal land occupation has no place in this enterprise; if it did, the Balfour Declaration would not be flaunted. Israel's return ought not to be held as affronts by the largest two belief groups of history; it is a contradiction of love and peace proclamations in the situations where it most applies.

The overwhelmed Jews who accepted all conditions handed them were in the midst of an existential precipice, and those in control were fully aware of their plight. Such actions merit defining and appraising to foster its corrections as a posterity marker; a step by step accounting, especially for the generations that have not been privy to this history and led astray, requires clarification and recounting.

False Witnesses.

The Christian communities are first-hand witnesses in this arena via belief and history, and thereby have obligations to both those faculties. It is primarily the onus of Christians to correct Britain and to apologize to the worldly multitude for bearing false witness. This appraisal will highlight a host of deceptions to produce an exposure of alignment of a conspiracy incurred since the 20th Century. These actions have brought great calamities to many people and nations and can be seen as extending globally. Thereby these are not presented as inciting or exaggerations, its aim to eradicate by exposure so such errors may be discarded, especially for those who hold that the truth will set them free.

Act 2.
'Deceptions'

• *Noun*; plural. The action of deceiving someone. "Obtaining property by deception"; "A thing that deceives"; "A range of elaborate deceptions." [Google]

• "Deception, beguilement, deceit, bluff, mystification and subterfuge are acts to propagate beliefs of things that are not true, or not the whole truth." [Wikipedia]

• "Whether these are errors or deceptions, the candidate can be harmed. Sometimes it's called propaganda and sometimes hypocrisy, lying and deception. Self-deception proves itself to be more powerful than deception." [Dictionary.com]

Deceptions do not happen accidently or via acts of nature. A deception is an intentional agenda of covering the truth; it is well planned and rehearsed. Deceptions are the most vital weapons in war; it includes any or all of propaganda, antithetical reporting, false accusations, corruption, bribery, fear, threats, force, castigation, diversion and fostering via an enlarged accumulated multitude. Its aim is to replace a disdained truth with a preferred falsehood. A host of devices are required to turn truth and history and sustain an antithetical account. Always, its claims have no evidence in reality when checked, or are vested in a visionary realm none can prove or disprove. By the time the deceived realizes it, the deception is already hard-wired and embedded in their DNA; it becomes akin to an inculcated religious belief and assumes a preferred premise to all other truths.

The deceived are almost impossible to extricate themselves from their inherited deception anymore, save for great effort by a few willing to brave a bad career move in a stirring quest for truth. Like a virus, a deception can infect a loved one or the gullible that trusted others without checking. Left unattended, it will extend and infiltrate elsewhere. Its antidote is elusive.

Trust, Trust - But Check, Check. The reader must not be deceived again by relying on this book's assessment alone; effort is needed to

118

equally check and expel a claim of deception. The pursuit of truth is not a simple matter when it encounters an already secured worldly multitude. Mighty Rome's greatest weapon was, more than its military might, its mastery of guile. There is a good reason the world found no first and second century archives of the Jews and Christians. Rome's emperors scrutinized all writers of any negative reporting with brutal focus and systematically destroyed all writings seen as anti-Roman. The Dead Sea Scrolls were saved via extra-ordinary measures. Rome wanted not truth disclosed, but its own preferred one of dominion whereby 'all roads lead to Rome'. [16]

Deceptions are travelling enterprises; else they would achieve no momentum and force. A series of historical, biblical and political deceptions that began in the early 20th Century are active and continuing, and these have become embedded in the human psyche. Deceptions can become a force of their own when allowed prevailing in one place, extending and impacting like the precedent of a legal tort that can apply elsewhere.

The damaging impacts of a false accusation become difficult to cast away. It is not an insignificant or localized issue; historical deceptions impact all aspects of humanity globally via their derivative subsequence. Nor can it be resolved by itself or by beliefs alone that numerously contradict each other. A deception will compound, enlarge and extend, with no sector of humanity free from its impacts. That Britain was the first nation to accept and thereby legitimize the name 'West Bank' to cover 3,000 year Hebrew town names will impact the British Empire and Christianity equally as it does others; thereby a deception of such historical and biblical proportions can extend and impact by its un-fathomed consequences.

• Deceptions emanating from the 20th Century of the Middle-east are based on a stratagem model of infiltration, one that can and has already encroached upon other nations. Deceptions are processed by stealth via infiltration and gifts in political machinations, the judiciary, the sciences, news-reporting and educational institutions. Even entertainments, sporting faculties, books and the new-age Apps all become rendered as replaceable with new paradigms. Here, the personal freedoms we assumed as untouchable and taken for granted become primal targets. Its effects are pervasive and far-reaching, because the covering of one truth inevitably requires thousands of other truths to be covered.

119

The *"HA!" Factor.*

In the modern world's recent history, the controversy of names became a foreboding issue of deception. The global phenomenon of name alterations into its own antithesis with such wide acceptance requires an examination in deciphering both its cause and its remedy. It is a journey which began some 4,000 years ago, before many of today's nations and beliefs had emerged; yet like a virus it has subsisted and embedded itself among all those sectors that crossed its path. Nowhere was the power of a name more impacting; it began as a recorded prediction that altered history and humanity with two alphabets: 'HA'

• "Neither shall thy name any more be called Abram, but thy name shall be Abra-HA-m (Gen. 17:5)

6. The Name Deception.

The name Palestine was a globally held reference to the homeland of the Jews, including in Muslim countries.

• In 1918-20 in the Azerbaijan Democratic Republic the Jewish communities published a Caucasian Jewish bulletin called "The Palestine" newspaper.

• The Middle East conflict was facilitated via name deceptions. The charges against Israel would be diminished without the corruption of names that are among histories' most known and recorded. West Bank; Arab Palestinians; East Jerusalem. All three names are new historical fictions created in the Mid-20th Centuries, its aim to overturn the heritage marks of another people. All three names, presented as attachments of an Arab nativity claim and occupation charges are equally fictional. These are new names intended to cover the previous historical names of another people's land. The impacts of these name corruptions affect all nations and their histories; it is a phenomenon that has nothing to do with Israel and thereby merits careful consideration.

Why Change Historical Names?

The new names are intended to give its reverse impression via the usurping of another peoples' heritage identity theft. Their allocations

120

are calculated implements designed to assist charges of land occupation which soon followed the name changes. West Bank and Arab Palestinians became the means to claim a 3-state in Palestine, itself one of a thread of deceptions by presenting this as a 2-state; Jordan was the 2-state the British declared as a 'Historic 2-state compromise' when the original Balfour Mandate was corrupted when oil was discovered. These are the views expressed by a host of prominent international lawyers. By altering the historical names of the land of the Jews it facilitates Israel's land being presented as occupied; such charges of occupation lose their credibility when these names are not altered. Palestinian Jews, as they were called prior to the 1960's, cannot be charged as occupying Palestine; likewise, the West Bank towns with Hebrew names like Hebron and Beth-Lehem cannot be presented as illegally occupied by Jews. Thereby, the names West Bank and Arabs as Palestinians were enacted to cater to the forthcoming charge of Israel's occupation of Arab Palestinian land. These were Jewish Palestinian lands declared in the Balfour Mandate and three scriptures and a vast array of historical archives prior to the name switch; Arabs were not called as Palestinians prior to 1960. The name East Jerusalem, enacted for the first time in history, caters to the splitting of Israel's capital, a claim no nation can survive. All three names signify the rejection of Israel's right to exist, as declared in numerous Arab group's charters. For the Arabs, its underlying premise catered to a Caliphate, a theological doctrine of dominion; for the British, it catered to commercial arrangements that justify dishonoring legal pledges and history, even at the cost of genocide. The slogans of extermination made by Haj Amin, the British appointee as the mayor of Jerusalem and founder of Hamas, continue with no response from the British who master-minded this situation by accepting these name changes:

• "In a final resolution, we would not see the presence of a single Israeli - civilian or soldier - on our lands," Abbas said in a briefing to mostly Egyptian journalists." - (Palestinian Authority President Mahmoud Abbas; Cairo Meeting with Mohamed Morsi)

Thereby, the name changes mark as a conspiracy that covers an underlying historical deception, one suppressed and shrouded from its underlying motives. Whether the worldly multitude was not fully privy or knowingly accepted these deceptions with indifference is a subjective issue. Yet their impacts that have become manifest globally speaks for itself; it legitimized a Caliphate in the Middle East that is

121

not limited to one nation or people. The terror in the region's only Christian state of Lebanon and the Copt and Armenian plight are also subsequent to a Caliphate doctrine.

Britain was the first country that approved the name West Bank on the most sacred land portions of the Jews, followed by Pakistan and Iraq. There is no issue that Britain, the Arab people, the UN and the world's scholars and theologians were unaware of the history of these names that Britain fostered, rendering it implausible that its motives were unclear. They contradicted ancient and recent history, the pledges of Britain's treaties, and of the Emir Faisal's acceptance of agreements with the Palestinian Jews in 1919; two years later oil was discovered and the situation turned dramatically for the Jews. The issue arises whether Britain respected the sanctity of the older sites of the Jews as well as the Christians; the sites of the Hebrew Patriarchs in Hebron, of Joseph's tomb in Shechem, Rachel's tomb and Jesus' birthplace in Bethlehem; these were fully disregarded by Britain. Whether by error or otherwise, Britain legitimized a Caliphate doctrine. Israel has been paying its price thus far, yet with definite omens of its extensions globally.

Emulating Mighty Rome.

The changing of a name can, via propaganda and inculcation, dislodge a prevailing paradigm, even one many thousands of years old and evidenced by more archeological relics than any other nation. Here, changing historical names become a means to change history, acting as destructive attacks on a nation and its people.

The term Palestinian has successfully entered the collective DNA of the world's multitude and become almost impossible to anymore associate Jews with the name they held for 2,000 years. As was seen with Mighty Rome, the power of a name is an ancient mode of historical negation when used as a strategic weapon. Rome's agenda for replacing Judea's name with Palestine was the total its extermination and this can be seen as repeatable in the modern world; a doctrine of dominion is not limited to one small nation.

That Britain is revered as a great nation cannot exclude that WW2 Germany was also one of the world's most emancipated nations; the rule is the higher a position the more severe the crime it participates in. While many Arab groups openly declare their aims of elimination

122

in their charters, Britain did this covertly by masterly stratagems. Both names of West Bank and Palestinian were enacted after a Holocaust in Europe in the 1940's; West Bank was created in 1950, Arabs as Palestinian in the 1960's. The parallels are heightened by the Britons and Arabs at the helm of both scenarios of this land's history, with the Roman legions and with WW2 Germany. There was a Roman siege and a British White Paper that made the Holocaust unstoppable; both preceded and influenced the Roman and the Nazi Holocausts. In both instances the name weapon was a pivotal factor and utilized as a war stratagem when the Jews were fully overwhelmed by the greatest of forces.

Global Impacts.

The name deception is fastidiously progressed with no correction in sight. Britain enjoys immunity from the Christian and Arab sector and unlikely to be confronted. The Jews, the original owners of the name Palestinian which was Judea, are never included in the discourse, such as 'previously a name held by the Jews', or that 'West Bank was previously Judah and Samaria', or that 'East Jerusalem is part of the 3,000 year capital of Israel'. The new names are presented with an assumption such prior history is not relevant, including one that subsisted only a decade ago from the new name enactments.

The name Palestine and its derivative Palestinian were both applied exclusively to the 'national home of the Jews' by Britain in all her legal documentations prior to this name's transfer in 1960; Britain was silent of this contradiction, indicating an alignment with the Arabs of this name usurping. Prior to Herzl's endeavors for Israel's re-establishment, Palestine had the same employ as Zionism; he uses the term Palestine as the homeland of the Jews in his writings. Yet Britain made the name Palestinian as antithetical of the Jews, overturning the Balfour Mandate when oil was discovered.

The issue is also complicated by its negative default impacts outside of the Jews; the new Palestinians that emerged in the 20th Century face their true Arab heritage being lost irrecoverably, with Christianity confronting even greater impacts than any other sector. How did:

• "And he arose, and took the young child and his mother, and came into *the land of Israel*." (Matt 2:20). Become:

• "The necessary legal steps to put an end to Israel's occupation of the Arab territories" - (The Synod of Bishops chaired by Benedict XVI; 24 October 2010.)

Israel's history has inter-twining trajectories; a historical name reversal cannot be made without inevitable impacts on history itself. While the Jews have sustained themselves in numerous exiles and destructions through the ages, it is questionable that Christianity can withstand a Jesus of Nazareth rendered as a Palestinian of the West Bank. Here, history per se becomes fluid and discretionary; if a deception can impact a 4,000 year history, it can equally do so a 2,000 year one. Its biggest victims become the Christian and Muslim people inculcated with manipulated depictions of their history and belief.

Sheikh Ahmad al-Adwan of Jordan, when asked if he recognized Jewish sovereignty of the Jews' historic land, explained:

• "Indeed, I recognize their sovereignty over their land. I believe in the Holy Koran, and this fact is stated many times in the book. 'We made the Children of Israel inheritors of such things.' [Koran 26:59] and additional verses in the Holy Book."

• The name abuses foster negative impacts on the Arab people in contradiction of the Quran and a host of Islamic theologians and scholars who decry the political manipulations of their history. Christian History is also contradicted by the charge of the Jerusalem Temple denial:

• 'A 10-year-old Russian boy, Matvei Tcepliaev, recently made an extraordinary discovery in Jerusalem. Working as a volunteer in the Temple Mount Sifting Project, he found a 3,000-year-old seal from the time of King David. The artefact was nestled in tons of earth that had been illegally excavated from below the Temple Mount by the Muslim Waqf. The Temple Mount is sacred ground for Jews, Muslims and Christians, but Jewish historical claims are denied by many Muslims.' - ("A Boy's Discovery' by Jerold S. Auerbach; WSJ)

• The chaos created in the nations by the abuse of Israel's historical names cannot in any wise be directed at Israel. Book publications have emerged by prominent scholars with ominous titles such as Londonistan and Eurabia, and new buzz terms such as No-Go Zone enclaves that have become a new reality; perhaps in like manner of the West Bank, East Jerusalem and Palestinian deceptions.[17]

124

A Viral Phenomenon.

If a name change in the 20th Century can render the most sacred land portions of the Jews with 3,000 year Hebrew names to become as an Arab Palestinian peoples' West Bank territory, then the nations of Europe, with relatively new names, can more easily be prevailed upon. Whose territories are the No-Go-Zones of Europe, and will the world one day encounter new names and never ceasing 2-state and 3-state demands in European countries; and why will East London not succumb to the name Londonistan when such has precedence in Palestine; or why will enclaves in France and Norway not become part of occupied territories by a surge of immigration aspiring autonomy after thirty years?

Otherwise, such impacts are aptly described as 'The Israel Experience' and able to extend as a global viral phenomenon. These are not hypothetical questions; they are firmly based on actual slogans declared in the streets of London and across Europe.

To view such a phenomenon as errors or circumstantial affectations becomes a difficult endeavor; it boldly exposed its premise, one that had to be fully supported by Britain to have any means of success. The most impacting factor of how and why such a name transfer from Jews to Arabs became justified is nowhere addressed in the discourse, when it ought to be made as pivotally relevant. Reasonably, Britain and the Bishop synod should have been aghast of such historical and scriptural impropriety, so should all Christians and the Arab people themselves; yet its astonishing reverse syndrome resulted and it was fully supported. It is a subjective issue for the people to consider their leaders' decisions; they cannot be directed at an overwhelmed Israel.

Consider it well. The name Palestine was arguably the most commonly known historical attribution less than a century ago (from 2015); one held by no other people as a national symbol than of the Jews and their homeland for 2,000 years, including in the 20th Century up to the 1960's. Subsequent to the silence, in 1964 the new Palestinians will claim a time immemorial history stemming 7,000 years in Canaan, altogether negating Rome's anointing this name on Judea and a validate history of both the Jews and Christians. It was followed by denials of the Jerusalem Temple, even that Jews have no connection with this land.

With Britain's promotion these name changes became condoned by a resultant multitude. They include the following luminaries as an indication of the onslaught Israel is subjected to:

The UN, Scholars, Historians, Encyclopaedias, Dictionaries, Kings, Queens, Presidents, Prime Ministers, Islamic Clergy, Popes, Bishops, the Media, Journalists, School Principles, Humanitarian Agencies, Environmentalists, Sport Champions and Music and Stage Artists.

Few will brave disagreement with such a large purpose driven assembly and use terms such as 'deceptions' directed at an array of esteemed luminaries, except that it all falls apart by the accounting of its historical veracity; it does so not by a few irrelevant or incidental occasions, but on all of its manifold thresholds. A vast measure of humanity embraces the 20th Century phenomenon of a Palestinian people as one with historical credibility. Yet there were never any people or nations called as Palestinians for 2,000 years other than the Jews; it is the name that was applied to the historical homeland of the Jews. Palestine is Judea; there was no country called as Palestine, nor any Arabs referred to by this name. There was also no nativity of an Arab people to this land (See, "The Refugee Deception"). It thus challenges the held premise how can the whole world be mistaken.

• The Arab Palestinian premise and its nativity claims are pursued with a determination not seen elsewhere of any other issues of the modern world; it is fulcrum and pivotal to the illegal occupation syndrome. The occupation charge becomes dysfunctional without the historical term 'Palestinian' being applied to the Arabs; that Palestine was Judea and that only Jews were called as Palestinians till the 1960's is shunned from the discourse. The Arab Palestinian is a phenomenon presented in all narratives and made as prominently prefixed adjectives always followed by 'occupied territory' and 'international law'. Yet its extent can be equally measured as highly and fully questionable when devout Islamic scholars and prominent figures differ with the worldly multitude and are not given adequate acknowledgement; many are subjected to grave character diminishing or a casting aside from the radar when their views are more credible than the politicized historical deceptions of this region:

• "There is no such thing as 'Palestine' in the Koran. Your demand for the Land of Israel is a falsehood and it constitutes an attack on the Koran, on the Jews and their land. Therefore you won't succeed, and Allah will fail you and humiliate you, because Allah is the one who

126

will protect the Jews (Sura 5 Verse 21), and that Jews are the inheritors of Israel (Sura 26 Verse 59)." - (Sheikh Ahmad Adwan, a Muslim scholar.)

As well, by a renowned President of a neighboring Islamic State:

⋅ "Never forget this one point: There is no such thing as a Palestinian people; there is no Palestinian entity." - (Syrian President Hafez Assad to the PLO leader Yassir Arafat.)

And by an American Statesman:

• "There was no Palestine state. We have invented a Palestinian people who are Arabs from the surrounding Arab community as a war against Israel and it is tragic" - (US Republican presidential candidate Newt Gingrich; Jewish Channel Cable TV; Reuters)

Thereby, the term 'deception' is not utilized for evoking undue attention or contention; the Arab Palestinian promotion is more than a myth and borders on a genocide premise targeting Israel, one that does not appear an error or a naive consequence. The figureheads denouncing this phenomenon may be few and credible, yet not scale-tipping of the accumulated multitude. A vast and growing sector of Christians and Muslims are not in concert with their leaders and the representatives of this paradigm; especially so those who examine the credibility that this issue relies upon when researching this history. The world now has open access to the historical archives that affirm the recent 20th Century Palestinian name shift from Jews to Arabs and of scholarly books by honest and able scholars. Ultimately the corruptions will be seen as more than an error.

Palestinian Nativity

• "The problem is that another people are trying to lay claim to that land through a narrative that is not only false but that relies on twisted facts and outright lies to try to make the case. The people making the treaties with the Jews (the British) went back on their word and gave the majority of the land (75% of the promised mandate) to the colonizers: essentially, the colonizers gave the land to other colonists."

- ("Broken Treaties: Palestinians are not indigenous people like Native Canadians" by Ryan Bellerose; Canada-Israel Friendship Association)

127

Extermination by a Name.

It appears unlikely any confusion can pertain of such an antithetical history that over-turns the name Palestine away from the historical homeland of the Jews, accepted with a disregard of its import and consequences. There should be no confusion of Rome's intentions when Judea was changed to Palestine; thus its analogy applying in the modern world's conflict is not a hypothetical one or one that can be disregarded. No confusion should prevail why this conflict is irresolvable; one side is facing an existential crisis as was seen with Rome some 2,000 years ago. It can reasonably be viewed as an extermination premise via a name change; its impacts of dire contradictions hover ominously on the nations who still wish to uphold their own histories and beliefs. The UN Security Council holds four out of five Christian countries controlling its veto powers (USA, UK, France, Russia; and China); the Vatican is a powerful impresser of a billion Catholics.

It appears implausible such a historical name corruption could prevail without the positive support, or an absence of reaction, from the Christian groupings, including the multi-denomination Churches, the Vatican, and their Political representatives. This says that as was Britain given the caretaker role in the 20th Century, so are Christian countries handed the onus of fostering an Arab Palestinian name as an antithetical symbol of the Jews. The most impacting issue concerns whether the legitimizing of such provisions in this region can stem its extending flow elsewhere, or increase them; if the latter then its onus cannot apply on anyone other than its supporters.

The internet has emerged at a poignant juncture; it can expose history as a new force and become a beacon of the truth, setting it free when others fail this responsibility; a lie can be investigated today as never before. The promoted assembly of a name dislodgement points only to a miss-represented theological and commercial enterprise as opposed one of historical veracity; it is one diabolically in contradiction of its own sublime premise of 'The truth shall set us free'.

Such is further reflected in the entire assembly of states that overwhelm the UN General Assembly by always voting one way against Israel no matter what the Motion. Here there are strong facilities and options of corrupting international laws. That this name transfer aligns with an extermination premise becomes better manifest

128

in its unfolding, with too many too silent of it also becoming its own vindication of its extending impacts.

A Rose by another Name.

In this scenario, a rose by another name is promoted as its antithesis; they form the basis of almost all UN Resolutions of international laws against Israel. Thus, whether it is a theological or political phenomenon appears as the osmosis of both, each with an absence of historical vindication. How then can the denial by Arabs with respect of both the Jerusalem Temple, and by the Christian community of the name applied to Judea, win such a widespread acceptance, and does it mean history will be changed just for Israel without impacts elsewhere; it is a paradigm stalking the modern world. Will it not impinge on the Gospel that mentions a Temple in Jerusalem; or of the Babylonian, Persian, Greek and Roman archives and the scholars that wrote of it? Why is an Ottoman king's archives concerning Jerusalem's ownership in contradiction of the modern world's determinations in the 20th Century; or why is the Christian community calling Arabs as Palestinians when they know it is much more than a mere falsehood; these are the challenges waiting to be confronted. What kind of roses grow in such a landscape requires a closer examination of the first case of this conflict.

7. The Balfour Deception.

Leopold Amery, Secretary to the British War Cabinet of 1917, testifies under oath to the Anglo-American Committee of Inquiry in January 1946 in the approving of the Balfour Declaration, and of Britain's overturning of her pledge made to the Jews. Secretary Amery:

• "The phrase 'the establishment in Palestine of a National Home for the Jewish people' was intended and understood by all concerned to mean at the time of the Balfour Declaration that Palestine would ultimately become a 'Jewish Commonwealth' or a 'Jewish State', if only Jews came and settled there in sufficient numbers."

Jordan: A British Corruption.

Emery's claims thereby make the creation of Jordan, not Israel, as an entity borne of corruption, one that emerged not by a nativity premise but of the overturning of a treaty by Britain. Namely, Emery is saying Jordan is an illegal state created by the splitting of Palestine by dishonoring a legal treaty, and thereby the charges on Israel as an occupier in Palestine are based on corruption. A 2-state division of Palestine was not intended by the original Balfour Declaration. Indeed the Jordanian monarch is a Saudi with no connectivity of a heritage in Palestine, the land first allocated in as one only state for the Jews; it is a British stratagem of 'leave them fighting' and ever in conflict. Nor was there any requirement of a 22nd regime state in the Middle East. Emery's testifying correctly aligned with Lord Balfour's views, as well as that of Churchill, the Emir Faisal and the response of betrayal by the Jews to Britain's flaunting of its treaty.

Emery's statement of oath marks the whole of Palestine as allocated for the Jews, with no mention of divisions or of an Arab kingdom in Palestine. Its flaunting explains an array of deceptions targeting the Jews, including Britain's follow-up White Paper Policy and the creation of West Bank; thereby the Balfour's corruption did not occur because of the failure of Jews to settle in sufficient numbers; indeed they were fully denied this option. Emery's 1946 statement exposes the British guile that claims to wait until the Jewish population increases, while also restraining it with its White Paper policy. Britain will overturn any possibility of the Jews acquiring sufficient numbers in contradiction of the Balfour Mandate; its actions will pursue the reverse.

• Although the issue of the Balfour corruption is in a state of suppression and historical denial by many, there is more than sufficient evidence Britain sold out the Jews when oil was discovered, then encouraged the in-flow of Arabs in the land allocated for the Jews to settle, causing untold damage to numerous other Arab and non-Arab groups in Arabia aside from the Jews. The creation of Jordan on 80% of the land pledged to the Jews for 'one only Jewish state' in Palestine affirms the Balfour deception, one that will reduce the mandated home for the Jews to a dangerously minuscule size, then extend this action with a series of de-legitimizing name changes, further land reductionisms and a mass immigration of Arabs. That this was a catastrophic century of two world wars, with nations confronting existential situations and the greatest loss of lives among all recorded warfare, Britain's obsession and determination of

130

focusing on an insignificant home for the Jews is both inexplicable and self evident. That Britain possessed a great disdain of a Jewish state, equating the Jews as equal enemies as the Nazis, is given by Britain's own representatives in de-classified archives.

Christian Support of Britain.

The enormity of the Balfour Declaration's deception is grossly underplayed by the leaders in the Christian community, one that has promoted a worldly opinion of its adverse provisions that became comprehensively accepted by the Christian people. The hidden deceptions are seldom in the vista, thereby requiring persistent research encumbrances despite that Israel is made as one of the most reported issues. It appears the result of both the political and theological impacts sustained from age-old times, and ushered via the corruptions of solemn pledges. The Balfour corruption's moral factor was varied from a people also having possession of other countries to go to, as is seen of the Christian and Islamic faiths; the Jews had no other country to go to other than a return to their historical home; they were fleeing Europe and Arabia, with all Christian countries slamming their doors shut to Jews on Britain's dictates and they obliged its dictum. While Britain had bigger issues in Europe, and the Arabs had likewise with the Ottomans, yet it is the Jews that become centre stage in this calamitous century. Every Christian country turned refugee ships back to Germany. France will deport 75, 000 Jews to the Nazi death camps. With Britain the instigator of barring Jews returning to Palestine, became the worst offender with some half million Jewish lives denied:

• "British post-war immigration policy deliberately excluded Jews. The process was designed to keep out large numbers of European Jews - perhaps 10 times as many as it let in. Around 70,000 had been admitted by the outbreak of the war, but British Jewish associations had some half a million more case files of those who had not." - (We've been here before, Anne Karpf, The Guardian, 8 June 2002.)

The flaunting of a solemn official pledge made before the world was not a necessary prudent deed within a precarious world war scenario, but one bordering on a premise of annihilation. The barring entry to Jews fleeing W.W.2 Europe emerged after the Balfour's granting and the subsequent carving away of 80% of Palestine, nullifying any justification of such an action; what is not accounted is Britain's own

131

measures to justify its direction. The British actions are the definitive and substantial cause of the Holocaust's large human toll, and the sell-out to a Caliphate doctrine in Arabia; the latter will also be the chief cause of the Caliphate's global extension. The Balfour Declaration's corruption should be seen as an enormous error and as the primal cause and reasoning of this conflict. The world would be a different one had Britain been halted from corrupting a solemn treaty made before the nations. That this conflict's true reason is not confronted and is flaunted from the discourse aligns why this conflict's resolving is far away and extending; it is un-feasible to negate what Britain so strongly fostered and legitimized against the Jews in Arabia from its advance outside Arabia.

The Balfour's corruption also accounts for the aftermath of a conflict that continued and enlarged and promises to continue impervious to any other means of restitution. Its cause has no alignment with Israel or the Arab rejection syndrome, and should be directed solely to a British flaunting of its own pledges and proclamations and those who supported its flaunting. Here, the resorting to Zionist plot recourse is fully devoid of any credibility and only entrenches the deception of shying away of its true causes; such applies even where the entire Middle East is seen as a Caliphate region, for this has extending agendas. The Zionists executed positive agreements with the Arab sectors and were welcomed as the sole benefactors of all of Palestine. The British decisions against the Jewish state are conducive to other reasoning; the inflaming of a precarious situation's exploiting as a war stratagem can be retrospectively realized today.

In 1920, three years after issuing its Balfour Declaration, the British overturned its formal pledge made to the Jews, dividing the landmass of Palestine into two states containing what became Modern Israel and a new state called Trans-Jordan; it was formalized as the Kingdom of Jordan in 1948 with the British removing some 80% of Palestine, defining its action as a 'historic 2-state compromise'. Significantly of this proclamation, the term 'Arabs' is used for the people of Jordan, affirming they were not known or regarded as 'Palestinians' in this juncture of the 20th Century. Although some previous Arab rejectionist movements attempted to align themselves to the name Palestine, the usurping of this name as a propaganda strategy was initiated by Arafat in the 1960's, a protégé of Hajj Amin. In 1948, the name 'Palestine' was aligned only with the Jews and the land allocated for them when the Kingdom of Jordan was created.

- "Before local Jews began calling themselves Israelis in 1948 (when the name "Israel" was chosen for the newly-established Jewish State), the term "Palestine" applied almost exclusively to Jews and the institutions founded by new Jewish immigrants in the first half of the 20th century, before the state's independence." - (Eli E. Hertz; Myths and Facts)

In 1948, Britain was not confused that the creation of Jordan was granted as a new implement, namely a compromise of the Balfour Mandate's one state in Palestine; it is the first time that 'Two states' are called for in Palestine. Although Trans-Jordan was implemented in 1923, it was a deviation from the Balfour Declaration of 1917 with the discovery of oil as its true cause, incurred at the expense of the Jews as Britain's soft target:

- "In 1923 the British "chopped off 75% of the proposed Jewish Palestinian homeland to form an Arab Palestinian nation of "Trans-Jordan," meaning "across the Jordan River". The British, due to the large oil deposits being discovered throughout the Arab Middle East turned a blind eye ('to Arab rejection of a Jewish state'). Although Churchill stated that the Mandate "is not susceptible of change" the British sliced 76% of the land, east of the Jordan River" - (The Division of The Mandate for Palestine; Jerusalem Org).

It is now known by the amendments that all of Palestine was marked as one only Jewish state; and that the Balfour Declaration was overturned three months after the San Remo Conference by Britain, not the Arabs:

- **The Treaty of San Remo and the Palestine Mandate.** "At the allied conference at San Remo, in April 1920, at which the Allied Powers determined the fate of the former Turkish possessions, the Balfour Declaration was approved, and it was agreed that a mandate to Britain should be formally given by the League of Nations over the area which now comprises Israel, Jordan and the Golan Heights, which was to be called the "Mandate of Palestine". The Balfour Declaration was to apply to the whole of the mandated territory. The Treaty also contemplated an "appropriate Jewish agency" to represent the Jewish population and this was established as the elected Jewish authority in Palestine under the title of "the Jewish Agency". (Conflicting Arab and Jewish Responses to the Balfour Declaration; IJS Org)

• "The treaty of San Remo which was ratified by the League of Nations in July 1922 was therefore amended in September 1922. The British Mandate still extended over the whole of Palestine on both sides of the Jordan River, but a clause was added excluding Transjordan from the operation of the Balfour Declaration, which was therefore now limited to the western side of the river." - (The Arab-Israeli Conflict Part 2: Building Tension in Palestine 1918-1939)

• "I want to underline that the primary objective of the Mandate for Palestine was to grant political rights in respect to Palestine, to the Jewish people (later called as the UN). Following the conquering of the Ottoman Empire in WW1, the rights of all the nations in Arabia were granted at the San Remo Conference in 1920; 21 Arab states and one Jewish state were born here and ratified by the League if Nations (later the UN), as binding and irreversible laws." - (Dr. Jaques Gauthier; International Human Rights lawyer and 25 year expert on Jerusalem under international law)

• "The League of Nations voted on a very special resolution. It decided to give recognition to the 'historical rights of the Jewish people, to reconstitute their national home. They are recognizing a pre-existing right and not creating a new right. In other words the historical rights of the Jewish people to this land were recognized by the great powers of the time." - (Dore Gold, Former Israeli UN Amb.)

• The new turning of the Balfour was proclaimed by Britain as a 'compromise'. The overwhelmed Jews had few choices here, except to display their deep shock at this new proclamation:

• "It will be a historic compromise to grant two states in Palestine - one for the Jews and one for the Arabs" - (Sir Winston Churchill)

What Compromise?

The term 'compromise' for the removal of 80% of a small land underlines its inappropriate, even confounding summation of Britain's choice of words; it begs, what percentage is not a compromise? Thereby, the creation of Jordan was the first 2-state division of this landmass and intended for 'the Arabs in Palestine' - a people yet not called by its derivative adjective Palestinian; Churchill and other British Ministers will confirm the Arabs are not natives but who descended as waves of new immigrants in the land. Now, some 20% of the landmass was allocated for the Jews, namely all land west, or

134

trans ('beyond'), of the Jordan River. Aside from Secretary Amery's oath identifying the Balfour Declaration was intended for one only Jewish state in Palestine, the continuing deception later by the British condoning additional 2-states in the same landmass again, namely the support of a 3-state in the newly created West Bank and accounting this as a 2-state, exposes the first 2-state deception. The usage of the term 'historical compromise' which removed 75% of the land allocated to the Jews can thus be viewed as an infamy.

The First Cause of the Conflict.

The Balfour corruption, or the division of Palestine into new states and new regions, can well be considered as the true cause of this conflict and the support of its underlined Caliphate. These divisions diminished the land portions of the Jews by more than 78% in favor of the Arabs, although Palestine was allocated as the national home of the Jews, and the Arabs accorded vast lands and countries in Arabia; it also disregarded the agreements and declarations between the Arab and Zionist sectors that accepted all of Palestine as one state for the Jews. In 1917 there was no stated premise or requirement of Jordan in the Balfour Declaration, as indeed it should have been explicitly included; its absence renders Jordan's creation as a violation. An analogy is a home purchase contract which does not cater to its sub-divisions. The situation does not change if the contract was altered by one party, and when its recipient has no choice options. Nor was the name Palestinian referred to Arabs in these contracts; these are the same people who Britain will later allocate the name it previously designated exclusively to the Jews.

When Arabs Became Palestinians.

The 1960's mark the juncture of the 20th Century when Jews are Palestinians, and Arabs are Arabs, and the turnaround by the British of this name transfer. There is no recorded history of such a people; it is a political decision that emerged from a meeting of Arab states at a conference initiated by Egypt's President Nasser in 1964; it will result in the focused name of the Palestinian Authority with Arafat its leader. Thereby, prior to 1960, there was no Arab Palestinian nativity by this name or by any historical census accounts when both Jordan and West Bank were created. Now, there was no illegal occupation of Palestinian lands; the reverse is the case, whereby the historical and

135

allocated lands of the Jews were occupied by the Arabs, namely what became the West Bank now illegally occupied by Egypt and Jordan. This was thus not about land, a factor fully known to Britain who will still support the name and occupation of the West Bank; again, the Balfour deception becomes clearer throughout Britain's actions. Hereafter, Britain will fully endorse the transfer of the name Palestinian from Jews to Arabs, arguably the greatest historical mendacity as her response to the Holocaust.

Subsequent to the name Palestine being a heritage mark of Judea, the historical homeland of the Jews till the 1960's, its reversal underlies the inherent calamitous foundation of the position undertaken by the British. The new designation of Arabs as Palestinians marks the premise Israel is illegally occupying its own historical homeland; it is thereby also the cause of questioning Israel's right to exist. In effect, Israel is asked to forgo a 4,000 year heritage for a new one created in the 20th Century by another people. Charging the Jews with denying their heritage is a fully misguided enterprise and clarifies the intractability of this conflict. Thereby, the Balfour corruption is the first and primal deception of this conflict and should be viewed as a most foreboding agenda, one that requires its long due merited exposition by the Christian community.

Why Did Britain Create Jordan?

The 2-state division of Palestine was and remains highly questionable of its requirement and why it was implemented. Its exaggerated size allocation of land depletion did not cease. Soon thereafter, Jordan illegal annexation west of the river also removed the most sacred land portions of the Jews; it symbolized the geographical and heritage demise for the Jewish state. Despite the volatile scenario of this region, Britain was not without adequate measures of response in rejecting the division of Palestine. A host of new Arab states were created that did not make Jordan's creation a requirement of additional land at the expense of the Jews, nor were a host of other non-Arab inhabitants of this region catered to by an additional Arab country in Palestine; they eagerly flocked to Palestine away from the regime states created by Britain.

Thereby 'why create Jordan' is a legitimate issue. It says that Britain given full control of this region as performing inappropriately. The creation of Jordan had no connectivity with displaced peoples and

136

points only to Britain's own interests. Jordan will bar the Arabs west of the river entry the first 2-state division, contradicting the only reasoning given of its creation.

Israel will hereafter lose her land and incur a refugee issue resultant from the most dubious causes of any refugees in recorded history; thereby why did Britain create Jordan. The underlying reason for Britain creating Jordan is best understood by her own aggressive promotion of sending Arabs in this region; a future deal had already been worked out of another state in Palestine.

Now, land was the only facility the Arabs did not need, and the only one the Jews could not survive without; they were fleeing both Europe and Arab controlled states in Arabia, both parties, Britain and the Arabs being fully aware the Jews faced a potential extermination premise at this juncture of history. No means of reasoning should transcend justification of genocide; indeed the causes of the enormous human toll of the holocaust derived from here; it was followed alongside a declared Arabian genocide that the Jews narrowly averted.

The carving away of such a large portion for Jordan was a calamity for the Jews. Britain's lack of first insisting and overseeing the Arabs west of the river, the leftover portion for Israel, be transferred to the state of Jordan exposed a dark side of Britain; it contradicted why Jordan was explicitly created; namely, Britain's historic 2-state compromise in Palestine - 'one state for the Jews and one for the Arabs'. The West Bank that Britain supported called for a 3-state in Palestine, and the Jews made as the violators and occupiers of their most sacred land portion. The rejectionist doctrines against a non-Arab state cannot be made as its justification; the hostile situation is the very reason Britain should have protected the Jewish state, not intensify its already precarious situation. Such basic protection for the Jews was Britain's fundamental responsibility in its role as a caretaker of this war's aftermath, one akin to being the captain of a ship in distress; Britain abandoned this ship after causing its distress numerously and successively. The corruption of the Balfour that created Jordan, which the Jews accepted, was by no means limited to the ceasing of further demands.

Had the British intended to foster a harmonious outcome, as should have been expected of such a worldly and experienced controlling power, there was not an absence of positive factors at her disposal to adequately do so. It says Britain had her own self serving motives that

137

transcended all else; the Jews were seen as expendable by the caretaker of this region. Britain will later justify her deeds against the Jews both in Europe and Arabia using the war priorities, which were indeed tremendous and existential, when sons and daughters from many faraway lands of Australia, New Zealand and America contributed great effort and lives, as did also the Jews. Yet Britain's deeds merit careful evaluation and scrutiny; Britain had to undertake much manipulation and severe impropriety against the Jews to justify her deeds and these were not resultant from the war priorities; they began and continued long after both world wars' impacts and indicate a variant underbelly of reasoning of her actions.

Now there was no war and no issue of Palestinians; Britain acted in opposition of the 1917 Emir Faisal agreement with the Jews after the 1914 ending of W.W.1, as well as the corruption of the Balfour Declaration made with the Jews; similarly, West Bank emerged after WW2. The Balfour Declaration was corrupted by editing the original text, affirming this was not subsequent to any war priorities. It came with the discovery of oil.

Britain's Subversive Textual Reading.

The original text:

• "Though the Balfour Declaration went through several drafts, the final version was issued on November 2, 1917, in a letter from Balfour to Lord Rothschild, president of the British Zionist Federation." - (By Jennifer Rosenberg, 20th Century History Expert).

The altered text:

• "The original text of the declaration had read "Palestine should be reconstituted as *the* National Home of the Jewish people." After Montagu's attack, the text was changed to read "the establishment *in* Palestine of a Home for the Jewish people." The single word "*in*" was used subsequently to justify removing all of Transjordan from the British Mandate that resulted from the Balfour Declaration. - [Chaim Weizmann, Trial and Error, 1949, p 257; Ami Isseroff, History of Zionism and the Creation of Israel]

The change from THE to IN was perfect guile; now any number of states can be created in Palestine, in affect rendering Palestine in the Balfour Declaration's 'the national home for the Jewish people' as a

138

mockery. All that was hereafter required was to change the term Palestine from referring to Arabs instead of the Jews. Historically, Palestine was always referred to as the name of the Jewish homeland in all British documents, in 1917, 1920, 1939 and 1948; it denoted only one understanding of the term *'the national home for the Jewish people'*.

In 1917, the Jews saw the term *'National'* signified *'one only state'* in Palestine. Indeed any reasonable reading should say the same, especially so after Britain provided only one state in all the other states she created in Arabia; it renders more than one state in Palestine an anomaly.

The alteration also rendered the 1917 agreement reached between the Arab and Zionist sectors as disregarded or negated, and emerged in direct contradiction of Lord Balfour's determinations which allocated all of Palestine as the Jewish state. While Lord Balfour dismissed even autonomous facilities for the Arab people within Palestine in 1917, the British were creating a new independent state in Palestine in 1920 to carve away 75% of its landmass. A most renowned British author, whose book of history affirms the original allocation of Palestine for the Jews, states of this matter, namely that all of Palestine, not part of Palestine, was earmarked for the Jews as a separate state from the Arab states:

• "Palestine was made a separate state within the British sphere, earmarked as a national home for the Jews. "(The Outline of History', by H.G. Wells)

In 1917, Jordan was not on the horizon in the Balfour text. The British were well aware that the Arabs who have accumulated in Palestine were recent immigrants; this growth was fully fostered and collaborated in by Britain against a state for the Jews. Britain will actively encourage thousands of Arabs into Palestine when she should have done the reverse to uphold her pledge to the Jews. The Arabs will be told a Jewish state will be foiled from happening. Thereby, the development of this land by the Jews attracted a large in-flow of migrants from many surrounding lands with British strong assistance. These will become the substantial account of Palestinian refugees and made as Israel's problem.

Thus, Britain's allocation of Jordan to a Saudi with no connection to Palestine or Palestinians will bar entry to the state created precisely for the Arab in-flow, in direct contradiction of Britain's 2-state proclamation, and with British support; this became the corruption of 'one state for the Jews and one for the Arabs' (Churchill). Thereby did Britain corrupt the Balfour Declaration numerously throughout her actions.

Surprisingly, Britain, the most proficient in her own English language and who re-mastered the Balfour text, did not see "the establishment *in* Palestine of a Home for the Jewish people" as did the Jews, or Lord Balfour, the Emir Faisal, and Secretary Emery; or else Britain claimed not to see. The Jews conducted global protests of the Balfour corruption, but to no avail. That the situation began to change from the Jews' understanding of the Balfour text is seen in Britain's intense debate over a stray word or two which may justify a reversal of its reading. It is self-negating if the term 'national' can subsist with more than one such entity in the same land. How many 'national homes' did Britain declare in Saudi Arabia and Iraq, for example; and why later emphasize the term 'two states' as a new *'historical compromise'* - an acknowledged departure from the Mandate, and self evident of its altered process.

A '2-state' in Palestine is not seen in the original texts when it should have been explicitly included should this be its intention; thereby, there would be no requirement for a proclamation of a new 'historic compromise'. More logically, the 2-state division would have been made in the same year of the Declaration in 1917, with no need for the determined meetings of negotiations between the Arab and Zionists whereby the whole of Palestine as one Jewish state was accepted. Instead, the British invested much Endeavour and extraordinary debates of the Balfour text alterations that ensued. These were hinged on the grammatical articles of A, IN and THE prefixes, namely of 'The' (one only) or 'A' (one of many) national homes in Palestine, a disingenuous employ considering that numerous 2-state requirements would render the Mandate superfluous. That such a debate ensued and was deliberated in the formation of a new textual reading affirms its underlying agenda of things to come.

Drafting the Balfour Texts. The British devoted much effort over the following decades to *deny* that a state was the intention by the term 'a national home' of the Palestine landmass; that this pertains to many states in Palestine and that the size of the additional states have no bearing. Thereby a Jewish state can be reduced to any size, even one that could not be sustainable or viable. However, in private many British officials agreed with the interpretation of the Jews that one only state would be established when a Jewish majority was achieved. The initial draft of the declaration, contained in a letter sent by Rothschild to Balfour, referred to the principles:

• *"that Palestine should be reconstituted as the National Home of the Jewish people."* Thereby, in the final text 'the' was replaced with 'a'; it offset committing the entirety of Palestine to the Jews as the purpose in the original version.

• "Similarly, an early draft did not include the commitment, which was later added and solely applying to a home for the Jews: *"that nothing should be done which might prejudice the rights of the non-Jewish communities."*

These focused and determined changes came about by Britain using the stray urgings of Edwin Samuel Montagu as its excuse, namely an influential anti-Zionist Jew in the British Administration and Secretary of the State for India, who merely expressed concern that the declaration without those changes could result in increased anti-Semitic persecution. Britain chose such urging as its own fully intended justification to turn the meaning of its Balfour Mandate; else this would not have been utilized. - (United Nations Special Committee on Palestine, UN Document A/364, 3 September 1947; Mansfield, Peter (1922). The Arabs. London Penguin Books. Pp.176-177).

Here, the inserted requirement not to prejudice the rights of non-Jewish inhabitants is correct and not the issue; its absence in all the other Arab states created by Britain is a serious issue. It allowed severe human rights abuses, expulsions and property confiscations for the Jews and all other non-Arab groups of the region. The Jews of Arabia will barely escape the same faith in Arabia as in Europe.

The alterations affirm that the original Mandate was for one only Jewish state, and that Britain engaged in guile after oil was discovered in Arabia; else Britain could not plausibly be swayed by a remark of Montagu which would negate a treaty made with the Jews. Indeed the tremendous reduction of land only rendered the Jews' plight more susceptible to attack, affirming this was an incorrect action. Britain was not lacking knowledge of the consequences of carving away over three-quarters of a small land, placing Israel in a situation that was unsustainable; its justification appears lacking of credibility. Britain's further lack of action of insisting Jordan must receive the Arabs East of the river affirmed Britain's deception, even of its own new pledge of a 2-state, the only given reason for creating Jordan. The inaction of Jordan's annexation questions the reason for creating this state; except that it will become the means for a 3-state in a new region called as 'West Bank', and soon thereafter the sudden emergence of a new Palestinian people two decades later. Both were anti-Israel implements. Thereby, the resultant situation for the Jews was far removed from the Balfour texts, with prominent Arab figures agreeing that Jordan was a fictional country and that Palestine was originally allotted as one only state for the Jews:

• "There was never any country called Jordan, these are all bogus names. They (Arabs) have taken that land and called it the British Mandate for Palestine, which is again an artificial name. There was the Balfour Mandate which included all that land including Jordan to the Jews." - (Secular Jordanian Leader Mudar Zahran; The Glazov Gang, Nov 8, 2013).

A 3-State in Palestine.

The reasoning for replacing the article 'The' with 'In' becomes clearer. The first 2-state, itself an illegal action borne out of overturning the Balfour treaty by grammatical subversion, will again be rendered obsolete. Hereafter, Britain's 'one state for the Jews and one for the Arabs' will be flaunted, this time by mathematical subversion. As a U.N. Security Council member, Britain's first 2-state creation of Jordan can be seen as a deception by her follow-up support of an additional state in the same land. In direct contradiction of her revised 2-state that created Trans-Jordan east of the river, a 3-state will emerge, accompanied by the usurping of the term Palestinian for the first time in the 1960s; it will be presented to the world as a native people displaced by Israel and made as international law.

The follow-up support of an additional state in the same land affirms the 2-state deception; that no Arabs with the title of Palestinian existed before affirms the nativity deception. Seen retrospectively, Britain de-legitimized Israel's rights as subservient and expendable after the creation of 21 Arab states. While Jordan's annexation was declared illegal by the UN and the Arab states, Britain's inaction to protect

142

Israel from a 3-state will ensure this conflict will be rendered irresolvable.

In the aftermath of the Balfour corruption, the Jews will face Britain's most devastating deed.

8. The White Paper Deception.

Worst Crime of all.

Britain's Two White Papers

Jews Barred from leaving Europe, 1939.

Jews Barred from Returning to Palestine, 1939.

Britain - The Holocaust - And Hajj Amin.

• "One of the great tragedies, or crimes - depending on who is asked - of the 20th century, can be laid at the feet of the English. This is either omitted from our history books or downplayed into insignificance. Of course, the British passed themselves off as disinterested noble guardians stuck between two irreconcilably irrational opponents, but what seems to have been their chief interest was protecting the Iraq-Haifa oil pipeline." - ('The White Paper of 1939' by Mike Konrad; American Thinker, June 2, 2013)

The Docks of Haifa.

A group of 90 British citizens travelled to Israel and gathered at the docks of Haifa. This was by no means an official government or royal sponsored delegation, but a group of British soldiers and British citizens who came of their own compulsion. Their speeches were recorded in a film called as 'The Sorry 90'. Some examples:

• "Remembering what happened here 68 years ago, the small ship crowded with 2,664 intending immigrants which had been captured

143

off-shore and moored by the dockside. The smell was considerable, with Jews of all ages and sizes trooped out to the concrete. I remember being astonished that such a tiny vessel could contain so many people and the conditions they endured during their voyage. I was close enough to be emotionally involved of the wrong our British nation was doing." - (Jeffrey Ore, British Army; delegation of the "Sorry 90")

• "We have taken our confession and prayer with deep sorrow for our nation's reneging of the Balfour Declaration and for turning our backs on the Jewish people during the British mandate. We praise the preservation of the political, spiritual and legal rights of the present state of Israel. The injustice, humiliation, cruelty and betrayal your people have suffered from our nation of Britain are indescribable. We are deeply sorry." - (Lady in white attire; delegation of the "Sorry 90")

• "Our task was to intercept any Jewish ships before they could land their passengers in Palestine. We had no interest in politics and it wasn't until many years later I recognized the failure of the system and the need for repentance of our failings" - (Tom Dale, British Army; delegation of the "Sorry 90")

• "We are sorry for the White Paper that all but closed the gates of escape from Europe. We are sorry for every ship that was turned away from these shores. We are sorry for holding you in detention and deportation camps. We are sorry we were untrustworthy friends for failing you when you most needed us" - (Lady Speaker; delegation of the "Sorry 90")

~~~~~~~~~~~~~~~~~~~~~~~~~~~~~~~~~~~

The overwhelmed Jews accepted Britain's 2-state division of Palestine. It removed 80% of the land allocated for one 'national Jewish home' for the creation of Jordan. Its given reason was to house the Arabs in Palestine ('one for the Jews and one for the Arabs'). The Jews accepted Britain's revised texts of the 1917 Balfour Declaration which they previously miss-understood and were corrected of its understanding by Britain in 1922. Now the Jews required Britain's corrected textual rendition to be ratified and implemented, desperately seeking a safe home in the 20% remaining land. Especially now in their simultaneous situation of desperation in both Europe and the Arab controlled regions in Arabia. Namely, the Jews were now focused on the new revised assurance of the text, with the article 'IN' instead of 'THE' home in Palestine, and 'A' instead of 'THE':

- *"His Majesty's government view with favor the establishment in Palestine of 'a' national home for the Jewish people, and will use their best endeavors to facilitate the achievement of this object.."*

Many Jews enlisted in the British army as a mark of alliance, under the flagship of the 'Jewish Palestine Brigade'. Thereby did the Zionist advocacy promotions in America also begin earnestly assisting in the implementing of the British Mandate's National Home for the Jews in Palestine, no matter of its diminished meager size. But the British responses of the Jews accepting Britain's edicts are far from over; they will enter their darkest hour of this history. Britain's deceptions will continue in compounding escalation.

What the Jews did not fathom was Chamberlain's agreement with Hitler and Hajj Amin was a recipe for the extermination of all Jews; that it rendered any British Mandate irrelevant. The Jews never anticipated that the Jews would face Hitler's Mein Kamp of extermination in Europe and the same proclaimed in Arabia - barred from leaving Europe and barred from entering Palestine. That all Christian and Arab states would slam their doors to any Jews fleeing Europe; that refugee ships would be blown up at sea or turned back to the camps of Europe; how utterly foolish of the Jews. They believed Britain was only at war with the Nazis; the Jews were wrong.

Following the corruption of the Balfour Declaration, Britain was focused on oil in the dire situation of facing a second world war; and after the war, oil was a precious means of wealth and power. The Jews will be made the soft target to pay its price. Britain now issued its 'White Paper Policy' in 1939 to again appease the regime states she created, even as most of the Arab states allied with Hitler, and were handed vast new states and 80% of Palestine. The White Paper policy was a numerously utilized factor of the British against the Jews, enacting restrictive immigration since the 1920's to appease the landlords of oil rich lands; it was in contradiction of her Balfour Declaration. But the 1939 White Paper was used as the final solution by Britain in conjunction with Hitler and the mayor of Jerusalem she appointed. It will bar the Jews from leaving Europe - Chamberlain did not require the safety of the Jews from Hitler; Britain was fully aware of the Jewish situation at this time for many years.

While Chamberlain made no provision for the Jews in his infamous agreement with Hitler, Hajj Amin will compel Britain to forbid any Christian country from receiving Jews; Britain granted this and complied. Britain was aware its appointed mayor was promoting the extermination of all Jews in Arabia. The barring of the Jews even from the 20% portion west of the Jordan was a violation of Britain's revised 2-states in Palestine division that allocated all land west of the river for the Jews. Namely, the Jews again correctly regarded the land left after 'Trans-Jordan' as the Jewish homeland. Britain will again differ in her explicit textual interpretation, this time regarding the most sacred land portion of the Jews, the same patch of land the Britons and Arabs were destroying a Holy Temple in Rome's legions 2,000 years ago.

• "In 1939, Great Britain reneged on the Balfour Declaration by issuing the White Paper, which stated that creating a Jewish state was no longer a British policy. It was Great Britain's change in policy toward Palestine and prevented millions of European Jews from escaping Nazi-occupied Europe to Palestine." - (By Jennifer Rosenberg, 20th Century History Expert; About-Education Org.)

The Nazis did it - Britain caused it.

The White Paper Policy is the greatest crime perpetrated upon the Jews and among the great crimes against humanity. Britain's action will be exploited by Hitler and Hajj Amin, the Jerusalem Mayor appointed by Britain. The situation is clouded in the fog of war who was exploiting whom, Britain or the Arabs against the Jews, or both in unison. There were two White Papers executed by Britain in 1939; one was instigated by the Jerusalem Mayor Hajj Amin who became a confidant of Adolf Hitler. A legitimate question is incumbent here, one that has been fully avoided by the Christian community. Is it possible that Chamberlain, the British PM who negotiated with Hitler, was unaware of his two White Paper policy impacts on the Jews? Or what are the conclusions to be derived when Britain declared that the Jews cannot be saved in Europe and the camps not be targeted, by reason of the preservation of her vital war assets; yet accepted the Jews barred from fleeing Europe and barred entry by Britain anywhere else, even using war ships to blast any that tried to escape, and compelling all nations to forbid entry to Jews? Britain never released the Minutes of the Meeting between Chamberlain and Hitler, or of

146

Hajj Amin and Hitler; yet some of these details will emerge from an unlikely source.

Britain's actions against the Jews not been widely recounted and examined, despite WW2 being a most discussed and reported issue becomes a curious lacking. Whether by default or otherwise, the British action that forbade the Jews fleeing Europe in World War II any entry in Palestine became the chief cause of the Holocaust's large human toll. The new edict allowed no exit from Europe and no refuge for the Jews to go to; it is highly implausible its consequences were not anticipated. Britain's action further compelled all Christian countries to close their doors to Jewish immigration; many refugee ships of Jews fleeing Europe were sent back to W.W.2 Nazi Germany or blown up in the ocean by British war ships. It culminated in the greatest human toll of the Jews with the Nazi regime exploiting the situation with an expedited response it termed as its 'Final Solution of the Jewish Problem'. Britain will not waste a bullet to respond, citing the Jews were not important to waste vital war assets. The White Paper Policy was an in-human act that constitutes a crime against humanity, representing a darker side of a great nation. There are dark shadows of a conspiracy here; Chamberlain was negotiating with the requirements of both Hitler and Hajj Amin with two White Papers emerging in 1939, with the Jews the targets of both. This assessment must correctly consider whether Britain was a covert enemy of the Jews at a most precarious period of history, or merely acting the only way feasible given the conditions which prevailed; there was a disastrous outcome either way.

Thereby it is an incumbent inquiry and one that should be left for posterity and to the reader's well considered conclusions: was there a broader well designed master plan here, one aside from the known intentions of Hitler or Hajj Amin, one that required an even better stratagem of guile? One perspective is that Britain had much to gain by acting against the Jews and much to lose if she did not, a view that must be backed by firm historical data. It is the advocacy recorded in the archives of Britain's Prime Minister during WW2 and that Britain will chose the first alternative. Thereby is such a conspiracy premise legitimately evoked and well founded, even to track the true cause of the modern world's chaos and mayhem. Unless, one favors the view the Jews are to blame for daring to still exist. Great Britain is untouchable.

World War II.

The Second World War began following Adolf Hitler's handshake of deception with the British Prime Minister Arthur Neville Chamberlain. As in Europe, the situation of the Jews deteriorated in Arabia where they lived for thousands of years; rampant persecution, murders and property confiscations erupted in the Arab controlled states of this region in parallel with Europe. Both the Jews of Europe and Arabia began fleeing to Palestine and other countries, now their only refuge vested in Britain's hands. In 1939, the biggest blow for the Jews will unfold. The deception of a White Paper Peace accord that was made to Britain by Adolf Hitler happened in the same year as Britain enacted another White Paper Policy for the Jews in Arabia. While the White Paper with Hitler may be a genuine misadventure for Europe and Britain, the one concerning the Jews has been highly shrouded and remains highly questionable.

Britain saw it necessary to abandon Israel and appease Nazi Germany and the regimes she created; yet long suppressed archives say it was more intended to appease the Arab demands. Its underlying reasoning and negotiations are shrouded, yet if aligned with Neville Chamberlain's hand-shake with Hitler it did not result in anything positive for humanity. Over 50 Million lives will perish in the European and Russian regions; and mass killings will erupt in Arabia; 50% of the Jew population will perish. Those Jews fleeing Europe will find they are now barred from entering the 20% land in Palestine promised by Britain's 2-state division, and barred from all Christian and Arab states that covered more than 50% of the earth. Britain's Prime Minister had to be aware that the Jews simultaneously faced the same situation of expulsion throughout the Middle East; and that almost all Christian countries globally barred Jewish refugee's entry, many turning the ships back to the German camps. Britain's two White Papers of 1939 gave the Jews few options.

• "This morning I had another talk with the German Chancellor, Herr Hitler, and here is the paper which bears his name upon it as well as mine. We regard the agreement signed last night… as symbolic of the desire of our two peoples never to go to war with one another again. I believe it is peace for our time. We thank you from the bottom of our hearts. Go home and get a nice quiet sleep."" - The British Prime Minister declaration, September 30, 1938.

Britain's White Paper with Hitler.

PM Chamberlain's infamous hand-shake with
Adolf Hitler; 1939.
Britain's White Paper with the Jews.

London Conference, St. James's Palace, February 1939. Arab
Palestinian delegates with Sir Neville Chamberlain presiding and
to his left, Malcolm MacDonald.

The Great 20TH Century Error.

Neville Chamberlain holds a white paper signed by both Hitler and himself; 1939.

A handshake of an agreement between Hitler and Chamberlain became the adverse policy issued for the Jews. Britain's flaunting of the Balfour provisions gave no provisions for the Jews with his agreement with Hitler; it became a stark alignment with her other White Paper Policy with the requirements of Hajj Amin that barred immigration into Arabia, even to the land left over after Jordan was created. Entry into Arabia was shut down, both for the Jews fleeing from Europe and for the Jews fleeing from the Arab controlled states:

• "A clerical error by the British Colonial Secretary Malcolm MacDonald, that was intended to be seen only by the Arab delegates, arrived at the office of Dr. Wiseman. In the letter, MacDonald promised severe limits on Jewish immigration and land purchases in Palestine, and no Jewish national home without Arab consent." - (The conference, London St. James Palace; Rafael Medoff/JNS.org).

• The Jewish world was stunned and shaken by Britain's edict. Global protests erupted. Conditioning the national home for the Jews, their very existence, on Hajj Amin's approval was a deathly employ and charges of genocide were issued by the most prominent Jews of the time:

150

- "A death sentence for the Jewish people." - Dr. Weizmann, WZO President.
- "The greatest betrayal perpetrated by the government of a civilized people in our generation." - Ben-Gurion, Israel's Prime Minister.
- "The "death sentence for the Jews" was handed down while the U.S. remained silent." - Dr. Rafael Medoff, JNS Org.
- "What a heinous, collective crime of history! An act of national perfidy which will dishonor the name of Britain" - (Lloyd George, the Prime Minister of Great Britain; national radio speech.)

Jews Protest Britain's White Paper Policy.

'A Heinous, Collective Crime of History' - British PM.

Consequences of Britain's other White Paper.

HMAS Power Unleashed on Jewish Refugees Fleeing Europe.

The Struma

The Struma, one of many ships of Jewish refugees fleeing Germany is torpedoed in the Black Sea by the British. All but one of the 769 Jewish refugees perished. - ('Holocaust at Sea' by Douglas Frantz and Catherine Collins.)

151

Britain deems Jews as Enemies.

The Jews who fled Germany's destroyer warships in whatever boats and ships they could secure were now hunted down by five of Britain's most powerful war assets, the newly produced destroyers of His Majesty's Royal Navy, including the HMS Hero warship (flagship), HMS Havock, HMS Henward, HMS Hotspur and HMS Ivanhoe. Such was the obsession of what can only be seen as a genocide premise inflicted on the Jews, for Britain ought to have no justifiable reason to bar their return to the only refuge assured and pledged to them, and similarly from all colonized countries under her control. Arab demands for such a response is hardly a meriting; the Jews had every right to enter the land accorded them and should have been facilitated to do so. Britain's Foreign Office instruction was that Jews are no less the enemies than Germans. Thereby Britain's colonies Australia, New Zealand, South Africa and India were also ordered to uphold the barring of Jewish refugees, evidencing only a genocide provision for the Jews fleeing Europe:

• "A Division of Destroyers supported by five smaller launches was being employed to ascertain that those who had escaped Hitler did not escape the British capture as they approached Palestine. - [Mr. Malcolm MacDonald, the Colonial Secretary, PRO House of Commons Debates, July 20, 1939].

• "The Allies would be 'relieving Hitler of an obligation to take care of these useless people.' - [Richard Kidston Law, Parliamentary Undersecretary of State for Foreign Affairs].

• "On September 1,1939, His Majesty's ship Lorna opened fire on a rickety overcrowded refugee ship, The Tiger Hill, crammed with 1417 survivors as she neared Palestine. "She did not, could not, heed the order to turn back toward Germany. The encounter between HMS Lorna and the Tiger Hill ended with a victory for the Royal Navy. (William Perl, Holocaust Conspiracy: An International Policy of Genocide. New York: Shapolsky Publishers, 1989, pp.85-87).

• The rejection of the refugee ship 'The Atlantic' resulted in 1700 Jews on it being sent back to Nazi-occupied Europe. Most ended in concentration camps and were exterminated.

• On November 25, 1940, a ship called Patria was sunk near Haifa carrying 1800 Jewish refugees to Palestine.

• The British played a double-edged deception against the Jews: "The British were secretly importing thousands of Arabs from all over the Arab world into Israel and by the time 1948 came it was a continuation of immorality not the beginning" - [Joan Peters, *'From Time Immemorial: The Origins of the Arab-Jewish Conflict over Palestine', 1984]*.

Thereby did two White Papers emerge that impacted the Jews in Europe and in Arabia. Such factors allow the strong indicator of Chamberlain's dual agreement with Hitler and Hajj Amin. Britain's White Paper Policy against the Jews became the most forthright indicator of two paradigms, indicating pledges made to both Hitler and the Arabs, and both relating to the Jews: 1. The determined focus on Jewish refugees fleeing Europe, especially using warships, renders the given reason not to bomb the Nazi camps as a means of preserving precious war assets as dubious. 2. The creation of Jordan, the West Bank and accepting Arabs as Palestinians are thus based on appeasing oil rich regime arrangements against the Jews. Britain must be seen as the last nation to accept such implements by virtue of the control given her and the agreements made with the Jews.

Global Caliphate Consequences.

Thereby, the premise of a Caliphate doctrine that rejects a minuscule state for the Jews, and its global spread in the 21st Century, must be correctly ascribed to Britain's deeds in the 20th Century. Britain's actions represent the dominant factor that condoned a Caliphate, and is the only one that could have prevented the Middle East becoming subject to such a doctrine. It is also evident that except for the merit of a Jewish state, and the restoring of Lebanon as an intended Christian state, it is not possible to stem a Caliphate in this region or its extension across the nations. Britain's silence, even support, of Jordan's destruction of synagogues, churches and a host of sacred sites and monuments, should be viewed as the reason of the depletion of these areas of Christians and Jews. Thereby, these errors should be corrected if any stability is contemplated in the global extensions. Fair and reasonable conditions of rule, including the negation of a perpetual 'emperor rule' governmental system, one that adequately safeguards the rights of minority inhabitants, should be made on the states created by Britain, and as a priority of any other issues. The latter is the truest cause of the world's refugee crisis in the modern world. It is noteworthy the new government of Egypt is progressing such a theme.

A Crime Against Humanity.

Britain's barring of the Jews must be seen as a crime against humanity; it was also illegal. It should not be withheld solely for a nation held greatly by Christians; Britain's miss-deeds are too numerous and successive.

In the Balfour text of 1917 there was no mention or provision of another state in Palestine, despite that it contained the article 'a' state instead of 'the' state. As noted by Britain's own officials, Britain acted in contradiction of its treaties and prominent figures such as Lord Balfour in the numerous divisions of Palestine as well as the Arabs prior to the appointing of Hajj Amin as the Mayor of Jerusalem. The agreements between the Zionist Jews and the Emir Faisal were accorded without any inference of another state in Palestine, and an acknowledgment of both the land and the titles Palestine and Palestinian were referred exclusively to the Jews; that Arabs also entered the region are not valid reasoning of a heritage name transfer and made as the antithesis of the Jews. Thereby, the inculcation upon a worldly multitude that use the terms Palestinian and West Bank as anti-Israel charges must be seen as errors committed by Britain; these are more than falsehoods and hold the most sinister implications by design. In a sense, Britain mocked not only the Jews but the entire worldly multitude, most of all the British people themselves with a poor legacy. The later deeds when oil was discovered renders the creation of Jordan thereby bordering on a deception, or else it is a most un-reasonable usage of the Balfour texts and intent. Any reasonable understanding says this text, although open to inexplicably subjective variant readings, says Palestine was promised to the Jews with no conditions of land divisions, only strong conditions of safe guarding the privileges and rights of all peoples. Britain's removal of 80% of Palestine for a 2-state division affirms the shock and dismay by the Jews of such a sudden decision; its darker side is that the immigration was substantially fostered by the British. Thereby, Britain chose to manipulate the textual understanding to placate the most unreasonable demands of the Arabs and accept any requirements against the Jews, even one bordering on the comprehensive and total annihilation of the Jews, a declared goal of the two parties Chamberlain negotiated with.

No Nation should be held as above the law, especially so a great one such as Britain that was handed a judgment portfolio. Israel, now a separate enclave from Jordan, and yet to declare her independence and an official naming of the land, accepted the British proposed 2-State compromise; it was by an overwhelming force on an overwhelmed people; a choice-less issue propelled by Britain. Jordan's creation, notwithstanding its subversive reading of the Balfour text, can be seen as corrupting an agreement under extreme duress. That Britain's 2-state division was followed by the White Paper Policy aligns with dire human rights abuse and may also be open to a conspiracy charge of genocide; if credible then the statutory period cannot impact, nor whether Britain holds a prominent seat in the UN Security Council. The issue is bigger than its impacts on the Jews and aligns with the underlying causational factors of the entire Middle East conflict and its continuing global impacts.

• The world must consider forthrightly what transpired following the first 2-state that created Jordan. The remaining 20% ought to have rendered the remaining portion of Palestine, the land west of the River Jordan, now among the smallest landmass of all states in Arabia, as the Jewish state with a further requirements of a third state as fully unreasonable and a continuing genocide premise. Britain ought to have been assisting the Jews to reach safely at the meager state left for them instead of implements its reverse provision. This was the only place the Jews could proceed to, yet it was now barred to them with battle hardy war ships; Britain took time out from a world war to blast boats of Jewish refugees fleeing the Nazis that Britain was at war with.

The White Paper Policy made the 2-state treaty an open deception and the flaunting of Britain's declared pledges that the Jews fully relied upon. It says Hitler was appeasing Hajj Amin, and Britain was appeasing both with a White Paper for each. The Jews were being targeted both in Europe and Arabia; it is difficult to raise another plausible explanation to justify such actions.

Essentially, the Jews now faced the same situation in Europe as they did in Arabia and confronted two calamities; an openly declared potential genocide in Arabia, and what became an actualized holocaust in Europe; both under Britain's watch. The reasoning for such a dual-wedged pursuit against the Jews will remain outside the scope of this presentation; however, its consequences are manifest as among the greatest disasters in human history. And the world's silence has resulted in an expanding disaster that continues as one unconnected with Jews or Israel. Namely, the acceptance of the terms West Bank and Arabs as Palestinians are master-plans of Britain and the Arabs, and equally impacting potentials as those of the Nazis; by subsequence they have the same impacts extending outside of the Jews.

Although the White Paper Policy was also supported by America [the S.S. St. Louis Tragedy of June 1939], it was America's soldiers that made the greatest effort to disclose what occurred following the White Paper Policy in 1939. General Eisenhower correctly foresaw the Holocaust denial that became widespread in Europe and Arabia. Eisenhower thus embarked on a campaign of distributing letters, photographs, films and archives to preserve this history's memory; it marks a variant disposition with Britain and Arabia.

"The Things I Saw Beggar Description."

In the United States Holocaust Memorial Museum in Washington DC, four monuments showcase its facade with quotes from its presidents, including President Dwight D. Eisenhower. General Eisenhower's Letter to General George Patton said:

• "The things I saw beggar description...The visual evidence and the verbal testimony of starvation, cruelty and bestiality were so overpowering...I made the visit deliberately, in order to be in a position to give first hand evidence of these things if ever, in the future, there develops a tendency to charge these allegations to propaganda."

- [Filed under: Germany, Holocaust, World War II. Tags: Captain Alois Liethen, General Dwight D. Eisenhower, General George S. Patton, General Omar Bradley, Merkers Mine, Ohrdruf, USHMM — furtherglory @ 6:44 pm]

Eisenhower also retrieved from the British Intelligence Adolf Hitler's Final Will, Political Statement, his suicide note and his marriage certificate, despatching these to the American President and requesting their display in a special museum monument. All blame by Hitler for the Second World War was placed on the Jews on behalf of the Aryan race ['Hitler's Final Will' is in the index section].

Declassified Letter from Eisenhower to Gen. Marshall.

In Europe

Eisenhower views burned bodies at Ohrdruf. Right: Eisenhower "deliberately" visited this shed.

In Arabia

850,000 Jewish refugees flee Arab controlled countries.

Holocaust and Refugee Denial.

'The fantastic lie that six million Jews were killed.'
- P.A. President.

Eisenhower correctly forecasted the future decades. As part of its rejectionist war with Israel, Holocaust and Jewish refugee denial became widespread in the Middle-East, ranging from outright denial to attributions of exaggerated Zionist Plots; also un0mentioned was the genocide vitriol of Hajj Amin and the charters of destruction in the PA charter. Notorious falsehoods in Arabia were promoted, including claims of blood libels and the Protocols of Zion, met with silence from Britain, the Vatican and the Russian and European communities where these falsehoods emerged from.

The Zionist Organization of America (ZOA) condemned the Palestinian Authority (PA) president and Fatah leader Mahmoud Abbas for reiterating his long-standing Holocaust denial. In 1984, Abbas published an Arabic language book derived from his thesis called 'The Other Side: the Secret Relationship between Nazism and Zionism' (Arabic: *al-Wajh al-Akhar: al-Alaqat as-Sirriya bayna an-Naziya wa's-Sihyuniya*). In this book, Abbas repudiated what he called "the Zionist fantasy, the fantastic lie that six million Jews were killed." (ZOA Press Release, Jan 29, 2013). Significantly of this lie, Abbas' organization was initiated by Hajj Amin, the mentor of the P.A., who had intimate ties with the Nazis.

Muslim leaders visit Auschwitz.

It is known that some 30 to 60 Million people of various nationalities perished, establishing that the numbers are vast and that the Jews were especially focused on with Hitler's Mein Kamp' book; it illustrated his determination to erase one race of people termed as 'The Final Solution to the Jewish Problem'. The genocide support was in fact a fundamental inculcation of Hajj Amin, and we learn this was a more entrenched doctrine than those of the Nazi regime that collaborated with Hitler.

Arabs Deny Arab Denial.

A more forthright first-hand Arab team also emerged, one that made a historic journey to Europe and denounced Mahmoud Abbas, Hamas and the Iranian and Syrian regimes. The President of the Islamic Society of North America issued a joint statement condemning denial or justification of the Holocaust and rejecting anti-Semitism in any form. A total of 14 Islamic leaders from Bosnia, India, Indonesia,

159

Jordan, the Palestinian territories, Saudi Arabia, Morocco, Nigeria, and Turkey were in Poland as part of an anti-genocide program organized by the US State Department's Office of International Religious Freedom on May 20, 2013. Their response to Abbas:

• "We acknowledge, as witnesses, that it is unacceptable to deny this historical reality and declare such denials or any justification of this tragedy as against the Islamic code of ethics."

• "If the British Mandate authorities did not lock the gates of the Land of Israel to the Jews of Eastern Europe, as they did even before Hitler decided to exterminate them, we can certainly assume that the extermination of the Jews, the Holocaust would not have happened. So Britain has a large part of the responsibility for the murdering of six million Jews, between the years 1939-1945, when WWII came to an end." - ("The Story Behind The Sorry Video" News Blaze; by Nurit Greenger, Author and Essayist)

Britain's White Paper is far from ceasing. It persists with the false allocation of Arabs as Palestinians, one that is an extermination premise for the state of Israel. It is a name deception that was devised as a master-plan; the Palestinian Jews will be forever charged of occupying Arab Palestinian land. The transfer of the Palestinian term from Jews to Arabs appeared soon after the White Paper Policy of 1939 with the initiation of a 2-state in 1948.

9. The Jordan Deception.

• "There was no intention in 1920 of forming the territory east of the river Jordan into an independent Arab state." - *(Kirkbride, Alexander; A crackle of thorns, London, 1956 p 19)*

Was Jordan's Creation Legal?

Kirkbride's remark is important in its alluding to the corruption of the Balfour Declaration. It gives an underlying premise of the flaunting of Britain's 1920 pledge and overturning its text three years later; Jordan and any divisions in Palestine was not intended in the 1917 Belfour Declaration. It is also the year when oil reserves became a prominent factor. Britain's entrusted responsibility was to act as a fair and honest care-taker of all groups in this region, and for the Jews to rely on it with all their future on the line. Equally, it was the situation of the

Jews to rely, trust and to depend on the pledges of Great Britain, a foremost Christian nation that was law based, a worldly power and empire given the appointment to settle this reason. For the Jews this was an existential matter.

The creation of Jordan de-legitimatized the veracity of a solemn worldly proclamation given to the Jews, a legal treaty; it's flaunting foretold a syndrome of deceit. It required the over-turning of an agreement that assured a calamitous situation of a people already encumbered in a precarious situation. The flaunting, qualifies for consideration as an illegal action based on its 'under duress' accommodation, and its violation of the human rights of the Jews; especially so in the aftermath of the Balfour text corruption, an indicator of its underlying intent.

Although any alignment with the Holocaust appears an extremely controversial view at this time, Britain will appoint Hajj Amin as Jerusalem's mayor and Chamberlain will issue two White Papers with Hitler; both anticipated inevitable consequences for the Jews, in Europe and Arabia. ("The White Paper Deception"). Whether by default or otherwise, the creation of Jordan thereby represents a larger template of the reason why its over-turning was a paradigm shift. In its wake emerged the White Paper Policy and the extensive Jewish human toll of the Holocaust, the West Bank annexation and the emergence of Arab Palestinians.

The First Cause.

The creation of Jordan and the division of Palestine can be viewed as the first cause of the Middle East Conflict and the flaunting of a pledge; it will have global impact and be deflected away from Britain. Yet there were sufficient reasons for Britain to regret and reconsider the Balfour corruption; instead this was promoted with greater zeal with disastrous results for the Jews, and by default, also impacting Christians and Arabs negatively. It is also the factor that legitimized and fueled a Caliphate premise in the Middle East. The land occupation was reversed on the Jews instead of the Arabs; and the refugee issue was allotted to Arabs instead of the Jews. Britain supported all those corruptions by bypassing the positive agreements with the Emir Faisal in 1919 and aligns with the most radical groups of the region.

Britain's inaction in protecting the security and rights of the Jews was absent in numerous instances. The creation of Jordan caused an endorsement of a continuing thread of actions negating Israel's existence. The over-turning of the Balfour was followed by a White Paper directed at the Jews in 1939; then the establishing of Trans-Jordan as an independent new state in 1946; then the illegal annexation west of the river in 1948 that became the West Bank; it was followed in 1967 with the transfer of the name Palestinian from Jews to Arabs and the pursuit in the splitting of Israel's 3,000 year capital.

That the creation of Jordan as the 22nd Arab state was a 2-state deception is borne out by another state west of the river as still accounted as a 2-state; because a 3-state allocation highlights Britain's 2-state that created Jordan as an open deception. Thereby, Britain, the first nation to approve of the term West Bank, promotes a 3-state in Palestine as a 2-state. None in the Christian community confronted this guile; a formal group called the Oslo Accords will give it worldly respectability. A continuation of 2-states in the same land is an indisputable code for the destruction of Israel.

All of these actions can be viewed as resultant from the primal corruption of Britain's 1917 Balfour Declaration; none of these would have occurred had Britain upheld her pledges. Equally, had the division of Palestine been rejected by the veto powers, none of deeds that continued thereafter would have been possible. Thereby, based on the Balfour corruption, Jordan can be seen as a superfluous and fictitious state with no history, one created solely to appease the Arabs for Britain's interests.

There was no shortage of lands for the Arab people. Jordan was created as 'one state for the Arabs in Palestine', yet Britain failed to confront Jordan's illegal annexation west of the river and Jordan's barring of the Arabs from the new state. These are illegal deeds, at least from the view of the stated declarations and pledges made by Britain. No nation should be held above the law; yet none of Britain's corruptions have seen a place in the discourse of this conflict, and such an outcome is unlikely notwithstanding its continuing global impacts.

The Judiciary/Ethical Application.

162

The term 'illegal or disputed occupation' as international law is based on a manipulated historicity, and thereby an inversion of the charge. Jordan illegally annexed west of the river and illegally changed its name to West Bank, covering this land's 3,000 year Hebrew town names. Name changes do not change history, or render an illegal charge to be transferred from the perpetrator to the victim, as is presented. It is how the term West Bank was implanted by Jordan via an illegal annexation and thus illegal in itself as the correct view. The official term of 'Disputed Territory' is often presented as Illegal and Occupied Territory; nor did these territories belong to the Arabs claiming them. Such deceptions are easily verifiable despite the enormous efforts to cover them by overwhelming the internet with terms such as 'Illegal Settlements' and 'Occupied Palestinian Territory.' These are deceptions that have been thrust upon a worldly multitude. In its wake an ill-famed propaganda enterprise developed to cover the British deeds. Legitimate organizations such as encyclopedias ought not to favor a majority or a political enterprise when describing history, but rather to be relied upon to define history by its validating and un-biased historical markers. An example:

• Quote: "The Israeli-Occupied Territories are the territories occupied by Israel during the Six-Day War of 1967 from Egypt, Jordan and Syria. They consist of the West Bank, including East Jerusalem, much of the Golan Heights, the Gaza Strip, and until 1982, the Sinai Peninsula" - (Richard Falk, UN Rapporteur; Wikipedia.)

Such reporting gives an incorrect impression, one made by gross omissions. The impacting factor of Jordan's illegal annexation of land west of the river, which predates 1967, is not included here as its opening preamble, or that this portion of land was legally allocated to Israel in 1917 (The Balfour Declaration) and in 1920 (The Palestine Mandate). West of the River refers to the land portion Jordan re-named as 'West Bank' by an illegal annexation, as is also stated in the UN archives. The choosing of preferred quotes and ignoring those of Mandates, international law advocates, even British Ministers is an un-balanced historical view:

• "The Jewish right of settlement in the whole of 'western' Palestine - the area 'west of the Jordan' - are parts of the mandate territory, now legally occupied by Israel with the consent of the Security Council." - ('The Future of Palestine', Professor Eugene Rostow, Institute for National Strategic Studies, November 1993. U.S. Under-Secretary of

State for Political Affairs, major text producer of UN Resolution 242.) [italics are added as pointers]

• "The Mandatory shall be responsible for seeing that no Palestine territory shall be ceded or leased to, or in any way placed under the control of the Government of any foreign power. ('Non-Jewish foreign power')" - (Article 5 of the Palestine Mandate)

Although stated elsewhere in the same encyclopedia, it gives an incorrect report when omitted from its chapter titled as "Israeli-Occupied Territories"; it appears elsewhere, not in the subject "Israel-Occupied Territories.", but in another section:

• "The annexation by Jordan was regarded as illegal and void by the Arab League and others. ("Occupation of the West Bank"; George Washington University. Law School (2005). George Washington International Law Review; George Washington University. p. 390.).

• Why then does the same encyclopedia use the heading 'Israeli Occupied Territory' elsewhere, instead of 'Jordan's Illegally Occupied Territory'. The description used does not begin with this history and can thereby render a miss-leading understanding. Correctly, the heading should be "Jordan's Illegal Occupation of Judah and Samaria," which is then the legitimate reporting of this history, because the names were changed under an illegal annexation. A host of worldly recognized sources affirm Jordan's illegal annexation of land allocated to the Jews:

• "This purported annexation was, however, widely regarded as illegal and void, by the Arab League and others, and was recognized only by Britain, Iraq and Pakistan. - (Benveni?tî, Eyāl 2004, The international law of occupation; Princeton University Press, p.108)

• "The mandate implicitly denies Arab claims to national political rights in the area in favor of the Jews; the mandated territory was in effect reserved to the Jewish people for their self-determination and political development, in acknowledgment of the historic connection of the Jewish people to the land." - (Lord Curzon, British Foreign Minister)

• "One of the biggest lies, which is feeding the wild incitement campaign that Israel has been dealing with over the last few years, is that Israel is unlawfully occupying Judea and Samaria, and that the presence of the settlements and of Israelis in Judea and Samaria is a

164

violation of international law." William Jacobson, professor at Cornell Law School and author of the blog Legal Insurrection, told The Blaze that there are "serious and substantial arguments that Israel does not illegally occupy the West Bank, as well as that Israel has not illegally transferred population into that territory." - ('Challenging the Long-Held Notion That Israeli Settlements Are 'Illegal'; The Blaze, *Feb. 24, 2014*)

It is incumbent on an encyclopedia to include aligning and relevant contextual reporting of history; Jordan's annexation and the original name of the territories are absent, thereby it is a diminished historical account. The same should also apply with the term Palestinian when directed away from Israel, because the Jews were exclusively referred to by this name for 2,000 years prior to the 1960's and such is not an irrelevant factor; it should be included in the definition of this name. Nor should an encyclopedia call first century Judea as Palestine, even if this is a widespread anomaly; 'first century Palestine' is a historical impossibility because this name was anointed on Judea in the second century; using a quote of the 5th century as its claim is also an incorrect employ (See "The Herodotus Deception").

A host of prominent scholars and professors possessing this region's first-hand knowledge have vouched the affects of the corruptions engaged in with history when it relates to Israel:

• "This fictitious history, which ignores all historical documentation and established historical methods, is based on systematic distortions of both ancient and modern history with the aim of denying Israel's right to exist." - [Fabricating Palestinian History, by David Bukay, Professor of Middle East Studies, University of Haifa, author of Islamic Fundamentalism and the Arab Political Culture/ Middle-East Quarterly, 2012]

• "Egypt & Jordan illegally occupied Gaza, East Jerusalem and the southern towns to preclude the creation of Israel." - (Anthropologist & Historian Francisco Gil-White)

• "Any attempt to negate the Jewish people's right to Palestine, and to deny them access and control in the area designated for the Jewish people by the League of Nations is a serious infringement of international law." - ("Mandate for Palestine - The Legal Aspects of Jewish Rights"; Myths and Facts; by Eli E. Hertz)

• "The "Palestinians" never had a legitimate claim to statehood in the first place. The "Palestinians" are Arabs, and Arabs already have 22 states. They will not get yet another inside Israeli lands. Any Palestinian wishing to enjoy national sovereignty is free to move to one of those 22 Arab states, but no Arab sovereignty will exist in Israeli territory, meaning the lands between the Jordan River and the Mediterranean Sea. The West Bank belongs to Israel and is Israeli in all ways. The West Bank is part of the Jewish national homeland, always was, and always will be." - (By Steven Plaut American-born Israeli associate professor of Business Administration at the University of Haifa and a writer; Time to Annex Judea and Samaria January, 17, 2013).

The Theological/Moral Application.

Aside from the legal view concerning mandates, there is also a theological premise based on its moral ethicality. Instead of justly safe-guarding the basic human rights of the Jews and honoring Mandates, they were subjected to numerous existential abuses promoted by Britain and the Arab ruling figureheads. By the fostering of the names West Bank and Arab Palestinians, the Jews were presented as the occupiers instead of the victims, enabling a reversal of both history and theology. Placing no equivalent conditions on the Arab states as were placed on Israel was a disregarding of the human rights of the Jewish refugees fleeing Europe; and the declaring by Britain that East Jerusalem as not a part of Israel, whereby no nation can survive such a premise, aligns with a destructive enterprise.

The Third Commandment in the Decalogue, observed in all Christian judiciary institutions, is a law about honesty, and correctly placed before all other moral and ethical laws in the bible. 'In vain' refers to the flaunting of a vow such as a declaration made before the nations of the world:

• "Thou shalt not take the name of the LORD thy God in vain; for the LORD will not hold him guiltless that taketh His name in vain." [Ex.20:6]
• "Thou shall not bear false witness." (Ex. 20:12)

Did Britain Commit Crimes?

166

Britain's deeds against the Jews can and should be questioned; especially so by the British people and the Christian community. The division of Palestine was a violation of the Balfour Declaration and the rights and safe-guard of the Jews. So was the White Paper Policy; both are enormous crimes. Chamberlain's White Paper that caused great calamity to many nations in W.W.2 has been appraised as a monumental error of trust, its primal blame resting on the deceit perpetrated by Hitler. Britain's other White Paper that targeted the Jews in Palestine was also a deceit, perhaps even more odiously by the absence of its confronting. Britain exploited her position as the controller of colonies and regimes, enjoying immunity for numerous wrong deeds against the Jews.

Thereby, the worldly multitude did not find Britain's act of barring Jews entry in Palestine or Jordan's creation as a corruption of her pledges; nor did they question why the only land allocated to the Jews was focused on to house the Arabs and not one of the numerous new Arab states. Merit is due to many British citizens who made great effort to expose their leaders' deceit; many also travelled to Israel to commemorate their grievances with ceremonies of apologies.

The creating of Jordan is a direct response to appeasing Arab demands for oil acquisitions and of a subsequent new Caliphate doctrine that has resurfaced in the Middle East. It is thus a vital and appropriate issue requiring examination why the Jews were targeted as no other nation.

Did Britain Commit Grave Crimes?

The White Paper Policy and Jordan's creation remain among the foremost un-confronted crimes of the modern world by both a judiciary and theological accounting. Here, a play of words was utilized deceptively in overturning the otherwise understood terms of 'one Jewish state in Palestine', and became interpreted by destructive premises of continuing 2-state demands and the splitting asunder of Israel's capital; no nation can withstand such an onslaught.

Britain's Balfour Declaration clearly becomes superfluous if numerous states in Palestine become its definition and aims, even the denial of Israel's right to exist. Thus the Jews were subjected to guile, with the Balfour reading's desecration not being about land or displaced Arab peoples, as has been disclosed in the charters of

167

numerous groups in the region. Here, a land displacement and nativity can only legitimately apply to the plight of the Jews; the Arabs qualifying the least of a requirement for more land or a refugees status. Nor can any Christians validate the historical Hebrew town's name and symbol replacements perpetrated under Britain's watch.

Oil.

Jordan was created because at Damean well No. 7, Arabian oil was discovered in commercial quantities in what is today Saudi Arabia; herein was the testing of Britain. Oil added the incentive to appease the newly created regime states with all their demands being met. There are moral and ethical limitations what can be accepted as reasonable to attain a nation's priority interests; Britain display none when it applied to the Jews, and by default caused damage to all peoples in the region. Thereby, the charge of illegal land occupation on Israel is a distortion of the facts; oil was used to inflict great crimes on the Jews and by default it promoted a Caliphate requirement.

Britain cooperated with such Arab demands in Palestine, as is assessed in Joan Peter's acclaimed book which portrays Britain as encouraging a mass immigration of Arabs into Palestine, in contradiction of Britain's Balfour Mandate pledge and its textual reading. Peter's book also meticulously overturns the Arab displacement and nativity charges, as does the British Peel Commission:

• "Peters demonstrates that Jews did not displace Arabs in Palestine - just the reverse: Arabs displaced Jews." (Orbituary, Joan Peters, United With Israel)

• "The Arab population shows a remarkable increase, partly due to the import of Jewish capital into Palestine and the growth of the [Jewish] National Home..." (*The Peel Commission Report - 1937*)

• Peters' findings appear historically correct; the Jews have no history of acquiring another people's lands and are theologically commanded against it; the reverse applies with a Caliphate doctrine. Britain's fostering of the Arabs to mass migrate to Palestine was thereby an existential attack on the Jews; it aligns with Britain's White Paper and the reason of Britain's inaction when the Arabs were barred by Jordan from entry in violation of Britain's 2-state pledge and in contradiction

168

of Jordan's creation: why create a 2-state if the Arabs remain in the Jewish state and are barred from entering the Arab state?

Thereby, Britain opened the means for the rejection of a Jewish state in Arabia by misappropriating the rights and the land allocated for the Jews, in a situation when the reverse decisions should have been adopted. Historically, Britain's negative deeds toward the Jews date back to the 13th Century, with the first expulsion of Jews exiled by Rome and the false charges of blood libels made on fully innocent people that caused many to perish by burning. Yet as an appointed caretaker in the 20th Century such history should have been cast aside; it was not.[18]

• The thread of deeds committed by Britain became the subsequent premise for a Caliphate provision that denies not only the Jews, but all peoples of different faiths in Arabia, regardless that they are among Arabia's oldest inhabitants. There was no requirement of land by the Arabs in the 20th Century; thus Britain, who was successful in over-turning the Ottoman Caliphate that rejected any non-Arab state in Arabia, was also successful in fostering its replacement with another Arab Caliphate provision in its place.

The Brotherhood.

The Islamic Brotherhood emerged under Britain's watch. The appointing of Hajj Amin as the mayor of Jerusalem, instead of a Jewish mayor that would align with the Balfour Pledge, will be followed by calamity for the Jews and all people of the region. These indicate errors that assisted the pogroms against the Jews and the declaration of Palestine's first land division in 1922 emerging; it was a legitimizing of a violent rejection of a Jewish state, one spurred by Hajj Amin in opposition to previous agreements between the Jews and the Arabs. In 1928, Hassan al-Banna, an Egyptian school teacher and scholar, will introduce a new trans-national organization with the motto of its namesake: "Believers are but Brothers". Thereby, non-believers, those of any other form of belief were fully compromised.

The Brotherhood will proclaim its Caliphate doctrine as the rejection of a Jewish state's right to exist, and it will later usurp another peoples' name as its strategic weapon via Arafat. The name Palestinian became the deception to charge Israel of occupying its own lands and used as a covert means to cover its Caliphate goal. The

169

name Palestinian was disdained before its emergence in the 1960's because it was the symbol of the Jews.

Britain maintained its inaction of both the rejection of its own pledge of a home in Palestine for the Jews, and the usurping of the historical names that belonged to the Jews for 2,000 years. Britain thereby contradicted history and all her documentation thus far issued, promoting a heritage denial of the Jews. The acceptance by Christians of such a name usurping of Palestinian by the Arabs is arguably one of the great astonishments in recorded history. It began with an adjective that became enormously successful with the support of the Christian community; it is the source that invented a new native people that proclaimed the displacement of another native people.

Herein was History over-turned; herein was Rome's name change stratagem reverted against the Jews. It is a faithful juncture and marks a foreboding history that evolved; here was the Arab Palestinian phenomenon invented.

Cometh the New Palestinians.

• Before the creation of Israel, it was actually the Jews who were referred to as Palestinians, not the Arabs. As a matter of fact, Arabs did not accept being called "Palestinians" because they did not want to be associated with Jews or with the British Mandate for Palestine: "We are not Jews, we are Arabs", they used to say in answer." Prior to 1967, no news headlines ever referred to Arabs as "Palestinians". The Middle East conflict was known as the Arab-Israeli Conflict and not the "Palestinian"-Israeli conflict." - ("When The Arabs Became The "Palestinians" - The Invention of a People"; By Michelle Cohen)

The term Palestinian evolved from the premise of a Caliphate doctrine that sought to negate a state for the Jews; and thereby also of all other groups than the Arabs. There was never an Arab people called as Palestinian prior to the 1960's; indeed every British document allocated this name exclusively to Jews and the home of the Jews. A new group will utilize the power of names as weapons and un-historical slogans such as time-immemorial, West Bank, illegal land occupation, native Palestinian displacement; even denials of the Roman Exile of the Jews, the Jerusalem Temple, the Holocaust and that Jews are not Jews. It will achieve the support of Britain and Europe at the UN and attain a worldly multitude in its inculcation. Yet

170

in 1948, the term Palestine is again directed by Britain as a 2-state for and of the Jews in its proclamations of the Kingdom of Jordan. Now, in 1948, the reference of Arabs as Palestinians is still yet notably absent:

• "It will be a historic compromise to grant two states in Palestine, one for the Jews and one for the Arabs." - (Churchill; 1948).

It is at this faithful juncture of history when Jordan emerged as a UN ratified state, as was the changing of this region's name to West Bank that its underlying agenda will unfold. From here will emerge a newly invented Palestinian people, as a historical changing of the guards. From here an ancient historical name is going to be transferred from one people to another new group and they will be assigned via the UN as natives Palestinians in opposition to the historical nativity of the Jews. None will assign this juncture as the source point of Christianity's depletion from the region; blaming the Jews will become the preferred targeting than blaming Britain. This onus must correctly rest on Britain, it's correction is due by the British people themselves, as was seen by the honorable British Army officers and citizens who journeyed to Haifa and acknowledged Britain's errors of the White Paper; theirs is a message to all British people, and by extension to the worldly community.

The advent of a worldly multitude that followed evolved from Britain's legitimizing of West Bank and of a new Palestinian people; it said the pre-1960 Jewish Palestinians were occupying the post-1960 Arab Palestinian land. It rendered the proclamations of Lord Balfour and Sir Winston Churchill as deceit. Britain's accepting of Arabs as Palestinians made the Jews as illegal occupiers of the land of the Jews, even a mockery of Britain's treaties and her history before the world of nations. It is highly implausible its consequences were not devised by a war strategy of extermination derived from the Roman era.[19]

Churchill also turned, succumbing to the higher devotion of greed; in effect rendering the edited Balfour Declaration as referring to numerous states in Palestine, that the Arab population must be handed rights, ignoring the enormous lands handed them and targeted the Jews. Here, a Jewish state, minuscule as she is, cannot be Jewish; a fully disingenuous charge considering the Jews faced an existential crises and Britain acting as a super power controlling numerous colonies. Churchill's new view harbors formidable omens, in effect negating a Jewish state in contradiction of all earlier proclamations:

171

• "Palestine should not be "as Jewish as England is English.""

Jordanians are not Palestinian.

Britain's secret pledges to the Arabs will materialize; waves of anti-Israel slogans and UN Resolutions will result. Alongside the 2-state called Jordan, a new 3-state will be claimed of the Jews and it will be accounted as a 2-state. Aside from the poor arithmetic, the question for whom is another state west of the river claimed, considering that Jordan was created to house the Arabs in Palestine ('One state for the Arabs and one for the Jews/Churchill). This anomaly will spur the separating the Arabs west and east of the river with the usurping of the Palestinian.

Here, Jordan cannot and should not be confused as the Palestinian 2-State or any of Jordan's Arabs as being Palestinian, even as many in Israel have become overwhelmed to accept. The historical integrity fully negates any Arabs as Palestinians; such can be concluded to all who investigate this history as an improvised falsehood of the 1960's and a device intended against the State of Israel.

'Arabs Palestinians' never existed, nor are they natives of Palestine. Thereby this name's usurping becomes a detrimental attack on Israel as its only agenda. There is no historical validation to a claim of any Arabs as aligned with the name Palestine or 'Palestinian'. Such was not in the historical lexicon when Trans-Jordan was created in 1922, nor when the Kingdom of Jordan was formalized in 1948, nor in 1951 when the term West Bank was enacted, or during the previous Ottoman period; it is a recently robbed name promoted to overturn 2,000 years of history.

All honest Christians and Arabs know this truth and that Jews are not occupying Arab lands, the inference of the term 'Arab Palestinians'. Britain has caused Christians and Muslims to contradict their own scriptures and history, even flaunting her own treaties as a war stratagem to 'leave them fighting'. It is the reason this presentation cannot condone or participate in this great deception, one that impacts Christians and Arabs more so than Israel and has caused many disasters in the modern world.

• "And thereafter We [Allah] said to the Children of Israel: 'Dwell securely in the Promised Land. And when the last warning will come

172

to pass, we will gather you together in a mingled crowd'." - Qur'an 17:104

• "Get up, take the child and his mother and go to the land of Israel." (Matt.2:20)

• Israel developed into a united kingdom under the leadership of King David (c.1000-960 BCE) (Ancient History Encly.)

• "From the end of the Jewish state in antiquity to the beginning of British rule, the area now designated by the name Palestine was not a country and had no frontiers, only administrative boundaries." — Professor Bernard Lewis, Commentary Magazine, 1975)

• The Philistines were not Arabs, they were not Semites. They had no connection, ethnic, linguistic or historical with Arabia or Arabs. (Tzemach Institute for Biblical Studies)

• The British chose to call the land they mandated as Palestine, and the Arabs picked it up as their nation's supposed ancient name, though they couldn't even pronounce it correctly and turned it into Falastin a fictional entity." — (Golda Meir. by Sarah Honig, Jerusalem Post, 1995)

The usurping of these historical symbols from the Jews is a formidable attack and designed to render Israel as forever occupying Arab land; its over-turning is incumbent on the honorable British and Arab people, and all Christians who hold the truth will set them free, and by the world community. Jordan and West Bank are not Palestinian and never were as such; Palestinian was the British name for the Jews and the name applied by Rome on Judea, the homeland of the Jews; it held for 2,000 years. There can be no positive outcome of covering one falsehood with another; there was never an Arab group at any time in history that was referred to as Palestinians; this name was exclusively applied to the Jews and their homeland.

Thus the usurping of the terms West Bank and Palestinian are aligned as new un-historical deceptions. The Royal house of Jordan is not from this region; it was transferred here by Britain from the Hashemite family of Saudi Arabia, itself a new state, its royal status also newly created in 1933. There is an absolute dearth of history here relating to the name Palestinian; Britain committed a host of corruptions to cover her Jordan deception. Prominent figures that deal with worldly issues say so:

173

• "75% of what the League of Nations promised the Jews in an invitation to return to their homeland was sold behind their backs creating the country of Jordan." - (Israel and the Palestinians; Correcting Horrible Historical Revision"; Courtesy The Bob Siegel Radio Show, March 22, 2015.)

Cause and Effects.

The error of corrupting the Balfour Declaration of 1917 cannot be overly emphasized as the cause of a tragic global catastrophe. The issue cannot be resolved without its overturning. The Balfour corruption and the White Paper Policy caused a monumental human toll that contributed to one of history's darkest periods; its impressions extend to numerous other trajectories and a host of other lands and people who become targeted by this error; arguably, its direst victims in the Middle East are the Arabs themselves, whose history will become compromised.

• While other Christian countries were engulfed in two world wars and unable to respond to Britain's deeds, there has been sufficient time to reappraise the silence in correcting past errors. Thus a great fog shrouds this juncture of history and the deeds of Britain extending further afield. Consider the period and its transit epochs.

The period of the Balfour Declaration came three years into the First World War in 1917; the 22 regimes that Britain created emerged from its aftermath, as did the premise of a new Caliphate that will replace a conquered one. The impacts were not limited to the Jews; the Arab people of the region were also compromised by deceptions, their freedoms and rights diminished, their plight remaining of internal ethnic battles resultant from inappropriate border lines drawn by Britain based on oil deposits instead of maintaining harmony of the people; the Arab states were not obligated by Britain to adhere to basic human rights laws for its people. The internal Arab group's discordances have extended beyond the Middle East borders in a chaotic rage that blames one and all for their woes. These results were not caused by Israel but the assigned caretaker of the region. Many assisted Britain in prevailing over the Ottoman Empire in WW1, then again in WW2 against the Nazi axle. Many became ensnared in a web of British agreements that culminated in the present world order. The Jews became the soft target of Britain's most focused victim as its

174

continuing legacy. This history's accounting is incumbent to be recalled for those not made privy to it.

World War 1.

It began in July 28, 1914, with Britain allied with France, Russia, Italy, Belgium, Japan and then with America as a late entry in the war. The Ottomans (Turkey) sided with the German-Austria-Hungary-Bulgaria axle. Britain's war strategy focused on the softest enemy, directed at the non-Arab Turkish Ottomans, an invasive power that now occupied most of the Arabian region with its Caliphate doctrine intended as an extension into Europe; the Ottomans conquered the Christian Byzantine Empire in 1204.

The British employed necessary guile that resulted in victory and the felling of the Ottoman Empire with positive and negative merits; they committed overlapping and contradictory pledges to all parties that assisted her in a complex triangle of agendas to gain their support in the war against the Turks.

• Britain recruited the assistance of the Arab armies who sought an Islamic Caliphate mode in opposition to the Ottomans for an independent Arab rule of Arabia; it denied any other peoples' rights to a state in this region. The Arabs were enticed by Britain with an approval of understandings of what they understood as a new Arab Caliphate provision; that all of the region would be handed to them. The British also invited the participation of the French who had interests in Syria, and the assistance of the Jews who had earnestly pursued a return to their historical land for many centuries and were now facing rising anti-Semitism in Europe. The Jews were given their much awaited pledge of a return of their historical homeland with American backing; thereby did the Balfour Declaration assure a Jewish homeland in Palestine. Herzl's willing of his dream to happen was now on the horizon for the Jews after a 2,000 year exile from their ancestral land.

The Arabs were promised independence and the Arabian territories for their assistance against the Ottoman Empire; France was promised Syria and Lebanon as its part in W.W.1; and the Jews were promised Palestine for their assistance in using Zionist advocating by their strong American lobbies to bring America into the war, and by enlisting in the British armies. Britain strongly pursued control of Iraq

175

for its vast oil resources. It was a recipe for conflict whereby each was convinced of pledges given them by Britain without disclosing such secret overlapping pledges also made to any of the other parties. The strategy was successful in prevailing over the tottering Ottoman Empire, while it incurred a host of other problematic legacies.

• When Britain won the war against the Turkish Ottomans and her contradicting pledges discovered, revolts erupted in Syria and Lebanon, as these were allocated to France; these states were in Arabia and also pledged to the Arabs. Riots also erupted in Palestine, whereby the Arabs also saw their cause of controlling all of Arabia as flaunted by pledges made to the Jews in the Balfour Mandate. In Palestine, the Jews constituted only 10% of the population, their numbers always being historically small, and the Arab population grown to some 700,000 by a focused migration from the surrounding regions. This was a migration caused by this land becoming highly developed by the Jews for the first time after many centuries of neglect. Britain's fostering of the Arabs to hinder the Jewish state, in contradiction of its pledges to the Jews, also assisted the migrant inflow. When this war ended and the British issued her Balfour Declaration in 1917, the fostering of a mass migration of Arabs will unfold a series of duplicitous deeds by Britain toward the Jews; all of these were preventable with minimal management. The Jews and the Arabs had already executed agreements, with no inclusion for a division of Palestine and no mention of Jordan or Arab Palestinians as a distinct new group. In the interim of W.W.1 and W.W.2 these treaties were enacted:

• 1920: The Balfour Declaration of 1917 was reaffirmed by the Conference of the Principal Allied Powers at San Remo.

• June 1922: "It is essential that it should know that the 'National home of the Jews' is in Palestine as of right and not on sufferance." - (Winston Churchill British Secretary of State for the Colonies.)

• July 24, 1922: "Whereas recognition has been given to the historical connection of the Jewish people with Palestine and to the grounds for reconstituting their national home in that country." - (by The League of Nations, the previous body of the UN, executed unanimously by 51 nations)

The creation of a 2-state and the White Paper emerged after new discoveries of oil. West Bank and Arabs called as Palestinians yet did

176

not yet occur in this period; now, Palestine was referred exclusively to the Jews. Not a single Arab Palestinian existed till the 1960's, nor the PA Authority, despite the formidable diatribe of Hajj Amin against the Jews. Now only the Jews were Palestinians.

World War II.

Although the Arabs were deceived by Britain, as were all other parties, their determined struggles to reject Israel had no legal, moral or historical grounds, nor one made out of necessity; it was based solely on a new interpretation of theology, substantially promoted by Hajj Amin and the affiliated Brotherhood of Egypt. Outside of a violent view of theology, the Arabs should have accepted Israel's return, as was acknowledged by the Ottomans and the Emir Faisal; the Arab peoples were amply rewarded with numerous new states; more than twenty were created, most of which never existing before. Thus Britain substantially performed the independent region of states it pledged to the Arab peoples.

Thereby, the Jews, who accepted a land loss of 80%, should have been allowed to have a small state; for just as the Arabs claimed displacement by the Ottomans, so were the Jews by such invasive powers foreign to Arabia, namely by the Greeks, Romans, the Crusaders and the Ottomans. The Jews never abandoned their homeland and maintained a small presence at all times, even under harsh conditions. Thus the Arab rejection was based not on their displacement, but the disregarding of the displacement of the Jews; it was the Arabs, not the Jews, occupying another peoples' land. It is proof this was a Caliphate doctrine, not of land occupation. By default, Britain supported a Caliphate doctrine when she flaunted the treaties made to the Jews. The denial of Jewish nativity by the Arabs, even one that the Quran states was the homeland of the Jews, was exploited fully by Britain and numerous Arab groups, with a global indifference to the plight of the Jews. While the Jews encountered a rejection by the Arabs, they were not invaders or occupiers of another peoples' land by any accounting. Israel was returned legally via both the British and the UN, with the international community of all nations and states voting in the motion that returned the Jews to their historical homeland.

Thereby, Israel is not an occupier of Arab lands; the reverse is the historical position whereby the Arabs invaded the land of the Jews in

177

the 7th Century and erected a Mosque on the Jerusalem Temple site that Rome destroyed. There was at all times a Jewish presence in Palestine; not all Jews left Palestine in the exiles caused by Babylon and Rome. The Jews never abandoned their land at any time before and thereafter the Ottoman period, affirming their nativity rights as subsisting of their historical homeland for 3,000 years. Thereby those Jews who returned from Europe and the Middle East were not invaders but returnees to their ancestral homeland; the Arabs were the invaders because the Jews at no time left their ancestral land:

• "The Romans sent the Jews into exile again for 1,878 years. However, for all that time there was a Jewish presence" - (Emanuel A. Winston, a Middle East analyst & commentator, January 7, 2001)

Scriptures have Tests.

All Arab states are well aware of Israel's historical position via ancient and modern history of the ownership of this small landmass being that of the Jews, as is also inscribed in both the Christian and Islamic Scriptures, and by the archives of the Greeks and the Romans. The rejection of a legally appointed Jewish state, one that has a validated historical ownership to this land, inclines with no other reasoning than a theological Caliphate doctrine. Thereby this is not about Israel's occupation of Arab lands; it is a worldly issue of a theological rejection that impacts all groups of humanity. The narratives of all scriptures say their revered figureheads were tested of the path they choose to see how they turn, as should be true with the nations. Adam and Eve were tested; Abraham was tested concerning Sodom and of slaughtering his son as a sacrifice; King David was tested; Queen Esther was tested. So are the nations also tested. In 1948 a historical truth and a biblical prophecy will become validated as a testing of the nations embedded in the Middle East conflict; the ground will talk.

The Omen of the Scrolls.

A theological premise is heavily under-laid in this region's peoples, and it drives their politics. Certainly, a message did emerge at this time, one deemed among the greatest historical finds in archaeology; yet its message in emerging when it did was not understood or denied by the nations. Its theological impact may be even greater for all

178

parties' considerations. Discovered by an Arab youth, the Dead Sea Scrolls exposed and aligned with the historical return of the Jews; both occurred the same year wherein a large parcel of ancient archives of the Hebrew Bible became un-earthed as Israel was re-established. The Scrolls fully represented a historical truth; an omen that transcended all parties, nations and the UN.

As with Moses being distracted by a lost sheep only to be directed to a burning bush that doesn't burn, so was an Arab youth distracted by the sound of a shattering jar when he pursued a lost sheep in the Qumran hills. The Scroll's ancient writings verified an exacting replication of today's Hebrew Bible, with a predicted prophecy of the re-emerging of the Jews' homeland. Here, an ancient theological scripture became an empirical historical exposition.

This was not an adverse message for any other people or belief, as the return of a small group of people and a minuscule landmass cannot be accounted as a threat; numerous new states were created for the Arabs and a minuscule portion was left for the Jews.

The Scrolls proclaimed both past history of the exile that forcefully uprooted the Jews from their land and their return, answering the denial of this land's ownership. It comes from a scripture that is validated and acknowledged by all three religions that emerged in this region with regard the term 'Israel in their own land' and a prediction it contained in hard writ; one also acknowledged in the New Testament and the Quran:

• "I will plant Israel in their own land, never again to be uprooted from the land I have given them," says the Lord your God. (Amos 9:14).

The Scrolls emerged amidst actions by the world community that rendered Israel's re-emergence as a most implausible one. Simultaneously, a new region in the most sacred heart-line of Israel will also emerge, one devised by Jordan. Britain's condoning of a fictional region called as West Bank on the most sacred portion of the Jews sought to overturn history and usher a host of wars, creating an irresolvable catastrophe. It is a war stratagem of 'Leave them divided and ever fighting' and it was successful; but not without impacting of global and inter-religious consequences. The Scrolls most impacting omen pertained to the illegal annexation of land west of the Jordan and the covering of its 3,000 year Hebrew town names.

179

10. THE 'WEST-BANK' DECEPTION.

• "In Judea and Samaria, the Jews are not foreign occupiers. We are not the British in India or the Belgium in the Congo. This is the land of our forefathers. No distortion of history can deny the 4,000 bond between the Jews and the land of the Jews." - [Israel's Prime Minister Benjamin Netanyahu speech; of Jordan's illegal changing the 4,000 year Hebrew names of Judah and Samaria to West Bank in 1951/ US Congress, Aug 25, 2012. PBS]

Erasing 3,000 Year Hebrew names.

The revered 3,000 year historical imprints of biblical history became covered up with a fictitious one; its implementing was made illegally by the Jordanian regime. The anointing of this land portion as West Bank is a tremendous corruption of history. It made the birthplaces of King David and Jesus Christ, instead of Bethlehem of Judea, as Bethlehem of West Bank; it isolated Hebron, the recorded birthplace of Israel away from the Jews and barred to them; and it flaunted Britain's own pledges and the world of nations that executed the San Remo Resolutions. Thereby it sought to negate Israel's 3,000 year heritage and replace it with one that evolved recently or that never existed before, via elicit name corruptions and the UN's two-year Arab Heritage criteria of the 3,000 year Hebrew icons. Surprisingly, it was not attended by the Christian communities, and its acceptance by the world and the UN is also confounding. The negation of Israel's most sacred land portion is akin to the negation of Israel. The title West Bank is an illegally anointed name, enacted when Jordan annexed west of the river, territory allocated as part of Israel. Thereby,

180

its recognition is based on the legitimizing of both an ancient and modern historical corruption, thus qualifying as a 'deception'.

Britain's actions of condoning the transfer of the name Palestinian marks the duality in its supporting of the West Bank name of this land; both are parallel deceptions, one following the other in close succession and indicative of a designed stratagem. It is not an exaggeration but fitting to class this action as a genocide premise via a heritage denial, a continuing display that was followed by the name transfer of Palestinian from Jews to Arabs, and the carving away of the most widely acknowledged biblical sites of the Jews, namely Judah and Samaria, as depicted in all historical maps and archives prior to 1948.

It is more than an illegal annexation by Jordan. Britain was a signatory to the Palestine Mandate that forbid further land displacement to the control away from the Jews; it was illegal:

• "The Mandatory shall be responsible for seeing that no Palestine territory shall be ceded or leased to, or in any way placed under the control of the Government of any foreign power." - (Article 5 of the Palestine Mandate)

• "This purported annexation (by Jordan) was, however, widely regarded as illegal and void, by the UN, the Arab League and others, and was recognized only by Britain, Iraq, and Pakistan. - (The international law of occupation; Princeton University Press, p.108)

In the White Paper Policy's aftermath, Britain and the Arab regimes never ceased attacking the Jews. In 1948, both factions continued referring to the land west of the Jordan as Palestine, namely Palestine now became Israel and Jordan, while both the British and the Arabs still referred to Jews as Palestinians, and again using the term Arabs, not Palestine or Palestinians for the territory and people of Jordan.

The British pledged Jordan as the land created for the Arab peoples 'east' of the River, and the rest of Palestine was for the Jews; this was Britain's proclaimed 2-state in her historic compromise of a 2-state in Palestine. Thereby, Britain's 2-State division should have rendered the land portion west of the Jordan as allotted to Israel, and the name Palestinian should have remained as applying only to Jews or the citizens of Israel; Britain did so, then turned on the Jews again. Churchill will describe the land of Palestine as exclusively the homeland of the Jews for 3,000 years, impressing that the Jews are not

181

invaders or illegal occupiers in Palestine, that Palestine is a reference to the Jews and their historical homeland, namely that the Arabs are not its native inhabitants:

• "The coming into being of a Jewish State in Palestine is an event in world history to be viewed in the perspective, not of a generation or a century, but in the perspective of a thousand, two thousand or even three thousand years." (Declared in the House of Commons on 26 January 1949; *Churchill by Himself*, p175).

Thereby, the term of occupation is one that rejected Churchill. Yet the eloquent proclamations of Churchill will later acquire a dual edge by succumbing to his nation's deeds; Britain will not implement them. The aspiring words of 'Historic compromise' and 'granting two states in Palestine' was now being flaunted again from the Balfour Declaration. Now a 3-state was emerging with another new name as a new region called as West Bank, and Britain will promote a 3-state as a 2-state. It becomes difficult to determine the true import and significance of Churchill's words and the deeds of Britain, whether this was his true view or one ceded to the British agenda that was overwhelming. While upholding Israel's 3,000 year history, Churchill was fully supporting of the new term of 'West Bank' on the heels of his historic, but not historical, 2-state division pledge that created Jordan. Clearly, the premise of a 2-state in Palestine is a contradiction with a West Bank region; it will emerge as a 3-state demand in Palestine by a new group called as Palestinians that will emerge for the first time in 1964, and it will be regarded as a native heritage title that transcends the nativity of Israel.

Thereby, the status of Churchill's proclamation of its 3,000 year history was negated and corrupted; Churchill will readily accept Jordan's erasing of the 3,000 Year Hebrew town names, while also casting a negative view of the Arab people, indicating a duality of speech difficult to quantify:

• "A degraded sensualist deprives this life of its grace and refinement, the next of its dignity and sanctity. The fact that in Mohammedan law every woman must belong to some man as his absolute property, either as a child, a wife, or a concubine, must delay the final extinction of slavery until the faith of Islam has ceased to be a great power among men. Individual Muslims may show splendid qualities, but the influence of the religion paralyses the social development of those

182

who follow it. No stronger retrograde force exists in the world." - (The River War, first edition, Vol II, pages 248-250 London).

A Half-Naked Fakir.

India, a land and people that benefited Britain enormously, also earned a double-edged underlying portfolio. Churchill determinedly battled against India's independence, describing Mahatma Gandhi as a "half-naked fakir" and Indians as a foul race. India is a 5,000 year nation, one that has not invaded other peoples' lands or destroyed native inhabitants, and one that has shown much hospitality to millions of refugees with open arms since time immemorial, even when Britain will forsake the Jewish refugees in its White Paper Policy that India welcomed.

Seeking independence is never a foul disposition; invading and exploiting other lands is. The diatribe against India continues, forgetting fully Britain's deeds toward the Jews:

• "Power will go to the hands of rascals, rogues and freebooters. All Indian leaders will be of low caliber and men of straw. They will have sweet tongues and silly hearts. They will fight amongst themselves for power and India will be lost in political squabbles. A day would come when even air and water would be taxed. India is merely a geographical expression. It is no more a single country than the equator." - ("Gandhi & Churchill: The Epic Rivalry That Destroyed an Empire and Forged Our Age" by Arthur Herman; The Nile Book Publishers.)

Britain's role as a caretaker of this region becomes confusing how it failed to foresee a series of actions incurred in her watch. For 3,000 years the land that became the West Bank was called Judah and Samaria till 1950; today Israel still rightly upholds these names as active and subsisting as her true heritage marks. For no amount of political manipulation should cover heritage annihilation, even by the acclaimed Churchill: the term 'West Bank' applying to this land was illegally created by Jordan under Britain's watch. Jordan's annexation west of the River was not recognized by the International community and the UN; yet Britain did recognize it. Very confusing.

Jordan also simultaneously barred all Arabs in this region from entry into Jordan, a contradiction of Britain's only given reason of its creation; yet Britain's proclamation of 'one state for the Arabs' in

Palestine was thereby a corruption that will meet silence from the Christian community. In 1948, following the UN establishment of Israel, the illegal occupation was not by Israel but the Arabs:

• "Egypt & Jordan illegally occupied Gaza, East Jerusalem and the southern towns to preclude the creation of Israel." [20]

The Dead Sea Scrolls message was correct. Both actions, the illegal name change of this historical land portion west of the river, and the barring of the Arabs into Jordan, were violations of Britain's 2-state proclamations. This action also created the false premise of Arab Refugees; falsely, because Britain's 2-state division of Palestine created a vast country called Jordan precisely to house the Arab peoples, those who migrated here recently and were not indigenous or native to Palestine, and because it contradicts Britain's proclamation of a 3,000 year history in Judea and Samaria. Britain should have been assisting the Jews in Europe and Arabia at this time, not engaging in their further demise.

Significantly of the agenda behind the creation of Jordan, had Britain voiced her objections, and had the Arabs in Palestine not been barred entry into Jordan, there would be no Arab refugee issue, no West Bank and no Palestinians today; the Arabs could have amply re-located to Jordan or the countries they came from. Britain failed to negate any of these illegal and un-historical implements. Here, it is required evidencing that the Arabs calling themselves as Palestinian natives of this land is also a deception.

The Palestinian Deception.

The census conclusions of 17th and 18th Century Palestine verify that the people west of the Jordan were not this land's ancient inhabitants; that these arrived here only after the Jews began developing this land. There was no reason for the Arabs west of the river not to go to Jordan or to the countries they came from, accept that they preferred to live with the Jews than the regimes created by Britain. The Arabs west of the River also had a host of new Arab states provided by Britain. The Palestinian name deception clarifies the reasoning why Jordan annexed west of the river and barred those Arabs from entry east of the river.

Thus, unlike any other refugees anyplace else, these cannot be allocated as refugees without a place to go. Instead of negating

184

Jordan's actions, Britain supported the illegal 'West Bank' annexation in the land that Britain pledged to the Jews on two separate occasions: in its Balfour Declaration of 1917; and when it created Jordan in 1948 at the UN as its historic 2-state division of Palestine; here there was no mention of a division of Palestine or of a Saudi Kingdom in Palestine. Hereafter Britain will actively promote a third state in Palestine; a new group of people will be created and it will adopt the name of an ancient one. Thereby, some 30% of the Arab peoples for whom Jordan was created were barred entry into Jordan and were accounted as refugees; these will swell with the British assistance and the UN's new refugee accounting of a two year habitation for any Arab and all their families. It is a factor that clearly defines entrenched corruptions and the intended rejection of Israel. Unlike Israel absorbing 850,000 Jewish refugees from Arab controlled lands, Jordan and the surrounding states barred the Arabs west of the river from returning. These will become Palestinian refugees.

Thus did the southern portion of Israel's most historical regions, including its towns' 3,000 year Hebrew names of Judah, Samaria, Nazareth, Bethlehem, Bath-El and parts of Jerusalem, become changed to West Bank; and Israel was charged as illegally occupying her most sacred lands. It is from this source point a plethora of new charges will emerge to become the most pronounced denunciations of the modern world against any nation; and new terms that will enter the world's vocabulary, media, libraries, education institutions, encyclopedia and religious sermons:

• 'Occupied Territory'.

• 'Disputed Territory'.

• 'Illegal Occupation'.

• 'Arab Palestinians'.

• 'East Jerusalem'.

• 'Palestinian Refugees'.

• 'Two-State'.

• 'Green Line'

• 'Oslo Plan'

Missing in the Discourse: The Balfour Mandate; the Palestinian Mandate; A Caliphate doctrine that forbids a state for the Jews;

185

charters of genocide; that Israel has never occupied another peoples' land throughout history; that the name Palestinian belonged to Jews for 2,000 years; that Arab Palestinians are not natives of this land; that Jordan was a 2-state in Palestine and the West Bank a 3-state. These are not irrelevant factors by any accounting, yet they are not in the discourse.

Of Poor Arithmetic.

Why is a 3-state in the same land called as a 2-state by Britain? Two factors answer this numerical deception:

• That a 3-state in the same landmass can be seen as false, an overt corruption of the previous 2-state British proclamations and appearing as an annihilationist premise; it would be awkward to implement with credibility.

• That a new region with a new name must be created to obscure its deception. It will appear highly farcical to claim lands with the names Judah and Samaria as illegally occupied by the Jews; these were the 3,000 year Hebrew names of the southern portion of Israel in 1950 and depicted in all geographical maps by those names.

Today, the Arab states entirely omit Israel from the map of Palestine and most western states omit the names Judah and Samaria. The West Bank creation is a major propaganda stratagem component, one that has no historical alignment with the land portion it claims by displacing a validated one of another people. The means of changing the Hebrew names of ancient towns allows Israel to always be accused of illegally occupying Israel, and thereby be subjected to more negative UN Resolutions than all nations combined. Such a paradigm will be implemented after Israel accepted all demands upon it by Britain. The Scrolls message was more than an archaeological relic because it fully negated the corruption of the West Bank creation; this aspect was disregarded by the world communities, yet it cannot be denied.

Jesus of the West Bank?

The 'Illegal Occupation' as slogans, banners and posters hoisted in protest marches throughout the world and cited in all assessments by a multitude of institutions and media, has no legal or historical

186

justification. These are instituted via recognized funding inducements and filler busting sessions of International Law at the UN that would not be tolerated in other instances with other peoples. Thereby it becomes a latent agenda to erase Israel's history and by default, the Christian one by negating their most sacred sites. Here, all the revered figures of Christianity become not from Israel but a fictional new region called as West Bank.

• "In 1948 General Glubb lead the Jordanian Arab Legion commanded mostly by British Officers to expel all the Jews from Hebron, East Jerusalem and the West Bank. Not only they did ethnic cleansing but they destroyed dozens of ancient synagogues and 60,000 Ancient Jewish Tombstones in the Sacred Ancient Jewish Cemetery of Mount of Olives to try to erase all evidence of Jewish History in the West Bank. In 1956, after his service in Jordan, the criminal General Glubb, responsible for ethnic cleansing of Jews, was knighted by the Queen. General Glubb was appointed Knight Commander of The Order of Bath by Queen Elizabeth." - (Knesset Should Declare British General Glubb A War Criminal; The Conservative Papers)

• "It was President Truman again who prevented the British from sharing out the mandate Palestine among their Arab clients, having already taken a big chunk of it to create an emirate for its Hashemite protégés" - (Milestones: 1945-1952; US State Dept; Office of the Historian)

The reason why none can produce a Muslim Palestinian prior to the 20th Century is finally not an issue to be denied anymore; it is a historical fact. Palestinians are an invented people of the 20th Century condoned by Britain and impressed upon a worldly community via deceptions. The Arabs of Palestine were not a people that inhabited this land from time immemorial, a claim made by Arafat and accommodated throughout the Christian community's leaders at the UN.

11. The Time Immemorial Deception.

Are Palestinians Native to Palestine?

Can two opposing people claim a 'time immemorial' nativity in the same land? Yes, but not at the same time. To claim any such ancient nativity both party's claims require evidencing, otherwise one is a deception. Here, even belief and majority rule is insufficient as both are open to error and corruption. A time immemorial premise can refer only to what evidential history says, and this can only be measured via validated writings and archaeological imprints or an empirical means other than belief.

Namely, it cannot be so because some are saying so without any imprints, nor can this presentation; an arms-length historical validation must apply. And such validation must ideally possess cross-references and multiple verifications of exemplary historical references when it is contradicted by another. Thereby, the 'time immemorial' claim must affirm either the Arabs or the Jews possessed an ancient sovereignty in this land.

For the Jews, their claim is of a habitation of some 4,000 years ago and a sovereignty rule 3,000 years ago. The references cited here are as exemplary; other similar references from numerous sources may be independently investigated. While the new generation may not be fully aware of these historical factors, there is no question all of their peers, Christians and the Arab peoples, including of their religious sectors, are fully aware of them. It is the reason this book uses the term 'Deceptions'.

Circa 2,000 Years Ago. It is historically validated the Arab people called as Palestinians in the 20th Century were not the inhabitants or ruling force of Judea when Rome invaded and destroyed Jerusalem and its Temple 2,000 years ago. In the Roman war with the Jews, the Arabs are mentioned as mercenaries in the Roman legions; these were not citizens of Judea. It is seen in the archives of Roman historians like Tacitus and Josephus, and in the Gospels and the Quran that Judea, previously called as Israel, was the land of the Jews. Judea, the land of the Jews, was re-named as Palestine by the Romans in the second Century (135 AD/CE); this was not the land of the Arabs. [21]

Circa 2, 600 Years Ago. The Arab people were also not the inhabitants or ruling force of Judah (the pre-Latin name of Judea) when Babylon invaded and destroyed the Jerusalem Temple in the 6th Century BCE. There are no Arabs mentioned in these historical archives. [22] **Circa 3,000 Years Ago.** The Arab people were not the inhabitants or ruling force of Israel, the land ruled by the Jews as a sovereign kingdom from 1002 BCE to 135 CE. Israel is the previous name of Judah, established by King David with Jerusalem as its

188

capital; Canaan was the previous name of this land. There are no Arabs that are mentioned in these historical archives. [23]

Thereby, there are no recorded imprints of Arabs ruling this land from the Canaanite to the Roman invasion period. We have no recorded Arab kings, cities, wars, language or writings in this land 3,000 years ago, or 4,000 years ago, or throughout all recorded history, and thereby it negates the 'time immemorial' claim for this period of history as a deception. The original Philistines, who invaded and ruled in Gaza for a short period, were not Arabs, nor were the pre-Hebrew Canaanites an Arab people. Here, the Dead Sea Scrolls dated up to 408 BCE, with some portions 600 BCE; the Tel Dan discovery; and the first and second temple period discovery of relics, also act as aligning evidences this was the 'land of the Jews', not of the Arabs.

• "Jewish sovereignty in the Land of Israel extended over 1400 years. It was the Jews who first implanted their culture and customs of their permanent settlement" - (Ibn Khaldun, one of the most creditable Arab historians; 1377 c.e.)

• "The Jews lived in the Land of Israel for seventeen hundred years virtually uninterrupted until the Roman destruction of its national polity in AD 70. At this point, Israel's population of over two and one-half million was abruptly decimated by massive slaughter and expulsion. But as late as AD 617, Jews controlled Jerusalem and a large portion of the Land. After that time, even though Arabs conquered the land, they were only a minority. Then through the centuries of Christian Crusader rule and the Mameluke period, the Land was still dominated by Jewish culture and customs until AD 1400 even though the Arabs eventually became a small majority." - (Bible Students Congregation of New Brunswick)

Roman War Proof.

Rome went to war with the Jews in the first century, destroying the Jerusalem Temple in the year 70 AD/CE. Rome changed the name of Judea to Palestine and expelled many of the Jews in the second century (135 AD/CE). That the Arabs were mercenaries recruited in the Roman legions and destroying the Jerusalem temple is validated by the archives of the Romans and the Greeks, as well as its corresponding archaeological discoveries. Namely, the Romans were engaged in a war with the Jews in their homeland of Judea in the first and second centuries; thereby this was thus not an Arab land. Israel was returned to her own land, not of an Arab land. There are no historical records of a civilization dating 7,000 years. Here, both the periods prior to 1002 BCE Israel (Canaan), and after the 2nd Century Roman conquest, should also be examined; the former to determine any imprints of Arabs or a Pre-Arab people from time immemorial in Canaan prior to 4,000 years, the latter whether Arabs were the natives of Palestine since the Roman destruction of Judea 2,000 years ago. An examination of such a period fully covers the term 'from time immemorial'.

Post Roman Palestine.

The Christians, not the Arabs, ruled Palestine after the Romans. The Jews, banned from Jerusalem under Christian rule that followed the Roman edict, were now inhabited in smaller numbers yet not fully displaced from the land. Seven centuries after the Roman war with the Jews, the emergent Islam invaded Palestine, but they did not rule Palestine before this time. [24] In 638 a church was destroyed by the invading Mohammedans and a mosque was erected in its place. [25] The Jews were inhabitants of Palestine under Islam and found relatively peaceful habitation and given their right of belief. The Islamic invasion in the 7th Century says this was not the prior land of Islam or the Arabs in the first seven centuries after Rome destroyed the Jerusalem Temple:

• "In 638, Umar, the first Islamic Caliph, requested to be led to the Temple Mount, an acknowledgment of Islam's acceptance of the Hebrew prophetic tradition. After reaching the Temple Mount, the caliph found himself disgusted on seeing the heaped garbage in the sacred enclosure that expressed Christian contempt for the Judaic faith. Umar ordered the area to be cleansed out of respect for the Jews, an act that also prepared the sacred Jewish site for Muslim worship" [26]

In 1099, the Crusaders stormed Jerusalem and re-established its new control; virtually all of the city's Muslim and Jewish populations were butchered. [27]

The Ayyubid Period (1187-1516)

190

The invasive wars continued between the forces of Christianity and Islam and of their sub-groups throughout the following centuries. Palestine's history witnessed the reigns of many invasions, including the 12th Century Saladin (Salah al-Din) who recaptured Jerusalem. This was followed by Saladin's nephew al-Malik al Muazzam Isa; then by Hohenstaufen Emperor Frederick II (1229-1244); the Turkish Khawarism conquest that exterminated the entire Christian population of Jerusalem of 7,000, except for 300 who survived by fleeing to Jaffa; then the further devastation by the Mongols. The emerging Turkish Mamluk's war with the Mongols was so destructive that it left Jerusalem as a neglected, isolated and ravaged city. On the eve of the Ottoman conquest, the city numbered forty-four madrasas and twenty zawias. [28]

While the Islamic forces substantially diminished the Christian rule, two significant factors can be established:

1. That although the major population of Jews were exiled throughout the nations in Arabia and across the Mediterranean seas (Europe), they always maintained a Jewish presence in Jerusalem and the surrounding cities consistently, including in Jerusalem, Megiddo, Hebron and Bethlehem.

2. That none of the forces that battled over Jerusalem for 2,000 years were the 'time immemorial' people of this land; many of these invading forces were not natives of Palestine; and following the Islamic invasion of the 7th Century, these were not Arab, including the Crusaders, the Mongols and the Ottoman Turks.

We know of the Jewish continuous habitation by examining their status in Arabia, Palestine and Jerusalem under the final invasive empire of the region, one that was not Arab and prevailed for four centuries previous to World War One.

The Ottoman Period (1516-1917)

Prior to W.W.1 the Jews were prominent inhabitants of Palestine under the previous Ottoman Empire. It is a positive affirmation of the 'time immemorial' history of the Jews with this land's historical records from the 9th Century, thereby negating that the Jews in Palestine as based on recent immigration from the Spanish Expulsion of the 15th Century. Although Spain's expulsion did create an in-flow and expanded population, they returned to an already prevailing

191

Jewish habitation in the Ottoman reign. The Jews prayed at the Jerusalem Temple site continuously throughout biblical times up to the Ottoman period; the last Islamic Sultan acknowledging Jerusalem as the ancient holy city of the Jews, not the Arabs, Christianity or Islam.

Jews of Jerusalem under the Ottoman Empire.

Ottoman Jews at the Western Wall - by Felix Bronfils, 1870.

Ottoman Period Jews.

The Jews are historically recorded in Palestine dating prior to the Ottoman rule, including in the Assyrian invasion (9th Century BCE); the Babylon invasion (6th Century BCE); the Greek invasion of Alexander the Great (300 BCE) under Ptolemy when the Hebrew Bible was first translated (the Septuagint Bible); and the Roman destruction and Christian rule up to the 7th Century AD/CE.

In the later Ottoman rule that began in 1516, the Jews were among the most entrenched and recognized people as the 'Yehoudim' (Jews) of the 'Land of Yisrael.' The Jews constituted most of the Ottoman Empire's doctors, lawyers, accountants and writers, and developed many of their great institutions in Ottoman controlled Palestine.

This history says the Jews, not the Arabs, are this land's inhabitants since the time predating the Assyrian invasion of the 9th Century BCE (3,400 years according to the Egyptian Amarna Letters); and the

192

previous 400 year period prior to WW1; thereby that the Arabs are not its natives from time immemorial as is claimed; the evidence allocates such a premise solely to the Jews. Thus the Arabs cannot qualify as native refuges of Palestine:

• The Scroll of Ahimaaz, which predates Ottoman rule, is of a Hebrew family chronicle in rhymed prose written by Ahimaaz ben Paltiel (1017-c.60); the scroll bears the Hebrew title "Sefer Yuhasin" ('Book of Genealogies'; Neubauer's ed., pp. 111-113, 132, 133). The narrative's text covers the 9th and 10th centuries when the author's forebears were leaders of their communities and well-known poets. The scroll of Ahimaaz mentions the location of the Jewish Temple as a Jewish prayer site; it was sanctioned as such under the Ottoman rule. - (The Oxford Dictionary of the Middle Ages).

• In Ottoman controlled Palestine, thirty Jewish communities existed in Haifa, Sh'chem, Hebron, Ramleh, Gaza, Jerusalem and many in the north, with Safed as a spiritual centre for esoteric Kabala study. The Sulchan Aruch, the most widely consulted 'Code of Jewish Law' ever written was authored in Safed by Yosef Karo in 1563. As well, many Kabbalistic texts were developed in Safed. - (Codex Judaica, Mattis Kantor 2005; History of the Jews in the Ottoman Empire.)

• Compared with other Ottoman subjects, they (the Jews) were the predominant power in commerce and trade as well in diplomacy and other high offices. In the 16th century especially, the Jews rose to prominence under the *millets*, the apogee of Jewish influence could arguably be the appointment of Joseph Nasi to Sanjak-bey (*governor*, a rank usually only bestowed upon Muslims) of the island of Naxos. - (Charles Issawi & Dmitri Gondicas; Ottoman Greeks in the Age of Nationalism, Princeton, (1999)

• The first Jewish synagogue linked to Ottoman rule is *Etz ha-Hayyim* (עץ החיים; Lit. Tree of Life) in Bursa which passed to Ottoman authority in 1324. The synagogue is still in use, although the modern Jewish population of Bursa has shrunk to about 140 people. - (International Jewish Cemetery Project; Turkey).

• It would not be difficult to put together the names of a very sizeable number of Jewish subjects or citizens who have attained to high rank, to power, to great financial influence, to significant and recognized intellectual attainment - (G.E. Von Grunebaum, "Eastern Jewry Under Islam, 1971, page 369.)

Left: Jewish Ottoman Doctor (1558 Woodcut, Nicolay de Nicolay; p.185); Right: Ottoman Jew, Paining 1675.

• "Most of the physicians were Jews, including court physicians such as Hakim Yakoub, Joseph and Moshe Hamon, Daniel Fonseka and Gabriel Buenauentura, to name only a few. One of the most significant innovations the Jews brought to the Ottomans was the printing press." Sulaiman the Magnificent (1520-66), like his predecessor Salim I., had a Jewish body-physician, Moses Hamon II., who accompanied his royal master on his campaigns. - (Life of Ottoman Jewry, Jewish World Libr.)

• "The Jews offered Hebrew prayers for success during battles with the presence of the Ottoman Prime Minister in synagogues" (London Illustrated News, 9-6-1877).

• The Jewish population in Jerusalem increased from 70 families to 1,500 at the beginning of the 16th century. That of Safed increased from 300 to 2,000 families and almost surpassed Jerusalem in importance. - (Ottoman Jews; Wiki)

• Suleiman the Magnificent was the Caliph of Islam and the tenth and longest-reigning Sultan of the Ottoman Empire, from 1520 to his death in 1566; he fully acknowledged and endorsed Jewish nativity of Palestine. In 1560, Suleiman gave the Jews official permission of the

194

right to pray at their Jewish Temple site." - (Western Wall Heritage Foundation, Retrieved Dec 16, 2007, Online Libr; The Kotel Org.)

• "Jews have lived in Turkey from very early times. There was a colony of them in Thessaly at the time of Alexander the Great; and later they are found scattered throughout the eastern Roman Empire." - (Adrianople; Byzantime Empire)

• "The earliest records of Jews in Turkey date back to 220 B.C.E. Turkish Jewry reached its population zenith — 200,000 members — on the eve of World War I." - (The Society for Research on Jewish Communities.)

• "The troubled history of Turkey (previously Ottoman Empire) during the 20th century and the process of transforming the old Ottoman Empire into a nationalist Islamic nation state after 1923, however, had a negative effect on the size of all remaining minorities, including the Jews." - (Turkey; Wiki).

• "The Land still was permeated with Jewish culture and customs. In AD 1400, there was still no evidence of Palestinian roots (Arab Palestinians) or established culture." - (Arab historian Khaldun, called one of the greatest historians of all time by Arnold Toynbee)

• **Ottoman Palestine was not Arab:** "At its core, the Ottoman Empire was a multi-ethnic state. The ruling family was Turkish, but the population was made up of Turks, Kurds, Greeks, Armenians, Bosnians, Serbians, Persians, Arabs, and others. A wide range of nationalist beliefs existed, but it is safe to say that those (of the entire Middle East) advocating for a complete break from Ottoman history and the establishment of ethnic nation-states were a small minority." - (Ottoman History, Palestine.)

Was Palestine the homeland of Palestinians?

There was never an Arab country called as Palestine, or an Arab Palestinian people prior to the 1960s when this name was usurped from the Jews. The name Palestine did not belong to Arabs; it was applied to Judea, then resurrected in the 20th Century by Britain. Both Palestine and Palestinian were names referred exclusively to the Jews and their historical homeland in Britain's official and legal documentation, and utilized as the counter to the Arab people.

According to Joan Peter's critically acclaimed book ("From Time Immemorial: The Origins of the Arab-Jewish Conflict over Palestine"), a large portion of the Arabs of Palestine were not natives of Palestine at the time of the formation of Israel in 1948, but had arrived in waves of immigration starting in the 19th century and continuing through the period of the British Mandate. Namely, there were never a native Arab Palestinian peoples in this land from time immemorial, nor a substantial number relative to the Jews throughout this recorded history.

Thereby, the Arab time-immemorial nativity claim in Canaan, Israel and Palestine is false and un-historical. The denial of the Jewish nativity is also false and un-historical. That these are deceptions and un-historical is also evidenced by the lack of any Arab institutions or native habitation by the term Palestinian; the nativity premise in Palestine is not seen by any other people than the Jews. Joan Peter's findings are also affirmed by an array of prominent historians, writers, theologians and numerous Arab scholars; the late Peters became subject to much vilifications for her historical portrayal of this history, one that began as a support of the Arabs, but that turned altogether after her ten year examination of Palestine's history.

A mission of the U.S. Senator Robert Kennedy also affirms the same; his first-hand reporting of this history will allegedly cost him his life by an assassination.

"Bobby" Kennedy, Israel, 1948.

• "Over 500,000 Arabs in the 12 years between 1932 and 1944 came into Palestine to take advantage of living conditions existing in no other Arab state. This is the only country in the near and Middle East where an Arab middle class is in existence" - (Robert Francis "Bobby" Kennedy, June 3, 1948; Boston Post). Robert Kennedy also wrote, "We must deal with the causes of the conflict by ensuring a permanent and enforceable guarantee of Israel's right to live secure from invasion, and free passage for ships of all nations through the Gulf of Aqaba and the Suez Canal…" [Robert Kennedy Supports Israel, RAAB Collection].

A Barren Swamp-Land.

The previous centuries affirm this land's population status in the Ottoman period as possessing a dynamic Jewish population. However, far from being a land of many other displaced peoples, Palestine was accounted by prominent Historical figures as one of the least

197

populated regions of the world prior to the Jews returning, affirming that the Arab people arrived later. The historical imprints affirm that the Arabs called as Palestinians in the 21st Century are recent 18th Century onward immigrants and not of a past population of Palestine:

• "Nothing there is to be seen but a little of the old walls, which is yet remaining and all the rest is grass, moss and weeds much like to a piece of rank or moist ground." - (Gunner Edward Webbe, Palestine Exploration Fund, Quarterly Statement, p. 86; de Haas, History, p. 338)

• "Palestine is a ruined and desolate land." - (Count Constantine François Volney, 18th century French author and historian)

• "The land in Palestine is lacking in people to till its fertile soil." - (British archaeologist Thomas Shaw, mid-1700s)

• "There is not a solitary village throughout its whole extent (valley of Jezreel, Galilea); not for thirty miles in either direction. One may ride ten miles hereabouts and not see ten human beings. Palestine sits in sackcloth and ashes… desolate and unlovely." - ("The Innocents Abroad", by Mark Twain, 1867).

Modern scholars of this history also reject the premise of Arab Palestinians as natives of Palestine:

• "The fact is that today's Palestinians are immigrants from the surrounding nations! I grew up well knowing the history and origins of today's Palestinians as being from Yemen, Saudi Arabia, Morocco, Christians from Greece, Muslim Sherkas from Russia and Muslims from Bosnia." - (Joseph Farah, "Myths of the Middle East")

• "The Arabs themselves, who are its inhabitants, cannot be considered but temporary residents. They pitched their tents in its grazing fields or built their places of refuge in its ruined cities. They created nothing in it. Since they were strangers to the land, they never became its masters. The desert wind that brought them hither could one day carry them away without their leaving behind them any sign of their passage through it. With slight exceptions they are probably all descendants of the old inhabitants of Syria." - (Stephen Olin, D.D., L.L.D., called one of the most noted of American theologians after his extensive travels in the Middle East wrote of the Arabs in Palestine.)

• "It is not true that there were "Palestinians" living in Israel since ancient times only to be displaced by European Jews in the 20th century. The Jews have an ancient claim to the land." - (Courtesy The Bob Siegel Radio Show Quote.)

Historical Census Accounts.

Five centuries of Palestine was described as deficient of any natural resources, including water for irrigation, forsaken and neglected by the previous Ottoman Empire. Chiefly, it was not the land of the Arabs or an Arab populated region or country; the last ruling reign of Palestine for 400 years was the Ottomans (A Turkish people), itself an invading force and not an Arab people.

The historical archives of Palestine say Jerusalem's population was predominately and overwhelmingly of Jews and Christians even when ruled by the Ottomans and that Palestine was left barren and un-catered for centuries prior to the Jews who alone developed this land; that the Jews began development of the land when news of a return consideration began to surface via early American Presidents and Herzl's endeavors. Such is accounted by historical imprints seen in the17[th] and 18th Century census accounts under the Ottomans. The Arab populations were substantially located in the Middle-East outside of Palestine, but yet under Ottoman rule. Much suppressed archives have now emerged that deny two fundamental factors; namely of any historical Arab Palestinian Native claims to this land, and the UN's adopted Historical population claims, as is seen in historical census reports of the Ottoman period.

[Titled "Palestina" (Original Latin name Palaestine *by Hadriani Relandi — its original professional name* Palaestina, ex monumentis veteribus illustrata, *published by Trajecti Batavorum: Ex Libraria G. Brodelet, 1714, scholar, geographer, cartographer and well known philologist, spoke perfect Hebrew, Arabic and ancient Greek]*:

17th Century Population Census Survey

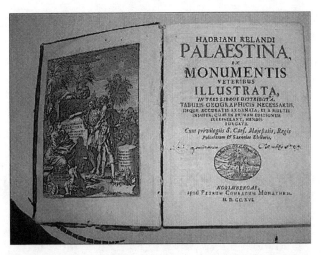

Historical Book of Muslim Census in Palestine.

In 1695, the cartographer Relandi was sent on a sightseeing geographical tour to Israel, the land at that time known as *Palestina*. He first mapped this historically known land's geography, then he arranged a population survey and census of each community. These are his most prominent conclusions:

• **Not one settlement in the Land of Israel has a name that is of Arabic origin.** Ramallah, for instance, was called Bet'allah (From the Hebrew name Beit El) and Hebron was called Hebron (Hevron/Hebrew name).

• **Most of the land was empty and desolate.** Most of the land was empty, desolate, and the inhabitants few in number and mostly concentrate in the towns Jerusalem, Acco, Tzfat, Jaffa, Tiberius and Gaza. Most of the inhabitants were Jews and the rest Christians. There were few Muslims, mostly nomad Bedouins. Nablus, known as Shechem (Hebrew name), was exceptional, where approximately 120 people, members of the Muslim Natsha family and approximately 70 Shomronites, lived. In the Galilee capital, Nazareth, lived approximately 700 Christians and in Jerusalem approximately 5000 people, mostly Jews and some Christians. The Muslims were as nomad Bedouins who arrived in the area as construction and agriculture labor reinforcement and as seasonal workers.

• **No Palestinian heritage or Palestinian nation.** The book totally contradicts any post-modern theory claiming a "Palestinian heritage," or Palestinian nation. The book strengthens the connection, relevance, pertinence, kinship of the Land of Israel to the Jews and the absolute

200

lack of belonging to the Arabs; no names of towns, no culture, no art, no history, and no evidence of Arabic rule; only huge robbery, pillaging and looting; stealing the Jews' holiest place, robbing the Jews of their Promised Land. - [English translation courtesy of Nurit Greenger. "Adrian Reland (1676-1718), Dutch Orientalist, was born at Ryp, studied at Utrecht and Leiden, and was professor of Oriental languages successively at Harderwijk (1699) and Utrecht (1701). His most important works were *Palaestina ex monumentis veteribus illustrata* (Utrecht, 1714), and *Antiquitates sacrae veterum Hebraeorum*."]

Arab Status in Palestine.

There is no issue that two people cannot be the inhabitants and ruling force in the same land at the same time. That one such claim is incorrect is validated by historical imprints. Scholars that are of high merit also agree one claim is false.

• "Historians and archaeologists have generally concluded that most, if not all, modern Palestinians are probably more closely related to the Arabs of Saudi Arabia, Yemen, Jordan, and other countries than they are to the ancient Jebusites, Canaanites, or Philistines." - (The American archaeologist Eric Cline in his book 'Jerusalem Besieged')

• "In 'From Time Immemorial', Joan exposed the fraud at the heart of the Palestinian national narrative — the claim of indigenous status in the land of Israel. As Joan showed, most of those who now refer to themselves as Palestinians were migrants from surrounding Arab lands who came to Israel as economic migrants beginning in the mid-19th century, and mainly during the period of the British Mandate in the land of Israel. That is, they came the same time the Jews did." - [Caroline Glick; Journalist, writer, Senior Fellow for Middle East Affairs of the Washington DC based Centre for Security Policy.]

Thereby, there appears no other description of the term 'deception' applying to the term 'Time Immemorial' of an Arab nativity in the land of Israel. There are no imprints of it in the historical thread; it accounts the usurping and transfer of the name Palestinian, and the changing of a parcel of land dotted with ancient Jewish sacred sites that was illegally altered to 'West Bank'. While such historical name manipulations are promoted by Britain who was in the controlling forefront of this region, no credible reasoning allows that the facts were not realized or known this was the exclusively held land of the Jews, both historically and legally via treaties and via the UN. These name deceptions numerously appear as a result of manipulations to overturn world history and the 20th Century legal agreements to achieve contradictive agendas and commercial interests. Thereby there is also a direct alignment of appeasement seen in the absence of any conditions placed on the regimes created by Britain; such machinations have fueled the loss of human rights for the Arab peoples ruled by lawlessness and inculcated with displacement teachings, harsh propaganda and a lacking of worldly knowledge. Yet this was a war stratagem of 'Leave the people fighting' by Britain who ultimately cannot be viewed a friend of the Arabs; it fuelled conflicts both within the Arab groups and with the Jews.

Britain's Fictional Borders.

The underlying strategy of creating borders antithetical to the region's sub-groups affected the Arabs more than any other sector. This was processed while Britain was servicing of every facility for the regimes she created, not the Arab peoples. An inevitable rage incurred by restrictions and hopelessness developed that extended elsewhere, a phenomenon that is already being witnessed globally by mass immigrations from the choicest lands with the greatest resources. Britain's devices included name transfers, treaty corruptions, propaganda and the exploiting of theological factors by appointing figures like Hajj Amin and encouraging mass immigration in Palestine while barring the Jews from returning. The Jews became Britain's expendable fall guy. With her excellent war-time investigative abilities and knowledge of the Arab groups and its geography, none would know more than Britain the Arabs claiming a nativity in Palestine was false, as stated by Churchill and other British Ministers. The Arabs were encouraged by Britain into the land allocated for the Jews; no passports or identification was required. Britain's actions are also exposed by those Arabs from the heart-line of Palestine.

• "As I lived in Palestine, everyone I knew could trace their heritage back to the original country their great grandparents came from. Today's Palestinians are immigrants from the surrounding nations! I grew up well knowing the history and origins of today's Palestinians as being from Yemen, Saudi Arabia, Morocco, Christians from Greece, Muslim Sherkas from Russia, Muslims from Bosnia, and the

202

Jordanians next door. My grandfather, who was a dignitary in Bethlehem, almost lost his life by Abdul Qader Al-Husseni (the leader of the Palestinian revolution) after being accused of selling land to Jews. He used to tell us that his village Beit Sahur (The Shepherds Fields) in Bethlehem County was empty before his father settled in the area with six other families. The town has now grown to 30,000 inhabitants."- (Walid, a Palestinian Arab defector, quoted from "Answering Islam")

12. The Refugee Deception.

Who Are the Refugees?

Are the Arabs or Jews the refugees of Palestine? This important question is well validated by history and many Arab Muslim experts, yet both remain disregarded. The only refugees of Palestine reported are of the Arabs, with no explanation how such a conclusion is arrived at. How can Arab Palestinians be from other Arab countries that are not Palestinian, as claimed by an award-winning Arab Journalist:

• "Not only do the Arab countries despise the Palestinians, they also want them to be the problem of Israel alone. That is why since 1948, Arab governments have refused to allow Palestinians permanently to settle in their countries and become equal citizens. Now these Arab countries are not only denying Palestinians their basic rights, they are also killing and torturing them, and subjecting them to ethnic cleansing." - (Ethnic Cleansing of 'Palestinians' by Khaled Abu Toameh, an Arab Muslim and a veteran award-winning journalist covering Palestinian affairs for nearly three decades, Senior Fellow at the Gatestone Institute. Yonkers Tribune)

The only error in Khaled Toameh's report is of the widespread deceptive term Palestinian attributed to the Arab people, even though it is noted as stated retrospectively as from 1948. His statement has a historical falsehood that underlies why this conflict has immense issues of resolving and why all have thus far failed; the pivotal deception in not confronted. Another factor is that none of the regimes could attain this result without Britain's full co-operation and assistance. There is strong reasoning of an arrangement in place which restricts negative subscriptions of the Arabs.

Herzl's Palestine.

Calling Arabs as Palestinians is akin to calling them as Judeans or Israelites; thereby such a name switch agenda is one of negation of one side's history and heritage. This name transfer is thereby a strategic weapon of deception used against Israel's existence, a premise often repeated in the Middle East with an apparent support in Europe and Britain seen the past 70 years at the UN and their media reporting.

The real refugees were not the Arabs but the Jews exiled by Rome from their homeland of Judea, which became named as Palestine. The Jews were also the refugees from Arab ruled lands where they lived for 2,600 years. Although the Jews chose Israel as their country's name, it is intriguing to consider what would result if they chose on the name Palestine, whether the Arabs would still call themselves by the name of the Jews. Herzl battled for the Jews' right of return using the 2,000 year symbol they were called by, referring Palestine by name as the Jewish state's return in his prophetic book:

• "Palestine is our ever-memorable historic home. The very name of Palestine would attract our people with a force of marvelous potency. - (The *Jewish State* by Theodor Herzl, 1896. Translated from German by Sylvie D'Avigdor.)

Jewish Refugees.

That the Arabs instead of the Jews are presented as the 20th Century's Palestinian refugees of this region marks the deception of its namesake. The Jews displaced from Arab controlled lands are greater than those Arabs displaced from Israel, in substance and mode of displacement; thereby the refugee claim is a reversal syndrome against the Jews. While the Arabs left of their own accord with the promise of return upon the destruction of the Jews by a multi-state Arab war, or even if fleeing a war scenario to save them - the displaced Jews were forced to leave via murder, pogroms and property confiscations without the advent of a war by the Jews in those lands. While the historical period of Arabs in Palestine is comparatively recent, the Jewish habitation in Arab lands is more than 2,500 years, even predating the Arab rule of these lands. And while the Arabs possessed more land options than any others, the Jews had none but their mandated homeland to return to. Such reasoning make the premise of

204

a heritage and physical annihilation aligning with the usurping of the term Palestinian; these make implausible the charges of land occupation and correspondingly, make credible the legitimate focus in rejecting the premise of Arabs as Palestinians.

Europe and Arab Hostilities.

The Jews were being exterminated in Europe and the same planned in Arabia. Both of these barred entry to the Jews in all places under Britain's watch. Thereby, the refugee deception is of a tremendous maligning against the Jews, as in the name transfer of Palestinian from Jews to the Arabs. The far more credible Jewish refugee history is also transferred to the Arabs. Even significant, those accepting the premise of Arab refugees cannot possibly be unaware of such a falsehood; perhaps their conclusions are based on different criteria that should be explored.

• "More than 700,000 Jews had left the Arab states. A large portion of nationalized Jewish real estate was left, for example, in the most posh neighborhoods of Cairo, Alexandria and Baghdad. The communal property of Egypt's Jews covered huge areas, including about half of the district of Maadi (a city of villas and gardens located about 20 kilometers from Cairo, where all the luxurious houses have turned into the residences of ambassadors from various countries." - ("Can Jewish Refugees claim billions from Arab states?" By Dr. Cohen, the son of Jewish refugees who fled Lebanon in the 1980s, managed to collect information about this aspect of the "nakba" of the Arab state's Jews as part of his studies; Ynet News)

• "Mr. President. Since 1948 Israel has received nearly one million immigrants, the great majority of whom are refugees, hailing from over 70 countries and from all corners of the world. The great majority of those who came to Israel during these ten years, came either from the post-war camps in Germany and Italy or from Arab-speaking countries." - (Golda Meir, Israeli PM; Speeches-USA).

Jordan's barring of the Arabs west of the Jordan River succeeded in creating an Arab refugee issue when it was least credible. The Arabs were handed an abundance of lands given them with no requirement for more; it indicates an improvised stratagem that was not about land. Britain will divide Palestine as one more land for the Arabs at the expense of the Jews. Instead of resolving this conflict it will cause a refugee problem, one again caused by Britain's inaction of requiring this as an end to the land issue.

Contrasting the plight of the Jewish refugees, the Arab refugees in Palestine appears intentional. The vast landmass handed to Jordan affirms the Arabs west of the river could very easily be housed in Jordan, else the given reason for creating Jordan in Palestine - 'one for the Arabs and one for the Jews' - must speak for itself. All other Arab states refused to accept those who came to Palestine from those lands.

Which Refugees?

The refugee term was focused on one set of Arab refugees and disregarded the 850,000 Jewish refugees from Arab lands, thereby choosing only one over the other. This occurs despite the historical position of the Jews being inhabitants of those lands for 2,600 years, in lands now ruled by the Arabs. There is no question the Arabs have not lived in Palestine for 2,600 years; Palestine was Judea 2,000 years ago and the Arabs were enlisted in the Roman legions and thus not this land's inhabitants.

More significantly, the modern history of Palestine equally refutes the status of an Arab native population, namely prior the end of the 19TH Century. The Jewish population was twice as big as that of the Arabs (See, Census Population Chart); and until the Jews began developing the land, it is described as among the most barren and isolation regions.

Thereby, which inhabitants of Palestine are the refugees is an incumbent issue; the Jews who lived here continuously for a historically evidenced 3000 years, or those who arrived at the end of the 19th Century. Based on such a position, it is a heavy injustice done to the Jews and would also be a heavy legacy for those who accept such anomalies when such an encounter crosses the borders of the Middle East.

The issue also harbors indications such anomalies were fully realized and measures were taken to overcome them via novel changes. The UN decided that the Arab refugees in Palestine don't have to be refugees, at least not how we understood its definition thus far.

The allocation of refugee status had to be altered for the first time in recorded history; it did not require native or historical habitation, the displacement from one's original homeland, or the lack of ancient land ownership provisions at its disposal. In Palestine, refugee became defined only that one migrated to Palestine two years ago and are thus deemed as already living in that region as natives. It contested the essence of the British Mandates of a historical connection of the Jews and Palestine, and the history of this region. In many countries, one cannot attain even temporary visa or citizenship by a two year measure.

• According to the United Nations weird standards, any person that spent TWO YEARS (!!!) in "Palestine" before 1948, with or without proof, is a "Palestinian", as well as all the descendants of that person. - (The True Identity of the So-called Palestinians; *Myths, Hypotheses and Facts*)

• "The definition of a refugee from Palestine in 1948 is a person who lived there for just two years: because many Arab residents in 1948 had immigrated so recently. The usual definition would have cut out a substantial portion of the persons who later claimed to be refugees from Palestine." - (Daniel Pipes *Commentary*, July 1984)

That such a criterion is allocated singularly to only one group of peoples in one land, regardless that it displaced another group's position, will lead to disputed and illegally occupied territory charges, and illegal settlements in contradiction of the mandated right of the Jews to settle west of the River Jordan. Thereby, an Arab refugee crisis emerged instead of the Jews of Palestine, in the land portion named by Jordan as West Bank, which the previous body of the UN fully acknowledged was of the Jews:

• "The League of Nations recognized that all the land west of the Jordan River as to be for a "Jewish National Home." (David Storobin; "Nazi Influence on the Middle East during WWII")

• "The Jewish right of settlement in the whole of western Palestine - the area west of the Jordan - are parts of the mandate territory, now legally occupied by Israel with the consent of the Security Council." - ('The Future of Palestine', Professor Eugene Rostow, Institute for National Strategic Studies, November 1993; U.S. Under-Secretary of State for Political Affairs, major text producer of UN Resolution 242.)

The Jews, inhabitants for 2,600 years in lands which became ruled by Arabs 1,500 years ago, were not accorded refugee status by the UN, or their plight even acknowledged in line with the Arab Palestinian refugees. Based on the UN allocation of Arab refugees, almost all Arab controlled states in the region have a debt and liability to the Jews, with equal claim for 2-state divisions. Such is the chaos derived by the decisions made by the UN and its member states of its Arab refugee provisions.

Arab Homes in Palestine.

Citizenship is not nativity or ancestry of a land, nor is proof of a home ownership or a passport by one's grandfather. These can still be recent immigrants that are natives of another land, especially so if those making such claims deny the true historical natives of that land. The Jews have home ownership in numerous lands of the Middle East dating up to 2,600 years since the Babylon Exile of the 6th Century BCE, yet the Jews are not natives of Egypt, Syria and Iraq, and cannot claim native ownership of those lands.

There is hardly any place where people are not present, be it the Arctic or the Sahara. Additionally, there are factual historical details of the recent Arab migration to this region. The premise of some Arabs with birth certificates and home ownership does not conclude to ancestral or native inhabitation, as has been presented. A father or grandfather living in Palestine does not signify nativity anymore than the Jews who have lived in numerous countries for many centuries yet cannot be classed as natives or claim its sovereignty.

The grandchildren of British people born in India are not native Indians; nor can they become Indian refugees that are transcendent of the Indian peoples, nor can they claim that land's ownership.

Thereby did the UN introduce new criteria of refugees solely for one people and all their descendents, wherever they reside in the world. It is aligned with some Arabs that are a few generations in Palestine and can point at a home in Israel where they once lived. The UN will yet reject the Jews living in Arab controlled lands since greater periods and not give them the same criteria. Such chaos can inevitably also extend across the nations with the same mode of chaos. The UN cannot display one law applying only for Palestine and Arabs and not for any other land. A host of Jews, Christians and other peoples in this region can equally produce such documents of home ownership, both in Palestine and in all parts of the Middle-East. Yet not all can validate a 3000 year habitation in Palestine; this is the unique historical connection of the Jews that Churchill and the Balfour Mandate referred to. Those Jews and Christians who owned homes in Syria, Iran, Yemen, Turkey, Saudi Arabia and Egypt do not claim ownership of those lands, notwithstanding they have far greater longevity credibility of its native inhabitants. The Jews and Copts predate Arabs in Arabia yet receive no similar statehood facilities by the UN as afforded the Arabs in Palestine; it affirms the extending impacts of the chaos directed at Israel.

Arafat, Abbas Are Not Palestinians.

The wife of Jordan's king is thereby not a native Palestinian but of a Kuwaiti aligned genealogy. The historical evidence says prior to a third generation grand-children history there was no Arab nativity in Palestine during the Ottoman period and that the Jews were more than double their population; the survey by the British in 1864 and historical reports of a barren Palestine say so.

The Jews are the only continuous un-broken ancestral natives of Palestine; the Arabs do not have such nativity.

Aside from the European Jews who were exiled across the Middle East, there were ancestral Jews in Palestine since the Babylon, Roman and Christian era who never left their land, accounting for a period of 3000 years. These include the Jews who returned under the Persian reign of Cyrus the Great and remained, as encountered by the Crusaders, Islam and in the Ottoman Empire. Palestine and Palestinian are thus the exclusive nativity marks of the Jews. Not any of the ministers of the Palestinian Authority are of a native habitation in Palestine, including of its founder Arafat.

• "The Person who is called as "Abu Mazen" (whose real name is Mahmoud Rida Abbas Mirza), is of Iranian origin. He is not Palestinian at all and is not from Safed, because he is of Iranian descent, from the city Bandar Khamin, the city of his grandfather, the founder of the Bahai religion. Rida Ullah Riza left to come to Palestine in the year 1882. - ("Abbas, ya Bahai, Get Lost!" Article by Muhammad Al-Tamimi. Quoted by Dr. Mordechai Kedar, Published Nov 22, 2012; The Jewish Press.)

Arabs are not Palestinian despite that some may have fathers born in the land or can produce passports and home ownership certificates. The Jews can do so across the Middle-East by far greater measures,

209

without resorting to the new UN criteria. Those Arabs calling themselves as Palestinians are not natives of Palestine:

• "...Far from being persecuted, the Arabs have crowded into the country [Palestine]." - (Winston Churchill; 1939)

• "In the Jewish settlement Rishon l'Tsion founded in 1882, by the year 1889, the forty Jewish families that settled there had attracted more than four hundred Arab families... many other Arab villages had sprouted in the same fashion." *(Joan Peters - From Time Immemorial p. 252)*

• "The Arab population shows a remarkable increase... partly due to the import of Jewish capital into Palestine and other factors associated with the growth of the [Jewish] National Home..." *(The Peel Commission Report - 1937)*

Theologically Based Refugees.

The fastidious and focused usage of another peoples' historically validated name exposes the absence of credibility in its nativity claim. It created millions of Arab Palestinians who were improvised by a new UN refugee criteria applied solely to the Arabs, with a disregard of legal treaties and the history of the Jews.

The changes of a land's ancient names affirm the claimant's lack of ancient habitation and of their recent status; it is an admission the previous named Palestinian people are the land's natives and thereby the 850,000 Jews from Arab lands are the refugees. Thereby, the Arabs are refugees from Arab lands, not of Palestine. The refugee allocation of Arabs as Palestinian is a historical deception that is targeted against the right of a state for the Jews; and by extension any other peoples. It is theologically based.

The refugee claim is furthered by the dubious arithmetic of accounting the West Bank as a 2-state instead of a 3-state; it is also astonishing that the Christian community accepts such anomalies.

The British declaration of the first two-state division of Palestine, with its stated terms of 'one for the Jews and one for the Arabs' pledge will be foiled by further 2-state measures and new transit agreements that expose an underlying disposition. The fostering of an Arab refugee allocation is a means to usher another 3rd state west of the river and based, not on a refugee or land issue, but on a Caliphate doctrine and commercial reasoning.

• No state any place has faced a greater tide of reductionism more obsessively or further away from Britain's original Balfour enactment that was validated by the world of nations. Thereby, numerous new transit agreements were enacted to negate precedent enactments, including the Peel Commission partition proposal of 1937; the UN partition plan adopted by its General Assembly on November 29, 1947; and the debacle of the Oslo agreement that accounted a 3-state in the same landmass of Palestine as a 2-state, one duly followed by many politicians and media today. These are additional provisions that seek to hide the original corruption that created Jordan, and are among the prime examples of punishing Israel instead of the perpetrators. Such provisions continued under extreme duress for the Jews between the periods of the two world wars.

The Green Line Deception.

A continuing insatiable trend is well seen again by penalizing Israel for accepting a ceasefire of a multi-state Arab war with an openly declared goal of genocide. Thus emerged the premise of the 1967 border lines, also called as the Green Line, whereby the ceasefire point Israel accepted are made as a semblance of Israel's borders. Such has correctly been described as 'Auschwitz Borders', a reference to the Nazi camps that crammed the Jews in train boxes. A ceasefire point is not a border, especially not when the winning side accepted it as a peace offering. The Green Line view is akin to one agreeing to stop battling a home invader when the police arrive, and declaring half of one's home ownership as forfeited and given to the perpetrator. The UN Resolution 242 states, concerning the 1967 war:

• "Israel was entitled to live in peace within secure borders and recognizable boundaries free from threats or acts of violence."

Israel's Balfour Borders.

Israel's borders were the Balfour Declaration lines, one that Lord Balfour fastidiously upheld, refusing even an autonomous Arab region anywhere in Palestine. The originally pledged borders declared as the national home for the Jews is never mentioned, when it should be the preamble of all discourse. The creation of Jordan, the first 2-state, required the prior acknowledgement of the legality of the 1917 Balfour Declaration, and this was duly processed at the UN; it evidences Israel's borders began at the Balfour lines, a fully historical pledge of 1917 that was corrupted by Britain in 1922 when oil was discovered.

Not recalling the Balfour borders, namely all of Palestine which originally included Jordan and the West Bank as one only state for the Jews, renders the creation of West Bank as the 2-state division of Palestine a violation and numerously defined as illegal. Thereafter, Israel's borders, even by grossly incorrect measure, can only become the second division of the first 2-state lines, namely west of the river, following the Kingdom of Jordan's creation in 1948. The region called as the West Bank was illegally occupied by Jordan; it is a portion of land historically and by legal treaty acknowledged as the most sacred land possessions of Israel; it was virtually devoid of Arab Palestinians in the 17th to 19th Centuries. When the violations of the Arabs are not displayed by the UN, and when other nations support such violations, the UN is mandated to correct them when Israel's position is more validated.

The on-going demands for new state divisions, and its accounting a 3-state as a 2-state, can be seen as a means of destruction no state can survive. It is also the underlying cause of a theological Caliphate doctrine that says no other faith must subsist in Arabia as a state. It is the primal cause of an extending Caliphate goal; its negation only possible by attending the corruptions against Israel and correcting them so it cannot be emulated in Palestine or elsewhere.

As with the deceptive name changing of this land's 3,000 year Hebrew titles to 'West Bank' in 1951, and the follow-up claim of 'Time Immemorial Palestinians', the refugee claims are an equally deceptive provision. The true refugees of the 20th century were not Arabs.

Jewish refugees fleeing persecution, murder and

property confiscations in Arabia.

Who's Right of Return?

A Right of Return that is based on a nativity claim correctly applies with the Jews, those who were previously displaced from their ancestral land. The issue of Arab refugees in the West Bank is a direct effect of Britain's inaction in correcting Jordan's illegal annexation west of the river in 1949 and the barring of the Arabs from entry in Jordan. Otherwise it begs the question, why did Britain created Jordan in Palestine? It contradicts Britain's pledges and its given reason 'One for the Jews and one for the Arabs'. The Balfour Mandate does not accuse Jews of displacing Arabs; it affirms the right of return as exclusively vested of the Jews.

Thereby, Jordan's illegal annexation and the name changing of this land portion as West Bank, and soon thereafter of Arabs as Palestinians who are barred entry to Jordan, were essential implements in forming a refugee crises as a sore unto Israel. From here emerged the one-sided premise of Arab refugees instead of the Jewish refugees from Arab lands; and Israel, instead of Jordan, becoming the occupier.

This became as international law at the UN. It resulted in an irresolvable situation of history, stemming from theological doctrines and corruption, with consequences for all nations and peoples. Its underlying result, one fully intentionally improvised, is seen in such debates between an esteemed scholar of history and an Arabic TV Station. Al-Jazeera TV Interview excerpts with Professor Mordechai Kedar, Dept. of Arabic Studies, Bar Ilan University, Tel Aviv:

Host: You cannot erase Jerusalem from the Koran.

Kedar: Jerusalem is not mentioned in the Koran, not even once, and you cannot re-write Jerusalem into the Kuran here on Al-Jazerra.

Host: Mr. Mordechai, the settlements, there are rumors of another 1,000 apartments and thus Jerusalem will include the whole of the West Bank, isn't that so?

Kedar: My brother, Israel does not count the apartments which Qatar is building in the Qatari peninsula. Jerusalem is Israel's eternal capital for 3,000 years and not of anyone else's business.

Host: International law contradicts everything you say. East Jerusalem is occupied. Everyone knows this.

213

Kadar: Jordan, until 1967, was the occupier. Israel can build whatever it likes in the West Bank.

Jordan, not Israel, was the illegal occupier of Judah and Samaria, one who changed the 3,000 year Hebrew names to West Bank in 1948 to enable the term 'settlements'. The Jews were the only people granted legal right of return and to settle in Palestine; and it was made irrevocable. There was never a right of return or any political rights granted to the Arab people with regard Palestine. Thereby, all of Britain's over-turning of the treaties established by the international community of nations remains illegal, according to scholars of international law and legal rights:

• "The facts are that the Jewish people got the right to Palestine because of their historical connection to this land. This is the primal aspect. It was neglected for years but in San Remo the international community realized that was a mistake and that the Jewish people should have full title to the land after the Ottoman Empire was dismantled. And it cannot be revoked because there is an article in the UN Charter, article 80, which preserves the rights of peoples; whatever rights they have acquired is forever. And on top of that there is the convention in the Vienna Convention of Treaties of 1966. It stipulated the treaty is sacred and even when it expires it remains with the Jewish people forever." - (Canadians for Israel's Legal Rights [CILR], Salomon Benzimra; CBN News)

Are Arabs Refugees?

While no people can wish to flaunt the plight of true refugees, no people in history had greater facilities and options than the Arabs called as Palestinian refugees. Contrastingly, none had fewer facilities than the Jewish refugees from Arab lands. The Jews were terrorized and expelled from Arab controlled lands of the Middle East. Thereby, the Jews, not the Arabs, can be defined as refugees with no place to go. The true cause of Arab refugees can only be pointed to Britain who failed to apply conditions of rule on the regime states as was done with Israel. It has resulted is a reversing of the refugee claim from the Jews to the Arabs, as is evidenced in the Middle East historical refugee accounts.

Jewish Refugees in the Arab World

	1948	1958	1968	1978	2011	2014
Algeria	140,000	130,000	1,500	1,000	<50	<50
Egypt	75,000	40,000	1,000	400	100	<40
Iraq	135,000	6,000	2,500	350	7	5-7
Libya	38,000	3,750	100	40	0	0
Morocco	265,000	200,000	50,000	18,000	4,000	2,000
Syria	30,000	5,000	4,000	4,500	100	17
Tunisia	105,000	80,000	10,000	7,000	1,500	1,500
Yemen/Aden	63,000	4,300	500	500	250	<90
Total	851,000	469,060	69,600	31,790	~6,200	3,704

[Fact-Sheet/ courtesy Jewish Virtual Library, American-Israeli Cooperative Enterprise]

13. The Arafat Deception.

• "There is not even the smallest indication of the existence of a Jewish temple on this place (Jerusalem Temple Mount) in the past. In the whole city there is not even a single stone indicating Jewish history." - Yasser Arafat; Camp David Summit, 2000.

The Christianity community should have been aghast at such statements; however, there was no repudiation or responses. Such claims are displayed across the world by the factor of silence of Christian leaders who yet supported Arafat. It is in parallel with the equally false notions of Arabs presented as Palestinians and Bethlehem as West Bank; these are contradictions of both the Christian and Islamic Scriptures and history. The Dead Sea Scrolls and the Roman archives remain the great exposure of such deceptions.

215

The Quran affirms Jerusalem as the Jews' holy city and gives elaborate construction details of King Solomon's Temple (Ch. 34:13); as well of the destruction of both the first and second temples (Ch.17:7).

Arafat [Mohammed Yasser Abdel Rahman] was an Egyptian citizen born prior to Israel's re-establishment. A member of the Islamic Brotherhood, a group established with the goal of Israel's extermination in its charter, Arafat will emerge to create a new people hailing itself as the dispossessed Palestinians from time immemorial. Yasser Arafat who led the Palestinian Liberation Organization, claiming his place of birth was Palestine and that he was related to the Jerusalem Husseini clan, has also been shown to be a deception. The most famous Palestinian refugee was born in Cairo and attended the Cairo University, as reported by French and Palestinian biographers and the historian Said Aburish, respectively.[29]

Arafat (second from right) with other civil engineering students in Cairo University, 1951

A Historical Deception.

There are those who do respond to open falsehoods against Israel:

• "There has never been a country called Palestine. This was a nickname for the Holy Land under the Romans. The people who today call themselves Palestinians are Arabs and they referred to themselves as Arabs for centuries until they were dubbed "Palestinians" as a publicity ploy by the terrorist and founder of the PLO, Yassir Arafat, who himself did not use the title "Palestinian" until after the year 1964." - (Courtesy Bob Siegel, 'The Historical truths behind the Israel

216

- Palestine conflict'; Communities Digital News; 22281/# OEizztbGfH Fpjx2L.99)

• "The PLO Reps join Arafat. Contradictions abound; Palestinian leaders claim to be descended from the Canaanites, the Philistines, the Jebusites and the first Christians. They also "hijacked" Jesus and ignored his Judean origin, at the same time claiming the Jews never were a people and never built the Holy Temples in Jerusalem." - Eli Hertz, Mandate for Palestine: The Legal Aspects of Jewish Rights; Daled Amos, Dec 28,11)

Both the Hebrew and non-Hebrew Canaanites were not an Arab people; and the Philistines were not a Semitic people. The ancient Egyptians and the Copts were also not Arab prior to the 7th Century invasion; nor were the Lebanese Phoenicians Arab. The Hebrew Bible that introduced the names Canaan, Jebusites, Palestine and Arab, say the ancient Jebusites and Philistines had historical connections with the Israelites and none with the Arabs. The Jebusites aligned with Joshua and later sold a hillside to King David which became part of the Jerusalem capital. This was a legal transaction between domestic groups of Canaan; it is similar to a government transacting lands owned by its citizens to build a bridge or a monument.

Both the Jebusites and Philistines became Israelites under King David and were exiled along with the ten tribes of Israel by Assyria. The Tel Dan discovery confirmed the 'House of David' dynasty as an Israelite nation. Thereby, there are significant historical factors that affirm Canaan, which became Israel and Judea, as the homeland of the Jews and not an Arab land. Such is evident that the claims are known as false by the Christianity community, yet they are not responded to; it is the strange plight of the Jews.

Theologically, it appears the changing of names of the landmass housing the most sacred figures of both the Hebrew and Christian groups, is an implement that seeks to overturn ancient history and theology via politically structured means in the 20th Century, rather than utilize historical, archaeological or archival proofing, or any other measures of resolving. Thus Jesus is seen as a Muslim; so is King David; figures born and buried in this land are now called as Muslim figures of the West Bank. History, as evidenced by all archaeological relics and ancient scriptures, says David and Jesus were born in Judea and spoke Hebrew; the Book of Acts (26:14) states Jesus' cross had Hebrew inscriptions. The Tel Dan discovery mentions the 'House of

David' by an enemy nation; and mounds of coins un-earthed from this region is embossed as 'Shekel of Israel'; thereby King David was a Hebrew Israelite. [30]

Half-Shekel Coins of Israel used in the Jerusalem Temple.

The world has not seen a relic or a single imprint that says this is an Arab Palestinian land; it is in contradiction of Arafat's statements and all the UN Resolutions, the historical data and the recorded archives of the Persian, Greek, Roman and Hebrew writings. When examined, it is also in contradiction of the treaties executed in the last two centuries of the modern world.

Today's issue is substantially a theological belief that has been activated via a political frontage. One can say it is more tragic for the Arabian people; they have been turned away from their true historical and ancestral veracity and subjected to a bold and blatant travesty, promoted by a fear of confronting such deceptions. Such deceptions and anomalies have seeped into the cultural beliefs of the Arabs as factual history, including by its scholars that the nations have failed to respond to correctly:

• "The Town of Hebron is an Arab Town. There were no Jews in it before 1967" - Edward Said, Islamic Academic.

• Abraham, as recorded in the Hebrew Bible, was a Hebrew, acknowledged so in ancient relics of Egypt and the Dead Sea Scrolls; both are historical evidences that predate the advent of Islam. Hebron was a sacred town of Judea under both Rome and Christianity, perhaps equally as Jerusalem. Abraham is recorded as purchasing the Michaela cave and its surrounding fields in Hebron, which was Canaan; it is the first recorded legal land transaction and the birthplace of Judaism; these mark a sovereign Jewish state that subsisted till

218

1,500 years later in the Roman reign. Many of Arafat's Egyptian Arab ancestors were recruited in those Roman legions that destroyed the Jerusalem Temple.

Numerous artifacts dating 3,000 years were discovered in the layers of the Hebron burial site of Abraham and Sarah; the large covering building structure of the cave was built by the King Herod, identifying the Hebron site as part of Judea more than 2,000 years ago. Other such legal ancient transactions are recorded in the Hebrew Scriptures. Abraham's grandson Jacob purchased Shechem (Nablus), where his son Joseph is recorded as buried; and David as purchasing the hilltop in Jerusalem from the Jebusites, who were not an Arab people. King David is recorded in ancient writings that he established Jerusalem as a Capital city, with its temple as built by his son King Solomon; a host of surrounding nations are listed in the enormous temple construction, with the notable absence of an Arab group.

Although these are theological archives, there are no negating counter archives of them and they are substantially validated by archaeological relics. There are no archives from the Arabic writing, which never existed at these periods that may justify Arafat's claims. It is highly implausible to give any credence to a counter claim 3,000 years later than is found in the Tel Dan relic.

The Temple builders are listed as the Phoenicians and the Jews. The Roman archives, the ancient Hebrew Scriptures, the Dead Sea Scrolls and the Christian Bible all affirm Hebron and Jerusalem as the land of Israel; the entire land is also acknowledged as possessions of the Jews by prominent Islamic scholars.

How Arafat Became a Palestinian.

• "The Palestinian people do not exist. The creation of a Palestinian state is only a means for continuing our struggle against the state of Israel for our Arab unity. Only for political and tactical reasons do we speak today about the existence of a Palestinian people, since Arab national interests demand that we posit the existence of a distinct 'Palestinian people' to oppose Zionism. For tactical reasons, Jordan, which is a sovereign state with defined borders, cannot raise claims to Haifa and Jaffa, while as a Palestinian, I can undoubtedly demand Haifa, Jaffa, Beer-Sheva and Jerusalem. However, the moment we reclaim our right to all of Palestine, we will not wait even a minute to unite Palestine and Jordan." - (Palestine Liberation Organization executive committee member Zahir Muhsein, Dutch newspaper "Trouw, March 31, 1977).

How Jesus Became a Palestinian.

• "Arafat declared that "Jesus was a Palestinian," a preposterous claim that echoes the words of Hanan Ashrawi, a Christian Arab who, in an interview during the 1991 Madrid Conference, said: "Jesus Christ was born in my country, in my land," and claimed that she was "the descendant of the first Christians," disciples who spread the gospel around Bethlehem some 600 years before the Arab conquest." - (The Legal Aspects of Jewish Rights; Daled Amos.)

The Gospels that Ashrawi refers to in fact calls Judea as 'Land of the Jews" (Matt.2:20), not land of the Palestinians. Such emboldened statements can be substantially attributed to the lack of response from the Christian community, even handing out honor degrees and promotions for what can be seen as manifest historical and theological deceptions.

There were no people or land called as Palestine or Palestinian in the first century. This name emerged in the 'second' century, namely by the Roman Emperor Hadrian in 135 AD/CE. That Jesus was not a Palestinian says the issue is a theological one and impossible to subsist historically.

14. The "Palestinian-Jesus" Deception.

The underlying agenda of a 'First Century Palestine' that is manipulated away from Judea and Israel is testified by numerous historical scholars.

• "There is a propaganda war going on now with regard to the term "Palestine". It is specifically employed to avoid the use of the name Israel, and must be considered an anti-Israel term." - (Thomas S. McCall, Th.M. in Old Testament studies.)

Jesus was born in Judea, which was not an Arab country 2,000 years ago in the first century. Judea was invaded by the Roman Empire and encountered a war with the Jews. There was no Palestine country or Palestinian people in the First Century. A Palestinian Jesus is a historical impossibility. The name Palestine was applied to Judea 100 years after Jesus of Nazareth was killed, namely this name was placed on Judea in the Second Century, in the year 135 AD/CE by the Roman Emperor Hadrian. In the First Century no country was called as Palestine and no people were called as Palestinian. Rome printed 1,000s of coins with "Judea Capta" - none that said "Palestina Capta."

After the Second Century, Palestine was referred only to the Jews for 2,000 years till the mid-20th Century. The Roman archives say the Arabs, who yet possessed no writings at this time, were fully embedded in the Roman legions in the Roman war with the Jews destroying the Jerusalem Temple. There can be nothing scholarly or historical of the term 'First Century Palestine', often stated with its disassociation from Israel and the Jews, namely from the very source that introduced the Philistine people in its Hebrew writings wherein this name emerged, and from the Hebrews who most interacted with this people some 4,000 years ago. The issue is further ignited when a Pope acknowledges Arabs as Palestinians. The Herodotus claim as the justification of a First Century Palestine is also a deception by many scholars harboring a variant agenda against Israel (see 'The Herodotus Deception').

Jesus of West Bank.

Although embraced and re-quoted by many scholars, media and educational institutions, a 'First Century Palestine' is an anti-historical, anti-Israel and anti-Christian usage. It is a deception of immense historical and biblical proportions, with an underlying premise of heritage and theological negation. The allocation of this biblical portion of land as West Bank and Jesus as an Arab Palestinian, are aligned with the erasure of both the Jews, and by its default, the Christian faiths alike. Shadi Khaloul is the first person recognized by Israel as an Aramaic Christian:

• "We are not Arabs. Christian Arab is a fake terminology created 100 years ago by a Pan Arab theology. We were forced to speak Arabic, but we are Aramaic Christians" - [Shadi Khaloul, Chairman, Aramaic Christian Society of Israel, Jerusalem Dateline, CBN].

That this conflict shrouds a theological doctrine presented via new political embellishments is nowhere better seen than when a 3,000 year religious symbol was targeted as a political weapon.

221

• "I would like to assure the Jewish community that the Uniting Church does not accept the view that Jesus was Palestinian. We affirm that Jesus **and most of his early followers were Jewish.**" - [**Peter Wertheim**, Executive Director of the ECAJ, and Stuart McMillan, President of the Uniting Church in Australia; "Jesus a Palestinian?" published by J-Wire with the kind permission of both of them.]

15. The Zionism Deception.

"Moses was the First Zionist"

Based on the premise a quest to return to one's homeland from a position of exile is a legitimate existential premise, one can align the most revered figure Moses with such a designation as Zionist. The return to the Promised Land from an Egyptian exile of the Israelites under Moses is its equally aligning measure.

Zion, (also called as Sion, Tzion or Mount Moriah / צִיּוֹן Ṣiyyôn Hebrew) is a synonym for Jerusalem, the Temple Mount and the nation of Israel. Zion is a prominently embedded term in the Hebrew Scriptures, affirming its ancient religious origins and significance, as well its Hebrew name and ownership:

• Jerusalem appears in the Hebrew Bible 669 times and Zion 154 times, or 823 times in all.

• The Christian Bible mentions Jerusalem 154 times and Zion 7 times.

• Jerusalem and Zion do not appear in the Islamic Scriptures.

Mount Zion is the high hill on which David built a citadel; it forms part of a hill top purchased from the Jebusites, one of the ancient Canaanite groups. It is on the southeast side of Jerusalem and became the holiest site for the Jews as the seat of the first and second Temples. Aside from scriptural narratives, there is no lacking historically of the Zion usage throughout 3,000 years of the Jews' history. No people make up such things; there are no perceivable positive benefits of it.

The term Zion was used by Herzl in like manner as David Ben-Gurion chose the name Israel; both are inherent theological and historical emblems of the Jews for 3,000 years. The allocation of Zionism being promoted as an occupation of another peoples' land is a deception; it is usually made without its connection of Zion being the Jews' 3,000 year symbol, not a new political enterprise; no such party exists.

Theologically, Zionism represents a covenant made to Abraham on Mount Moriah (Heb/ Gen. 22:2), just as Israel, the name change that was bestowed on the Patriarch Jacob, represents the covenant made to him at Bethel (Gen 28:10). Thereby, Zion or Zionism equates with Israel or Israelism; the rejection of the former is the same as of the latter. Zion represented the cry of the Jews when Babylon invaded and exiled the Jews in the 6th Century BCE; and thereafter during times of crises when dislodged from their homeland:

• "By the rivers of Babylon, there we sat down, yea, we wept, when we remembered T'zion." (Psalm 137:1)

King David aligned Salem to Zion and Jerusalem ('In Salem also is set His tabernacle and His dwelling-place in Zion'.Ps.76:3); as does the First Century historian Flavius Josephus. Thus the term Zionism is based on a pre-dating 3,000 year biblical emblem from the Hebrew Scriptures and a legitimate historical quest of returning to one's own land from an exiled position. Zionism is fully unrelated to a host of foreboding charges that have been allocated to it; namely, anti-Zionism seeks to make the return to one's homeland as a criminal premise and a crime against humanity, rather than its existential application of a people.

Anti-Zionism is Anti-Semitism.

Theodore Herzl's pursuit of Zionism, namely the re-establishment and return of Israel, was thereby not an un-natural or un-historical premise; it emerged after the French Dreyfus affair when the people chanted 'Death to the Jews'.

Zionism was focused upon in the 20th Century when charges of the Jews illegally occupying Israel began to flourish again with the Brotherhood Charter that promoted 'Death to the Jews'. The Brotherhood, of which Mahmood Abbas is a member, is based on false historical charges that include the denial of the Jerusalem Temple and the usurping of the name Palestinian that was applied exclusively to the Jews and land of Judea. Thus was the ancient symbol of Zionism focused upon in the 20th Century and presented as one of illegally occupying Arab land; the reverse applies.

Anti-Zionism is a Genocide Premise.

That Anti-Zionism can be viewed as a genocide summation is based on the persecution and mass murder of Jews in exiled lands, while barring their return to the land they were exiled from. There appears no alternative understanding from what was seen in Europe and Arabia; those who professed and committed annihilation of the Jews in their exiled lands are also those who deny the victim's right to live in their own land that the Jews were forcibly displaced from. Such is also why Israel has been subjected to name changes of her historical emblems and lands, also an ancient mode of genocide.

The underlying factor of its aspiration is that Anti-Zionists do not accept Israel occupying Israel, and have made Jewish Palestine derived from Judea as non-Jewish Palestinian relating to the Arabs. A growing worldly multitude is emerging anew that is not in concert with their leaders and representatives that support such claims; it is especially seen with Christians who are alarmed when the land that Jesus was born in is made as West Bank, and the Baha'i and the Lebanese Phoenicians who are demeaned as un-believers.

The term Zionism, derivative from Zion, was coined by Nathan Birnbaum in 1890. Zionism became the chosen name of a movement founded by Theodore Herzl in 1896 a natural selection of Israel's symbolism; it embodied the 2,000 year quest of the return of the Jews back to their historical land from which they were displaced by the Roman Empire. Supporters of this movement are called Zionists.

Both the early American Presidents and Britain used the names Zion and Israel as the name of this land when they documented the Jews' connection with Israel. Thus anti-Zionism underlies a theological Caliphate doctrine that denies Israel's right to exist by using this name as a political device.

When Arabs Welcomed the Zionists.

In 1919, prior to the Brotherhood's enactment and the discovery of oil, the Emir Feisal (Son of Hussein Bin Ali, Sharif of Mecca), made this welcoming of the Zionist movement, the Zionists and its 'national ideals' usage by the Emir:

• "I want to take this opportunity of my first contact with American Zionists to tell you what I have often been able to say to Dr. Weizmann in Arabia and Europe. We feel that the Arabs and Jews are

224

cousins in having suffered similar oppressions at the hands of powers stronger than themselves, and by a happy coincidence have been able to take the first step towards the attainment of their national ideals together. Our deputation here in Paris is fully acquainted with the proposals submitted yesterday by the Zionist Organization to the Peace Conference, and we regard them as moderate and proper. We will do our best, in so far as we are concerned, to help them through: we will wish the Jews a most hearty welcome home." - (Letter from Emir Feisal (Son of Hussein Bin Ali, Sharif of Mecca | Great grandson of the prophet Muhammad) to Felix Frankfurter, associate of Dr. Chaim Weizmann. Feisal-Frankfurter Correspondence; March 1919.)

The UN Equates Zionism With Racism.

The UN Resolution said an ancient Hebrew religious symbol used by Jews is racism; thereby the UN subscribed to anti-Semitism, itself one of the most overt forms of racism. Zion can be compared with Jerusalem and Israel; or the prayer chants all religious groups perform. The negative allocation of the term Zionism is thus a later development when the premise of the Islamic Brother emerged, one that was aligned with the Nazi Party via Hajj Amin el-Husseini, and a new Palestinian people that emerged in the mid-20th Century; it was followed by equating Zionism with racism which was ratified by the UN. Judging from the widespread anti-Zionist revolution throughout the Arab world, it appears the UN decision was a corruption to please those members while knowing this was a false and detrimental premise. Many respected figureheads and states clarified their responses:

• "The United States does not acknowledge, it will not abide by, it will never acquiesce in this infamous act." - (Daniel Moynihan, U.S. Senator, in response to UN "Zionism is Racism" Resolution, 1975)

• "Zionism springs from an even deeper motive than Jewish suffering. It is rooted in a Jewish Spiritual tradition whose maintenance and development are for Jews the basis of their continued existence as a community" - Albert Einstein, Nobel Prize Laureate; Manchester Guardian, 1929)

• "When people criticize Zionists, they mean Jews. You're talking Anti-Semitism." - Martin King. (Lipset, 1968).

225

• "There is no difference whatever between anti-Semitism and the denial of Israel's statehood." - (Abba Eban, Israeli Ambassador; New York Times, 1975).

• "We must stand with all our might to protect Israel's right to exist, its territorial integrity and the right to use whatever sea lanes it needs. Israel is one of the great outposts of democracy and a marvelous example of what can be done, how desert land can be transformed into an oasis." - (Martin King; Annual convention of Rabbinical Assembly, 1968)

• "Mr. Balfour, if you were offered Paris instead of London, would you take it? Jerusalem was our own when London was a marsh." - Chaim Weizmann, President of Israel (Quoted in 1915; Commentary Magazine 2009).

• "Send a message to the Jews scattered around the world that Christians are not oblivious of their faith, are not unmindful of the service they rendered to the great religions of the world and most of all to Christianity and that we desire to give them that opportunity of developing, in peace and tranquility, those great gifts which hitherto they have been compelled to bring to the fruition in countries that know not their language and belong not to their race." (Lord Balfour; House of Lords in 1922).

The UN itself committed racism against the state of Israel and the Jews by its infamous Resolution 3379, adopted November 1975. It aligned with the Arab premise as a negation of Israel's right to exist. Such is aligned with Hamas and the PLO Charter that rejects a state for the Jews and any other of a different faith. The UN Resolution was defeated and rescinded with assistance from America in 1991. The premise reappears in variant other anti-Israel modes of Resolutions issued by the UN.

Quote by Ardent Zionist Martin Luther King; 1965:

• "How could there be anti-Semitism among negroes when our Jewish friends have demonstrated their commitment to the principle of tolerance and brotherhood, not only in the form of sizable contributions but in many other tangible ways and often at great personal sacrifice. Can we ever express our appreciation to the rabbis who chose to give moral witness with us in Saint Augustine during our recent protest against segregation in that unhappy city? Need I remind anyone of the awful beatings suffered by Rabbi Arthur

Lelyveld of Cleveland when he joined the civil rights workers there in Hattieburg, Mississippi? And who can ever forget the sacrifice of two Jewish lives, Andrew Goodman and Michael Schwerner, in the swamps of Mississippi? It would be impossible to record the contributions the Jewish people have made towards the negro's struggle for freedom - it was so great" - (Read by Pastor Linden Allen, President of Total Life Ministries; "Black-Jewish Alliance" presented by Laurie Cordoza-Moore; WND]

Rosa Parks.

In 1975, Rosa Parks and a host of African American civil rights advocates signed an open letter in a bold statement of support for Israel:

• "Zionism is not racism, but the legitimate expression of the Jewish people's self determination. From our 400 year experience with slavery, segregation and discrimination we know that Zionism is not racism. Together with other Americans, we enthusiastically join in reaffirming the right of Israel to exist as a sovereign state..."

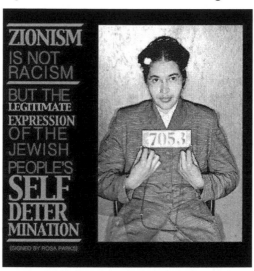

Rosa Parks, Civil Rights Advocate.

16. The Herodotus Deception.

The Great Scholarly Manipulation.

The quoting of a 5th Century BCE Greek Historian by his remark of 'Syria Palaistinê' and thereby that there was a first century Palestine is a new historical distortion that underlies a deception. This claim is used to justify the avoidance and negation of quoting a first century Judea, that this land was part of the Jews but of Syria, and that Jesus was an Arab Palestinian. Numerous anti-Israel scholars and theologians have embraced this historical mendacity as a political agenda to deceive, via selective media, history books and some encyclopedias that call First Century Judea as Palestine via this Herodotus usage.

There was no country called Palestine in the first century; Rome applied this name in the 2nd Century. Judea was never a part of Syria; nor was Jesus an Arab Palestinian. The Herodotus reference was a stray mention by a Greek writer with no impact of how this land was called or referred to in the first century, other than applying to the land of Israel; yet many scholars have pounced upon this singular quote as a new politically devised manipulation to promote an anti-Israel history.

All Scholars are not scholarly.

It is borne out of gross omissions and political manipulation that is difficult to account as a sincere error. Omitted by these scholars who use their title to deceive, is that Herodotus was referring only to the Jews in his description of 'the circumcised people' and the 'people who observed the Sabbath' in his usage of Palaistinê. (Herodotus, *Histories* 2.104). There was never a Syria-Palaistinê state or such a people in Horodotus' time or any other time. Thereby the inversion of aligning Herodotus' Palaistinê to 20th Century Palestinians is a deception. Ultimately, it seeks to promote Arabs as Palestinians and as natives of Palestine, both premises being false.

Herodotus was a Greek writer who first contextually aligned this name to the homeland of the Jews. It appears doubtful a historian can derive such an adverse conclusion other than he referred to Judea, even with minimalist consideration. Five centuries after Herodotus, Rome minted 1000's of coins embossed with "Judea Capta"; not "Palestine Capta" or "Syria Capta" or "Syria- Palaistinê". These coin relics are commonplace in numerous museums and history books. The emblem of "Judea Capta" were overlaid on coins that said 'State of

Israel' ('Medinat Yisrael' in Hebrew letters), the name of this land before Rome called it Judea:

Both Sides of Shekel Coin Relics of Israel.

• "When Titus destroyed Jerusalem in 70 A.D., the Roman government struck coins with the phrase "Judea Capta," meaning Judea has been captured. The term Palestine was never used in the early Roman designations." (Zvi Rivai, Zola Levitt Ministries).

Robert Spencer, author of New York Times bestseller books, (including "The Political Guide to Islam" and "The Truth About Muhammad") refers to the book "Zealot: The Life and Times of Jesus of Nazareth" by Reza Aslan:

• "Aslan refers numerous times throughout his book to Jesus living in "first-century Palestine." He has defended this usage in interviews by claiming that that was the Roman name for the area during Jesus' time. But in fact, Jesus lived not in first-century Palestine, but in first-century Judea, a place that no one called "Palestine." The Romans renamed it "Palestine" after emptying the area of Jews after the Bar Kokhba Revolt in 135 A.D. (2nd Century). Aslan's usage is an anachronism, and given his venomous opposition to the state of Israel, perhaps a politically motivated one at that. - ("Five Falsehoods in Reza Aslan's *Zealot: The Life and Times of Jesus of Nazareth"*, By *Robert Spencer, PJ Media,* September 2, 2013)

• Quote: "Herodotus used Palaistinê to refer not to the Land of the Philistines, but to the Land of Israel. His understanding of the geographical extent of Palestine is reflected in his reference to the population of Palaistinê as being 'circumcised'. However, the Philistines, as we know from the Bible, were not circumcised. The Israelites, of course, were circumcised. Hadrian officially renamed Judea Syria Palaestina after his Roman armies suppressed the Bar-

Kokhba Revolt (the Second Jewish Revolt) in 135 C.E.; this is commonly viewed as a move intended to sever the connection of the Jews to their historical homeland." - (David Jacobson, 'When Palestine Meant Israel')

Thus the Herodotus writing is used deceptively by many scholars, or else with a surprising deficiency of history. Also surprising is that some prominent media facilitates such provisions.

First Century Palestine is Fiction.

Both the Roman and Greek writers, which are post-Herodotus, used the name Judea (Iudaea, from the Greek Ioudaia), not Palestine, as is freely quoted when referring to this land in our modern lexicon. It is highly implausible scholars can be confused that first century Judea was never called as Palestine. 'First Century Palestine' is a fictional premise; its reference had no historical reality or impacts. Judea was not an Arab land in the first century.

'When Palestine Meant Israel'

The modern world's adaptation of Palestine as a reference other than of the homeland of the Jews is based on a manipulation of dubious historical employ.

The Palestina usage referred to the Greek's Philistine kin as marking the first European invasion of Arabia from across the seas in the time of Abraham; it was a 'take-over' inference of the later invasion by the early Greeks, including of the notorious Antiochus who attempted to change the name of Jerusalem and failed, one who made Syria as a conquered base following Alexander's invasion. Herodotus did not refer to any Arabian people other than the Jews as the inhabitants of Judea, as is misconstrued by some scholars.

In all historical instances and archives, and all references of Palestina and Syria- Palaistinê by ancient writers, these were directed to the Jews and the land of the Jews and by the name Judea:

• "Jerusalem is by far the most illustrious city of the East, not merely of *Judea*." ['Natural History' by Pliny the Elder; First Century]

• **Philo**, the Jewish philosopher of Alexandria, allocates Palestinian as the populous nation of the *Jews (Stern,* Greek and Latin Authors, *p. 349).*

230

• **The poet Ovid** (First Century) writes of "the seventh day feast that the Syrian of Palestine observes" - namely the unique Jewish Sabbath observances.

• **Aristotle** was similarly also referring to the Jews in his reference to the Dead Sea; as was the Latin poet Statius, and the writer Dio Chrysostom. Aristotle's comments of 'the waters in which neither man nor beast can sink, and which are bitter and salty and do not support fish' leaves no doubt he is referring to the Dead Sea of Israel. - (Menachem Stern, Greek and Latin Authors on Jews and Judaism, vol. 1, From Herodotus to Plutarch; Jerusalem: Israel Academy of Sciences and Humanities, 1974, pp. 6-7 and note 2).

• "Like Herodotus, Aristotle gives the strong impression that when he uses the term Palestine he is referring to the Land of Israel. In his description of the Dead Sea, Aristotle says that it is situated in Palestine. 4. The Land of the Philistines, however, was separated from the Dead Sea by the hills and wilderness of Judea, so Aristotle could hardly have intended the two to be directly connected! He, too, seemed to identify the Land of Israel as Palestine." - (David Jacobson, 'When Palestine Meant Israel', Bar 27:03; Archive Today)

The Greek and Roman Historians of 2,000 years ago, including Tacitus, Pliny, Suetonius, Plutarch and Ptolemy, who requested of the Jews the first translation of the Hebrew Bible in 300 BCE ('The Septuagint'), also used the name Judea, not Palestine of this land's name:

• "*Judaea* was divided. The Samaritans came under Felix and the Galileans under Ventidius " [Roman Historian Tacitus, The Annals, XII: 54]

• The New Testament never used the term Palestine, referring to the Jews as 'The people of Israel' and 'The land of Israel' more than once:

• 'And he arose, and took the young child and his mother, and came into the land of **Israel**.' [Matt. 2:21 and 22].

• "You will be my witnesses in Jerusalem and in all **Judea and Samaria**" (Acts 1:18)

The oldest existing manuscript of Herodotus that some authors refer to as their evidence is dated 10th Century AD/CE, which is 1,300 years after he is said to have lived in 425 BCE. While copies may be authentic, this is more recent than numerous earlier documents which

231

contradict these scholars' reporting, including the older copies of the Gospels that use the name of Israel for this land, as do the Roman archives and the Dead Sea Scrolls.

The First Century Palestine Myth.

When Horodotus used the name Palestine it was referred to Judea - the land of the Jews, a reference to the land that the Greek's Philistine kin once invaded. The Romans later officially applied the name Palestine on Judea in the second century, not the first century, as a mockery relating to the ancient 4,000 year old enemies of the Hebrews. There was never a First Century Palestine, nor did the Romans conduct a war with Arabs in this period; the Romans went to war with Judea, land of the Jews, with the Arabs enlisted as Roman mercenaries in its war legions.

The Roman naming was derived when a Greek mentioned the ancient enemies of the Hebrews and it was thereby adopted by Hadrian; it fully negates any description of 'First Century Palestine' and renders Judea's connection with Syria as a historical fiction.

It is thereby a modern political manipulation directing Herodotus' remark to an Arab group that never called themselves as Palestinian before 1964; the re-allocation of this name to another group 2,000 years later thereby affirms the political manipulation of history it seeks to impose.

Numerous anti-Israel scholars and theologians have embraced this historical mendacity, including the media, history books and encyclopedias that call First Century Judea as Palestine via this Herodotus usage.

The Greek and Roman Empires were conquering and invading forces and both were thus establishing Judea, along with Syria ('Syria-Palaistinê), as their own war spoil in cohesion; yet both these empires referred to Judea as the land of the Jews, a people both empires were closely interacted with by numerous battles and philosophical exchanges.

The Philistines were conquered by King David six centuries earlier than Herodotus and they never appeared again as a force in history; namely, there were no such Philistine or Palestinian people in Herodotus' time, as is incorrectly inferred by some authors and media publications. Josephus wrote in his 'Against Apion' response, correcting Herodotus and negating any confusion this was the homeland of the Jews, not of his Philistine Greek kin:

• "Nor, indeed, was Herodotus of Halicarnassus unacquainted with our nation, but mentions it after a way of his own." ‾ (Josephus, "Against Apion" Book 16).

Although the name of Judea was changed to Palestine in the 2nd Century by the Roman Emperor Hadrian, its reference thereafter was exclusively directed to the land of the Jews and remained so up to the 20th Century in the British, French, American and Jewish documents.

Rome was not at war with Syria or the Philistines but the Jews in this juncture of history. The name anointing of Palestine occurred after the obsessive extent of Jerusalem's destruction, in the aftermath of a war with heavy casualties on both sides in Hadrian's battles with the Bar Kochba Jewish revolt. It was followed by Rome's barring of the Hebrew belief and language and forbidding Jews from Jerusalem. However, the Jews did not leave and continued living in Jerusalem, as is seen with the Crusader and Islamic invasions of this land with the Jews who remained. The misplacing of the term Palestine and Palestinian away from Israel and the Jews in modern times is an anti-historical and anti-Israel premise, with the Herodotus example as its justification:

• "It seems clear that by choosing a seemingly neutral name - one juxtaposing that of a neighboring province (Syria) with the revived name of an ancient geographical entity (The Philistines), Hadrian was intending to suppress any connection between the Jewish people and that land" - [Historian, Ariel Lewin].

A Palestinian Jesus.

Prior to Rome, the previous Greek Empire also attempted to change the name of Jerusalem; it was a failed attempt, this city's name being too famed in the region to be negated. Rome later emulated the Greek's name erasing scheme on Judea in the second century; thus quoting 'first century Palestine' is a fiction, in like manner by the premise of a Palestinian Jesus. 'First Century Palestine' is an over-kill to further seek to erase the name of Israel from the historical radar, as was done by Rome; it is bearing false witness and incurring poor baggage on scholars and the Christians and Muslim peoples via falsified Anti-Israel premises disguised as history.

233

The often stated reference of a 'Palestinian Jesus' upon the revered figurehead who lived in first century Judea is a historical impossibility, also aligned with the misrepresentation of the Herodotus alignment. The name Palestine was applied to Judea by the Roman Emperor Hadrian in the second century (135 AD/CE), a hundred years after Jesus was killed [circa 30-31 AD/CE). No Jews or any other people in Judea could thus be called Palestinians in the first century.

Thereby, its alignment with 20th Century Arabs is un-historical, as is any reference to Jesus or anyone else who lived in first century Judea as a Palestinian. It is a negation doctrine of the Jewish and Christian history and their faiths. Jesus was not a Palestinian but a Jew living in first century Judea a hundred years before Rome's name change occurred. Similarly, Arab Palestinians is a 20th Century phenomenon, not a historical people cited by Herodotus 2,500 years ago.

17. The Occupation Deception.

Greatest Deception of All.

Although Israel was invaded throughout her history and her people exiled numerously, never before was the ownership of the Jews' homeland disputed by any invading forces. Never before was the charge of "Disputed Territory" ever raised by the nations that battled with the Jews 3,000 years.

The charge of illegal or questioned land occupation made on the Jewish state is a modern world phenomenon of the 20th Century. It is antithetical of history, both ancient and modern. That the Jew's most sacred land portion is deemed as 'Occupied Territory', after its ancient name changed to West Bank, illegally, is perhaps the clearest form of all in measuring the occupation charge. Thereby, the examination of how, when and why the charge of occupation arose aligns with the premise of the greatest deception of all.

Israel is in the forefront of a phenomenon impacting on many of the Middle East's most ancient period inhabitants, many pre-dating the Arabs, with signs and omens such is not limited to one region or people.

234

• "The Yazidi in Iraq and the Christian Copts in Egypt are not "occupiers" or "settlers;" neither are the Jews in Israel. They are both victims of a common enemy that seems to want a Middle East free of Muslims" - (Gatestone Institute International Public Policy; Ezequil Doiny)

In the 13th Century BCE, Ancient Egypt's Merneptah Stele boasted of a war and proclaiming that "Israel's seed is no more." Yet Egypt never charged the Jews of any illegal occupation and saw the Jews return to Canaan, the land they were born in, raised Kings and Priests, wrote books of their history, built cities and establish Jerusalem as a capital holy city with a huge Temple that rivaled all other monuments of the ancient world. Canaan became Israel 3,000 years ago under King David on 1002 BCE. In the 6th Century BCE, the Babylon Empire invaded Israel, destroyed its temple and exiled most of the Jews. Yet Babylon never charged the Jews of an illegal occupation of this land. In the same 6th Century the Jews returned from their Babylonian exile via the subsequent Persian Empire that conquered Babylon. The Jews were not charged with illegal occupation of this land. The Persian King acknowledged the Jews' homeland and granted them the right of return and assisted in the rebuilding of their temple. Modern Israel's Postal Service issued a postage stamp honoring the Persian King Cyrus and his granting the Jews the right to return to their land.

הצהרת כורש
The Cyrus Declaration
منشـور کورش · بیـان کـورش
ישראל
ISRAEL اسرائيل
₪8.30
התשע"ה 2015
ראות אבודרהם דדון
מי בְכֶם מִכָּל עַמּו...
וְיַעַל לִירוּשָלַם
עזרא א, ג
Anyone of you of all His people...
and let him go up to Jerusalem
Ezra 1:3
מטבע יהד

The Cyrus Declaration, 538 BCE.

A clay cylinder discovered 1879 in the ancient city of Babylon (Iraq) contains this Persian dynasty public edict in ancient Akkadian writing, also recorded in the Book of Ezra:

• "In the first year of King Cyrus of Persia… the Lord roused the spirit of King Cyrus of Persia to issue a proclamation throughout his realm by word of mouth and in writing as follows: Thus said King Cyrus of Persia: The Lord God of Heaven has given me all the kingdoms of the earth and has charged me with building Him a house in Jerusalem, which is in Judah. Anyone of you of all His people, may his God be with him, and let him go up to Jerusalem that is in Judah and build the House of the Lord God of Israel, the God that is in Jerusalem" (Ezra, chapter 1).

Two thousand years ago Mighty Rome invaded this land and minted 1,000's of gold and silver coins embossed with "Judea Capta" slogans,

236

signifying this was the conquered land of the Jews. Rome never charged the Jews of illegally occupying another peoples' land.

One hundred years ago, the previous Ottoman Empire acknowledged Jerusalem as the Jews' sacred capital and that Palestine was surely the land of the Jews.

In the 20th Century the American, British, French and the Arab Emirs proclaimed Palestine as the national home of the Jews. Even the Nazis put up posters and billboards of "Jews go to Palestine".

Big Questions.

If the world's greatest empires throughout history never charged the Jews of occupying another peoples' land, there are big question hovering in the modern world. Some questions:

Why does the UN charge Israel as occupying Judah and Samaria, which the Romans called as Judea, which previous name was Israel, which name was changed to West Bank in 1950?

Why is the term 'Palestinian' made as an exclusive reference to Arabs, when it was anointed on Judea, the ancestral homeland of the Jews, and held that way for 2,000 years till 1960?

Why did the Arabs and all Christian states accept, and then reject the Jews' land rights when both their scriptures and histories, and their treaties of the early 20th Century, said that Palestine, which was Judea, is the historical land of the Jews?

Why is the accounting of a 3-state in Palestine presented as a 2-state?

Such questions are not controversial, irrelevant or circumstantial, but incumbent, and should be the topside preamble of the world's most debated issue. Yet these are not in the discourse.

Israel and the Jews have been a controversy throughout the past 4,000 years, even before many of the nations that are active today existed as an identifiable force, and many other great nations have since vacated history. No nation ever questioned the veracity of the land of the Jews, not even their greatest invaders; it is a new phenomenon of the modern times.

The history of Palestine is the history of Israel, and in turn of two of the largest belief groups that battled each other for her minuscule land and heritage for centuries; both are now in the forefront claiming

237

Israel is illegally occupying Israel. Yet what does history say of the claims made by those occupying more than 50% of the earth's landmass - in relatively recent vintage, and of those who support them so vigorously? Thereby, the occupation charge will be examined; via history - both ancient and modern; and via the judiciary - both the veracity and legality of international laws enacted against Israel. Let's begin with a name.

Palestine is Israel.

Judea's previous name was Israel. It is a nation that defied all the laws of history by returning after 2,000 years, and it has upset the worldly status quo. As part of its baggage, as though a witnessing was required, the Hebrew language was also returned; it is one that no other nation spoke or wrote; one that is not 2,000 but 4,000 years old. Hebrew was the language of the Hebrews throughout their history since Abraham's time; this writing has been un-earthed in 3,000 relics; and some of the inscriptions in the Dead Sea Scroll package date up to 600 BCE.

The Arabs never spoke Hebrew throughout their history, yet deny Jews as Jews in the modern world and a temple in Jerusalem. Immediately, Israel faces a contradiction of charges from Christianity and Islam's histories and beliefs, whereby both cannot be right; yet both support each other in the occupation charges.

Thereby this is a nation that bears the world's most impacting history, its trajectories uniquely extending across the nations. The charge of the Jews occupying Palestine illegally makes Israel's history a most imperative study today. Chiefly, Israel foretells of a future scenario impacting much more than one land and one people. And it has erupted throughout the world's nations with a dire message to confront; that it is a worldly issue un-connected with Israel and occupation. Some of the most prominent minds of the times say so.

• "We're talking about global jihadists, and their desire is to destroy us and to destroy our way of life." - (Mr. Ben Carson, US Presidential Candidate; Meet The Press, NBC News, Nov.11, 2015)

All of Palestine.

238

In the early 20th Century both the British and the Arabs acknowledged the historical connection of the Jews with Palestine and declared the entire land as one Jewish state - all of Palestine, including today's Jordan and the West Bank. They enacted treaties and agreements to return the Jews to their historical land. Soon thereafter, both overturned their agreements. Jewish Palestine became Arab Palestine from time immemorial, and as occupied by the Zionist Jews. It says something happened at this junction of history that is barely reported or officially debated.

This presentation contains numerous references of treaties and pledges that identify Israel's return as based on the ancient 'historical connection of the Jews' to Palestine as their homeland; and the legal treaties and pledges that declared so, that have been corrupted. The 'historical connection' was the primal clause that was legally executed with the world powers and the community of nations; 51 nations. It aligned with centuries of census records of a continuous habitation of the Jews in the land and a vast array of conforming archaeological relics. One relic was an especially poignant revelation.

Israel's most vital exposition is the Dead Sea Scrolls, accounted as among history's greatest discoveries. The Scrolls rendered the charge of occupation an irrefutable deception. It depicted a 3,000 year old continuous history of Jewish habitation in Palestine, stemming long before the Romans changed the name of Judea 2,000 years ago.

Israel, a minuscule landmass was returned in 1948, when the Arabs were handed 22 states, none of which existed a hundred years ago. Britain's Lord Balfour called Palestine a little notch of a land that none could be bothered about; indeed this was a barren, isolated land in the 19th Century, malaria infested with no agriculture, irrigation of electricity. The Scrolls posed whether the worldly angst hinged on another few cubits of land, or does something else apply here. The conflict should have ended with the Balfour Mandate, or else definitely later with the first 2-state compromise that created Jordan on 80% of the landmass originally allocated for 'one only state for the Jews'. But it didn't; it wouldn't. The term 'occupation' reigns unmoved, unceasing and untouchable, as though it transcended all else.

Thereby, there appears no alternative that other factors than a little notch of land may apply with the occupation charge. What other factors can apply to turn Israel's legal return into an illegal one; or to

239

conclude with the charge of occupation on the only state able to affirm her land ownership as no other in this region; it is an incumbent examination. Yet, when Israel's history with the nations is denied it becomes a contradiction of history per se, extending and impacting half of humanity. Here, history is not the only factors that make Israel's return validated; the 20th century international laws also do so; these were also over-turned.

The UN's 'Disputed Territory' charge is often misconstrued as an 'Illegal Occupation'. It has become the world's most pursued problem, one concerning a tiny measure of landmass, propelled by those handed enormous measures of lands as new states. Of all the states created by Britain in the 20th Century, Israel is the only one that existed previously; Israel was also returned via a legal process more legitimate than any other, with all nations voting in the UN Motion. The issue is further compounded by the absence of any previous owners of this land other than the Jews and transitional invasive forces. Yet the charge is accepted by a vast array of nations of the region and beyond. It appears most implausible as a land occupation or people displacement issue.

The charges on Israel are a phenomenon which like is not seen anywhere else. It attains a mark of chaos that Israel is charged both with occupying a small sector of land, as well as being an illegal state with no right to exist, depending on who is asked. Israel remains among the oldest continuously active historical nation whose history is most known; yet one also most questioned. History says that Palestine is the name anointed on Judea by the Romans, and Jews were called by this name for 2,000 years till 1960. It begs the question: can Israel be charged with occupying Palestine if this name was not usurped? This should not be a problem if the Arabs are native to Palestine and can use another name not aligned with the Jews. But are Arabs or the Jews the natives of Palestine, the often given reasoning? Here, what does history say, must apply.

Natives of Palestine.

History says there was no occupation by Israel of another peoples' land. Because no other people had a Palestinian state; no such state ever existed. Nor was there another people as natives, as has been so promoted. History says that the Jews are the only continuous ancestral natives of Palestine. Surprised? There is a marked variance of a

240

transitional immigrating people and one that remained since the Roman era 2,000 years ago; even from 3,000 years ago. Not all of the Jews were exiled from Palestine; some remained as witness to their homeland ownership in the midst of numerous invading forces, archived by the Crusaders, Mohammedans and numerous other nations; it is especially seen in the last Ottoman reign. While the Arabs were one of the peoples since the Islamic invasion in the 7th Century, in the 1800's this land was almost vacant of habitation; the land swelled with mass immigrants and ancestral natives in the 19th Century.

Prior to the Ottomans, the land had an array of multicultural inhabitants; the Arabs were one of them and the Christians and Lebanese predated them in Palestine. The Jews, often in smaller numbers under harsh conditions, were there throughout and never abandoned their land. Thereby was Palestine declared the historical home of one people; all of Palestine.

In the early 20th Century all of Palestine was allocated for one Jewish state, with no other people were listed as a historically connected people with this land; this was not an error. No other people inhabited Palestine as did the Jews. Thereafter, Palestine was divided; this land was drastically reduced in size by Britain without any resultant satisfaction or peace; the conflict intensified. Britain's dividing of Palestine by corrupting treaties is correctly the first cause of this conflict; it was not a legal action and was not based on any ethical or moral principles. It was also not based on rights applicable to displaced peoples ("The Refugee Deception").

The Balfour Declaration of 1917 is aligned with the American Proposal for a Jewish Homeland dated January 21, 1919; it said all of Palestine must be mandated as one only Jewish state, separate and independent from the new states created by Britain. The Tentative Report and Recommendations of the American Delegation to the Peace Conference included the following segments:

1. That there be a separate state of Palestine.

2. That the state of Palestine be placed under Britain as a Mandatory of the League of Nations.

3. That the Jews be invited to settle there in Palestine, being assured by the Conference of all proper assistance in doing so. That it will be

the policy of the League of Nations to recognize Palestine as a Jewish state. - (American Proposal for Jewish Homeland, January 21, 1919)

Thereby did the Jews trust the nations and began returning; the Jews, defined as the 'people of the book' in the Quran, acted as a law abiding people. While the Arabs were promised almost the entire Middle East region by Britain, the rejection of Israel and the minuscule landmass allotted her should not have resulted by a need for land by the Arabs or claims of Israel's illegal occupation; after all the Arabs were given numerous new states that never existed before. Such a result is better seen as a theological rejection than of land; because all other factors of rejecting a Jewish state's return are without merit. Such is claimed by the Arabs themselves who negotiated with the British in achieving a provision that rejects a non-Arab state. The Sharif of Mecca, King Hussein Ibn Ali, claimed he had been offered the entire Levant if he fought on the side of the British. Palestine was not included, according to Churchill, presumably due to the American recommendations.[31] The 'Disputed Territory' claim emerged later as a politically devised phenomenon when vast oil wells were discovered and was followed by agreements between Britain and the Arab chieftains; these terms substantially approved a new Arab Caliphate to replace the Ottoman Empire. Britain would be rewarded for it.

Although Britain issued the Balfour Declaration, other arrangements were also made thereafter with the Arabs of its negation; much of these have been suppressed from the discourse. These British arrangements explain that the Middle East conflict is not related to Israel or land occupation; that it is based on commercial basis as the price for a Caliphate in the Middle East. Israel just happened to be a state that contradicts the Sharif of Mecca's wishes which were theologically based and disguised as a land issue. Letters exchanged between Sir Henry McMahon, Britain's High Commissioner in Cairo and the Sharif of Mecca Husayn bin Ali in 1916, explain some of the mutually acceptable terms:

• 'The Arab Government of the Sharif will acknowledge that England shall have the preference in all economic enterprises in the Arab countries whenever conditions of enterprises are equal. We accept the terms of Lord Kitchener, supplied to you via Ali Effendi. You accepted fully for the independence of Arabia and its inhabitants, together with our approval of the Arab Caliphate when it is declared. We affirm again now that His Majesty's Government would welcome the resumption of the Caliphate by an Arab of true race. I confirm your rejection will be only of those who have contradicted the rights of the Caliphate in which are included the rights of all Moslems.' [32]

Therein were Lord Balfour's terms being negated and replaced with that of Lord Kitchener ("The Balfour Deception"). That a Caliphate agenda was fully embedded and continues, and that such is not related to any land occupation by Israel, is affirmed by its designs being global:

• "We place our hope that our triumph will not be restricted to Palestine, but to the banner of the Caliphate over the Vatican, the Rome of today" - (Dr. Subhi Al-Yaziji, Dean of Koranic Studies, Islamic University of Haza; Al-Aqsa TV, Hamas-Gaza)

The Wrong Man.

One of the detrimental actions against the Jews, and thereby the facilitating of a Caliphate, was of the wrong man being appointed as the Grand Mufti of Jerusalem by Britain. Based on the 1917 Balfour Declaration's essential provisions, Jerusalem merited a Jewish mayor. Britain's error will usher the darkest side of humanity, affirming the motives for the deception of an occupation charge, and that this conflict is not an Israel issue. It is a global one and it has erupted afar with no alignment with Israel.

Hajj Amin's appointment caused the fuelling of widespread revolts, pogroms, murders and chants of genocide, as though the Jews suddenly entered from left field of nowhere and had no history or legal rights. From here will emerge the denial of the Jerusalem Temple, the Holocaust and the entire history of Israel; from here the corruption of the Balfour derives its reasoning. It was followed with Britain's White Paper Policy, the support of a new West Bank region and a new people called as Arab Palestinians.

History will become distorted as never before. Palestine will cease being viewed as historically connected with Jews or Judea or the 'national home of the Jews.' The Palestine that was Judea will become Arab Palestine since time immemorial. History will be altered with a name switch. Britain will have blood on her hands; the Holocaust will have a thread that aligns with Hajj Amin's alliance with Hitler and Lord Chamberlain.

Under the notorious Hajj Amin the charge of illegal occupation flourished soon after the Balfour Mandate was issued and positive agreements were signed between the Jews and the Arabs. Britain will divide Palestine into two states in contradiction of the Balfour, then hail Jordan's illegal annexation of southern Israel that was renamed as the West Bank in 1950. A new region called as East Jerusalem will emerge, soon followed by Arabs as Palestinians for the first time in 1964.

Instead of Jordan being charged, Israel will be accused of occupying the most sacred portion of her land and another state will be demanded. The present occupation charge is for a 3-state in Palestine, one deceptively presented as a 2-state; and this, known to the UN and all the Christian community, is a facade when the charters of the Arab groups are considered. It all aligns with a theologically motivated compulsion of Israel's demise.

Britain and the Arabs will promote the support of a worldly multitude and by successively diminishing Palestine's land size to the most dangerous extremities for the Jews with no sign of quelling. It becomes implausible to view the actions of Britain as unrelated to the negation of a Jewish state; thereby it is also tediously implausible not to have perceived a default Caliphate doctrine hovering and the oil factor as its price. Instead of confronting what is a worldly impacting premise, Britain, the appointed caretaker of this region, focused only on Israel. The Balfour Declaration and all British proclamations by Churchill will become as a mockery. The charge of illegal occupation and its aligning international laws is a diabolical outcome because Israel is among the most widely acknowledged and recorded homelands of any people, and the Jews are not known to have ever occupied another peoples' land. The quest of changing a country's borders was perceived in the ancient realm of a heinous crime.

• Palestine was legally mandated as one separate state and to be un-divided; forever. In the early 20th Century Israel's borders were the Balfour lines; its inference is the Arabs in Palestine were largely recent immigrants secured by Britain throughout the period, in contradiction of its pledges to the Jews.

• "In the period leading up to 1922 the British preferred cheaper foreign labor and they employed fifteen thousand foreigners (mostly from Egypt and Syria) and only five hundred Jews. The increasing numbers of these two populations would soon lead to a significant clash." - ("The Myth of Jewish Colonialism: Demographics and Development in Palestine" By David Wollenberg).

Relatively, all of Palestine was not a large landmass for one nation with no other states. The charges of Israel's land size become disproportionate considering her borders have been diminished to the most extreme and dangerous marks. The land west of the river Jordan was as virtually barren as west of the river was under the Ottomans and allocated as one state in Palestine. And although all of today's Jordan was not part of historical Israel, it should have still been allocated to the Jews considering the vast lands handed to the Arabs and the legal mandate given to Britain to assist the settlement of Jews to return from around the nations. Yet the diminishing of land sizes held by the Jews did not diminish the conflict, affirming it was not a land issue.

The demands applied on Israel today are derived from multiple 2-state divisions, aligning with Israel having no right to exist, conducted via name changes that present an antithetical history. The land claims shrouded an underlying Caliphate agenda. Retrospectively, it is now correct to see that the Balfour Declaration's flaunting was and remains both the cause of a Caliphate doctrine and a corruption by Britain. Thereby, what is accepted against Israel cannot be stemmed from an extending global syndrome unless these are corrected. While the nations see such a requirement as unfeasible, it is the formula of a mass immigration stratagem used to achieve such a result; and it is more than a local issue concerning only the Jews. First the Saturday people, then the Sunday people; its agenda is self declared. Consider the matter well. The occupation charges on Israel are not based on land or nativity factors but solely on name changes, without any historical or legal veracity; a native people will never usurp another peoples' historical symbol as with the term Palestinian, or revoke the names of its ancient towns as with West Bank. While all the new states that Britain created in the 20th Century have fictional borders improvised by impromptu lines in the sand to cause regional and cultural in-fighting, Israel's borders can be historically verified by ancient archives from numerous empires, by factual historical imprints and by some one million archaeological relics. West Bank and Arab Palestinians are historical fictions and agenda based.

Thereby, changing the names of Hebrew towns to West Bank exposes a lack of credibility, and Britain's accepting of such means places very poor baggage on her people and legacy. The occupation charges represent a reversed historical paradigm mid-way in the same 20th century. These are very bold deceptions borne out of an anticipated immunity enjoyed by Britain as a Christian nation; yet its onus must rest on those who remained silent to correct her. It is history's message why we have a conflict without cause and a land claim where there is no reasoning of land; the correct cause is not in the discourse.

Revelation.

In the modern history of Palestine a revelation emerged the same year Israel was re-established. The Dead Sea Scrolls is more than a historical or theological manifestation; it is an indisputable factor of proof, one that affirmed Israel is not illegally occupying her own homeland, that this was the native land of the Jews some 4,000 years ago, describing a host of Kings, cities, monuments and wars in the native written language of Israel that was not used by any other nation. Thereby, the Scrolls proved to be a historical time-machine that aligned with a vast treasure trove of archaeological relics. The message of the Scrolls was either missed or disregarded as it fully negated an occupation charge. However, the land division was really never the issue; Israel's return was. Otherwise, why would the Arabs usurp ancient historical names of the Jews, other than a negation of a 4,000 year nation and of their own historical veracity. Here, the occupation charge aligns only with a theological doctrine, one set in the constraints of un-ending 2-state charges and a chaos not seen in any other example of history; perhaps intentionally driven so.

A Complicated Roadmap.

The understanding of the numerous treaties and agreements of the Israeli-Arab conflict is a long and winding road, one studded with intricate inter-connecting clauses and 'subject-to' conditions. However, a simplified analogy can assist in un-complicating this maze.

Imagine that John Doe purchases a house in 10 Myrtle Street. Thereafter, he is told his house must be divided into two houses, and that 80% of his home is to be removed. John Doe is aghast; he was never advised of such a possibility in his purchase contract. He is referred to the word 'in', namely that his purchase was for a house 'in'

246

10 Myrtle Street; that it allows such a division whereby his house will remain as one in 10 Myrtle Street but not the only one.

He complains such a pivotal requirement was not made explicit, but then he reluctantly agrees, and 80% of his house is sold to someone else via a 2-House contract. Next, some of the occupants of House-2 are left in John's house and barred from entering in House 2. Next, House 2 annexes another 10% of John Doe's house. He is now told another House 2 is required to house the displaced refugees barred from entering House-2.

Such is a reasonable account when House-1 is seen as Palestine; House-2 as Jordan and the second House-2 as the West Bank.

What Illegal Occupation?

Israel did not illegally occupy Egypt from the Copts, or Krakow from Poland, or Kashmir from India, despite being inhabitants in those lands for many centuries. The historical record says Israel has never occupied another people's land in all her 4,000 year recorded history; yet Israel is the world's most accused country of illegally occupying another peoples' land. Ironically, Israel cannot occupy another peoples' land for a theological premise as well; it is one in reverse of the Caliphate doctrine. A host of reverse systems pervade this conflict. In the 1960's Jewish Palestinians became Arab Palestinians. Here, the occupier of a historical name of another people became presented as the occupied; a new improvised heritage definition replaced a historically validated one. The original status prior to such heritage replacement, or that Palestine is Judea and Samaria, are never mentioned alongside the charges; perhaps because they render those charges as problematic in presenting Israel as the occupier. Thus, at the very least, the charges are a lie-by-omission. More accurately, the charges have become diabolical; the two largest belief groups stand by their histories and beliefs, yet contradict them in the reality of the modern world. Thereby, this is not a problem resting with Israel to resolve, but on those who flaunted their histories.

• Britain's conclusion in 1950 became that Israel should be charged of illegally occupying the West Bank instead of Jordan. Missing from the discourse is that Jordan illegally annexed west of the river, the Jews' most sacred and historical portion of land and changed its name to West Bank under Britain's watch. Britain condoned an illegal action and placed the charge on its victim; she reversed the charge of occupation, a corruption that was processed at the UN and now deemed as international law. To right these wrongs, a re-consideration has enormous potential merit, especially when undertaken by the foremost participants of this issue, the Arab and British people themselves; a few bold and forthright ones have pursued such a path. The foremost implication is that the illegal charge constructed at the UN is itself illegal; if the UN's 'Zionism is Racism' charge was corrected, so can another equally entrenched UN wrong be corrected. The real issue is an absence of will to anymore confront such a longstanding error. These wrongs are not based on isolated assumptions but reflect the views of an academy of scholars of good repute from widespread sectors.

A host of distinguished figures reject the UN determinations, some also denying its very judiciary implements as a violation of international law. The occupation charges made on Israel are deemed as both historically false and as illegally adopted by the UN and the western and Arab states that accepted them. Such views merit good consideration of the sincerity, expertise and statures of those denouncing the charges of illegal occupation; they represent a comprehensive array of institutions:

• "The oft-used term "occupied Palestinian territories" is totally inaccurate and false. The territories are neither occupied nor Palestinian. Claims by the UN, European capitals, organizations and individuals that Israeli settlement activity is in violation of international law therefore have no legal basis whatsoever." - [Courtesy of Israel's Ambassador to Canada and Negotiator in Peace Agreements with Egypt, Jordan and Lebanon, Alan Baker; 'The Legal Basis of Israel's Rights; courtesy JCPA Org]

• "There are serious and substantial arguments that Israel does not illegally occupy the West Bank, as well as that Israel has not illegally transferred population into that territory." - ("Legal Insurrection: Challenging the Long-Held Notion That Israeli Settlements Are 'Illegal." by William Jacobson, professor at Cornell Law School; The Blaze, *Feb. 24, 2014)*

• "I would like to see which international law has declared them illegal" - (Australian Foreign Minister Julie Bishop; "Don't call settlements illegal under international law"; Times of Israel)

248

• "Unfortunately, most of the nations' deceptions is regarding Israel… about the name of the country, and the size of the country and the world is convinced this is not Israel, this is Palestine, all those lies, and this whole Palestinian ethos that was born only in the 20th century, all of that caused so many churches even in America to actually turn their back to Israel and start believing in horrible doctrines" - ('The Deception In The Church'; Olive Tree Ministries. Jan Markell and Eric Barger talk with Amir Tsarfati.)

• "Most fair minded people are aware this is a fundamental theological mission of global dominion." - (Pastor Steven Brodin, Fair Bank Fellowship Church, Dallas Tx.; Black Congressional Pastor's Caucus; Conservative Tribune.)

Politicizing Theology. While theologies merit respect, the theological and historical factors can be strange partners and often result in deception when made as a political device. It is especially so when Israel is subjected to two totally contradicting theologies that harbor instances of one common denominator against the Jews, rendering both the two largest belief systems equally encumbered and mutually exclusive of each other. Here, honest and objective investigative consideration is essential when faiths clash and leave nowhere to turn; such advice emanates from a source cherished by many and one that also aligned with the Dead Sea Scrolls emerging when it did:

• "Come now, and let us reason together, says the Lord" (Isaiah, 1:18)

Disputed Territory, the originally charged claim, became a covert synonym for 'Occupied Territory'; osmosis soon followed in a pre-empting defiance of its own legal status. The issue is compounded because the original 'Disputed Territory' charge was itself baseless and should have been directed at Jordan, not Israel. Israel did not illegally annex west of the river; Jordan did.

The charge is based on the most dubious premises and enacted as law by those with little arm's length from the issue and via the filler-busting of the UN process. The rejection of Israel, a slogan numerously proclaimed in the Middle-East, align with the often declared goal of a Caliphate doctrine, usually displayed with chants of 'We will dominate' and the rejection of a non-Arab state in the region, even those that are among the oldest inhabitants and nations in the Middle East. Otherwise, it is not plausible for such an obsession to subsist over one meager landmass, a half of 1% of this region, by those holding the 99.5% of the land largess acquired in the 20th Century via Britain.

Why was a state for the region's ancient Copts not attended instead of Jordan, and why Lebanon was not adequately protected; these are issues incurred under Britain's watch and merit good consideration. History affirms there was never an Arab state called as Palestine the past 2,000 years, nor is an Arab Palestinian nativity claim validated other than by recent name changes; such nativity is especially not seen during the Roman reign or the previous 400 year Ottoman rule.

Thereby, this is an un-historical theological doctrine that is presented via political machinations, one that is the reverse practiced by the Jews. The Jews are uniquely commanded in Holy Writ not to take a cubit of another peoples' land, even that of its immediate borders, thereby contradicting the claim of illegal occupation west of the river from the theological view. A reverse theological premise of dominion contrasts those held by the Jews. Israel has abided her theological commands throughout her history, and cannot and never did accept other lands even when offered with assurances of a far better existential provision. To wit:

• "Take ye good heed unto yourselves therefore; contend not with them; for I will not give you of their land, no, not so much as for the sole of the foot to tread on; because I have given mount Seir unto Esau for a possession. And the LORD said unto me: 'Be not at enmity with Moab, neither contend with them in battle; for I will not give thee of his land for a possession". [Duet. 2/4]

Politicizing History .

Political policies cannot alter past history. Israel is a nation born and incepted in Canaan almost 4,000 years ago, the land which became 'Israel' then Judah or Judea in Latinized form; its name was changed to Palestine by Rome. This name was not applied to an Arab land; this history was abused recently by those most known of it. Britons and the Arabs were paid mercenaries in the Roman legions and witnessed this event (Flavius Josephus); they also presided when Israel was returned in the 20th Century (The Balfour Declaration). Namely, the name Palestine was held for 2,000 years as a synonym for the national home of the Jews, including in both the British and Arab peoples' documentation of the 20th Century (The Balfour Declaration; the

Faisal-Zionist Agreement and the San Remo Conference Resolutions). Both Britain and the Arab states are thus in denial of their past and present histories, their charges derived by Britain's overturning of previous legal agreements when oil was discovered. These are attempts to change history via Roman devices of names, using guile and propaganda. History itself exposes the similarities of Rome's imprints employed and supported by Britain without regard of its widespread global implications for humanity. Britain should reconsider the infamy of propaganda she spread globally; such is worthy of an otherwise great nation. Many great nations fell by such errors and this be made far away from Britain.

Arabs are not Palestinians.

The Arabs are not Palestinians because this name was applied exclusively to the Jews and their homeland; it is a deception because this history is fully known to the UN, Britain, Europe, Russia, America, the Vatican and any who would perform minimal investigation of this history. Hebrew names with a 3,000 year heritage asset were changed to West Bank in 1950 to support a doctrine of dominion; there is no West Bank referred to prior to 1950 anywhere in history or in the Dead Sea Scrolls.

The West Bank name is a historical fiction, a recent deception of charging Israel of illegally occupying Israel's most sacred land portion. This name was not enacted due to borders or land requirements but one that seeks to hide an underlying negation of Israel's history. It can be credibly argued the usurping of the names Palestinian and West Bank are akin to a Roman genocidal aspiration, one numerously declared so and enshrined in charters of Arab states and groups, and fully known to Britain and the UN.

Arabs are not Canaanites.

The Philistines, the source point of the name Palestine, were not a Canaanite or Arabian people; nor were the Canaanites, the Jews or the ancient Egyptians an Arab people. All historical imprints say despite their numerous enforced exiles, the Jews are the only identifiable active descendents of Canaan, by their historical origins, the Hebrew Scriptures and language, and by archives and archeological reliefs worldwide. [33]

Restoring Britain.

Israel has very substantially abided all legal provisions, more so than any other nation. Palestine was returned to the Jews via mandated treaties and the UN body, with all states voting in the motion via legal process. The region called as West Bank, along with its namesake, was illegally derived and should not be included as a violation by Israel. Israel, west of the river, is thereby not illegally occupying another peoples' land; the Arabs are doing so. Britain must come clean; for the merit of her nation's honor instead of her political and commercial preferences, even when this has become an enormously difficult task to confront anymore. The charges of occupation are improvised and arose after Britain's creation of Jordan and the corruption of the names West Bank and Palestinian. There can be hardly any honor for Britain in being the first nation to accept the overturning of 3,000 Hebrew town names to West Bank. This act, fostered and promoted by Britain, was thereby followed within 30 years by the usurping of the name Palestinian from Jews to Arabs, and by the demand of a 3-state; there are no occupation charges outside this parameter, yet such a path appears will continue unless corrected by Britain and the British people. A 3-state in Palestine, presented as a 2-state, can legitimately be viewed as an intended negation of Israel; the name West Bank and the transfer of the name Palestinian from Jews to Arabs affirms its reasoning, one that allows Israel to forever be charged as illegally occupying Palestinian land.

A closer examination of such a thread of deeds shows that Jordan and Britain conspired to cause such a false paradigm to satisfy Britain's arrangements with her created regimes, rather than of any illegal occupation factor.

Why "West Bank"?

The usurping of the name West Bank is a corruption of history and self affirms its reasoning. Here, Israel is charged with illegally occupying Jerusalem and Hebron, among numerous other sacred sites of the Hebrew prophets that are recorded in all three scriptures of this region and in the Dead Sea Scrolls. Thereby, the name usurping of West Bank and Arab Palestinians are deceptions intended to give these credence by using non-Hebrew names that would not succeed otherwise. Here, the name changes and name transfers align as an essential requirement of intent and do not appear as benign. A closer examination shows the charges stem from theological, not historical or geographical premises, and supported for commercial gains of Britain. Its acceptance says the UN body does not offer protection to the rights of all people of the Middle East, thereby contradicting its mandate.

The charge upon Israel is thus based on the process of historical and heritage elimination to appease Britain and Arab interests; thereby was the Balfour Declaration corrupted with its immense disregard of the overwhelmed Jews or the honoring of solemn pledges.

• "Jordan had no reason to be a state on its own rather than a state of Palestine or Saudi Arabia, except that it better served Britain's interest to do so" (*King Abdullah, Britain and the Making of Jordan*; Cambridge University Press, 1987; by Prof. Mary Wilson, p.3.)

Israel's Return.

Some have equated Israel's return as inapplicable, with comparisons to lands globally invaded and usurped by other nations who were not historically aligned to those lands. Such an analogy is incorrect; the Jews were not invading a new land but were 'returning' to their historical lands instead. Nor can an exiled people still actively subsisting and displaced by force and mass murder become negated of such a return by the statutory period (The Judiciary of War Laws).

It Was Not About Land.

It was not at no time about land because the West Bank was not controlled by Israel when the Arab states embarked on a series of wars with the Jewish state. In 1948 and up to 1967, Gaza was occupied by Egypt and the West Bank by Jordan, both occupations deemed illegally by the UN, both being west of the river, when Israel was subjected to an array of Arab states with a declared goal of wars of annihilation.

• "Israel should be annihilated and this is our ultimate slogan." - (The Iranian Parliament Speaker's Adviser for International Affairs Hussein Sheikholeslam, quoted by Iran's Fars news agency; "Israel should be annihilated, Iranian official says"; Jpost)

When the UN actively participates in the corruption of Israel's rights, instead of protecting the lofty faculties enshrined in its Mandate, it legitimizes the same consequences on all other peoples of the region.

The UN's greatest victims may be the Arab people whose basic human rights are violated by its silence of the regimes mode of rule. The UN Resolutions on Israel, which now number more than any other nation, is not about land; it caters to a declared agenda to diminish the rights of the region's inhabitants and any other belief system, even those that are its most ancient. A new view of a theology has emerged, interpreted in its harshest form and used to justify murder and castigation based on different belief adherents; it is also used to deflect all blame on Israel. Many have made cautionary addresses at the UN podium to no avail:

• "The UN adopted the Universal Declaration of Human Rights, which declares everyone has the right to manifest their religion, in the world summit outcome of September 2005, paragraph 139, and the responsibility to protect people from genocide, ethnic cleansing and crimes against humanity. The persecuted Christians are the caged canary of the modern world - so where are the UN Resolutions to protect the most persecuted people on earth?" - Jonathan Cahn Speech to the UN.)

• "I come before you as a survivor of terrorism. I was ten years old when they blew up my home, burying me wounded under the rubble. My only crime was that I was a Christian. At ten years old I learnt the meaning of the word 'infidel' - (Brigitte Gabriel, Act For America Org; Speech to the UN, April 17, 2015).

The UN and its Members have thereby chosen to inflict harsh measures on Israel instead of all other issues facing humanity. Resolutions of Zionism as Racism are hardly related to occupied and disputed Territory charges, yet it arose in alignment with the region's harsh new theological premises. These include targeting the ancient heart-line of the Jews' most sacred and fundamental region when west of the river was illegally annexed with no Resolution against Jordan; the same applies of the illegal and un-historical name change of 'West Bank'. Such can credibly be defined as a doctrine that emulates the Romans that committed a great destruction, including a holocaust in Judea in the year 70, when it too changed this land's name to Palestine.

It is thus evident Israel's castigation does not appear about land or displaced Arabs as is presented in the UN Resolutions as international law, but represents a far more sinister agenda. If the Jews were land robbers, every nation they lived in would know of such a history of the Jews and this presentation could not refute such charges. The charge of illegal occupation is made solely referring to the Jews' most sacred historical land, its size of no consequences to those given vast lands and requiring no more. Yet the nature of the demands cannot be anything other than targeting Israel's very existence when Israel's capital is also the central focus of a West Bank landmass. Based on an underlying Caliphate pursuit and the widespread turmoil outside of the Middle East where land is not an issue, the demands of displaced refugees and the name usurping appear as deceptions that have extending global designs.

• The creation of Jordan in 80% of Palestine fostered and anticipated Israel's instability by removing such a large portion of mandated land handed to a Saudi figurehead. This was the flaunting of the rights of the Jews west of the river by Britain when they were fully helpless. An array of corruptions, primarily focused on Israel, marks the plight of all inhabitants of the region by its consequences and that the charges made on Israel are illegal:

• "The "Mandate for Palestine," an historical League of Nations document, laid down the Jewish legal right to settle anywhere in western Palestine, between the Jordan River and the Mediterranean Sea, an entitlement unaltered in international law. The "Mandate for Palestine" was not a naive vision briefly embraced by the international community. Fifty-one member countries - the entire League of Nations - unanimously declared on July 24, 1922: "Whereas recognition has been given to the historical connection of the Jewish people with Palestine and to the grounds for reconstituting their national home in that country." (Myths and Facts Org)

• "Prior to this usage of the name "West Bank", the region was commonly referred to as Judea and Samaria, its long-standing name. For example, U.N. Resolution 181, the 1947 partition plan, explicitly refers to the central section of the Arab State as "the hill country of Samaria and Judea". The neo-Latin name *Cisjordan* or *Cis-Jordan*, is literally "on this side of the River Jordan" - (Judea and Samaria, CS McGill)

• "Israel has the right to build settlements in the West Bank" - (President of Israel, Reuven Rivkin)

The West Bank is a fictitious region that emerged by Britain's failure to correct Jordan's illegal annexation of this land portion. It occurred on the heels of Britain's White Paper Policy and the corruption of the Balfour Declaration which left a meager 20% of Palestine for the Jews. Britain's White Paper consequences can well be accounted as fostering the greatest crime of the 20th Century, with the West Bank as its follow-on corruption. To wit:

• The name changes of 3,000 year Hebrew towns in Judah and Samaria to 'West Bank' as a region separate from Israel remains illegal and can be accounted as a means to negate Israel's existence with continuing 2-state demands. That Jordan was Britain's first 2-state, the premise of a 3-state called as West Bank, accounted as a 2-state in the same landmass, affirms its corruption.

• The Palestinian name transfer, a derivative of Palestine, namely which was Judea, is presented as the antithesis of the Jewish homeland as a means to negate Israel's existence with a name corruption.

• The false 'Time Immemorial Palestinian Natives' premise of those that came from the surrounding states after the Jews began developing the land, encouraged by Britain as portrayed in Joan Peter's book, equally aligns with a native people status corruption. The previous Ottoman Empire did not call Arabs, but the Jews, as Palestinians.

• The UN's Heritage designation allocation of West Bank to a new group aligns with a negation of Israel's ancient history and allocated to a new one with no heritage; the UN cannot produce an Arab called as a Palestinian prior to the 20th Century, affirming its heritage corruption.

• A 'Refugee Problem' focused on the Arabs instead of the Jews who were harshly expelled from Arab controlled lands they lived in for over 2,500 years affirms its refugee allocation corruption.

• The equated Zionism with Racism UN Resolution, later rescinded, was also an aspiration to negate Israel's existence via the corrupted view of a 3,000 year historical and religious symbol.

Contrastingly, the UN issued no Resolutions of the multiple wars and military attacks upon Israel, despite that these were accompanied by openly declared goals of genocide on a UN established state. The Arab leaders embarked on war against Israel's existence which is genocide, and threats of war and such annihilation claims are illegal as they are contrary to the UN Charter, Article 2 Section 4:

• "All Members shall refrain in their international relations from the threat or use of force against the territorial integrity or political independence of any state, or in any other manner inconsistent with the Purposes of the United Nations"

The Scrolls Expose.

It appears clear there was never any issue of occupied land as has been presented by the UN Resolutions. This is abundantly manifest with the region called as West Bank, a corruption in direct proportion of the name usurping of Palestinian; both signify a genocide application than a land dispute. The Dead Sea Scrolls transcends what the UN presents, affirming both charges are false.

Following the outcome of the UN Resolution that favored Israel's return, the Arabs embarked on multi-state wars despite voting in the UN Motion.

The resultant rhetoric was absolute and formidable, and fully devoid of any relevance to refugees or land; it was a time when Jordan and Egypt occupied Gaza and the West Bank illegal, and prior to any charges of occupation emerging. The UN should have issued at least 50 Resolutions after these grave crimes, rejecting the attacks by states who voted in the UN Motion, the name changes of ancient Hebrew regions and the illegal occupation by Egypt and Jordan.

Despite the acceptance of Jordan's creation on 80% of the land that was allocated for the Jews, the eruptions of multi-state Arab wars were launched on the embryonic state of Israel, with equally harsh rhetoric as was seen in W.W.II Nazi Germany. The declarations of genocide appeared before the premise of Arab Palestinians emerged and when the entire region called as the West Bank was in Arab hands. Thereby, this was not about land but a rejection based on a numerously declared Caliphate provision. Consider the notable examples of genocide declared on all Jews and prior to the terms 'Disputed Territory' and 'Illegal Occupation' emerging; it is amid such times when Britain targeted the Jews:

• "I declare a holy war my Moslem brothers. Murder the Jews! Murder them all!" - (From Hajj Amin El Hussein Mufti of Jerusalem.)

• "We shall never call for nor accept peace. We shall only accept war. We have resolved to drench this land with your (Jews) blood, to oust you as aggressor, to throw you into the sea." - (Then-Syrian Defense Minister Hafez Hassad, May 24, 1966, who later became Syria's president. (Martin Gilbert, *Atlas of the Arab-Israeli Conflict,* Oxford University Press, New York, 1993. pg. 63).

• "There are fifty million Arabs. What does it matter if we lose ten million people to kill all of the Jews? The price is worth it." - (Abid Saud King of Saudi Arabia 1947).

• "This will be a war of extermination and momentous massacre, which will be spoken of like the Mongolian Massacres." - **(Azam** Pasha, Secretary General of the Arabs League 1947).

• "Our basic objective will be the destruction of Israel. We will not accept any coexistence with Israel. The war with Israel is in effect since 1948." - (Egyptian President Nasser; Leibler; p60).

• "If the refugees return to Israel, Israel will cease to exist." - (Egyptian President Gamal Abdel Nasser Interview, Neue Zuercher Zeitung, Germany, September 1, 1960).

• "The existence of Israel is an error which must be rectified. This is our opportunity to wipe out the ignominy which has been with us. Our goal is clear - to wipe Israel off the map." - (President Abdel Rahman Aref of Iraq, May 31, 1967).

• "Muslims Will Rule America, Britain… and the Entire World; Israel is a Cancer; Jews are a Virus Resembling AIDS; Muslims will finish them off" [Palestinian Authority TV Sermon, May 13, 2005).

• "We will never recognize the Jewishness of the state of Israel," - (Palestinian Authority Chairman Mahmoud Abbas declared at a meeting of Arab foreign ministers and was quoted by Channel 10 News, INN).

Dhimmitude is a religious premise that was coined by Bat Yeor in 1983; it relates to a doctrine of conquering lands, including by war, initiated from the Arabic word 'Dhimmi' (Protected); and 'Dhimma' (Treaty). The war chants clarified fully that the issue was not of 'occupied territories' as claimed by the UN Resolutions and enacted as international law. The chants of genocide predate the creation of a West Bank because these lands were held by Arabs. The charges are thus a corruption of the sacredness of both law and history, because Israel was not occupying any lands of another people other than its most sacred historical portion, as was legally accepted in the Balfour

Mandate. The reverse is the case; Jordan and Egypt illegally held the West Bank region when Israel was attacked. Israel was returned not on the British Mandate but on the prima facie factor of the Jews' connection to this land; Britain accepted this status when given caretaker rights to issue such a mandate for the Jews by the world powers and the American recommendations.

Denials of other Beliefs.

The vitriol and rejection was not limited to Israel and the Jews. It implied that no other religion can be accommodated in the middle-east. It is a Caliphate doctrine. Christians are also equated as un-believers ('Infidels') and others like the Baha'i are equated as Heretics. Although the Jews faced threats accompanied by declarations of genocide, the UN and Britain failed to respond and instead focused on Israel, issuing more Resolutions against the new state than all the world's countries combined.

The illegal settlement is the West Bank, a situation caused by Jordan and Britain against the state for the Jews. Thereby, Britain supported a Caliphate when it failed to correct Jordan's illegal annexation and also flaunted her 2-state pledge:

Of International Law.

• "Concerning the West Bank, we often hear the terms occupied territory, 1967 borders and illegal settlements. But from whom did Israel capture the West Bank, from the Palestinians? In 1967 no Palestinian state existed. The UN Resolution 242 rejected repeated attempts to call Israel as the aggressor or to demand unilateral

259

withdrawal to the 1967 borders. UN Resolution 242 called for a negotiated settlement based on secure & defensible borders for Israel. But what was Jordan doing in the West Bank in the first place? Jordan simply occupied this area and changed the names of Judea and Samaria to West Bank and almost no one recognizes the legality of Jordan's occupation, not even any Arab states. So if Jordan had no legal claim to the land and Palestine did not exist, whose territory is it? Israel's claim to this land was recognized by world renowned jurists of the International Court of Justice, and that is why Israel's construction of houses in the West Bank should not be considered illegal." - [Israeli Ambassador to the US and Deputy FM Danny Yaalon, "The Truth about the West Bank"].

Calls for genocide of the Jews and that Israel has no right to exist were not confronted. No Resolutions emerged; these were condoned and legitimized by increased demands on Israel instead. It occurred with a focused and obsessive determination not seen in any other worldly issues, and when many others merited far greater attention. Here, there was no respite seen even in the midst of two world wars; that such flaunting had no alignment with the veracity of the charges now appear retrospectively clear. Consider then if the illegal occupation was by Israel or Jordan:

West Bank is Not Arab Land.

A nation cannot credibly be charged of illegally occupying its own land. Israel was returned based on her acknowledged 'historical connection to Palestine'; and especially so when it is demanded by those with no historical or legal claims. Jordan was never the owner of the West Bank; it is a new state created by Britain in the 20th Century in contradiction of her original Mandates. Britain's proclamations and treaties, executed in the San Remo Resolutions of 25 April 1920 by the principal Allied and associated powers after the First World War were not made benignly or subject to revoking.

• The League of Nations and the British had designated the land called "Palestine" for the "Jewish National Home" — east and west of the Jordan River. - (The Mandate for Palestine, 1928, pp. 66, 204—210).

• Arthur Balfour's memorandum of August 11, 1919, stated: "Palestine should extend into the lands lying east of the Jordan."

• Britain flaunts the Balfour with a 2-state division of Palestine for oil gains: "In 1923, the British divided the "Palestine" portion of the

260

Ottoman Empire into two administrative districts. Britain made a deal with the Hashemite Kingdom, to obtain control over Suez Canal and oil reserves in Kerkut. The trans-Jordan (77% of the Palestinian Mandate; Trans -East of the river) was given to the Saudi Arabian king's brother.

• Jordan flaunts Britain's 2-state division and annexed east of the river. In April 1948, just before the formal hostilities were launched against Israel's statehood, Abdullah of Transjordan declared: "Palestine and Transjordan are one, for Palestine is the coastline and Transjordan the hinterland of the same country."

• From 1948 to 1967, Jordan illegally occupied west of the river and changed this region's name to West Bank. Additionally, Jordan embarked in a multi-state Arab war the same year with a slogan of driving Israel into the sea. That Israel returned back this land is what is now called as Israel's Occupation of Arab land. This was not Arab land: "Thus Jordan's occupation of the Old City-and indeed of the whole of the area west of the Jordan river-entirely lacked legal justification; and being defective in this way could not form any basis for Jordan validly to fill the sovereignty vacuum in the Old City [and whole of the area west of the Jordan River]."

• Professor Eugene Rostow, past Dean of Yale Law School, U.S. under Secretary of State for Political Affairs, and a key draftee of UN Resolution 242, concluded that the Fourth Geneva Convention is not applicable to Israel's legal position and notes: "The opposition to Jewish settlements in the West Bank also relied on a legal argument - that such settlements violated the Fourth Geneva Convention forbidding the occupying power from transferring its own citizens into the occupied territories. How that Convention could apply to Jews who already had a legal right, protected by Article 80 of the United Nations Charter, to live in the West Bank, East Jerusalem, and the Gaza Strip, was never explained." It seems that the International Court of Justice never explained it either.

It is clear the land occupation has been disguised via political and geographical deceptions, based on the examination of legal documents. Thereby, an occupation charge against Israel west of the river is open solely to theological requirements on another people's possessions and commercial gains. It is a region more connected with Israel than any other sectors and of course this would be known by both Britain and the Arabs. The theological charge is also likewise flaunted; both the Gospel and Quran declare ownership of this land resting with the Jews. Here, condoning such a doctrine against Israel has extended as a global theological syndrome; because it was not defended against Israel.

• **The Judiciary Factor.** The West Bank and East Jerusalem, indefensible as being part of Israel by the Dead Sea Scrolls, was allocated by the legally enacted treaties as parts of Israel's territory, determined so in two legal documents, namely in Britain's Balfour Declaration of 1917; and in its division of two states that created Jordan in 1948. Of note, Trans-Jordan was not part of the 1917 Balfour Declaration; this was amended in a later supplement via the 16 September 1922 memorandum. [34]

Thus, west of the River was Mandated Israel territory, and cannot be classified as occupied or disputed territory; such is based on an illegal annexation by Jordan, not by Israel, and accommodated by later editing of original legal documents and pledges by Britain with the discovery of oil. The said land occupation was enacted by an annexation and a name change of 'West Bank'. The invention of a region called 'East' Jerusalem is also a recent travesty with no historical validity.

The 1967 Green Line Debacle. Wars of annihilation were declared and enacted on the appointed state of Israel after the Arab states voted in its UN Motion and the results favored Israel. The UN failed to issue any Resolutions against the Arab states that violated the UN's Motion of its voting results. Israel thereby prevailed in wars of a declared genocide goal and in a 1967 war accepted a cease-fire. The cease-fire line was accepted by both parties only on the bases it was not a political border, ensuring any demands on Israel from the region called West Bank are not enforceable. Thereby, Israel is not required to forgo her most sacred region, based on such invasive wars that declared genocide, and thus this cease fire mark (The Green Line) has no legal or historical basis. Here, Israel did not acquire new land; rather it received back the land allocated to her, which was illegally annexed by Jordan and the region's name changed to West Bank.

The 3-State Debacle. The UN Resolution 242 called for 'Secure and Defensible Borders' guaranteed to Israel; a 3-state is a violation of Israel's sustainability, geographically, and by the splitting of its Capital that no country can sustain. The Balfour Mandate forbids Jews being barred from the West Bank or any part of Palestine or any

262

country in Arabia. A 3-state, presented as a 2-state is a deception; it fully disregards the 2-state creation of Jordan in Palestine. The barring of Jews from Jordan and other Arab controlled states should be seen as a racist premise; its cause legitimized by Britain's lack of conditions of rule on the states she created. Part of the Balfour Declaration states conditions on Israel which are not seen in the Arab states but should be:

• "It being clearly understood that nothing shall be done which may prejudice the civil and religious rights of existing non-Jewish communities in Palestine, or the rights and political status enjoyed by Jews in any other country."

• A resident Aramaic Priest and a prominent Professor of Law's definition of Occupied Territory contradict the charges embodied as International Law, as do prominent law professors:

• "When people talk about occupied territories' I ask myself, 'what do they mean?' It is the Arab cities that occupy Jewish land. From Nablus (Shechem) in the North to Bethlehem and Hebron in the South, these are the Biblical cities of the Jewish forefathers, Abraham, Isaac and Jacob." - (Reclaiming Judea; Fr Gabriel Naddaf, Israeli Christian Aramaic Priest of Nazareth)

• "Of all the countries that have come into existence in the last century no country's birth certificate is more legitimate than that of Israel. Its leaders were obsessed in making it legal, step by legal step." - (Alan Dershowitch, Prof. of Law at Harvard University)

It's Not About Occupation.

It is also not about land, refugees, nativity, Israel, Zionism, UN Resolutions, West Bank, Palestine or Palestinians. The Arab Officials say so:

• "Jewish sovereignty is profoundly blasphemous under Islamic law. This situation must obtain in all lands once conquered by a Muslim army, no matter how long ago, and whether or not the current rulers of the place follow Islam. Perforce, the existence of the Zionist Entity violates Islamic law, and thus violates the religious rights of Muslims to enjoy legal sanction for the oppression and extermination of Jews."

- ("The Existence of Jews Violates My Religious Rights" By Mahmoud al-Zahar, Hamas Official; Pre-Occupied Territory Org)

It's not about Jews.

• "Recently, the Islamic State released a map of the areas it plans on expanding into over the next five years. The map includes Portugal, Spain, Hungary, the Czech Republic, Slovakia, Greece, Bulgaria, Ukraine, Romania, Armenia, Georgia, Crete, Cyprus and parts of Russia. The reason these European states are included is simple. According to Islamic Law, once a country has been conquered (or "opened" as it's called in the euphemistic Arabic), it becomes Islamic in perpetuity. This, incidentally, is the real reason Muslims despise Israel. It is not due to sympathy for the Palestinians. The "caliphate" has been reborn and is expanding before the west". - ("The 'Refugee Crises': Muslim History vs. Western Fantasy". By Raymond Ibrahim, Middle East and Terrorism)

The charges on the most legally appointed nation is not about any occupation of Arab lands by Israel. It's a Caliphate doctrine, says a Middle East expert, and here, the term 'stupid' can respectfully apply as its cautionary notice:

• "Let's wake up and tell the truth. The truth is that we are a Jihad target for Hamas and the PLO, each one using its own methods of trying to dissemble and pull the wool over our eyes, and if we fall - thanks in part to the European money pouring into the arteries of the PA Jihad - Europe will be the next objective of that very same Jihad, which is already in the midst of exporting itself to Europe by means of massive Muslim immigration to the aging and deteriorating continent - ["It's Jihad, Stupid" by Dr. Mordechai Kedar, senior lecturer, Department of Arabic at Bar-Ilan University. Arutz Sheva]

Act 3:
'WHO ARE 'PALESTINIANS'?

18. A 4000 Year Historical Enquiry.

**Moshe Dayan & Abdullah el-Tell reach
a cease fire agreement; 1948**

The Israeli military leader says:

• "Jewish villages were built in the place of Arab villages. You do not even know the names of these Arab villages, and I do not blame you because geography books no longer exist. Not only do the books not exist, the Arab villages are not there either. Nahlal arose in the place of Mahlul; Kibbutz Gvat in the place of Jibta; Kibbutz Sarid in the place of Huneifis; and Kefar Yehushua in the place of Tal al-Shuman." — (Moshe Dayan, Israeli Politician and Military Leader, April 1969, Ha'aretz; quoted in Edward Said, 'Zionism from the Standpoint of Its Victims', Social Text, Volume 1, 1979, 7-58.)

There is no contention that Arab people lived in Palestine when Israel was established in 1948, or during the Ottoman Empire's reign, or in the previous centuries. The Arabs were in this land after the 7th Century via the Islamic invasion, and stayed in short intervals and in variant numbers and conducted battles with the previous Christian invaders of this land. Thereby, history says this was not the land of Islam or Christianity, nor of the numerous migrating peoples they brought with them. Both were battling for the land of another people. The Jews.

The Greeks, Lebanese, Armenians, Persians, Turks, Bosnians and many other peoples also lived in Palestine at various periods. Such is fully accepted by Israel and affirmed by historical imprints. There can be hardly any place where people do not live, especially so in the ancient lands of Arabia where even harsh deserts have been conquered for habitation. However, such a description can be used deceptively. The Arabs are claiming a land that is not theirs; such is the topside preamble of this issue that is obscured. When this land's history is accounted correctly, it says the Arabs that claim nativity by virtue of immigration are in fact not native to Palestine; the same applies to the numerous non-Arab peoples who also lived here. They lived in this land alongside the only ancestral inhabitants of Palestine that the Arabs deny. The Jews.

The Big Omissions.

Not all the Jews were exiled by Rome in the 2nd Century or by the Babylonians in the 6th Century BCE. The issue is not of what is claimed, but what is omitted; namely, that the Jews also lived in this land, continuously and constantly, for more than 3,000 years in an un-broken historical thread, without pause, even up to the previous Ottoman reign, and the British rule of the 20th Century.

In 1984 a British survey said the Jewish population was twice the size of Arabs. Joan Peters' critically acclaimed book ('From Time Immemorial: The Origins of the Arab-Jewish Conflict over Palestine'), gives a detailed accounting the present Arabs in Palestine are recent immigrants from other states. And a host of Historians agree the physical Jewish bond remained unbroken with their homeland. These factual historical provisions are denied by the Arabs, thereby rendering the situation not of displaced peoples but of the negation of a 3,000 year people. A land occupation charge is falsely promoted of a people that have no history of land occupation.

• "Jerusalem's Jewish connection dates back more than 3,000 years. Even after Jews lost control of the city in 70 CE, a Jewish spiritual and physical bond with Jerusalem remained unbroken, despite 2,000 years of dispersion." - ('Jerusalem in a Nutshell' by Eli E. Hertz, Middle East Historian and author; Myths and Facts Org.)

A Most Barren Land.

The Arabs who claim they were displaced are rejecting the claimants of this land's owners. There was no Arab state or native Arab population in Palestine. In the 18th Century this land is described among the most barren and isolated regions of the world, almost devoid of a population. The historical record says so; it also says the few settlements in Palestine were of the Jews who remained since the Roman exile of most of Judea's population. The Crusaders, the Islamic invasion and a host of other invading non-Arab nations affirm the Jewish presence in Palestine for 2,000 years up to the Ottoman and British periods.

The other omission is that one could have immigrated to Palestine in the 19th Century, bought a home, or simply erected one in this barren land without permission, even to have a family and grandchildren and obtain a Palestinian passport; it would be a regional passport because Palestine was never an official state. Clearly, such a migration cannot claim an ancestral or native habitation as credible relative to the Jews.

This land had no controlling government or security walls to bar entry to anyone for many periods. The historical record says this is also what occurred; a large in-flow of Arabs began migrating as the land was starting to be developed by the Jews who hearkened to the endeavors of Herzl and the early US Presidents' call for a return of the Jews and a Palestinian Jewish homeland. Palestine is the name of the homeland of the Jews, not the Arabs; the Arabs usurped this name recently and deny the rights of the Jews in their homeland. Therefore, the displacement factor must be directed to the Jews.

The whole of Palestine, accept for some sectors like Jerusalem, Hebron and town enclaves the Jews lived, was among the most isolated and barren regions of the world; its populations would have been relatively inconsequential; the population of the Jews would have also been small, yet significant. Thereby, the correct issue is that many people from various countries lived here; and foremost among them were the land's original and native inhabitant; the Jews. Otherwise, any definition which does not say so at the outset appears as incorrect by omission.

Jewish Nativity.

There is a dire issue in calling those who migrated recently to this region as native inhabitants or any inference this was the native land of the Arabs. History also says the 'time immemorial' claims of Arab nativity, the recently usurped Jewish referenced name of Palestinian, and the overturning of the Jews' ancient Hebrew town names as West Bank, are recently enacted implements that is designed with a means to render historical credibility when such is absent. The nativity claim is held only by the Jews.

The Balfour Declaration that acknowledged the Jews' unique historical connection with this land was accepted by the Arab chieftains, with no opposition from any sector in both ancient and modern periods prior to Hajj Amin's appointment as the Jerusalem Mayor by Britain.

There were Jews in Middle East countries controlled by Arabs prior to the Arab race emerging; there have been no voices of similar displacements for land ownership for the Jews - nor for many other peoples like the Copts who have also lived in the Middle East for many millenniums.

There are no record of Arabs in ancient Egypt and Babylon, yet there are of the Jews. Egypt, Saudi Arabia (Mecca), Yemen, Syria, Iran (Persia) had established, successful Jewish populations for 2,600 years up to the Mid-20th Century. The Jews made no claims of nativity to any of those lands, as is seen by the Arabs relating to Palestine. The other variant is while the Arabs invaded Palestine, the Jews were not in Arab lands via invasions; they were driven there prior to the Pre-Islamic Arabs since the 6th Century BCE.

The Jews represent a 3,000 year nation and are recorded in three scriptures, in hundreds of historical archives and thousands of archaeological relics. The Jews cannot be credibly left out as the Middle East primal inhabitants or denied of Palestine as their homeland. The Dead Sea Scrolls fully established Israel as one of the few existing original holders of a sovereign state in the region. Thereby there are significant historical and moral omissions in the charges and claims that impact this conflict. The premise of Arabs as Palestinians and as displaced peoples of Palestine is a historical oxymoron.

Refugee Status.

The history of the Jews is also evidenced in the modern period's legal treaties of Israel's return that were formalized with the world powers of nations, including with the Arab Representatives. The Jews are thus the only returning refugees with a resolution to settle in this land, a variant from giving sanctuary to Arabs who are not the original inhabitants and thereby not returnees.

The refugee status of the Jews cannot be omitted from the preamble. Nor can any refugee status be morally or ethically credible when allocated to those abounding with options and facilities after being handed 22 vast states in Arabia that never existed before. Such facilities are avoided or barred from the discourse because it questions the credibility of the charges made on Israel; it thereby also evades an underlying Caliphate doctrine that has spread globally in the 21St Century.

The premise of Arab refugees west of the river Jordan can well be described as the least credible refugees in recorded history. Despite having numerous states to return to, and the creation of Jordan, why they are still accounted as refugees lacks credibility; namely, why are those handed more than 99% of the Middle East landmass in such torment of less than 0.5% held by Israel.

Thereby, the refugee claim of Arabs in Palestine should be directed not at Israel but the Arab and western states that have promoted the world's longest and most inappropriate refugee status; they gave no attention to the true Jewish refugees of larger and more deserving magnitude, those who faced genocide and were forced to flee leaving all possessions behind; and even worse in Europe. Those making charges on Israel were fully aligned with the Nazis that exterminated Jews; it appears implausible of a most meager land issue.

The credence of the Arab Palestinian claims should be a legitimate inquiry, one that is not based on preferred political premises but factual history, with the equivalent provisions applying for both parties. Its absence of confronting indicates why none have been able to resolve this issue. By the same claims, the Jews are refugees from land displacements of all the surrounding states of the Middle East. An Arab refugee and displaced people designation that concludes native land ownership of a people would render the Jews as ancient natives of numerous lands now controlled by Arabs. The Jews become more eligible for sovereign portions in those lands. Unlike the Arabs who migrated to Palestine recently, the Jews have lived in Arabian lands for more than 2,600 years. They were not offered refugee or displacement categories or statehood, nor did they seek such. Here, the

269

status of Arab claims as displaced Palestinians require its historical examination accounted.

Arab Palestinian History.

The issue of who are Palestinians is thereby reliant on the historical imprints both in the modern and ancient world, as opposed the determinations of recent vintage that were promoted less than a hundred years ago in the 1960's. Such a period is not conducive to a nativity, its corruption resulting in disastrous results and upheavals for all people of the region. The history of Arab Palestinians is an essential inquiry because its historical credibility impacts all peoples of the Middle East and is extending globally in the modern world.

The historical record says the fundamental problematic issue is that Arabs are not Palestinians; this has been made almost impossible to rectify anymore because its promotion has become akin to a theological belief, and such has little regard for historical veracity. In the modern world this belief has become ingrained as a political premise, rendering it an even more powerful implement. Yet it is the modern world's great deception and thereby also its pitfall.

The task of erasing this historical falsehood is difficult to confront; yet not attending it raises greater future difficulties for all peoples, and all historical, political and theological sectors, both in this region and further afield. The Arabs used the mass immigration into this land of a recent period to improvise their claims; it is a declared provision not limited to this region and has crossed the Middle East borders. When wars of annihilations failed to drive Israel into the sea, the Arabs in Palestine were barred from returning to their native lands, and the name Palestinian was usurped from the Jews as its stratagem. Arab Palestinians is a new phenomenon with no history and based on a declared Caliphate doctrine.

• "No Palestinian Arab People existed at the start of 1920. Palestine, then a secular way of saying Eretz Yisrael or Terra Sancta, embodied a purely Jewish and Christian concept, one utterly foreign to Moslems, even repugnant to them" - ("Pre-State Israel: The Origins of the Palestinian Arabs" by Daniel Pipe; Jewish Virtual Library]

Consider why it was required by the Arabs to use this name when it was held exclusively by the Jews and disdained by the Arabs. It answers itself and is self declared by the Arabs; it refers to a Caliphate

270

doctrine of dominion, not on a land claim or a nativity history of Arab Palestinians. It is an issue fastidiously avoided, yet its impact is of great relevance and impact to all nations. It says the Jews were native to this land by this name title, not of recent vintage but for 2,000 years, and such is superseded by later emerging theological belief criteria. It also says such is not limited to the Jews.

Here, the absence of usurping the symbol held by the Jews renders the Arab nativity and refugee paradigms negated by virtue the Palestinian name and the land being originally held by the Jews. Both people cannot claim equivalent status of the same space-time and the same landmass. Thereby by claiming the name of the Jews, Palestine's ancestral people, it is an admission of the predating historical natives of this land. Here, a usurped name is utilized to infer an ancestry from time immemorial that is devoid of history. This land's history says Arabs are not Palestinians. A native people do not adopt another peoples' native symbols.

• "A lot of advocacy seems almost staged. I refer to it as "manufactured outrage". I find that if there is a cause that you strongly believe in, you don't have to manufacture anything. You just advocate for it. So when people find out they have been misled they get very upset." - ("Don't Apologize for Defending Israel", by Ryan Bellerose, founder of Canadians For Accountability, a native rights advocacy group. by: Ilana Shneider, CIJ News)

Without the name usurping, there can be no Arab Palestinians; thereby rendering this usage as a strategic design that caters to a belief, not an illegal occupation by the Jews. The Arabs were not the native inhabitants or descendents of Canaan, Israel, Judea or Palestine; this was not the land of native Arabs when the Babylonian, Greek and Roman empires invaded Judea, nor when Palestine was ruled by the previous Ottoman Empire for 400 years; the census surveys of the past centuries say so.

While the issue is complicated by a dominant mosque structure in Jerusalem, this does not conclude in ownership of another peoples' homeland. The reverse ownership applies; a dominant temple of the Jews stood in its prior place. This land also has numerous churches, a Baha'i temple and relics of Greek and Roman monuments, yet those were not a mark of nativity or land ownership, nor can such apply for the Arabs. A belief provision was inculcated by Hajj Amin to fuel incitement in the 20th Century, gold plating the Mosque and collecting funds from Islamic states to cause a religious conflict. Hajj Amin's appointment as the mayor of Jerusalem represents Britain's failings that will impact on many peoples and nations globally. The un-biased faculty of historical veracity must apply in determining who the Palestinians are and why this Jewish name reference was stolen in the 1960's.

Identifying Palestinians.

The historical record validates that a substantially barren and Malaria infested wasteland was returned to the Jews in the 20th Century, after centuries of such deliberations with Europe, America, Britain and the Arabs. The words 'return' and 'national home' were embedded in the documents of the world's nations; both the names Palestine and its derivative adjective Palestinian was accorded to the Jews. Thereby, some relevant questions apply how Arabs became as the Palestinians and the Jews charged as occupying Arab Palestinian lands.

In the former Ottoman Empire its Sultans and mayors fully acknowledged Palestine as the historical homeland of the Jews, a description essentially the same seen in the British and American archives. Chiefly, there is no instance of any reference to Arabs as Palestinians prior to the 20th Century. It begs why this name was taken later if the Arabs saw themselves, not the Jews, as the Palestinian natives. The historical record says no Arab dynasty used the term Palestinian for the Arabs. It is a recent premise invented by Arafat following a meeting of the Arab league in Cairo in 1964; its aim to destroy Israel with a name weapon used as a nativity of the land of the Jews when numerous wars failed to reach such an objective. There was no Arab nativity in Palestine.

Here, it is relevant to examine what constitutes nativity and why the name Palestinian was turned from Jews to Arabs. Namely, what does History say of the alignment of Jews and the name Palestinian, compared with the Arabs - from the first recorded imprints of this history up to the modern times; and whether the Arabs were ever in this land 4,000 years ago as is numerously claimed. Thereby, the ancient land of Canaan is the first point of examination.

Jews are Canaanites.

272

History says the Arabs do not have any record of imprints in ancient Egypt or Canaan, positions which are open to any independent investigation. Historically, the Jews are the only surviving and validated Hebrew Canaanites incepted and created in that land and they do possess such abundant imprints, despite their turbulent exiles and dispersions. Thus it is reasonable the Arabs who have never been exiled from Arabia should also possess their historical native imprints as well. There was no Arabic writing till the 7th Century, so we should seek other nations reporting on Arabs; however such imprints of Arabs in the Canaanite period are fully vacant in the historical thread. It is a large anomaly.

The Jews are a people that integrated with many nations via their exiles and by the absorbing of many mixed inherited imprints, a generic syndrome with all peoples subjected to such means. Yet the Jews possess historical validation of their homeland, from their own writings and via cross-nation writings. The history of the Jews identifies all the nations they were dispersed to and returned from, and their connectivity with their homeland; from Ancient Egypt, the Assyrians, and Babylon - prior to the emergence of Arabs; and of the Greeks and Romans, and from Christianity, extending up to the recent Ottoman and British presence of the 20th Century. Namely, the Jews have hard copy archives and relics that evidence their historical interactions with those nations, and all align with Canaan. Contrastingly, the premise of Arab Palestinians and a claim of a nativity and refugee status in Palestine are limited to recent 20th Century provisions. It is an anomaly.

There has been a host of strong efforts to foster an Arab Palestinian people; it is also one that the Arabs deny the Jews as being Jews and of their Canaanite heritage, even including that Jews are non-Semitic and are Europeans, or that they converted and abandoned their faith, or that the Jews are Khazars, a 5th Century mixed people with traces of the nation of Mongolia. Such claims also deny all the forces that invaded this land for 3,000 years who interacted with the Jews. The Arabs also claim the Jews converted and lost their individual belief status. Yet history says the Jews did not surrender their beliefs as is claimed; the reverse is the case, whereby the Arabs did forsake their previous religion and became either Muslims or Christians, with the Jews being among the only people who did not do so. It is an amazing claim considering the Arabs were in the Roman legions witnessing that the Jews were exiled because of their rejection to abandon their

273

faith. The Jews were the stiff-neck people who rejected conversion under the most difficult situations:

• "So you are the only people who reject my divinity!" (Roman Emperor Caligula; 37 AD/CE).

In today's new age communication phenomenon, the internet is swamped with such false tags and postings of Jews not being Jews and as European invaders, as a war propaganda enterprise intended to obscure the history of the Jews; it takes many pages to near the truth in a search investigation. Yet most of the Jews were not dispersed to Europe, but to the Middle East via Babylon 2,600 years ago. The Jews saw the emergence of the first Arabs before the Greek emergence in Arabia. The term Arab was introduced in the Hebrew writings prior to the Greeks using this name.

The foremost victims of false propaganda are the new generation youth impacted by the internet saturation and the inculcations on children in the Arab sectors, and by those media encouraged by their governments to spread such propaganda. Almost all of Europe and Britain's media are heavily immersed in promoting a false narrative against Israel and this is exploited by the Arabs.

By subsequence, the usurping of names to sustain a false heritage by denying another emerged. It compromises the history and belief of both Judaism and Christianity by the denial of the nativity of the Jews to this land and of the Jerusalem Temple as recorded in the Gospel, as well as the rights of other native inhabitants of this region, including of the Arab peoples held in this warp of deceptions. The UN should not be supporting such historical distortions as it is accused of by numerous sources, especially when it is aware of its intents and goals.

Jews in Palestine.

The unique Hebrew language is the world's oldest active one, used exclusively by the Jews throughout their history, with an accumulation of ancient books and their cross-reference archives of many other ancient nations. The Dead Sea Scrolls and all ancient archives fully identify the nativity of the Jews and their homeland with a 4,000 year language. Despite invasions by numerous forces, the Jews were historically embedded in Canaan, Israel, Judea and Palestine - the numerous names accorded to this land. While the Jews were numerously dispersed throughout the nations, there was never a time

274

when Palestine did not possess Jews. The nativity to this land by the Jews is affirmable as no other people can of their history. Aside from the Roman exile to Europe, the Jews substantially remained in Arabia and possess a 3000 year recorded history as one of this region's oldest inhabitants. The Hebrew writings introduced the Philistines that became anglicized as Palestinians and the first recording of the term 'Arab'. The Jews are thereby not a recent group in Arabia that occupied another peoples' land.

Palestinian refers to Jews.

The name Palestine, which comes from the Hebrew Peleshet, was applied on Judea, the land of the Jews, not on an Arab land. Thereby the nativity claim, aligned with the name Palestine and its derivative Palestinian, is of the Jews. It became Arab recently, fifty years ago in the 1960's, via support from Britain, as is the case with the name West Bank.

The historical record says the Jews, the Copts and the Lebanese are older inhabitants of the Middle East than the Arabs, prevailing even prior to this region's name being changed from Cush to Arabia by the Greeks in 300 BCE. Israel is a name that dates back over 3,000 years by the Hebrew narratives and mentioned in ancient Egyptian relics. Israel became a sovereign state by this name in 1002 BCE under the reign of King David.

Arab Palestinian Origin.

This honor must be considered as a British provision and the inaction of the Christian community that promoted such historical mendacity; it followed on the heels of Britain being the first nation to approve the name and region called as West Bank in 1950. The title of Arabs as Palestinians is a phenomenon that began recently in the mid-20th Century (1964), first via a conference held in Egypt that formed the Palestinian Authority with Arafat its President, followed by his claim of an Arab based Canaan habitation since time immemorial, alongside denials of a Jerusalem Temple and that Jesus was a Palestinian. It was a plan of attack via a name, after numerous wars of annihilation failed to dislodge Israel. Exploiting age old bigotry, it was widely embraced by many Christian states or un-defended adequately; it is the causative source point of Arab Palestinians and it could not prevail had the

Christian community responded to this historical and theological travesty.

The goal of the Palestinian name usurping was to align Arabs to Canaan via a propaganda stratagem that needs no historical validation; none exists; and it is in contradiction of all existing historical imprints. Its most astonishing factor is its support by Christianity, this land's foremost witnesses being in contradiction of its own history and scriptures.

Arabs are not Palestinian.

Arabs are not Palestinian because Palestine is Judea and Israel is Judea which was re-named Palestine. Palestine was not an Arab state at any time in history. Israel, Judea and Palestine are the historical attachments of Jews and their homeland; when this name is used as antithetical to Israel it is like saying Arabs are Israelis. It is thereby saying Israel has no right to exist.

Judea's inhabitants were not Arab; it was a people who were Hebrews and spoke and wrote in Hebrew. The Dead Sea Scrolls render the history of Palestine as Judea irrefutably. It is not an opinion and transcends belief; its rejection being the strongest mark of disbelief and an un-believer.

The Jews are recorded as incorporating battles with numerous empires and incurring numerous exiles and of returning back to their land throughout their 4,000 year history. Thereby Israel is not a foreign or occupying force in the Middle East, but one of its oldest surviving people. It acts as a validating of its returnee status to their historical homeland, via a legal process in concert with the world's nations and negating of any land occupation charges.

The Christian community, in this instant, has failed the noble pledge of the truth setting one free by supporting what is the modern world's great deception against the nation of Israel. And the Arabs are certainly aware of it; else they would not have exploited such a historical travesty. Its unfortunate impact is the loading of poor baggage on its own people.

Flaunting the Antidote.

Equally, such a paradigm is not embraced by all Christians today, as has been displayed in numerous quotes throughout this presentation. More significantly, it is strongly rejected as well by prominent Islamic scholars and Clerics. However, the 'Arab Palestinian' deception has been so successful that its correction appears akin to overturning a religious belief; yet it is the modern world's great deception. Here, the Jews were taken advantage of when they were fully incapacitated to respond; its victim cannot become the culprit of the actions of others.

Here, even the 2,000 year Dead Sea Scrolls' irrefutable truth had no impact. Yet it appears only a bold and forthright correction is its antidote, with no alternatives at hand. Only the over-turning of this name's abuse can render sanity. Its proof may be seen if Arabs cease being called as Palestinians; such would also disqualify the occupation myth by its absence of credibility; it also says if the name West Bank is restored to the land's 3,000 year Hebrew names, occupation charges on Israel is automatically muted. Such are the real reasons these names were usurped, thus they will not be corrected.

The Jews were called Palestinians for 2,000 years, up to the Ottoman period and by the British who enlisted 26,000 Jews as the Jewish Palestinian Brigade in WW2, one decade before this name was usurped under Britain's watch. Thereby, the only antidote for this conflict is flaunted; it has become too shaming to attend, too overwhelming even for Israel to address anymore. Arabs as Palestinians, and thereby the antithesis of Israel, is embedded in the world's lexicons; it cannot be extricated even by strong will to do so. Yet the other side of the coin says its future impacts are not slowing down but extending, and the Christians and Arabs are its greatest victims. The question how long such an obvious falsehood can prevail can only be answered how it prevailed so long and so fastidiously.

Silence to one deception will inevitably cause other deceptions. The Arab Palestinian deception ushered the un-historical premises of time immemorial native Palestinians that seeks to negate the time immemorial Jews of Palestine. By subsequence it overturns the Gospels and what many respected Islamic theologians say is in contradiction of the Quran Scriptures. This presentation that relies foremost on historical imprints is in full agreement with such conclusions.

The usurping of names of another peoples' history has become the only basis of charging Israel as an occupier in Israel. Sadly, it marks a continuing syndrome of the silence of a host of other deceptions, including the blood libels and Protocols of Zion falsehoods that are awash throughout the Arab world for decades. Arab Palestinians became its legacy and the poor baggage on the shoulders of otherwise decent Christians and Arabs.

Thus, unless such errors are over-turned the conflict will continue and extend further afield. If a name weapon can prevail over Jerusalem, Hebron, Bethlehem and Nazareth, it can more readily do so in the more recent titles of London, Paris, Kashmir and New Orleans.

Israel and Egypt.

The original title of Palestinian is not of Arab or this region's people; it is of a foreign invading people. The Amarna Letters from Egypt and the Egyptian Merneptah Stele records the words 'Israel, Hebrews and Palestinians' (*Peleshet/ Peleshtim*) that is dated as 3,400 and 3,200 years ago respectively. These relics do not mention Arabs; nor do the empires of Assyria, Babylon or the Greek and Roman Empires. There is no record of an Arab by the title of Palestinian prior to the 20th Century. It is an anomaly for any ancient people's claim, one that is not subject to the absence of Arabic writings; there is no mention of Arab Palestinians by any other nation that did possess writings.

The historical records and archives say the Arabs as Palestinians are a new group introduced in the 20th Century, a mixed people from the surrounding regions that infiltrated here when the land began to be developed by the Jews. There is a case to be made the invention of a new Palestinian group was created to support a Caliphate doctrine, one that rejects any other belief in Arabia, even one as minuscule a landmass as Israel and possessing ancient roots in this region. A Caliphate is a global design.

The usurping of the Palestinian name in the 20th Century is a stratagem device implemented to uphold a theological doctrine; because the Arabs were given over twenty new states and cannot claim to need more land. Thereby, the charges against Israel and all other inhabitants of the region are not based on historical grounds of nativity or past homeland status; they are based on a rejection or a denial of history.

History Devoid of Arab Palestinians.

278

An Arab Palestinian group is not evidential in the previous 400 year Ottoman period. The Ottomans, a devout Islamic Empire, referred Palestine exclusively to the Jews who were in the land along with numerous other peoples under this reign. All of the British documents also referred to the Jews as the people of Palestine, using the term Arabs for the Arab people. As well, the premise of a Palestinian nation, state, people, belief, native habitation or land relics have no imprints via history, theology, archaeology or any archives of writings from any source. No other group of people poses such an anomaly in history, especially one claiming a nativity stemming many thousands of years.

That a worldly multitude accepts the premise of Arabs as Palestinian does not itself render such as meriting historical credibility. It is a deception that is evidenced with minimal research of the historical records, one promoted by the British Empire to all its colonies across the world; these falsehoods were British and Arab inculcated when the Jews were in an existential predicament both in Europe and Arabia.

Thereafter, a propaganda war of protest marches emerged globally, using the term Palestinians as fully antithetical to the Jews. It caused an overwhelmed Israel not to use the name accorded them for 2,000 years; it is among one of her gravest errors. The Palestinian Post, a prominent Israeli Newspaper, changed its name to The Jerusalem Post in 1950. As well, a host of Jewish institutions dropped the prefix of Palestine from their titles. It resulted in an Arab Palestinian 'time immemorial' claim that rejects any historical connection of Israel and 'the land of the Jews'. Its impacts on Christianity's history and beliefs are an inevitable future outcome.

7,000 Year Nativity Claims.

The Palestinian Authority President Mahmud Abbas, a mentor and Lieutenant of Arafat, calls himself a Palestinian with a 7,000 year history in the land of Palestine, in an addressing that fully negates Israel's history:

• "We said to him [Netanyahu], when he claimed the Jews have a historical right dating back to 3000 years B.C.E., we say that the nation of Palestine upon the land of Canaan had a 7,000-year history. This is the truth that must be said: Netanyahu, you are incidental in history. We are the people of history. We are the owners of history." -

(PA President Mahmoud Abbas, Palestinian al-Fatah TV, May 14, 2011).

Abbas' statement negates the validated history of Israel by asserting a 7,000 year premise that is vacant of any validation, thus promoting a fictional one. The truth is that almost all of the Palestinian Authority ministers are themselves not Palestinian; many not even Arab, a vital issue that was of no interest to its supporters. Mahmud Abbas is a recent generation Iranian, a nation that is not Arab. Contrary to Abbas' 7,000 year nativity claim, and unlike all other nations, there are no imprints of a Palestinian city, capital, language, coins, postage stamps or a national anthem; all such factors are evidential only with the Jews aligning with the name Palestine. Thereby, the charge of Israel occupying Arab Palestinian land has no credibility via historical validation.

The condoning of a Palestinian people other than the Jews is thereby a premise borne out of manifest historical denial; its most astonishing facet is the silence of Christians of such claims, the pivotal factor of its growth and legitimacy. Radical and novel means to accept the Palestinian narrative have developed via non-historical manipulation and enacted as international law. This is seen despite that such acceptance wantonly negates the evidential history that the world is fully aware of concerning the Jews and Israel. However, not everyone accepts the provocative dispensations directed upon Israel's history or of its credibility accorded as international law:

• "The Palestinians have not lived in the country (of Palestine) for generations, but rather are immigrants who arrived relatively recently. The hurried acceptance of the Palestinian applications by the UN is a serious violation of international law. - [Courtesy of Amb. Alan Baker, Director of the Institute for Contemporary Affairs, JCPA; "Palestinian Deception and the Unwarranted Trust of the West: The Case of Palestinian Accession to International Conventions"]

• "No 'Palestinian Arab people' existed at the start of 1920; Palestine, then a secular way of saying Eretz Yisrael or Terra Sancta, embodied a purely Jewish and Christian concept, one utterly foreign to Moslems, even repugnant to them" - [Daniel Pipes; "Pre-State Israel: The Origins of the Palestinian Arabs"; American-Israel Cooperative Enterprise]

• "There has never been a civilization or a nation referred to as "Palestine" and the very notion of a "Palestinian Arab nation" having ancient attachments to the Holy Land going back to time immemorial is one of the biggest hoaxes ever perpetrated upon the world!" - (Rockwell Lazareth, (c) Masada2000.org.)

In 1939, Winston Churchill affirmed the recent Arab migration flow after the issue of the Balfour Mandate of 1917; the Jews marking a majority in Jerusalem by a British census survey of 1864 as twice the Arab population. The Arab in-flow began after the census accounting date as the land was being developed again after 2,000 years:

• "So far from being persecuted, the Arabs have crowded into the country and multiplied."

In the early 20th Century the USA Congress also affirmed the historical status of this land. Chiefly, here there is no mention of Arabs as Palestinians; the land of Palestine is referred to the Jews as its native ancestral inhabitants:

• "Palestine of today, the land we now know as Palestine was peopled by the Jews from the dawn of history until the Roman era. It is the ancestral homeland of the Jewish people. They were driven from it by force by the relentless Roman military machine and for centuries prevented from returning. At different periods various alien people succeeded them, but the Jewish race had left an indelible impress upon the land. Every name, every landmark, every monument, and every trace of whatever civilization remaining there is still Jewish. And it has ever since remained a hope, a longing, as expressed in their prayers for these nearly 2,000 years. No other people have ever claimed Palestine as their national home." - [Mr. Appleby, representative of New Jersey's 3rd Congressional district in the United States House of Representatives; 1922]

Israel's first woman President reflects the same historical appraisal of the Arab Palestinian premise soon after its emergence in the 1960's:

• "There is no such thing as a Palestinian people. It is not as if we came and threw them out and took their country. Palestinian people never existed in Palestine!" - (Golda Meir, statement to The Sunday Times, 15 June, 1969).

A New Group.

The Canaanites, the Hebrews, the Egyptians, the Phoenicians, the Copts and the Persians were not Arabs. The term Arab is a term applied by the Greeks and adapted from the Hebrew Book of Nehemiah. That there was never an Arab group called as Palestinians prior to the 20th Century, the issue remains, why then was this name chosen by the Arabs, even when it was as disdained as the term Zionist in the 20th Century. Such adaptations of name usurping are never seen with the historical names by other cultures; usually the reverse occurs whereby the original historical names are restored when independence from an occupying force results. The Indian city of 'Bombay' becomes 'Mumbai' in Post-British India. The New Palestinians have usurped a 2,000 year name of another people's land, with the intention of acquiring a land that was not their own and rejecting any non-Arab states in Arabia. The situation includes an underlying cadence that over-steers the Caliphate premise; namely, the Arab disdain of the Jews and a coveting of their land are encountered long before it became a religion in the 7th Century. Such a historical syndrome is exemplified in the Hebrew Book of Nehemiah that first introduced the term 'Arab' in 450 BCE (2:19). Here there is a land discordance that prevailed 1,000 years before the advent of Islam. Later, the Arabs recruited in the Roman legions were also seen by the Roman Commander Titus as possessing the harshest disdain of the Jews (Josephus Wars, Book V, Ch 13, 4).

Six centuries later, when Islam emerged and invaded the land of the Jews, a mosque was erected in the Jerusalem's Temple site; such an act is a held belief of take-over by a theological doctrine, with a disdain of the Jews as predating.

The New Palestinians of the 20th Century are not saying this was the land of the Jews and then it was vacated by invading forces. Both Arafat and Abbas deny this was ever the land of the Jews or that a Temple stood in Jerusalem, even though the Islamic Scriptures clearly affirm this was indeed the land of the Jews and that the Islamic prophet ascended from the Temple site. The Arabs of the modern world are saying this was their land from time immemorial, that they were inhabitants of this land for 7,000 years; such constitutes perhaps the greatest historical falsehood and a negation of a fully validated history. Even more astonishing, the world at large has no corrective response, thereby it legitimized a Caliphate doctrine by the act of silence. Israel cannot be made to confront a Caliphate doctrine alone; it applies to all nations globally, including all Arab peoples.

282

An Invented People.

The Arab people were not native inhabitants of this land. A host of prominent Islamic figures have rejected the premise of a Palestinian people that has been embraced by a worldly multitude:

• "Arabs are clearly apprehensive that general awareness of the nonexistence of a past Palestinian state historically jeopardizes their case for creating one in the present. The lack of a distinctive Palestinian national identity apart from the wider Arab identity has been argued by many Arabs themselves." - (Courtesy Andrea Levin, 'Touching A Nerve — Palestinian Origins', Camera Media Analysis, December 22, 2011)

• "I don't think there is a Palestinian Nation at all. I think there is an Arab Nation, I always thought so and I didn't change my mind. I don't think there is a Palestinian Nation; I think it's a Colonial invented Palestinian Nation. When were there any Palestinians? Where did it come from?" - (Azmi Bishara, former Israeli Arab Knesset Member, TV Interview, 2009)

• Prior to Israel's re-establishment in 1948, the Arab peoples displayed a disdain of the terms Palestine and its derivative Palestinian:

• "Palestine' is alien to us. It is the Zionists who introduced it." — (Local Arab leader to the British Peel Commission, 1937).

• "There is no such thing as 'Palestine' in history, absolutely not." - (Arab-American historian and Princeton University Professor, Philip Hitti, who testifying before the Anglo-American Committee in 1946)

• "The characterization of Palestinian nationalism as 'artificial' does not come from Zionist adversaries but from classic Arab sources. In the period before and after the issuance of the Balfour Declaration, Arab nationalists consistently protested the use of the name 'Palestine' or the adjective 'Palestinian' to demark them from other Arabs in the region." - (Late author and scholar Marie Syrkin, 1970's essay).

Like a tort of law, that which is legitimized in one place can apply elsewhere by its extension. Above all considerations, those given control and responsibility of the events of this turbulent period should be held more accountable than anyone else.

19. Britain's Failings.

It is among the greatest nations in history. One that created the English language that held sway over all, one who initiated and propelled humanity forward with the Industrial Revolution. Britain was the educator of modern civilization and its foremost world power, both the colonizer and elevator of remote lands. It is a nation that was able to use her powers for great good and great bad, and she did so in all thresholds that she trod.

Britain confronted two World Wars in the 20th Century and the rise of the destructive Nazi power, facing her own potential demise in its process; she was positioned in its forefront. Britain was also privy to another menace in the Middle East inclined on a similar destruction of the Jews - they depended and relied fully on Britain.

It was Britain that master-minded the defeat of the Ottoman Empire in Arabia as she did of the Nazi machine in Europe, acting as one of the substantial savior of humanity from a spreading darkness. It was also a time when a darker side of Britain lurked in the fog; there was a reverse syndrome for the Jews, both in Europe and the Middle East. Even a great nation is not above the law, nor free from the consequences that befell other great empires that perpetrated intolerable and unacceptable deeds. Here, it is incumbent to account both the difficulties faced by Britain in a most turbulent region and the actions and deeds she committed in its consequence.

For whatever reasons that can apply in the enormous turbulence faced by Britain, both in Europe and Arabia, her greatest failings can be measured by her response to the Arab demands upon the Jews; it marks a litmus test as the true cause of the modern world's turmoil today. Britain was privy to what was witnessed in Europe when such similar ideologies made equivalent hell-fire charges and aspirations in Arabia under her watch.

Hajj Amin el Husseini, an Arab figurehead with the same declared position of Hitler, was appointed by Britain as the Grand Mufti of Jerusalem, when this city was mandated as part of the national home of the Jews. This appointment defines an intent that emerged on the heels of the discovery of oil; it becomes evident with a series of follow-up deeds.

Hajj Amin was allied with the Brotherhood to pressure Britain against accommodating a Jewish state. It was evident Hajj Amin's nihilist racism was not about land, illegal occupation or the displacement of any Arab people in the year 1920; the Arabs were handed over 90% of the Middle East landmass. Britain was better aware of Hajj Amin's history and plans against the Jews than anyone else; his radio broadcasts from Nazi Germany was fully known to Britain, and its impacts on the Jews - yet his appointment as Grand Mayor of Jerusalem was not re-considered.

• "God's Holy Book (the Qur'an) contains God's own word and divine ordinance for the Jews, a race accursed by God according to His Holy Book, and destined to final destruction and eternal damnation hereafter, and we commend to His Majesty's government to read and carefully peruse that portion which deals with the Jews and especially what is to be their fate in the end. For God's words are unalterable and must be." - (King Ibn Saud of Saudi Arabia, interviewed by Col H.R.P. Dickson, British Political Agent in Kuwait.)

The British who stood against the Nazi ideology in Europe succumbed readily to a theological premise of annihilation for the Jews in Arabia. With the discovery of oil in 1920, Britain agreed with the Arabs and formed an alliance against the Jews. It resulted in a host of measures that will cause great disasters, its worst Britain's White Paper policy and the treacherous diminishing of the land size allocated to the Jews in 1917. Britain did so with the dishonoring of her pledge made to the Jews before the world's nations.

Palestine was reduced to a minuscule land portion that was dangerously meager for the Jews to subsist as a state. It is incumbent to re-consider the division of Palestine as illegal and immoral, as also the legitimizing of a Caliphate by its subsequence, a doctrine that rejects a non-Arab state in the Middle East; numerous opinions by scholars and historians say so.

A Caliphate Reborn.

Today's chaos and mayhem afflicting the nations can well be argued as the rejection of a state for the Jews and their annihilation as sprouted from Britain's appointed mayor. A new Arab Caliphate doctrine emerged as a replacement of the previous Ottoman Caliphate;

its impacts will not be limited to the Jews who are incorrectly charged with land occupation. As the appointed caretaker of the region, Britain's responses merit good consideration for such consequences that were supported against the Jews.

While Britain issued her White Paper policy that barred the Jews fleeing Europe, illegally and in contradiction of the Balfour Mandate, Britain simultaneously barred them from entering Palestine. Now, Hajj Amin proceeded to Germany impressing Adolf Hitler for the extermination of the Jews rather than expulsion from Europe. Long suppressed and de-classified archives tell it.

Britain's Prime Minister Lord Chamberlain was fully aware of the Nazi-Hajj collaboration, yet he will issue two white papers, one with Hitler that fully disregarded the plight of the Jews in his negotiations; another with Hajj Amin that equally focused on the extermination of the Jews in Arabia. Both White Papers occurred simultaneously in 1939, both manifesting the same syndrome toward the Jews; both papers consequences were fully known. Delving into this history and its suppressed archives says these were not errors of miss-judgment. One of history's greatest nations failed in this juncture of history. Here, a nihilistic theological premise of a Caliphate was being established that negated the Jews' land and their basic human rights. As well, the pledges made by Britain which the Jews fully relied upon as their only source of survival were flaunted away. It soon became clarified what would inevitably follow; and it did.

In the big picture, Britain's failings transcend any other justifications and considerations, and will impact the Jews' situation in Europe and Arabia with outcomes that should have been readily anticipated. British Intelligence was fully focused of the situation of the Jews in Europe and Arabia.

By default, the British also failed to understand the true import of the holy tirade against the Jews; that the Sunday people will be next in line after the Saturday people, for such is the basis of a Caliphate, wherein no state of another belief can prevail. If it is argued that Britain's actions against the Jews are not directly related to the global chaos and mayhem that now engulfs the world, it is not arguable a Caliphate is the reason behind the deeds suffered by the Jews, and that such a doctrine is manifest today as an extended global syndrome, and that Britain was at the helm throughout. Both the rejection of a state for the Jews and the goal of a Caliphate of global dominion were declared by the Arabs themselves under Britain's watch in the 20th Century, and it is globally manifest in the 21st.

Britain's errors are not accounted adequately. Such is most assuredly because this was a Christian nation and the colonies she established saw Britain as their kin source and first provider. While Britain was understandably reliant on the new oil asset in a war torn century, Britain exploited age-old syndromes against the Jews both in Europe and the Middle-East, and committed grave wrongs in the most desperate hour of the Jews.

These are failures of such magnitude that the notion a retrospective view being easy to apply cannot impact, or that the dire war situation transcended all else; these appear an incorrect view. Such failures merit their accounting when the miss-deeds are comprehensive, manifold, widespread and continuing unabated. Had Britain's deeds been confronted and corrected by other nations that remained silent, her errors would not have continued; the 20th Century would not have been among the worst in history; and arguably, the modern world's chaos and mayhem seen today would have been either avoided or much tempered. Such never happened. All was shrouded in the fog of the world's wars, with no due reappraisal and accounting. It is a shrouding that continued even when the fog had cleared.

A history turning phase occurred under Britain's watch with the emergence of vast discoveries of oil and the appointment of Hajj Amin as Jerusalem's mayor. Britain's deeds against the Jews were perpetrated with the full support of the Christian community, with a disregard of the sublime premise 'the truth shall set you free'. Many of this generation do not know of it, including the honorable British people who were entrenched in the devastation of two world wars. Britain's actions are not conditional to WW1 when Britain claimed she needed assistance of the Arabs against the Ottoman Empire. Now, in the 1940's, the Jews were enlisted in Britain's armies as the Palestinian Brigade and most of the Arab states were allied with Hitler.

An Accounting.

On the heels of the discovery of oil, Britain will initiate the greatest deceptions on humanity against the Jews, one that imitates those of Rome 2,000 years ago. The corruption of the Balfour, with its

287

paradoxical 2-state division in the land that was allocated for 'one only state for the Jews' emerged, emerged with the removal of 80% of an already small landmass. Such was Britain's stated measure of a 'historic compromise'; it appears as a mocking of the Jews. It will be followed by an edict that barred Jews from entering the 20% land left for them, even while rejecting to assist them in Europe and barring their return to the small notch of a land that Lord Balfour thought none would bother about.

Britain's 2-state compromise will be followed with a 3-state in the most sacred land portion of the Jews as a new West Bank territory, then by Britain switching Jewish Palestine for Arab Palestinian, in contradiction of all her proclamations enshrined in her declarations and treaties. If such a thread of deeds are seen as circumstantial, or that this assessment is miss-guided, these are only its periphery. In the retrospective big picture Britain's deeds are arguably the cause of the Holocaust's huge human toll and the continuing turmoil of the modern world. Britain's Ministers will declare the Jews as equal enemies of the Nazis. Britain cannot be regarded outside the box as has been thus far; such an assessment can only be derived by a closer examination of the events and historical archives of this period.

Palestine, that was Judea, the Roman name for the homeland of the Jews, became the antithesis of their homeland under Britain's watch; a new people will be supported of this name. It will forever render Israel as illegally occupying another peoples' land. The Jews that Britain called as Palestinian will become the Jews occupying Arab Palestinian lands. This was a mockery never anticipated. Britain will pursue the splitting asunder of Jerusalem, a situation resultant from the creation of a region called as West Bank. A new region called East Jerusalem will emerge and 3,000 Hebrew towns such as Bethlehem and Nazareth will be regarded as Arab land. It will also result in extending impacts on Christianity. The New Palestinians have thus acquired a fictitious historical allocation that will assure a replacement premise of the Jews in their own land.

Britain's actions, or inactions, should be accounted as onerous; there is none to blame but the source given authority to settle this region and those Christian states that failed to respond, a condition Britain will exploit to the fullest.

For let none be confused what was given the Jews that created such relentless targeting; a swamp land that cannot in any wise be equated with what was later developed by the sweat of the brow.

A Barren, Isolated, Neglected Land.

Left: Jerusalem 1800's. Right: Tent Dwelling in Jericho.

Right of Return.

Based on a virtually absent population in the 1800's, as is reported by a host of prominent visiting figures, Palestine was not the land of the Arabs. At this time the Ottoman Empire ruled this land and the Turks, an invading force, were not Arab. The Ottoman Sultans mention Palestine as the indisputable land of the Jews. And while Palestine was barren of a population, Jerusalem, Hebron and some other towns did contain ancient Jewish communities; the Ottoman rulers declared Palestine as the indisputable homeland of the Jews.

In the later part of this century, a census chart which includes a British survey of 1864 says the population of the Jews in Jerusalem was twice the number of Arabs who began to arrive here. The census chart also accounts the Jewish inhabitants of Palestine for 3,000 years as a continuously subsisting people, and that no other people share such a status.

The same chart also discloses how the Arab population in the city of Jerusalem grew from 4,000 in 1864 to 281,000 in 2011, a 70% increase in 150 years; it affirms these are new immigrants from the surrounding Arab states. Thereby, these are not refugees or natives of Palestine, but the Arab people that immigrated here for better working conditions.

Such immigration inflow will extend even in greater measures in the rest of Palestine. These will become the Arab peoples who were exploited in the 20th Century by their own countries that barred them entry, including by the Jordanian regime that Britain created to house the Arab immigrants. The more honest truth is that Britain strongly facilitated and assisted a mass immigration west of the river, as exposed in Joan Peter's book. These were not returnees or natives, as has been promoted to the worldly multitude; nor were these Arab Palestinians, a name usurped later in the 1960's.

The Jews, this land's ancestral people who were exiled by Rome and thereby constituting the true returnees, faced great forces by Britain and the Arabs, both of whom were embedded in the Roman legions, a factor that historically validates the Arabs cannot in any wise be classed as returnees of Judea. Both barred the Jews from returning to their land, while Britain fostered the mass inflow of Arabs who were not this land's returnees.

It is a time when the Jews were held hostage in Europe and Arabia, for no crime other than that they were Jews. While the Nazis hoisted signs in Germany of "Jews go to Palestine" - they will be barred by Britain from entry in Palestine. It is poor historical and theological baggage placed on the shoulders of the otherwise good Christian people and those who sacrificed all in the war effort; they merited better from their leaders.

What British or Christian can truly be confused about the homeland of the Jews: Judea is Palestine and Britain referred Palestinians exclusively to Jews in WW2. Nazareth and Hebron are not West Bank. A 3-State in Palestine is not a 2-state.

In 1939, Britain's White Paper Policy is equitable with propelling an anticipated genocide in Arabia that was assured in the interview with Col H.R.P. Dickson, British Political Agent, inciting the Arabs with Arabic terminology and ensuring history's greatest calamity upon the Jews.

• "Our hatred for the Jews dates from God's condemnation of them for their persecution and rejection of Isa (Jesus Christ)"

However, let us not blame God or Isa or Jesus for condemning the Jews and accusing them of occupying their homeland. The truth is that Britain was hardly an honest broker in the Middle East or in Europe when it concerned the Jews. If a source point has to be selected as the chaos of the modern world today, none can compete with Britain's deeds in its fostering and succumbing to the paradigm against a minuscule Jewish state.

No conditions of rule will be made upon the Arab states Britain created, unleashing a Pandora's Box of disasters for decades to come, for the Arab people and all others in the region. Here, all blame will be cast on the Jews who were made solely heavy laden with Britain's conditions for a homeland. There are many good Christians in the world that may not be fully aware of the actions perpetrated on the Jews in the 20th Century. The truth is that those who flaunt vows and treaties are liable both via Christian and Jewish theology and their judiciaries. Flaunting a vow or contract that has existential impacts is the flaunting of the truth that sets one free. Honesty cannot be displaced from being the prefix to belief and the law:

• "Thou shalt not take the name of the LORD thy God in vain; for the LORD will not hold him guiltless that taketh His name in vain." - (Ex.20/6)

• "Then you shall know the truth and the truth shall set you free" (John 8:32)

Israel was not occupying another peoples' land at any time and any place throughout their history. This was told Britain when the Dead Sea Scrolls emerged in the same year Britain flaunted her oaths with the creation of Jordan, which Israel accepted under duress; and the West Bank, which Israel does not accept, also made under duress. It is up to the Christian and Arab peoples to decide their leaders' errors; both targeting a small nation is not a mark of power over such a minuscule patch of land.

A listing, if not a cleansing of Britain's errors, and the responses of silence from the Christian and Arab world of it, is appropriate and incumbent, especially so for the two most powerful and largest religious groups in history.

The Middle-East Policy.

It is a common phrase used to justify the reasoning why the western world's policy toward Israel is wrong by the Arabs. In fact, it is only wrong by the Jews and fully biased toward the Arabs. For how does it favor Israel when the British themselves assisted the illegality of the

West Bank that negates the Jews' most sacred land portion, an action that covered 3,000 year Hebrew town names, then encouraging mass immigration in the land which belongs to Israel and mandated so? The policy harms Israel, not the Arabs. Consider what is absent in the policy:

• That Israel is a legitimate nation with a 3,000 year history in this region, including the land called as West Bank.

• That Israel has no record of ever occupying another peoples' land.

• That great errors, or great compromises, were made to the Arabs with 22 new states and 80% of Palestine.

• That if 22 Arab states can prevail as Islamic, that Israel can be a Jewish state.

• That the term Palestinian, which is Judea, was exclusively referred to the Jews for 2,000 years till 1967, including by the British and the Arabs.

• That there were greater numbers of Jewish refugees with no place to return to other than Palestine, than the Arabs who had numerous Arab countries to return to.

• That only the Jews, not the Arabs, evidence a 3,000 year continuous habitation in Palestine.

• That the 'Right of Return' to Palestine is vested only with the Jews by the historical evidences.

• That Christians are witness the Arabs were wrong in denying the Jerusalem Temple or charging Jews with no connection to Palestine.

• That a theological basis and commercial oil arrangements is not the way of deciding history and treaties when it supports a declared genocide.

• That the corruption of the Balfour was a crime that spurred a Caliphate that is extending globally.

• That the Dead Sea Scrolls irrefutably proved the west and the Arab policy against Israel as incorrect for charging the Jews as occupiers of the region west of the river Jordan.

When Britain Called Jews as Palestinians.

During both World Wars, the term Palestinian was only used as a reference to Jews and their ancestral homeland by Britain and the Arabs. Prior to this period, almost the entire Arabian region was ruled by the Ottomans for 400 years; there were no countries or separate states in this period. Now only regions and provinces were referred to in a Caliphate mode of rule. There were no Arab people called as Palestinians or an Arab Palestinian state under the Ottoman rule or any time in history; Palestine was the name the Sultans used for 'land of the Jews'; so did Britain, America and France. All references to Palestine remained only as a retrospective metaphor relating to the Jewish homeland, with no other significance of another people applying to this name for 2,000 years.

Nor did the Arabs flock to this region before the Jews began developing what was described in the 18th Century as one of the most barren and neglected patch of land. The name transfer from Jews to Arabs occurred after the Arab migration to this land by those who were not native to Palestine but immigrants from the surrounding region. This history is known to Britain and the Arabs; the Roman archives disclose both peoples were prominently embedded in the Roman legions in the first century destruction of Jerusalem of 70 CE, and the second century name-change ceremony of Judea to Palestine in 135 CE. [35] Thereby, there was a collaboration of deceit conducted against the overwhelmed Jews, one unfitting of a great nation as Britain. It was fully known that in the early 20th Century there were no Arab Palestinians; every proclamation and official documentation by Britain referred Palestine exclusively to the Jews.

The Al-Aqsa Mosque in Jerusalem had no gold-plated dome in the early 20th Century; this was implemented under Britain's watch by an Arab Mayor appointed by Britain, when the Balfour Mandate was issued to the Jews, not the Arabs, for a return. These are errors that targeted Israel by a world power handed control of Palestine.

In the fog of W.W.II Britain will corrupt her pledges and proclamations to the Jews, with what appears as a willful design more so than a miss-understanding or lack of ability to correct such errors. Britain caused the term Palestinian to represent the antithesis of the homeland of the Jews by her support. This too was supported by the Christian community, albeit with many Christians inheriting this deceptive employ unintentionally. The silence of Christians will contradict the Gospel's name of this land and of the Dead Sea Scrolls.

This denial of first century history will result in great trauma for the Jews, and it has now extended as a global syndrome by its subsequence in areas and situations that are fully un-related to the Jews or Israel. More correctly, its predominant cause can be seen as the absence of any conditions applied by Britain on the Arab states and thereby the extension of a Caliphate that spread from the Middle East across the seas and borders.

Now, the Jews confronted the world's two most powerful belief groups targeting them in both Europe and Arabia. Here, not even the Dead Sea Scrolls that fully impressed the world of this land's true historical owners shall set the Jews free against such a determined dual force. Britain accounted the Jews as expendable in her foreign policy. Here, not even an opening door offered by the Arabs themselves was hearkened to.

Faisal: Palestine is One Jewish State.

Following the defeat of the Ottomans, Britain created numerous new Islamic states and pledged one Jewish state in Arabia in 1917. A Mandate for a state for the Jews was initiated and supported by the world of nations before Britain was handed control of the region. The Arab figureheads also fully welcomed the Zionist Jews returning to their homeland; after some deliberations Palestine was fully accepted as a Jewish state without any reference to Jordan, West Bank or Arab Palestinians. The term Arabs was always used to denote the Arab peoples, with Palestine referring to the Jews; wherein did this change happen of dividing Palestine when 22 Arab states were created, and the transfer of the term Palestinian from Jews to Arabs, thus becomes onerous and merits a full accounting.

The historical archives convey that Britain had adequate means to inculcate a more cordial interaction with the Arabs than an alignment with Hajj Amin being appointed as the Jerusalem mayor. This decision will ensure the Brotherhood, Hamas and similar groupings to evolve. Significantly, it appears Britain was fully complicit in furthering an already heated conflict that developed, when the Jews and their 2,000 year Zionist dream was becoming acknowledged positively and welcomed by the Arabs:

The Emir Feisal Welcomes the Zionist Jews.

Arab Delegation, Paris Peace Conference

Agreement Between Emir Feisal and Dr. Weizmann Faisal-Weizmann;

3 January 1919:

Preamble. His Royal Highness the Emir Feisal, representing and acting on behalf of the Arab Kingdom of Hedjaz, and Dr. Chaim Weizmann, representing and acting on behalf of the Zionist Organization, mindful of the racial kinship and ancient bonds existing between the Arabs and the Jewish people, and realizing that the surest means of working out the consummation of their natural aspirations is through the closest possible collaboration in the development of the Arab State and Palestine, and being desirous further of confirming the good understanding which exists between them, have agreed upon the following:

Article IV:

All necessary measures shall be taken to encourage and stimulate immigration of Jews into Palestine on a large scale, and as quickly as possible to settle Jewish immigrants upon the land through closer settlement and intensive cultivation of the soil. In taking such measures the Arab peasant and tenant farmers shall be protected in their rights and shall be assisted in forwarding their economic development.

Letter of reply from Felix Frankfurter to Emir Feisal:

Paris Peace Conference. March 5, 1919.

Royal Highness,

Allow me, on behalf of the Zionist Organization, to acknowledge your recent letter with deep appreciation. Those of us who come from the United States have already been gratified by the friendly relations and the active cooperation maintained between you and the Zionist leaders, particularly Dr. Weizmann. We knew it could not be otherwise; we knew that the aspirations of the Arab and the Jewish peoples were parallel, that each aspired to re-establish its nationality in its own homeland, each making its own distinctive contribution to civilization, each seeking its own peaceful mode of life. The Arabs and Jews are neighbors in territory; we cannot but live side by side as friends.

Very respectfully, (Sgd.) Felix Frankfurter.

Why Jordan?

In the aftermath of the Faisal-Weizmann Agreement, Britain flaunted her Balfour proclamation to the Jews. It is not a small matter of a nation's overturning of its pledge declared before the world; it ought not to be disregarded as the first error of this conflict's primal cause. Britain flaunted her responsibility despite the support of the Arabs in this juncture of history, and it will alter the path of history when oil was discovered. Britain's editing of the original Balfour texts to allow Jordan's creation was and remains the cause of the Middle East conflict.

With the focus on oil discovered in Saudi Arabia Britain appeased and exploited the Arabs that emerged with Hajj Amin's incitement of 'Death to the Jews'. It appeared surprising to the Jews that Britain would appoint such a mayor for Jerusalem after issuing the Balfour Mandate and the Faisal-Zionist agreement, with the clear knowledge of Hajj Amin's anti-Semitism and chants of genocide. Britain fostered riots against the Jews and used it as the reason to divide Palestine with the creation of a new Trans-Jordan 2-state in the land it allocated for the Jews. Britain's action of flaunting her Balfour Declaration left the Jews in a traumatic phase of bewilderment; it was condemned by the Zionist leaders. Britain carved away 80% of the land, and what was left for the Jews was dangerously inadequate by its meagerness. Thereby, Palestine was divided to house the Arabs that Britain herself

296

promoted to mass immigrate in the land allocated for the Jews (Joan Peters).

In a new declaration, Britain proclaimed a new design for a 2-state in Palestine, justified by the manipulation of the original Balfour texts:

• 'One state for the Jews and one state for the Arabs' (Churchill).

This action was the first 2-state division of Palestine in a series of land divisions against Israel and the first causative factor of a conflict that will extend with no resolve in sight. Henceforth, Britain will foster and legitimize a tremendous array of falsehoods against the Jews; of occupying another peoples' land and the formidable Arab position against Israel's existence will be postured as the hapless plight of displaced native Palestinians under an illegal occupation. The previous 'unique connection of the Jews to Palestine' was swept aside. That it was the Arabs who rejected any peace with the Jews, and that Britain flaunted her pledges in its accommodation, will be suppressed and cast out of the narratives.

Thus there are valid reasons for questioning a narrative that has entered the world's lexicon by Britain's flaunting of a pledge in such a precarious time for the Jews. These are some of the key factors of the division of Palestine and the first cause of this conflict; it can also be seen as the subsequent cause of a Caliphate doctrine being evoked that will extend globally upon the nations:

• Why did the Hashemite family acquire so many lands from Britain, and still handed one more at the expense of the Jews - the only people with a Mandate of return, the only nation that existed previously?

• Why was a far flung member of the Saudi family brought to Palestine and given a state called Jordan, when the Hashemite family was not Palestinian?

• Why was Britain silent of Jordan's illegal annexing west of the river and made as Israel's failings, instead of Jordan and Britain - carving off 80% of Palestine was not sufficient?

• Why was Jordan's barring of the Arabs east of the river not seen as a corruption of Britain's given reason for creating Jordan - 'a historic 2-state compromise to house the Arabs of Palestine' - as declared?

• Why is Britain later condoning another third state in Palestine via an illegally created name of a West Bank region west of the river, accounting a 3-state in the same land as a 2-state?

• Why was the Christian community silent, even supporting Britain's actions of the false names of Palestinian and West Bank that emerged soon after the creation of Jordan?

An Illegal Land Compromise.

Although Israel accepted Britain's 2-state division with its extraordinary language of 'compromise' used for the extraction of 80% of Palestine, it was implemented under extreme duress with no options applying for the Jews. It equates with an enforcement under 'extreme duress' - a fully judiciary provision that qualifies its illegality.

The Balfour Declaration was indeed established as a legal Mandate, one that was corrupted by Britain. Here, whatever causes related to Britain's actions, removing $3/4^{th}$ of this landmass for a new Arab state was yet insufficient to satisfy a series of further demands upon the Jews. The creation of a 3rd state in Palestine, called as West Bank, for which Britain became the first nation to approve, was in violation of the Palestine Mandate.

• Article 5 of the Mandate clearly states that "The Mandatory [Great Britain] shall be responsible for seeing that no Palestine territory shall be ceded or leased to, or in any way placed under the control of the Government of any foreign power."

Further:

• Article 6 states that "the Administration of Palestine, while ensuring that the rights and position of other sections of the population are not prejudiced, shall facilitate Jewish immigration under suitable conditions and shall encourage, in co-operation with the Jewish agency referred to in Article 4, close settlement by Jews on the land, including State lands and waste lands not required for public purposes."

Accordingly, this article makes clear that Jewish settlements are not only permissible, but actually encouraged. Jewish settlements in Judea and Samaria (i.e., the West Bank) are perfectly legal. The use of the phrase "Occupied Palestinian Territories" is a disingenuous term that misleads the international community, while encouraging Palestinian Arabs, with the right to use all measures to attack Israel, including the use of terrorism. (League of Nations; Mandate for Palestine Org.)

The territory of Palestine, all of it, was exclusively assigned for the Jewish National Home. Thereby its justifications should be examined of what was known by Britain of its reasoning for corrupting all pledges and issuing policies that violated the human rights of the Jews both in Europe and Arabia, and of the land allocated to them.

What Britain Knew...

Britain's failures were two-pronged concerning the Jews, occurring both in Arabia and Europe simultaneously. There is validated reasoning to see Britain had intimate knowledge and intelligence of the conditions of its operations. During W.W 2 the British commissioned legendary film director Alfred Hitchcock to survey and document Europe's camp horrors, but decided not to release or to make known the film's gruesome contents. This important film was buried away for new political reasons after the war's aftermath; yet it stands as evidence the plight of the Jews was known to Britain before the 1945 film was produced. In 1941, Churchill called the atrocities against the Jews as 'a crime without a name'. Churchill also knew of the European pogroms, urging General Anton Denikin to prevent the ill treatment of the innocent Jewish population. Throughout the 1930s, Churchill decried the virulent anti-Semitism of Nazi Germany just as forcefully as he opposed the policy of appeasement. Britain was also privy to numerous reports by Jewish refugees who escaped Europe; it failed to induce any British empathy; the plights of the Jews were made worsened both in Europe and Arabia.

A Warning Cry.

In 1939, in the very year of Britain's White Paper Policy, Szmul Zygielbojm managed to escape from Poland and issue his warning cry to British newspapers and the BBC, revealing the full horror of the unfolding Holocaust. Zygielbojm told the BBC:

• "It will actually be a shame to go on living, to belong to the human race, if steps are not taken to halt the greatest crime in human history. In the name of millions of helpless, innocent, doomed people in the ghettos, whose unseen hands are stretched out to the world, I beseech you, you whose conscience is still alive: expunge the raging shame which is being perpetrated against the human race."

Realizing that the Allies were not going to act and learning that his wife Manya and son Tuvla had died in Warsaw, he decided on suicide with an overdose of Sodium Amytal at his home in west London. His suicide note said:

• "I cannot continue to live and to be silent while the remnants of Polish Jewry, whose representative I am, are being murdered. By my death, I wish to give expression to my most profound protest against the inaction in which the world watches and permits the destruction of the Jewish people." - (R. Hanes, Shmuel Mordekhai (Arthur) Zigelboim, Commemoration Book Chelm; Translation of Yisker-bukh Chelm, published in Yiddish in Johannesburg, 1954; p. 287-294)

Britain's war measures knowledgeably failed the Jews both in Europe and Arabia, well aware of the war's primal people targeted by the Nazis and the Arabs. When Britain over-turned her pledge by choosing a subversive view of her Mandate, it ushered an action that will plunge the world in irresolvable conflict. Had Britain refrained from corrupting her pledge to the Jews, there would not be any issues concerning Palestinians or land occupation; here, the corruption of the Balfour Mandate legitimized a theological Caliphate doctrine that rejected any non-Arab state in Arabia. Britain employed her war strategy to 'leave the people fighting' and promoting all Arab woes on Israel.

Britain erred in assuming a Caliphate would only impact the Jews, and of accepting Israel's historical name corruptions under her watch. It sent a formidable message to the Jews. Palestine was the land documented in the Balfour Mandate of 1917 as a 'National Home' for the Jews, with no anticipation of another Arab state or a West Bank region within Palestine.

Thereafter were changes inserted in the Mandate text such as 'in Palestine' and 'a national home'. If the term deception is found excessive, such textual editing of pledges renders Britain's proclamations of a 3,000 year historical right of Palestine, declared when Jordan and Arab Palestinians yet never existed, and when Palestine was referred only to the Jews, as provocative double-speak, with a disregard of its consequences. A host of atrocities by Jordan that flaunted Britain's 2-state was also not confronted, making the justifications of such actions as inexplicable.

Britain erred again in Europe. Britain most knew of the plight of the Jews and did not assist. On the contrary, the Jews' plight was rendered hopeless by Britain's White Paper Policy, followed by merciless land miss-appropriations in Palestine and the encouraging of mass Arab immigration into the land left for the Jews. It is difficult to account Britain's actions as circumstantial; these actions emerged earlier in 1920, aligning with the discovery of oil and the creation of Trans-Jordan. Rightly, Britain had the onus of correcting the Arab states to absorb the Arabs in Palestine, but she did the reverse; such actions negated the reasoning of a state for the Jews.

Thereby, the Jews faced Britain's double-prong devastation both in Europe and Arabia. It will culminate in Chamberlain's two White Paper Policies in 1939, both incurring horrific impacts on the Jews and great devastation globally, both in Europe, Arabia and in Britain itself. The absence of the recognition of these errors allows its impacts to grow and extend, allowing no other means of stemming the chaos and mayhem in the modern world. Casting all blame on a fictitious occupation issue on Israel that only drives the world on the wrong lane of the highway.

Britain's Other Mega-Fail.

Had democratically inclined Britain that was battling the Nazi dictatorial regime insisted on the most basic governing conditions applying for the new Regime states that she established, as was made upon the Jewish state and thus a most reasonable anticipation of Britain's care-taker requirements, a varied situation would have resulted. Britain failed to apply the conditions on the Arab regimes as she did on Israel; namely:

• "…It being clearly understood that nothing shall be done which may prejudice the civil and religious rights of existing non-Jewish communities in Palestine, or the rights and political status enjoyed by Jews in any other country."

Thereby, the states Britain created have no obligation to protect the basic human rights of the people of the Middle East. The rights of the Copts, the Baha'i, the Christians and the Arab peoples under one-party rule in perpetuity resulted. And the one-party rulers will require retaining their perpetuity by deflecting all the world's woes on Israel. Britain, a democratic nation, cannot allocate such errors to the culture of this region; not while abusing those cultures with fictitious borders that will subject the people forever fighting, and signing oil deals with those regimes. Here, the plight of the Jews, including the Arabs and all of Arabia's peoples, would have otherwise not been so tragic; especially, it would not have erupted as the chaos and mayhem witnessed in the 21st Century and continues with no resolution possible. Most impacting, had Britain remained steadfast to her pledges, the Jews fleeing from Europe would have had a refuge to go to prior to the Holocaust's great toll occurring; Britain's White Paper Policy in 1939 foiled this opportunity for the Jews. Arguably, this can be viewed as among the lowest point in Britain's history, whereby a formal pledge was flaunted to incur the direst consequences on the Jews.

The Daily Telegraph headlined in 1939 as Chamberlain shook hands with Hitler:

• 'Germans murder 700,000 Jews in Poland'.

Britain responded with two White Paper Policies that sealed the tragedy of the Jews with Hitler, and the other with Hajj Amin. While the Jews faced a holocaust in Europe, they narrowly escaped the same faith in the Middle East. It happened under Britain's watch.

Britain's Caliphate Legacy.

The overwhelmed Jews facing extermination in W.W.II Europe and persecution in the Arab states had accepted Britain's 2-state division of Palestine that carved away three forth of the land. Thereby, all further demands on the Jews should have ceased here by all sectors. Yet the rejection of a minuscule non-Arab state in Arabia erupted under a British emboldened force, even after 22 new Arab states were created. It fuelled bloody killings and demands to forbid any entry to the Jews fleeing war torn Europe. Great Britain obliged this demand.

Britain will issue its infamous 'White Paper Policy' in response to Arab demands to cease Jewish immigration, using warships to blast refugees in the oceans. There is the encumbrance here of commercial oil arrangements which clearly impact; it says that Hajj Amin was not the primal figure that impressed Britain. A backdrop of appeasement will extend beyond Israel; India will also lose a third of her land.

Britain's White Papers became a flagrant flaunting of Britain's own 2-State proclamation that created Trans-Jordan and barred entry to the Jews fleeing the Nazi onslaught with no place to go, not even the meager 20% left over for the Jews in Palestine. It incurred one of history's greatest atrocities. Such was the animosity accorded the Jews it showed no boundaries of humanity's negative inclinations. It appears difficult to equate such deeds with the claim of a small measure of land previously held by the Ottomans, not the Arabs of this region, as its cause. Those who held the most substantial portions of the Middle-East landmass, over 99% of it, thus became emboldened to target the most meager allotment of land for the Jews. One truth has been borne out despite all means to cover it. This was not about occupied land by Israel, but all lands. The global scenario of the 21st century says so.

Britain will bow to a Caliphate doctrine, flaunting the ancient history of the Jews affirmed in all her pledges and proclamations. Its causes will be removed from Britain and the Arabs by placing all blame on the Jews; the premise of a national home for the Jews, now an existential factor for them, will become Britain and the Arab's most fundamental cause of fury. While the people of Britain and her colonies expended many lives and effort in wars with great merit, there was also a darker side abiding in this great nation. Britain's two White Papers will employ two of the most notorious figures against the Jews; none of these deeds have been raised in the modern world's most reported issue.

Hajj Amin al-Husseini

Britain would have been the least of all nations to be unaware of the direst consequences of its actions concerning Hajj Amin al-Husseini. He was the most prominent Arab figure in Palestine during the Mandatory period, his Nazi-like vitriol against the Jews being fully exposed with death chants and radio broadcasts from Germany. Hajj Amin was appointed Mayor of Jerusalem by the British in 1921, one year after the discovery of oil in Saudi Arabia; it was seen as a most controversial and foreboding appointment. Britain made no attempt to isolate Hajj Amin's incitement or to remove him from the post of mayor.

Apart from the warnings and suicide note of Szmul Zygielbojm, a disclosure will emerge from the Nazis themselves. It questions how much Britain knew and what was negotiated by Chamberlain with both Hitler and Hajj Amin concerning the Jews. In Europe an increased and planned acceleration of the emigration of the Jews from the Reich territory was initiated; namely, at this time the decision was the expulsion of Jews from Germany. But Hajj Amin will proceed to meet with Adolf Hitler and form a different agenda with far more foreboding impacts than the Reich's Jewish problem. The archives of the Nuremberg War Crimes Trial reveal the Arab Mayor's dark influence in the Nazi Holocaust and the genocide of the Jews, the Serbs and the Roma [gypsies]. De-classified documents reveal that Britain was fully privy to such details.

Hajj Mufti Amin al-Husseini and Adolf Hitler.

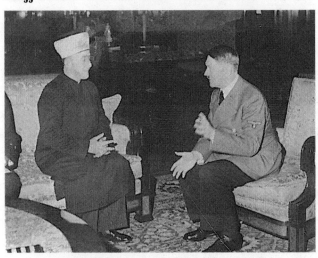

**Hajj Amin favored extermination
rather than deportment of the Jews.**

304

Before 1941, The Nazis had not yet decided to exterminate the Jews, initially wanting to expel them from Europe; such is claimed by the German Nazis themselves. In 1933 onwards, German Nazi Slogans began to appear only of boycotts and deportment of the Jews:

• "Don't Buy from Jews!" (*Kauf nicht bei Juden!*)

And

• "JEWS GO TO PALESTINE" (*Geh nach Palästina!*).

Initial Slogans in Nazi Germany.

Boycott and Expulsions:
"Jews Go To Palestine" (*Geh Nach Palästina!*)

THE WANSEE PROTOCOL

a) the expulsion of the Jews from every sphere of life of the German people;

b) the expulsion of the Jews from the living space of the German people. - [The Holocaust: Selected Documents in Eighteen Volumes; Vol. 11: The Wansee Protocol and a later 1944 Report on Auschwitz by the Office of Strategic Services (New York: Garland, 1982), 18-32./ Official U.S. government translation prepared for evidence in trials at Nuremberg].

Nuremberg Trial Memorandum.

When al-Husseini arrived in Berlin, he and Hitler sat to decide the extermination of the Jews, as registered in the Nazi Minutes of the meeting; Memorandum of an official of the FM Secretariat in the presence of Reich Minister Grobba in Berlin [fuh 57a.g.Rs; Berlin, Nov 30, 1941].

• **The Hitler-Hajj Amin Deal**: Germany will destroy the entire Jewish people from Europe till the Southern end of Caucasia; then the fuehrer will give Al-Husseini, appointed as Grand Mufti of Jerusalem by Britain, sole authority to destroy all Jews in the Middle-East.

In the Nuremberg War Crimes Tribunal of 1945, Deiter Wisliceny, right hand man of Adolf Eichmann, testified as follows:

• "According to my opinion, the Grand Mufti played an important role in the decision of Germany's extermination of the Jews; the importance of this must not be disregarded. The Mufti repeatedly suggested, before Hitler, Ribbentorpe & Himmler did, of the extermination of the Jews. He considered this the most comfortable solution to the Palestine problem. He was Eichmann's best friend and constantly incited him to exterminate the Jews. The Mufti is the originators of the systematic destruction of the European Jewry, and he became a permanent member, partner & advisor of Eichmann in this program."

- (Based on the book "The Collapse of the West - The Next Holocaust And Its Consequences" - By Anthropologist & Historian Francisco Gil-White.)

There can be no issue of diminishing Hitler's 'Mein Kamp'; he and the Nazi machine would not need encouraging. And while the statement made by Wisliceny warrants qualification that he may have been seeking leniency to impart such information in the Nuremberg Trial, he cannot be disregarded; the numerous deeds and declarations of Hajj al-Husseini against the Jews say so because genocide was his catchcry with equivalent ferocity as Hitler. The charge on Husseini will appear credible to anyone researching his history; its legacy is seen in numerous Arab groups that emerged and harbor charters of genocide. This was an inappropriate appointment by the British.

Husseini also travelled to Iran and Nazi-supporting Iraq in 1941, causing the massacre and depletion of 2 Million Jews, Serbs and Romas (Gypsy groups). In Nazi occupied Yugoslavia, Bosnia & Kosovo, Husseini also oversaw the training of troops in such genocide measures. Amin Al-Husseini made his radio broadcasts from Berlin to the Middle-East:

• "I declare a Holy War, My Muslim Brothers! Murder the Jews! Murder them all!"

Hajj Amin al-Husseini was an Arab Nationalist leader who fled to W.W.2 Germany, consolidating with Hitler, Himmler and Von Ribbentrop and persuading them to extend the Nazi anti-Jewish extermination program in Europe with its follow-up in the Arab world. It was Hussein's mode of extinguishing the premise of a Jewish state in Arabia, and resulted in the rejectionist Arab groups that will spur unfettered extremism and vilification to the Jews in the region.

Greeting Bosnian Waffen-SS volunteers with a Nazi salute.

It is the premise of a Caliphate; the Jews became its victims only because they were given the right to return as an independent state, while the same would result had the Copts or any other peoples be handed a state. The Husseini doctrines are embedded in numerous Arab group charters and seen in protest marches globally. Yet they are not limited to the Jews or one region, and thereby manifest as not concerning land occupation, as have been so erroneously presented.

The Brotherhood Founding.

• Hassan al-Banna founded the Muslim Brotherhood in the city of Ismailia in March 1928 - (Muslim Brotherhood/ Wiki).

• Amin Al-Husseini became the most prominent member of the Muslim Brotherhood in 1928. - (Tell the Children the Truth, History of the Muslim Brotherhood).

• Hamas, a nationalist-Islamist spinoff of Egypt's Muslim Brotherhood was founded in 1987 - (Zachary Loud, Council on Foreign Relations).

Britain Abandons Israel.

Britain was fully aware of the actions and promotions of Hajj Amin:

• "It is now known that the British administration was collaborating with the young Hajj al-Husseini with inside intelligence and advice on how to sabotage the Jews." - (Robert Mock MD; Bible Researchers).

• "British Officer Meinertzhagen reported later that Hajj Amin had been informed by British Colonel Waters-Taylor four days before the Easter pogrom in Jerusalem that 'he had a great opportunity at Easter to show the world that the Arabs of Palestine would not tolerate Jewish domination in Palestine; that Palestine was unpopular not only with the Palestine Administration but in Whitehall; and if disturbances of sufficient violence occurred in Jerusalem at Easter, both General Bols and General Allenby would advocate the abandonment of the Jewish Home." - (Joan Peters, former White House consultant to the Middle East, *"From Time Immemorial"* JKAP Publication, Chicago, 1984 quoting Colonel R. Meinertzhagen, *Middle East Diary*, 1917-1956 (London, 1959, pg 81-82).

The usage of the term 'Jewish domination' of the historical land of the Jews, which Britain already reduced to a 20% notch after Britain proclaimed so eloquently in its proclamations and treaties as the historical home of the Jews, thereby marks Britain's incitement stratagem against the Jews. It initiated and exploited the first Arab intifada (uprising) syndrome, first presented as 'The Israeli-Arab Conflict'; later as the 'Israeli-Palestinian Conflict' after this name usurping by Arafat in 1964. Far from dominion, the crime of the Jews was that they held a notch of landmass reduced to a size not viewable on a map of the Middle East; it earned them Britain's most eloquent mode of deceit.

An ironic situation developed. Husseini led the war against the Jews with Britain's fostering and the assistance of the Nazis. Thereby Hazam Pasha, Secretary General of the Arab League, announced an extermination agenda in Arabia against the Jews in the Middle-East. It fully mirrored the situation in Europe and gives the reasoning of the Arab collaboration with the Nazis. Hazam Pasha:

• "This will be a war of extermination and momentous massacre, which will be spoken of as the Mongolian & Crusader massacres." (Hazam Pasha)

• "Dozens of aging Nazis did indeed trek to Cairo, to prepare the Arabs for the war with the Jews" - (Historian Timothy Naftali).

• Many Germans who came to the Middle-East, conscious of Hitler's ideology, did not want the Arabs to be reminded of individuals who did not measure up to the Nazi concept of a superior Aryan "master race." Whether the Arabs would measure up to the Aryan genetic purity concept of Hitler is also a matter of ironic retrospection. It said, in part:

• "Wartime was the best occasion for the elimination of the incurably ill. The physically and mentally handicapped are "useless" to society, a threat to Aryan genetic purity, and, ultimately, unworthy of life." - Adolf Hitler; Mein Kamph ['My Struggle'].

A Crime without a Name.

In retrospection, what factors justified Britain's White Paper Policy against the Jews to satisfy the situation she confronted in Europe and Arabia remains inexplicable if not onerous. It is the year of two White

Papers emerging, one with Hitler and the other with the Arabs; both were executed by Britain in unison; both were primarily focused on the Jews. The issue remains, what consequences Britain expected by its decisions' impact for the Jews, both in Europe and in Arabia. Whether Chamberlain even raised the matter of the Jews, or was it mentioned and accepted. Such issues are not discussed and thereby they remain highly emotive and suspicious; yet these are pivotal issues.

There is a successive graduation of events marking the two White Papers. The following are notable 'Key Dates' that enlighten, beginning from 1939 onward, when Britain knew of both the Arab and Hitler's deeds against the Jews. Britain yet barred the Jews fleeing Europe from entering the Middle-East, including to the meager 20% landmass allocated for a Jewish homeland, as well as to all her colonies across the world to bar entry to Jewish refugees fleeing Europe. The Jews were similarly charged with all manner of barring in Arabia as did Hitler in Europe:

October 1939; Hitler Authorizes Killing of the Impaired.

Adolf Hitler authorizes the beginning of the "euthanasia" program—the systematic killing of those Germans whom the Nazis deem "unworthy of life." The order is backdated to the beginning of the war (September 1, 1939). At first, doctors and staff in hospitals are encouraged to neglect patients. Thus, patients die of starvation and diseases. Later, groups of "consultants" visit hospitals and decide who will die. Those patients are sent to various "euthanasia" killing centres in Greater Germany and killed by lethal injection or in gas chambers.

August 3, 1941; Catholic Bishop Denounces Euthanasia.

By 1941, the supposedly secret "euthanasia" program is generally known about in Germany. Bishop Clemens August Graf von Galen of Muenster denounces the killings in a public sermon on August 3, 1941. Other public figures and clergy will also raise objections to the killings.

August 24, 1941; Hitler Officially Orders End To "Euthanasia."

Mounting public criticism of the "euthanasia" killings prompts Adolf Hitler to order the end of the program. Gas chambers in the various "euthanasia" killing centers are dismantled. By this time, about 70,000 German and Austrian physically or mentally impaired patients have been killed. Although the "euthanasia" program is officially ended, the killing of physically or mentally impaired people continues in secret in individual cases.

Extenuating Impacts.

By subsequence, the impacts on Israel extend to other trajectories. As with the Nazi regime, the Jews were only the first target in Arabia. A Caliphate doctrine that is supported against the Jews cannot stop with the Jews, not in Europe or Arabia. The impacts on those other than Jews soon became apparent; by implication it will impact Christianity.

The West Bank landmass is not an Islamic land; it contains the most prominently featured sacred sectors of the Hebrew Scriptures. The new region of 'West Bank' that Britain and Jordan created, illegally, also produced Christianity's most revered figures and held its most sacred sites. It is the land that produced Jesus and Christianity, a religion that pre-dates Islam in Arabia and is also subject to a Caliphate. Such are the extenuating impacts which are witnessed globally today. However, Israel's claim is not based only on scriptures. The Dead Sea Scrolls is an archeologically validated relic that gave the world irrefutable and un-contestable proof west of the river Jordan is not the land that was stolen from Arabs; the reverse applies from the historical view and the Balfour Mandate of the 20th Century. The West Bank deception that targets Israel is not about Israel. It is about a Caliphate fostered by Britain with the mistaken ideology it will only target the state of the Jews, and thereby positively secure Britain's commercial arrangements with the Arabs.

The Ottomans were not Arab or Semitic; they were an invading people engaged in a Caliphate doctrine and not the original owners or inhabitants of this land. After the Ottoman 400 year reign fell and Britain handed a caretaker position to form mandates of the region, there was no requirement to create another 2-state division in Palestine after numerous Arab states were newly created in the region. The states created by Britain were not all merited to an overwhelming Arab population; these states emerged subsequent to oil discoveries. Many other groups merited a state and their human rights protection that never happened. Britain's actions thereby fostered a Caliphate premise, by default or otherwise, in the placating of the regimes it created. While it was a difficult task for Britain to control the volatile situation she faced in Arabia, there is also good reason to render her

311

actions as the most disastrous that was possible, one that was fully and reasonably avoidable. The Jews trusted and depended on Britain's assurances and treaties, pledging their full support. In 1939, Chaim Weizmann, the first president of Israel, and of the international Jewish Agency and the World Zionist Organization, addressed the British Prime Minister Neville Chamberlain in a letter published in *The London Times* on September 6, 1939:

• "I wish to confirm, in the most explicit manner, the declarations which I and my colleagues have made during the last month, and especially in the last week, that the Jews stand by Great Britain and will fight on the side of the democracies. Our urgent desire is to give effect to these declarations. We wish to do so in a way entirely consonant with the general scheme of British action, and therefore would place ourselves, in matters big and small, under the coordinating direction of His Majesty's Government. The Jewish Agency is ready to enter into immediate arrangements for utilizing Jewish manpower, technical ability, resources, etc."

It was of no avail. Britain's response was the 'White Paper Policy' that same year; it left the Jews facing the Nazi doctrines in Europe and of Hajj Amin in Arabia, assuring them of no place to go as a refuge from their declared two-prong annihilation. Here there were adequate signs and omens of an obvious requirement to place conditions on the regime states that would protect the rights of all peoples in Arabia. It appears the largest loss of lives and basic human right privileges were suffered by the Arab populations of the Middle-East under the British created regimes, for the same reason.

Ancient land portions were divided to foster conflicts between long-standing Islamic theological sects; gratuitous and impromptu borders were created to please the regimes appointed by Britain instead of the inhabitants. The same situation was also seen in India, resulting in an equally irresolvable conflict and loss of life and lands by the placating of the regimes created by Britain. In India, Gandhi will be demonized by Britain for pursuing an independent democratic India.

Of Unconditional Regime Rule.

Unlike the manifold stringent conditions placed upon Israel in the Balfour Mandate, such was absent from the treaties that created the new regime states, in effect granting vast landmasses as the personal properties of rulers appointed by Britain in perpetuity of reign. Like pet camels and Persian rugs, vast countries with abounding oil resources were handed as gifts. Jordan was created, many deeming it illegally, for the utmost inconsequential reason that had no connection with Palestine and to offset an unrelated British mishap with the French during WW1. We find India, once a colony of Britain and a larger populace than the entire Middle-East, successfully upheld democracy and required no sole ruling kings. The magic word for Britain was oil, and it transcended democracy and any responsibilities of catering to the people of the Middle-East or India. Here, the very issue of Palestinian refugees underlined the people fleeing from regime controlled states to Palestine, instead of the improvised inculcation of the Jews being illegally occupying Arab lands.

The Arabs were fleeing from regimes created by Britain is the more credible reasoning. The regimes, now securing their own positions, will foster the antithesis and disdain of democracy, a faculty that was supposedly the entrenched backbone of Britain's war with the Nazis, but not so with the peoples of Arabia.

At the very least, Britain should have made conditions that protected the people of this region, even without using the term 'democracy', which also does not appear in the Balfour, yet conditions Israel to respect the rights of all inhabitants. The Arab peoples will pay its price, becoming one of history's least productive peoples under oppressive dictatorial regimes. Here, the Zionists, not Britain's failure to apply minimal conditions of rule on the regimes she created, will be presented as the cause of all woes in Arabia.

Britain's actions indicates a failure in the responsibilities entrusted to her, incurring an assured conflict for the numerous nations and inhabitants of Arabia that were of different faith, yet native to this region for many thousands of years. Yet such stratagems were uncalled for; these were not Britain's war adversaries but those who participated in Britain's success against the Ottomans and fully relied on her pledges and proclamations.

Britain's actions will remain unaccounted by the world's Christian community; a worldly multitude will be inculcated to cover all wrongs by blaming Israel. But not without future consequences that will have global impacts.

Britain Invents Arab Palestinians.

• "It is easier to say I love Palestinians than to say I hate Jews" - (Exiled Jordanian Political Activist Mudar Zahran, Confederation Latino-Americana Macabi, CLAM).

This assessment makes the first time charge it was Britain that established Arabs as Palestinians. How Britain's Jewish Palestinians in WW2 became Arab Palestinians in the 1960's, is an incumbent issue for the world, and poignantly so for those who hold that the truth will set you free. It was under Britain's watch and promotion that a new Arab group called Palestinians was invented in the 20th Century. Arafat, the Brotherhood, the Arab world and the UN could not have succeeded without Britain's accepting, fostering and promotion of such an anti-historical provision. Consider the thread of events in a fully designed plan that culminated in the modern world's greatest deception.

1. **The 1948 War of Independence.** "In May 1948, Israel became an independent state after Israel was recognized by the UN as a country in its own right within the Middle East. Israel was attacked on the same day it declared its independence - May 14th. The combined armies of Egypt, Lebanon, Syria and Iraq attacked Israel. With such a force, few would have given the new country any chance of survival." - (Citation: C N Trueman, "Israel And The 1948 War"; The History Learning Site, UK.)

• **Annexation.** "West of the river Jordan was allocated as land of Israel and separate from Jordan." - ("Separation of Trans-Jordan From Palestine; Jerusalem Cathedra 1: 284-313)

• "Following a multi-state Arab attack on Israel one day after her UN approved establishment in 1948, Jordan annexed west of the river. It was in violation of the UN and in contradiction of the British treaty that created Jordan on 80% of Palestine." - ("The annexation was regarded as illegal and void by almost all nations, including the UN and the Arab League. It was recognized only by Britain, Iraq and Pakistan." - (George Washington University Law School, p.390, 2005).

• **A Name Change.** Jordan then changed the Hebrew names of this ancient land to 'West Bank' via an illegal occupation, and barred some 30% of Arabs west of the river from entry into Jordan. Britain was the first nation to approve the name change. - ("The territory is

314

also known within Israel by its biblical names, Judea and Samaria."
Encly. Britannica).

• **A Name Transfer.** The above three actions created a new annexed region, with a new name and an Arab population west of the river in the territory of Israel that Jordan barred entry to; all three actions were illegal; all three were supported by Britain. This still required one important factor to advance an underlying design. Now, it is the late 50's and the Arab Palestinians have not emerged; now, Israel's Jerusalem Post media was still called as 'The Palestinian Post'. The 2,000 year name held by the Jews as an exclusive reference to their ancestral land, enshrined in the Hebrew and Christian scriptures and numerous British treaties and essays by America's Presidents, was usurped by an Egyptian born agent of the Brotherhood.

• **1959. Arafat forms *Fatah*.** "As a graduate engineer Arafat moved to Kuwait, where he eventually established himself as a successful contractor. In 1959, he and his friend Khalil al-Wazir began publishing a magazine called "Our Palestine", and then formed a five-man underground cell which adopted the name *Fatah* , an acronym for "Palestine Liberation Movement", with the initials reversed to form the word "victory"(rather than "death" if not reversed). Khalil al-Wazir was later to become the "military" leader of Fatah, and known as "Abu Jihad. The PLO was created in 1964 under the leadership of Ahmed Shukheiry, a Palestinian lawyer, at a conference in East Jerusalem attended by the Arab foreign ministers. Its founding manifesto stated that it was formed "to attain the objective of liquidating Israel". As Shukheiry put it, immediately before the 1967 war, "Those who survive will remain in Palestine, but I estimate that none of them will survive." The title of the organization included the word "Palestine" rather than "Palestinian", since it was seen as a pan-Arab organization dedicated to the liberation of Palestine, rather than a Palestinian movement, and its leadership was appointed by the Arab League. - (YASSER ARAFAT 1929-2004; IJS Org)

At this juncture all Britain had to do was shout, and not too loudly either, along the following means:

• "Hey, hold on just a minute. Arabs as Palestinians is un-historical, it is a contradiction of all we declared and a negation of the 2-state we mandated. We British have never seen Arabs as Palestinians - it is the name we used for the Jews. We British cannot accept such a heritage name reversal."

315

It didn't happen. It should have, considering that Arabs as Palestinians is a deathly agenda for Israel and in violation of everything Britain thus far incorporated as caretaker of this region. It is the 'how, when and why' factors that caused the emergence of a new Palestinian group that never existed in history till this juncture. It is correctly one of Britain's many failures and onus. It is tempting to speculate this was the plan of Jordan's annexation and the name West Bank as precursors to the usurping of the name Palestinian by the Arabs, and with the British involved in such a stratagem; otherwise both those two deeds would have and should have been responded to by Britain.

Three Deeds that Changed History.

A New Region was born via an illegal annexure with the full support of Britain, as was seen with the name West Bank a decade earlier under Britain's watch. Despite the allocation of 80% of Palestine, Jordan annexed the southern region west of the river. Britain's 2-state historic compromise of 'one state for the Jews and one for the Arabs' was corrupted. The annexation was not recognized by the UN or the world community, yet Britain became the first nation to accept Jordan's illegal occupation and a new fictitious name that covered 3,000 year Hebrew town names. It says Britain did not like the Jews; she made no effort to reject or oppose this action which was in direct violation of her second 2-state pledge. In effect Britain opened the door to un-ending 2-states west of the river, or till there was none left, and a new people that was bent on dislodging the Jewish state. Many Synagogues and Churches were destroyed by Jordan; toilet tiles were made of sacred tomb stones in this biblically historical region and the Jews were barred from their most sacred site. Britain's co-operation with Jordan's illegal annexation and the name West Bank is the initiation of a stratagem for a new 3rd state in Palestine and the emergence of Arab Palestinians; the latter relied on the former of its credibility, and Britain fully assisted both. Here, Britain was responsible for the three steps she supported but should have fully rejected, in defiance of its corruption of her own 2-state pledge and all her declarations who was a Palestinian. To wit:

1. **A 3-state is born.** Jordan implanted the new name of 'West Bank' on the annexed region west of the River in 1950; the annexation was illegal. It is a landmass that contained Israel and Christianity's ancient biblical towns and sacred sites, including East Jerusalem, Bethlehem,

316

Nazareth and Hebron. Britain's failure to respond becomes the consequences that will usher a new people that never existed before, one that will render the name applied to Judea by the Romans as the antithesis of the homeland of the Jews.

2. **Palestinians are born.** Jordan now barred the Arabs in its new West Bank region from entering Jordan, thereby contradicting the only reason of its creation by Britain's 2-state compromise of 1948; it illustrates a master plan unfolding. It is at this juncture when the term Palestinian yet never existed, whence will emerge this most historical deception on the world community.

3. **Native Refugees are born.** In conjunction of a new region called West Bank, and Jordan and the Arab states barring their own people from returning to the countries they came from, a new stateless refugee group with no place to go will emerge. It is a class of Arabs that will become the displaced native Palestinians by a foreign invading people called the Zionist Entity. Zionism is Racism will be enacted at the UN. Israel's history and all of Britain's pledges will be fully disregarded and denied.

These denials will extend pervasively, including with the Jerusalem Temple made as a Zionist myth, that the Jews are not Jews; of holocaust denial and the promotion of blood libels and the Protocols of Zion will flourish. None of the Christian states will respond. Thus was born the Arab Palestinians. Thus did Britain invent Arabs as Palestinians and Jews as occupiers of Judea and Samaria, which was named as Palestine by the Romans; with the Britons and the Arabs its witnesses 2,000 years ago.

Thereby Israel will now face another state, a third state in Palestine, and a new people bearing the name of the historical land of the Jews embedded in the landmass left for them. Israel will become an illegal occupier of Israel and be accused of displacing a non-native people who will usurp the name of Palestine by its derived Adjective.

None will take Britain to task of her inaction and supporting of this manifest corruption; especially not the Royal House of Britain, the Vatican or any Christian country. Palestine will become a non-Jewish Arab mark that will contradict 2,000 years of history and all of Britain's earlier proclamations.

Why Names Were Changed.

There is no question that Israel could not be accused of illegally occupying a region of cities and towns with ancient Hebrew names. Had the original names of Judah and Samaria remained un-changed, any premise of the land not belonging to Israel would have been seen as devoid of credibility and highly farcical. Thereby the name West Bank was a required implementation in usurping the name Palestinian; it required a native people from time immemorial, and it invented one.

Retrospectively, Britain ought not to have condoned so readily; the impacts for Christianity that relied on its scriptures and history will be compromised; an extending Caliphate that has spread across the Christian nations will unleash chaos and mayhem; Israel will become the fall guy for Britain's failings. Thereby, it is the primal onus of the British people to correct the legacy they inherited by their leadership's errors in the 20th Century. The restoration of Israel's historical names is a first step: Nazareth and Bethlehem are not West Bank; Arabs are not Palestinian or native to Palestine. The Jews are the only historically validated continuous natives of this land for 3,000 years since Israel was established in 1002 BCE, and for 2,000 years since the Roman destruction in 70 CE.

Jerusalem.

Changing a long held historical name is the greatest exposure of a usurping. This is seen with the names West Bank and Palestinian, attempted in history's most acknowledged city. Jerusalem is called as Al Quds (Beit Al Quds; Arabic) by the Arabs; this holy city's name was not successful to alter by the Greeks and the Romans, it being too well established as a Jewish holy city. Such a name change phenomenon was also seen when the Greek Antiochus attempted to change the name of Jerusalem in 175 BCE; it failed to take hold. Equally, many Arabs deny the existence of the Jerusalem Temple, inculcating a historical falsehood to its people, justifying this as a doctrine known as Taqiyah; despite that the Quran acknowledges this as a possession of the Jews.

Likewise, the term Palestinian, derived from Palestine, could not be applied to Arab Muslims without the annexation and name change of West Bank; it required a people, even one that can be made as natives of the land. Thereby the stage was now set for a propaganda promotion upon a global multitude; it will achieve great success with the backing of Britain and the U.N. in its forefront. Even holy Popes will proclaim the new names of West Bank, a 3-state accounted as a 2-state and Arabs as Palestinians.

Mahmoud Abbas, the mentor of Arafat, and their claim that Arab Palestinians had a 7,000-year history in the land of Canaan, will emerge with the slogan of 'from time immemorial'. All historical archives render such a premise as among the greatest falsehoods of the modern world. The Canaanites and ancient Egyptians were not Arabs. The Jews were one of the Canaanite groups, born and created in that land; there are no Arabs recorded in Canaan from any source. Yet a 4,000 year worldly known history is going to change with a new one created less than 100 years ago in the 20th Century. Both Arafat and Abbas deny the Jerusalem Temple and the Holocaust; thereby it denies the Dead Sea Scrolls which dating precedes Christianity and Islam; as well denied is all the history of the Persians, Greeks and Romans. Such a situation begs the question, how did such a phenomenon become accepted by Christians and Muslims; will they both bend such large un-truths with hammers and nails to turn them into truth?

At this time in the 20th Century, Britain was one of the world's foremost empires that controlled an array of colonies, including India, Australia, New Zealand and segments of South America and the Middle-East. Britain could have articulated the stance of a new world view more than any other. But sadly, this nation chose to foster a worldly multitude against the world's most overwhelmed one of the time. The British inaction of removing Jordan's illegal annexation from west of the river, the supporting of the new West Bank name, and of accommodating Jordan's barring entry of the Arabs in the new state created for such a reason, will be followed by fully appeasing a new Arab stratagem, namely of condoning and adopting an official transfer of the name 'Palestinian' away from the Jews. This cannot be presented as a result of British confusion or circumstantial requirements to negate such means; rather, Britain chose to act against the Jews when it was un-required and un-thinkable. And the Jews had no means to counter such great forces.

Had Britain, a foremost power at this time, both militarily and by her literary excellence, performed actions to negate the unwarranted demands and false claims upon Israel, it would not be plausible for Arabs to usurp the name 'Palestinian'; they would not be able to challenge even a meager stance of correction from Britain. It never happened; Britain turned history upside down against the Jews.

As a Christian nation, Britain enjoyed the alliance of all Christians world-wide; namely, Britain had immunity of its actions not being confronted by other Christians. Britannia ruled. Thus a worldly multitude was formed that accepted and aligned with an array of actions promoted by one of history's most powerful nations of this period. Thus did Britain foster the Palestinian myth with the inculcated support of the nations and her formidable media enterprises. There was no stopping Britain and none tried.

Britain's Worldly Multitude.

The Jews will see no respite in the aftermath of Britain's actions or from Europe and Arabia's obsessions against Israel. This state's landmass will be contracted to the lowest geographical levels, rendering the premise of land occupation more applicable to negating Israel's right to exist. It is the beginning of the inculcation of a large multitude that will usher and legitimize a conflict based on fully un-historical premises, the flaunting of treaties and proclamations, and the determined targeting of the land allocated to the Jews.

Britain's worldly media enterprise will toe the line and foster a new global paradigm of a fictional history against the Jews. Israel will face a greater force than the Roman Empire upon Judea 2,000 years ago, and be subjected to an onslaught as no other nation and targeted from all trajectories.

Thereby did the Palestinians and West Bank enter the historical map in the 20th Century, where once the Jews held the title of Palestine and of the previous names of this land's ancient towns. The 4,000 year names recorded in the Hebrew Bible will be changed: Beit El, recorded in the Hebrew Bible as the place where Jacob's name was changed to Israel, will become as Ramallah; and the 4,000 year name of Hebron, the birthplace of Judaism, and the 3,000 year name of Jerusalem established by King David as Israel's Capital, will be seen as located in a new region called West Bank, one that was created illegally by Jordan in 1951. Thereby, Jesus of Nazareth will become Jesus of the West Bank. Such is the power of a name's abuse.[36]

No-Go Zones and West Bank.

The names West Bank and Arab Palestinians will become a mockery of the Balfour Declarations and Lord Balfour. It will also encumber unanticipated forces. By subsequence it will impact Britain, Europe and the Christian world as none other could. The West Bank underlies a syndrome of dominion that is not limited to Israel. Can it happen elsewhere? Yes; it has precedence and given legitimacy. The same can threaten a global extension and be dubbed as No-Go Zones in all Christian states, with its stark similarity how the terms West Bank and Palestinian impacted Israel.

No-Go Zones can be viewed as enclaves of autonomy derived via mass immigration, infiltration and minority law privileges. A one-way population flow inevitably results in claims for 2-state divisions and it does not stop at such perimeters. It happened in India and Palestine; Kashmir and West Bank are claimed after both those nations lost vast land masses. Such an outcome can be seen as more readily emulated across the European nations by virtue of those nations having supported such formulae.

No country is immune from what became legitimized by Britain against a minuscule nation called Israel. That such deeds have become ingrained in the DNA of a worldly multitude, now unable to turn it aside anymore, is its most foreboding feature for humanity. Such chaos and upheaval can be directed to no other cause than of Britain's actions against the Jews. There appears no credible or legitimate reasoning for the manipulated usurping of the historical name of Palestine other than the discovery of oil and a historical obsession to deny the state of Israel's existence. Its other dimension was not envisioned, one that was hardly about land, as has been presented.

The Default Caliphate.

It is a theological doctrine of domination, one that impacts the rights of all peoples of Arabia from having an independent state. It resulted by default as a Caliphate agenda in the Middle-East by Britain's actions and inactions, targeting the negation of Israel's right to exist, and the absence of any conditions placed on the numerous states Britain created. The world cannot challenge a Caliphate elsewhere when it supports it against Israel and other peoples in Arabia. Otherwise, why is this minuscule land of the Jews, an insignificant half of 1% of the region's landmass, be so obsessively focused upon when a host of Arabian states were newly created in the 20th century? It remains the central issue of this conflict.

Contrastingly, although Israel existed as a sovereign country 3,000 years ago and returned legally by a world majority's voting Motion, it remains the only one to be denied of her history.

It is a conflict that could have been resolved had Britain acted as an honest broker. None of the complainant parties needed a few more kilometers of land more so than the Jews; none less so than those handed numerous vast states. Its justification will become the cause of a wholly fictional one of an invented Palestinian people whose land has been illegally occupied by Israel; it will also cast a shadow on other inhabitants of this region. The scenario's underbelly is the legitimizing of a Caliphate where no other belief can prevail; not even one legally established with a track record more than 3,000 years of historical validation.

Consider the implications if the people of Japan were called as Chinese, or Russians as Germans, or Indians as Pakistanis, and that

322

such was appropriated at the UN, as is made upon the Jews. It would ensure a never ending conflict via a fully manipulated and dubious legality. The device of changing a nation's ancestral trademarks renders her as an illegitimate entity; it is the same provision that Israel has no right to exist. Such will always render Israel to be charged as illegally occupying Israel. The situation in Palestine is almost a mirror image in India, with the displacement of peoples in an exodus regarded among the greatest in modern human history and both transpiring under Britain's watch; the situation in Palestine is thus not a hypothetical one, nor when it occurs any other place.

Israel will now confront a new means of her annihilation by a multitude at the UN, an office made unanswerable to any other, armed with an overflow of members ensuring Israel will always be overcome with a surety. Israel's legalized return via the UN will be declared as an illegal occupation of a land via name usurpations and successive 2-state demands in the same landmass. A series of new charges and the over-turning of history will be implemented and legitimized as worldly law.

The impacts of a Caliphate do not appear to cease from extending globally; the Israel Experience crossed borders, impounding on shores afar by a strange force of its own. When the world's law office was fully corrupted, by satirical parody, Frank N. Stein made a U-Turn.

20. The UN Failings.

The New Killing Fields.

• "An alien observing the United Nations debates, reading its resolutions and walking its halls, could well conclude that a principal purpose of the world body is to censure a tiny country called Israel." - (UN, Israel & Anti-Semitism, UN WATCH - Monitoring the UN, Promoting Human Rights.)

The world's law office was the only hope of support against a large assembly attacking one small nation; yet it became that nation's greatest attacker. The UN's support of Arabs as Palestinians, the condoning of the name West Bank on the ancient historical towns of Israel, and its accounting of a 3-state as a 2-state in the same landmass are deceptions that should not have been supported by this office.

These are manipulations fostered by nations who have historically embraced persecutions and corruptions against Israel. These are also anti-Human Rights and racist provisions that are employed by historically racist groups. Such distortions should not be supported by a world law body enacted to promote justice, equality and cohesion for humanity. It is why the UN was established.

The UN would not be able to justify its accepted charges on Israel if held to scrutiny by another unbiased source. Apart from the opinions of an array of international law advocates presented in this book, a growing outcry has emerged that says the UN is not above the law; that its personnel, operatives and groups merit enquiry and independent supervision:

• "The UN Is Absolutely Corrupt". Claudia Rossett received acclaim for her stunning revelations in the pages of the *Wall Street Journal* about the U.N. Oil for food scandal, one of the largest financial frauds in recent history. Her revelations led to a series of Congressional Hearings about UN corruption and two awards: the 2005 Eric Breindel and the Mightier Pen awards. - (The UN Is Absolutely Corrupt; by Jerry Gordon. Feb. 2009, The New English Review.)

• "The UN's Human Rights Council condemns Israel more than the rest of the world combined. The very agenda of the Council, unchanged for each meeting, stacks the odds against Israel as it is the only country singled out for special criticism. Nestled amongst items including "Human rights bodies and mechanisms" and "Human rights situations that require the Council's attention" is agenda item 7: "Human rights situation in Palestine and other occupied Arab territories." (*by Donna Rachel Edmunds*; Breitbart, London.)

• "Corruption is at the heart of the United Nations." - (The Economist, Aug 9th 2005).

• United in hate, corruption and scandal. "The United Nations, so far, has called 10 emergency sessions eight of them against Israel. In 1967, the UN made no effort to stop a genocidal invasion of Israel by the combined forces of Egypt, Syria and Jordan. But after Israel sent these three aggressors back to think again, it had an emergency special session to criticize and condemn Israel." - United in hate, corruption and scandal. By *Bret Harte, 24/11/2014.* Australian Morning Mail.)

• "Ex-U.N. General Assembly head, five others face U.S. bribery case." - (Nat Raymond and Joseph AX; Oct 7, 2015Reuters.)

• "Whereas Arab states have traditionally used the UN forum to demonize and isolate Israel (for example, they routinely attempt to deny Israel its credentials), they now believe they enjoy 'Western' support which emboldens them." - (Morris Abram, Chairman, United Nations Watch, 1997)

• Such conclusions do not appear the result of poor knowledge of history or of international laws by the UN; they incline more as corruptions of its mandate and can be seen as violations and crimes against humanity. The UN has exploited the powers given it. Grave wrongs have been committed against Israel by the UN in accommodating falsehoods by a corrupted majority that it would be fully aware are inclined with theologically based doctrines and commercial gains, not on law or history. The UN has succumbed to 'payola' - gifts that corrupt and beget false charges made as Resolutions and international laws.

The UN has aligned itself with such miss-deeds throughout its organization with no plausible reasoning other than rendering it culpable.

This office has been numerously described as anti-Semitic in its supporting of charges by those with declared theological doctrines of annihilation and with nations that support such doctrines. The UN does not debate the charges with independent sources or examines the veracity of the charges, accommodating the accusers with executive mode privileges. The President of Human Rights Voices spokesperson enumerated the UN as an anti-Semitic body:

• "Fifty percent of the Emergency Special sessions of the General Assembly over six decades were convened to denounce Israel. No emergency special session has been called on any other state in over thirty years. That's anti-Semitism. Seventy percent of all the 2013 General Assembly Resolutions criticizing specific countries for human rights abuses were about Israel. That's anti-Semitism. The Human Rights Council has a fixed agenda with one item to condemn Israel at every session, and one item to consider the other 192 U.N. member states, if required. That's anti-Semitism." - (Panelist Anne Bayefsky, director of the Touro Institute on Human Rights]

Historical Name Corruptions. The UN failed the people that most needed its assistance. Condoning Israel as the antithesis of the name Palestinian is an un-historical anti-Israel premise. When the UN was initiated in 1942, its name coined by United States President Franklin D. Roosevelt, and replacing the League of Nations, there were no people other than the Jews called as Palestinians; has the UN lost its past archives? That such a name transfer from Jews to Arabs in the 1960's was a stratagem of heritage denial by Britain and the Arabs should have aroused the UN of its motives and intentions; it should have been questioned.

The UN should have corrected this deception, not support it. Such a name transfer emerged anew as international law by the UN's failure to correct the lethal mendacity engaged in the manipulation of Israel's historical symbol, and thereby it allowed the corruption of both law and history with a well organized propaganda machine against one nation. The UN would be well aware of the propaganda in the Arab world and of Britain; its personnel are embedded in these enclaves from where they do their reporting. Israel is thereby left with no avenue of justice to turn to. Humanity cannot function when the world body becomes steeped in corruptions.

Democracy Corruption. Substantial blame can be placed on the UN Members who have condoned an overwhelming negation of Israel's rights via illicit voting power. In the UN's assembly halls there is a large sector of nations that vote against Israel no matter what the motion. That is not a democratic process. Israel is charged of occupying its own lands by those who have usurped historical names of Israel, incurred by the illegal transfer of names and treaty corruptions. Such charges have been supported by the UN, with America often being the only nation that has periodically overcome this assembly.

Israel is an ancient nation that has made the greatest contribution to the law. Its laws of justice, equality and liberty are all enshrined in the modern world's judiciary institutions, including the law of democracy. The Hebrew laws of democracy are the oldest and most superior, extending further than 'Let the majority decide' that is open to abuse. Let none be misled by ancient appearing language; these laws are fully applicable in the modern world's judiciary, to the extent there is no democracy without these laws:

• Thou shalt not utter a false report; put not thy hand with the wicked to be an unrighteous witness (Ex.23:1).

• Thou shalt not follow a multitude to do evil; neither shalt thou bear witness in a cause to turn aside after a multitude to pervert justice. [Ex. 23:2]

• Thou shalt take no gift; for a gift blindeth them that have sight, and perverteth the words of the righteous. [Ex. 23: 8]

• To give the decision according to the majority, when there is a difference of opinion among the members of the Court as to matters of law (Ex. 23:2)

• That one who possesses evidence shall testify (Lev. 5:1).

• Not to testify falsely (Ex. 20:13)

• To examine witnesses thoroughly (Deut. 13:15)

Wherefrom did the UN countenance Arabs as native Palestinians when both past and recent history says the Jews are the only people able to demonstrate such a provision of nativity; or what accounting allows a 3-state in the same land to be presented as a 2-state; and why allow the 3,000 names of Israel's towns to be changed via Jordan's illegal annexation. What compelled the UN to alter the heritage status of one group to two years and disregard the other with a heritage status more than 3,000 years; why were Arab refugees given greater focus than Jewish refugees. These are corruptions of both law and history.

Law and justice must be seen to exhibit the essential provision of an office mandated as a worldly body; the UN must abide by laws enshrined in the judiciary. The UN has chosen to appease a corrupt multitude and mocked the essence of democracy and the source where most of the world's judiciary laws are derived from.

Nativity Corruption.

This region's history is known and set out in history books and the UN archives via its predecessor that it took over, The League of Nations. When the Jews began developing this land again, Arabs from the surrounding countries flocked here when it was a barren, isolated region; these were Arabs fleeing from Arab controlled lands seeking a better life. Instead of applying human rights ruling conditions on the Regime states to enhance the plight of the Arab people, the UN focused all of its bearing on Israel. Its reasoning appears suspicious. The UN premise of condoning a Palestinian nativity is false; it is seen

327

by the UN's requirement of newly enacted nativity definition as a contradiction of the term. Namely, it replaced the true nativity of the Jews to this land with a recent one based on new novel criteria of a two year period. The UN declared anyone staying in Palestine for two years is a native Palestinian, including their descendents. The Jews are the only people able to evidence a 3,000 year un-broken habitation in Palestine; no other people can make such a claim. History says Palestine is Judea; it was never an Arab state. This unusual process of nativity manipulation to improvise newly created refugees that apply only to Arabs of Palestine is the UN's definitive exposure of corruption.

Refugee Corruption. Who would the UN nominate the least applicable people in all recorded history as refugees? The UN is well aware these are recent immigrants since the 19th century with more options and facilities than any other; those who are intentionally barred from 22 Arab states created a hundred years ago by the British for the Arab people. The UN condoned new definitions of refugees as it did with its nativity and heritage factors, to the extent it is implausible to accept such was secured legitimately or without great corruption. The logical way was to enable the Arabs who came to Palestine to be catered to and attended by the regimes; it should not be used as a destruction of Israel. The UN disregarded the Jewish natives that were greater in number with a habitation of over 2,600 years, and fleeing from Arab controlled lands.

A 3-State Corruption. By condoning the Arabs as refugees instead of the Jewish refugees that were of greater number and with no place to go, the UN approved a covert design intended of Israel's destruction. Namely, a third state west of the river was becoming implemented in the dangerously diminished land size left for Israel, by those with no requirement of more land. There is no better evidence than the UN calling a 3-state in the same land as a 2-state, a reflection of mimicking the British-Arab line. The 2-state which created Jordan in Palestine had to be legally ratified at the UN; 80% of Palestine was removed with the proclamation:

• "It will be a historic compromise to grant two states in Palestine - one for the Jews and one for the Arabs"

Thereby, another state in Palestine cannot be accounted as a 2-state. One land cannot have more than one partition and be accounted as

328

'one' partition plan. The UN should not countenance a 3-state in Palestine presented as a 2-state.

Palestinian Name Corruption.

The transfer of the name Palestinian from Jews to Arabs becomes exposed by the absence of its most basic validation requirement. The UN and all its members cannot produce an Arab called as a native Palestinian prior to the 20th Century. One who knows tells us why:

• "The Palestinians have not lived in the country (of Palestine) for generations, but rather are immigrants who arrived relatively recently. The hurried acceptance of the Palestinian applications by the UN is a serious violation of international law. - (Courtesy of Amb. Alan Baker, Director of the Institute for Contemporary Affairs, JCPA; "Palestinian Deception and the Unwarranted Trust of the West: The Case of Palestinian Accession to International Conventions")

• "During the period of the Mandate (1917-1950 AD/CE), it was the Jewish population that was known as "*Palestinians*" - including those who served in the British Army in World War II." - (The History and Meaning of "Palestine" and "Palestinians; Tzemach Institute for Biblical Studies.

The Jewish Palestinian Brigade.

Palestinian Jews fighting for the British government.

• 'The only military unit to serve in W.W.II in the British Army - and, in fact, - in all the Allied forces - as an independent, national Jewish military formation, the Jewish Palestinian Brigade Group comprised of Jews from Eretz Yisrael (then called as Palestine) and had its own emblem. The Brigade was the final by the yishuv and the Zionist Movement to achieve recognized participation and recognition of the Jewish people in the war against Nazi Germany. In 1940, the Jews of Palestine were permitted to enlist in the Jewish companies attached to the East Kent Regiment [the "Buffs"] - (Jewish Defense Organizations, Jewish Virtual Library.)

• "The losses were staggering for the British; the war was not going well. A British brigade, unknown at the time to General Koenig, was hastily sent to hold the far end of the line near Bir-el Harmat. They were a battalion of mine layers, poorly armed and provisioned, without heavy weapons or anti-aircraft equipment but with a grim, tooth clenched determination. They were a battalion of 400 Jewish Palestinians under the command of Major Liebmann from Tel Aviv. It was May 26, 1942. The Jewish fighters dug in. Noticing the strange flag flying, the German asked who they were. To the amazement of the German officer, Major Liebmann told him they were free Palestinian Jews fighting for the British government. They would not surrender. The flag was the flag of the Jewish people." - ('WW2 History: Tobruk & the Palestinian Jewish Brigade of the British Army'; JASHP.Org)

Palestine is the name applied to Judea, which was Israel; this was not an Arab land. Rome did not go to war with the Arabs or against an Arab country. This was also not an Arab land during the previous 400 year Ottoman reign, negating any semblance of an Arab Palestinian nativity. The Jews were the Ottoman's most prominent people of Palestine, and referred to by this name.

The UN succumbed to a corrupt majority with a disregard of any due diligence to verify the British-Arab designs it accepted against Israel. Thereby, an anti-Israel usage of this name was allowed to flourish as historical and as international law.

The UN acceptance of such historical corruptions afforded Arafat a privileged accommodation to promote the Palestinian falsehoods to the world community; it did so knowing the genocide charter in the Palestinian Authority. The UN encouraged the name Palestinian, an exclusive reference to the land of the Jews for 2,000 years, to become distorted as the antithesis of Israel. The UN contradicts every nation's historical archives, including those of the Ottomans who refer

Palestine exclusively to the land of the Jews. Yusif al-Khalidi is an Arab Muslim scholar who was appointed a mayor in the Ottoman reign:

• "The idea itself is natural, fine and just. Who can challenge the rights of the Jews in Palestine? Good Lord, historically it is really your land. What a wonderful spectacle that will be when a people as resourceful as the Jews will once again be an independent nation, honored and complacent, able to make its contribution to needy humanity in the fields of morals, as in the past" - (Ottoman Reign Jerusalem Mayor and Scholar Yusif al-Khalidi; 1842-1906. Letter to Chief Rabbi of France Zadok Cahn. From "The First Aliyah" Jewish History Org; The Elder of Ziyon)

The UN silence when it should not be silent also fostered the false occupation charge displayed in protest marches and the media. The new name of 'West Bank' that became as 'Disputed Territory', will incorrectly acquire an 'Illegally Occupied Palestinian Territory' status, without its correction by the UN. As well, a new 3-state claim east of the river Palestine will be presented as a 2-state in the same landmass. Thereby, the UN sanitized and legitimized a false and dangerous agenda that de-legitimizes a 3,000 year nation that was legally established at the UN with all nations participating.

The 'West Bank' name was adopted in 1950 and later declared as Disputed and Territory of the Palestinians, a law that Israel disputes. The UN also accepted the premise of a fictional new area called 'East Jerusalem', of the 3,000 year capital of Israel, a city that no nation ever declared as their Capital. The 'West Bank' also contains Hebron, the birthplace of the Judaism and one of history's earliest recorded land transactions (Gen. 23:16); the burial grounds of six Hebrew Patriarchs and Matriarchs of Israel; the Hebrew Patriarch Jacob's wife Rachel in Bethlehem (Gen. 35:19-20); and her son Joseph's tomb in Shechem (Ex. 13:19). Heritage does not get any more convincing.

Bethlehem contains the sacred sites of both the Jews and Christians, including the birthplace of Jesus as recorded in the Gospels of Matthew and Luke. These are the 4,000 year heritage components of Israel, recorded in the archives of the Greeks and Romans, the Dead Sea Scrolls, and the American and British documents; all of these are in contradiction of the UN Resolutions against Israel. Judea, which became Palestine was the 'Land of the Jews' (Matt.2:20), not of the Arabs; it was never an Arab country.

The Heritage Corruption.

A Resolution by UNESCO, which declared the region called West Bank as 'an integral part of the occupied Palestinian territories', caused a rift at the U.N. by Israel. This land portion is the historical biblical land of the Jews, as recorded in all historical archives, including in the Dead Sea Scrolls and an estimated one million archaeological relics world-wide. Thereby it begs which planet's history the UN is referring to.

The nominating of heritage marks in Israel to a people not ancestral of this land indicates the UN corruption of the heritage premise. The UNESCO decision thereby de-legitimizes both ancient and modern history and is absent of any historical veracity. The term 'heritage' is first applicable to its well recorded original ancient history more so than a later one that was based on invasion.

Bethlehem's Church of the Nativity is at the centre of a fight between Israelis and Palestinians. UNESCO recently declared the church an endangered World Heritage Site in Palestine. Israelis and evangelical Christians are upset by UNESCO's decision, saying the move isn't about protecting the landmark but about de-legitimizing Israel. The Church of Nativity is of Judea, 'Land of the Jews' prior to its name becoming as Palestine. Judea was not an Arab land.

• "The Palestinians have a built-in U.N. majority which I call as "The Flat Earth Society". If they proposed the Earth was flat, most nations would vote for it. They're anti-Israel and a lot of U.N. forums, they're able to pass all sorts of resolutions that de-legitimize Israel and by-pass the peace talks." - (David Parsons, International Christian Embassy, CBN)

One of the world's leading human rights advocate, Anne Bayefsky, further accused the United Nations and its member nations of anti-Semitism, a charge that is un-fitting a world body because the same can be leveled of others. It is difficult to deny this charge based on the UN history toward Israel:

• "Inciting murderous intolerance towards the Jewish people" during an unprecedented speech at the international headquarters in New York City. - (Scholar to UN: You Are 'the Leading Global Purveyor of Anti-Semitism'; the Washington Free Beacon)

Right of Return Corruption.

332

The UN condoned a refugee deception that produced the premise of millions of Arabs as Palestinians and as natives of this land via a corrupted two year definition of the term; it used name transfers and false resolutions of occupation inversed on the land's true natives. The UN thereby aligned itself with the genocide goals seen in Arab charters and in protests across the nations. In effect, the UN is rendering Israel's right to exist as potentially negated by virtue it is illegally occupying Palestinian land. The Jews were not accorded a Right of Return to all the Arab ruled lands they inhabited for thousands of years, nor accounted the losses suffered by them; thereby the UN inclines with inequality and promotes anti-Semitism.

When the historical census is examined, it says only the Jews can evidence a nativity that reaches back to their 3,000 year ancestral homeland, and that the name Palestinian has no connection with the Arab peoples or any state they ever possessed; even more significantly, it says the Arabs were not connected to this land as natives and that such manipulations are based on theological premises.

That the Jews have a unique un-broken continuous habitation in Palestine is evidenced by the Roman archives, the Crusaders, the 7th Century Islamic invasion and leading up to the last Ottoman reign; none of them mention Arabs connected with Palestine. This land's ownership was affirmed by the Dead Sea Scrolls discovery; it should be seen as transcending any UN Resolution corruptions of law and history.

The UN Accountability.

Humanity faces a chaotic future when its central law body becomes a centre for miss-information and corruption. Those UN members that have an entrenched history of corruption would not want any changes in the world body. They would like to continue filler-busting and voting their own UN presidents and dictate their Resolutions and International Laws to their chosen president. Thereby is a 3-state accounted as a 2-state in Palestine, and a two year nativity devised especially for the Arabs, and the land's ancestral people, the Jews, made as their own land's occupiers.

The UN changed the Arab-Israeli conflict into a Palestinian-Israeli to promote a false premise Israel is illegally occupying Palestine, and Arabs, not the Jews, have a historical connection with this land.

Considering the global impacts of its decisions, the UN should not be made as above the law by virtue of its members alone - such a premise is open to abuse and corruption. Both the UN and its members' positions should be subject to an independent, rotating council of historians and legal entities with equal power in monitoring any corruptions, as is seen with a Congress and an Executive ruling appointment. Thereby, the UN becomes a processor, not the sole judgment of laws that reflects a corrupted assembly. An arm's length council that oversees illicit demands and historically evidenced deceptions is a vital implement for humanity, as is seen in the faculties of medicine and all other vital institutions of humanity.

A closed door court ruled by an aligned majority that votes one way no matter what the motion, one that seeks to overwhelm and deny another nation's right to exist, is both legally and morally antithetical of a law office. The charters of genocide in many Arab groups are fully known to the UN body, with no negative Resolutions ever issued against them. The members and the personnel of the UN should be made accountable and subject to a legitimate set of governing guidelines via an independent, arms length and rotating overseer.

The UN has abused its powers and overwhelmed the only democratic state in the region with more negative Resolutions than all other countries. These were the result of serial historical corruptions implemented on Israel and highlighted by the usurping of the name Palestinian and the condoning of successive 2-state demands as international law, a term endlessly chanted against Israel. Thereby, Israel has no avenue of obtaining justice, a situation which can also impact other nations by its precedence factors.

According to prominent Arabian figureheads with first-hand experience in this region, the UN premise of Arab refugees appears both deceptive and selective of one only state:

• "A Humanitarian agenda has been transformed to a Political agenda with the collaboration of the UN. Over 5 Million Muslims were expelled from Europe in 19-20th century; 50 Million transferred from India; 1.1 Million Kurds displaced by the Ottomans; 2.2 Million Christians displaced from Iraq; 800,000 Jews from Arab states." - (Derek Deek, Israel's VP to Norway and Druze Poet from Jaffa; House of Literature Speech, 2114).

• 21. Global Impacts.

Causes and Effects.

It is difficult to consider another term than 'deceptions' as the causes and effects applying in this conflict. Thereby, attending the causes remains the only path of correcting its effects. Such a definition becomes credible by the existential demands placed singularly on one country and the process modes adopted. There is little credibility when so much is focused on the smallest nation by the largest ones, for the most minuscule patch of land by those holding too much. Clearly, these are racist theological premises that seek to transcend historical provisions.

The only facility that Israel does not possess and the only one demanded of her - land - becomes highly questionable by those that least require additional land; nor will such demands being fulfilled resolve or stem such requirements. These have become manifest in the modern world as global theological premises.

Changing historical names extended the issue into widespread and unanticipated proportions; ominous equations of Eurabia and Londonistan emerged. No-Go Zones became new buzz terms. Further, an improvised and un-historical land charge has been made as a global issue that transcends all else - as a means of extending an underlying agenda that is fully un-aligned with land or the minuscule state of Israel. Israel, Palestine and Palestinians are not aligned with the cause of millions of Arab refugees driven from the Middle East and made as enclaves across Europe. These are intended deceptions and the UN has not assisted in denouncing such schemes, rather it has been its foremost promoter.

Arabs are not Palestinians. The UN should have been the primal source that ought to have negated this great deception along with its underlying agenda. Palestine is the 2,000 year emblem of another nation usurped in the 20th Century. The notion that because Arabs live in Palestine alongside the Jews, they are naturally Palestinians is not correct. It is a ploy used to align with the negation of Israel. There is no Palestine anymore; the land is made of Israel and Jordan, and the term Palestinian belongs to Israel.

The term Palestine has no alignment with Arabs; indeed it is the antithesis of the Arabs who were in the Roman legions destroying

335

Jerusalem. This name was applied to Judea, not an Arab land; the Arabs usurped this name recently to continue a global agenda. Thereby, all sectors that support this deception must consider why such a deceptive path was undertaken and why the UN failed to act as a legitimate source of the law. Here there is an immense reeking of corruption, one that accounts for the greatest deception facing the modern world.

Arabs presented as Palestinians is a manipulated falsehood promoted as a historical truth; it is a corruption of historical veracity and a covert genocide premise underlying a Caliphate doctrine. The chaos of this name's corruption has extended globally, and has become an enormous difficulty to correct; however the effects of a Caliphate is not limited to Israel, nor can it be eliminated without attending its causes. Its effects can cross borders. They have.

• "Words are powerful. Every single person who uses the terminology as defined by the Arabs who wish to establish the State of Palestine is complicit. You are literally, wiping Israel off the map. It's really not that complicated. Palestine was always Israel. Palestinians were Jews. For the love of Zion, my grandmother was a Palestinian. I have the documents to prove it." ("My grandmother the Palestinian"; by Forest Rain. WP)

The same applies to the name West Bank that was changed by Jordan and hailed by Britain in 1950 to hide this region's 3,000 year Hebrew names. It is the most sacred holy sites of the Jews, with almost no holy sites existing in Israel outside these borders; and such is fully known by Britain, the UN and the Arabs. What legacy will accompany those who perpetrated such infamy is not a subjective issue but an easily verifiable one on today's information highway.

Causes.

That four out of five Christian countries hold veto powers at the UN Security Council, incurs a presumed responsibility and moral obligation. Had the Christian countries rejected such a flaunting of a historical name transfer from Jews to Arabs, as they all should have even if to preserve Christianity's own history, such an identity theft would have been squashed at the UN. However this never happened and none came to the rescue of the Jews or of history per se.

A Roman Pope responsible to one billion Catholics and embracing such an astonishing historical falsehood will leave a poor legacy on the Christian community. Today, a growing population of Christians rejects such an employ, even embarrassed of it by the actions of their representatives; numerous Christian theologians, historians, international lawyers and a prominent US Presidential candidate has denounced it. The Roman Emperor Hadrian who applied this name on Judea can be said to be spinning in his tomb as an appropriate metaphoric consideration.

The UN's attempts of flaunting and changing history cannot be limited to one people or one region; it has global trajectories and impacts and such an effect has already begun. The world's borders are falling away. Causes and effects apply. If the truth will set us free - a falsehood will do the reverse.

22. Israel's Failings.

An Identity Theft.

The calling of Arabs as Palestinians should have been responded to by Israel in the most determined stand of rejection it could muster. It should have been assessed as a heritage destroying weapon equivalent to all the attacks of wars Israel sustained; its consequences are equally, if not far more grave, for Israel's future. It was a Roman mode attack that was inflicted on the homeland of the Jews and its devastating impacts lasted 2,000 years and lingers. Britain and Arafat resurrected it again in the 20th century. Israel ought to have responded as though it was an existential attack and not accepted it.

Equally, Israel should have likewise rejected the name 'West Bank' upon the ancient heart-line of the 3,000 year Hebrew towns and cities, as well as the accounting of a 3-state as a 2-state. Most certainly, the Christian community should have responded likewise and corrected the deceptions enacted by Britain and Jordan. More correctly, the world should have resisted such a foreboding enterprise. Here, the failings of Israel also mark the failings of those who could but did not perform what they should have. It is also a record what Israel was subjected to by those handed power and facility.

Overwhelming Israel.

~~Yet Israel's deficiency here must be qualified to align with the~~ overwhelming reality of the forces she confronted. The Jews were totally helpless and fully depended on the goodwill by the Christian and Arab community to negate such measures. It never happened. This grave inculcated attack via the power of a name's abuse on Israel continues today, its extending trajectories impacting both Christians and the Arabs; their true biblical history has been compromised by subsequence.

It is fully appropriate to highlight the lack of voice of the Vatican and other Christian groups of condoning Palestinians as the antithesis of Judea - the Land of the Jews. It contradicts the Gospels, the Roman archives, the Quran and of history. Its grave impacts are not excusable as cultural or politically correct realities; it is poor baggage placed on otherwise God fearing people who abide by the sacred premise of the truth, for the truth cannot set us free when it is abandoned in its most required testing.

Today, a large and growing number of Christians and Muslims are not in concert with their representatives in this conflict's manifestations. The retention of any rights for both Jews and Christians, and their sacred structures in Israel still standing and protected, cannot be attributed to the merits of any other party than of Israel today, safeguarded under the most difficult conditions.

The Historical syndrome to erase Israel from history is an old one. While it is seen as a religious war, it is also a politicized one of animosity occurring prior to today's religions that harbor such doctrines. The syndrome pre-dates both the Christian and Islamic religions, as recorded in the Flavius Josephus writings of the First Century; as well as in the Hebrew Book of Nehemiah dated as 450 BCE which describes such animosity and land usurping. It later entered into religious theologies, affirming the premise of the Palestinian premise, both historically and theologically, as the greatest deception of the modern world. Nor can its repercussions outside of Israel be stemmed or denied.

How the most minuscule nation of some seven million become the greatest threat to 3.7 Billion Christians and Arabs holding more than 60% of the earth's landmass - and what does this have to do with a name usurping - is not an inconsequential issue. It hovers large and its true impacts have not yet materialized. It is more than a limited, domestic historical abrasion.

• "… The conflict with the Zionist enemy has never been a border issue, nor an interstate conflict, but rather a total confrontation concerning the survival of our [Arab] nationalism against threats posed by the Israeli entity." - (Syrian columnist Khayri Hama, Syrian daily Al-Ba'th, July 26, 1994)

Lest we forget, Israel's borders were originally marked by the Balfour lines. However Britain's actions are understood, the numerous corruptions of her own pledges, the issuing of her White Paper Policy and the condoning of the term 'West Bank' and 'Palestinian' away from the Jews and Israel, impacted not just Israel but many peoples of Arabia and history per se. Britain lost the prefix of 'Great' the day she corrupted the Balfour; it was perpetrated for 30 barrels of oil and age-old anti-Semitism.

The larger hovering issue of consideration is its alignment with a Caliphate, one incurred by the British actions, whether intentionally or otherwise; such a consideration also answers the only antidote possible, namely, what results when these name usurpations are negated and can a Caliphate be viable without it. These are not Israel's errors; however they do concern Israel's very existence, and by extension any other people, the modern world's manifest conditions of the inhabitants of the Middle East region. If the Arabs as Palestinians never existed and is a hoax, why was this name adopted?

• "The Palestinian people do not exist. Only for political and tactical reasons do we speak about the existence of a distinct Palestinian people". - Zahir Muhsein, leader of the Al-Saiqa Organization, interview in the Dutch Newspaper "Trouw".

• "The British did not fulfill the promise of the Balfour Declaration to create a Jewish homeland. Instead, to reward the Hashemite family for its assistance during the war, Winston Churchill severed Eastern Palestine from its western part to establish the Emirate of Transjordan (later the Hashemite Kingdom of Jordan) and install one of the Saudi family's leaders, Abdullah, as its ruler" - (Raphael Israeli; 'Impacts of Palestinian Nationalism on Israel, Jewish Virtual Library)

The Default Factor.

By default, the terms West Bank and Palestinians are a greater attack upon Christians and Muslims than for Jews; such is true by population substance and the true heritage foundations of both becoming diminished. While the Jews have somehow survived numerous exiles out of Israel, it is doubtful that Christianity can survive a Jesus of a Palestinian West Bank, previously a Jesus of Nazareth. Equally, just as Christians contradict their Gospel with West Bank, the Muslims are also in contradiction of their own Quranic Scriptures when Israel is presented as an Islamic land of Arab Palestinians. Here, both the Gospels and the Quran are being denied. These are not errors of Israel. As well, the modern world treaties of the 20th Century that were sworn before the world have been flaunted.

Were the Jews wrong to trust the word of Britain and the Arabs who executed agreements; or were the Jews wrong for depending on Christians and Muslims? Today, both these sectors know the deception they harbor and their mutually contradicting paradigms that have no bearing on Israel; they must laugh at each other when one leaves the room, a paradigm that is not reassuring for the future.

Aside from the historical and judiciary factors, the theological basis is likewise compromised. Belief incurs tests to determine how one turns; such is seen with humanity's first recorded human parentage, down to Abraham, Moses, Job and thereby true for the revered figures of all religions. Here, by the very factors underlying such beliefs, the Decalogue correctly lists honesty, the 3rd Commandment, as transcending and precedent of all laws and beliefs. For there can be no belief without the prerequisite of honesty applying.

The act of indulging in an oath in vain, namely the flaunting of a solemn contract, with no fear of God or of the judiciary laws of humanity, has not become obsolete or to be held as too naïve to matter anymore. It is not a small matter; honesty was forsaken concerning Israel when the nations given power were tested. Honesty is especially relevant in vows and agreements declared before the world and made in vain:

• "Thou shall not take the name of the LORD thy God in vain; for the Lord will not hold him guiltless that taketh His name in vain" - [Ex. 20:6].

• "Thou shall not bear false witness" [Ex. 20:16].

• "Thou shall not steal" [Ex. 20:15].

• "Thou shall not covet" [Ex. 20:17].

The vast assembly of historians and theologians, including a host of Islamic scholars, substantially accept the historical factors presented in this appraisal. A recap:

• That Palestine is the name applied by Rome upon Judea, the land of the Jews, 2,000 years ago in the year 135 AD/CE by the Roman Emperor Hadrian.

• That the land was also previously called as Israel and was the sovereign homeland of the Jews. (Flavius Josephus; Matt. 2:20; The Dead Sea Scrolls)

• That Palestine was Judea, the Roman name for 'Land of the Jews' - and has thus far been validated by some one million archaeological relics and archives world-wide. [37]

• That it is not debatable the Britons and the Pre-Islamic Arabs were both embedded in the Roman Legions as mercenaries during both the destruction of the Jerusalem Temple and the name anointing of this land by Rome, affirming its denial as a deception of their histories. [38]

• That a mosque, with its rich ornamentation the work of Syrian Christian artists in the 7th Century, and its dome gold plating in the 20th Century, was erected on the destroyed Jerusalem Temple site when the Jews were displaced from their homeland by Rome; it is cited by prominent Islamic Historians. [39]

• That two of the largest theological groups who hold possession of most of the earth's landmass are engaged in the fostering of falsehoods over a minuscule land held by Israel, its rightful owners and inhabitants. [40]

• That accepting deceptions in one location will impact other locations by subsequence.

• That ultimately, those who rely on a lie cannot be seen as holding a Godly belief.

Corrupting Holy Scriptures.

The Gospel cannot be changed by the name West Bank, and the Quran cannot be changed by denying Jerusalem as a holy city of the Jews. Thereby the default factor can impact Christianity and Islam more so than Jews, with the flaunting of historical truth impacting their scriptural and historical protocols.

Corrupting Historical Records.

Israel was not returned to Palestine illegally, as is falsely charged, and not so by war, but via the world's nations voting in the UN Motion, including by all Christian and Islamic states. Israel was returned when it was least possible, when the Jews were fully helpless confronting both a holocaust in Europe and a declared genocide in Arabia; when the Jews were both barred from leaving WW2 Europe and from returning to their own land as promised in the Balfour Mandate.

Zionism was not its cause or the detested premise it is portrayed as today; prominent delegations Muslim Rulers headed by the Emir Faisal welcomed Zionism and Israel's return to her historical homeland in Paris when the Balfour Mandate was issued in 1917. The Ottoman Empire fully declared Palestine as the land of the Jews; so did the British, American and French powers.

Corrupting Palestinians.

It is historically validated there was no Arab people known as Palestinians for 2,000 years or in the early 20th Century; that Palestine was at all times referred exclusively to the Jews till the Mid-20th Century by Britain; that there was no Palestinian state before Israel's return to Palestine; that the Ottomans who invaded this land were not Arab and fully acknowledged Palestine belongs to the Jews; that Palestine was inhabited by a host of peoples other than Arabs. That the nativity and refugee factors were manipulated as was the name Palestinian, because the Jews are the only people who can validate their habitation in Palestine continuously for 3,000 years; 3,000 years of population survey charts say so. The corruption of history was overturned by a thread of deceptions that targeted one nation.

• There was never an Arab Palestinian prior to the 20th Century, nor can a historical alignment become credible in such a small period of less than 30 years before this name was usurped.

• "Most of the Arabs living in the land had migrated there only in the previous thirty years attracted by the jobs created by the Jews who were building and farming. - ('*From Time Immemorial*' by Joan Peters, p. 244)

• "The characterization of Palestinian nationalism as 'artificial' does not come from Zionist adversaries but from classic Arab sources. In the period before and after the issuance of the Balfour Declaration Arab nationalists consistently protested the use of the name 'Palestine' or the adjective 'Palestinian.'" - (Late author and scholar Marie Syrkin , 1970's essay)

The occupation deception is directly aligned with the 'Palestinian name deception' and what it signifies; it is a Caliphate doctrine. Israel should have, but could not, stem the inculcated worldly multitude she confronted in the aftermath of W.W.2. Others could, but it never happened.

23. Modern Israel.

Inventing East Jerusalem.

There was never a place called 'East' Jerusalem. Like West Bank and Palestinian, East Jerusalem is a newly invented term in contradiction of history and all the previously made declarations by Britain. When Britain became the first nation, along with Pakistan, to recognize Jordan's changing of Israel's Hebrew town names to West Bank, it says an East Jerusalem never existed previously. It is an existential attack no nation can survive. Jerusalem is a wholly Jewish creation, established prior to any historical imprints of the Arab peoples existing ('Who Are Arabs?')

• "You ought to let the Jews have Jerusalem; it was they who made it famous" - (Winston Churchill to Diplomat Evelyn Shuckburgh, Descent to Suez, Diaries 1951-56)

Britain altogether failed to act as a responsible controller of this region. The fostering of Jerusalem being split asunder marks a biblical and historical calamity. Jordan illegally occupied East Jerusalem which is located west of the River, thereby occupying portions of lands allocated to the Jews and changing its 3,000 year Hebrew names illegally. Jordan thus deceptively changed the name of this portion of land to 'West Bank' in 1951 as a means of negating Israel's existence. Thereby, Britain's condoning is an attempt to cover her inaction of the illegal annexation west of the river under her watch. When the Britons and Arabs were in Rome's legions there was only one Jerusalem that was destroyed. The modern State of Israel is not based on an illegal annexation or as an occupier of another peoples' lands, because Israel was legally re-established to her historical homeland (the texts).

• "We regard it our duty to declare that Jerusalem is an organic and inseparable part of the State of Israel and an inseparable part of the history of Israel and of the faith of Israel" - Ben Gurion, Israeli Prime Minister Knesset speech, Dec 1949.

Unlike nations that conquer new lands by force and massacre, Israel was returned via a treaty enacted with the League of Nations (the previous name of the UN), with the entire world of nations voting in the Motion. In 1948, there was no Palestinian state other than the Palestine region cited in the Balfour Mandate, nor was the Arabs called as Palestinians at this time; there was also no such entities as West Bank and East Jerusalem, newly invented terms following Jordan's illegal annexation that Britain failed to correct. The Arabs in the region were not natives of this land, as is validated by history, for Rome did not destroy an Arab city but a Jewish one called as Judea. In the Mid-20th Century, even after Modern Israel was established, the name Palestine remained one referring exclusively aligned to the Land of Israel in 1951; it is evidenced with historical icons of the 20th century, illustrating no other people than the Jews were previously called by this name, exposing Jordan's miss-appropriations even after it was handed some 80% of Palestine.

Jewish Palestine Symbols.

The Jerusalem Post, Israeli Newspaper, was called as The Palestinian Post in 1951.

Hebrew Currency produced by the Anglo Palestine Company, owned by the Jewish Agency. [E.Y. refers to Eretz Yisrael/Land of Israel]

In the 20th Century the name Palestine was a Jewish Israeli symbol in a host of her state's icons:

• The Jerusalem Post newspaper was called "The Palestine Post" and issued in both Hebrew and English in 1951.

• Today's Israel Philharmonic Orchestra, founded in 1936 by German Jewish refugees who fled Nazi Germany, was called the "Palestine Symphony Orchestra," composed of 70 Palestinian Jews.

• Bank Leumi L'Israel was called the "Anglo-Palestine Bank," a Jewish Company.

• The Jewish Agency was called the "Jewish Agency for Palestine."

• The United Jewish Appeal (UJA) was established in 1939 as a merger of the "United Palestine Appeal" and the fundraising arm of the Joint Distribution Committee.

• A Princeton University professor of Semitic literature Philip Hitti (1886-1978), one of the greatest Arabic historians of the ninth century and author of 'The History of the Arabs,' testifying on behalf of the Arab cause, told the Anglo-American Committee of Inquiry on Palestine in 1946:

• "There is no 'Palestine' in history." - ('The Artificiality of the Historical Palestinian Identity'; Eli E. Hertz, Myths and Facts Org.)

A host of distortions and deceptions occurred to overturn Israel's history in the 20th Century by condoning, fostering and legitimizing a new un-historical one. These distortions were promoted as international law by corruptions of greed and monetary gifts to achieve theological doctrines. The acceptance of the name transfer of

Palestine away from the Jews has seeped into our civilization's psyche so we cannot anymore separate its inculcation from its historical veracity; the deceiver and the deceived have become inseparable from the deception anymore. Yet it is false in all its thresholds, as illustrated throughout this presentation.

Now the only remaining factor is to examine the origins of those claiming to be Palestinians. Namely, the history of Arab Palestinians claiming to be from and of Palestine, from time immemorial, with a 7,000 year history as proclaimed by the President of the Palestinian Authority. Such proclamations are best defined by examining the history of the Arab people themselves. Namely, what is the history of the people called as Arabs, and when and wherefrom did they emerge; do some Arabian groups predate Arabs, and were there any Arabs in the time of the Philistines some 4,000 years ago?

These are the fundamental, legitimate and incumbent questions that should be examined in like mode as is done of all groups from the ancient periods, such as the Chinese, Indians, Africans, native aboriginals and the Jews. Are there any imprints of the Arab people connected with Ishmael and Abraham?

24. A 4,000 YEAR ENQUIREY.

All Arabians are not Arab.

Arabia is a region, as with South America; it is the name the Greeks applied to Cush, the previous name of this region. The term Arab is varied from 'Arabian', namely, one can be from Arabia but not be Arab. It is analogous to Spain being European but not all Europeans being Spanish. Although the Arab people are a conglomeration of many ancient mixed groups of Arabia, its component groups possessed different traits and languages and predate the Arabs. The Hebrew Bible is the only source we have that gives a genealogy account of these ancient groups and their names and origins; it also mentions Arabs and Philistines numerously; and the first origins of nations such as France and Spain by their former Hebrew names. Cush is the grandson of Noah via his son Ham:

• And the sons of Ham are Cush, and Mizraim, and Put, and Canaan. (Gen. 10:6)

It says the groups that evolved from the sons of Cush predate Abraham and Ishmael; thereby also the Hebrews who emerged via a later generation of Noah named as Shem; as well as the Arabs; even the origins of the ancient Egyptians who are derivative of Ham.

There is no proof of the figures of Abraham, Ishmael and Moses; however the factor of a historical written record is a highly impacting provision and equally not disprovable; it is the basis of this examination. Thereby it can be said, even though there is no proof of Noah, it is the only record we have of such genealogies, listed in a scientifically appearing protocol, and with no record of opposition.

The Noah genealogy's records say that numerous groups emerged in the region from this point and constitute the mixed groups in the land of Cush. We have scant, isolated or insubstantial historical evidences of recorded human history or recorded speech dialogue prior to the Genesis Hebrew dating namely of some 5776 years or under 6,000 years; this is varied from a pre-speech endowed humanity.

The groups that are prior to the name of Cush being changed to Arabia is our starting point. Subsequently, groups like the Egyptians,

347

Babylonians, Hittites, Moabites, Medianites, Phoenicians and the Hebrews predate Arabia and the Arabs - based substantially on these names recorded as older than 3,000 years and prior to the names Arabia and Arab emerging. The name Shem appears soon thereafter in this period:

• And the sons of Cush: Seba, and Havilah, and Sabtah, and Raamah, and Sabteca; and the sons of Raamah: Sheba, and Dedan. (Gen. 10:7)

The same source also says, earlier, that Ham and Shem were brothers, sons of Noah:

• Now these are the generations of the sons of Noah: Shem, Ham, and Japheth; and unto them were sons born after the flood. (10:1)

The Canaanite groups also predated the Hebrews that evolved from Shem:

• "and the Jebusite, and the Amorite, and the Girgashite" (Gen. 10:16)

These are given as the first recorded speech endowed groups. Almost all of them have disappeared, along with all trace of their original identities of language, writings, belief structures and other traits. However, not all these groups were Arabs from Cush; they veered and became varied with different traits, colors and languages. Most of these groups became Arabized when Islam emerged and the Arabic language was mandated throughout the region; they subsequently lost their original individual traits. The Canaanites, Egyptians [Copts], Phoenicians (Lebanese) and Hebrews were not Arab; the Egyptians became Arabized in the 7th Century when conquered by Islam.

Arabization in the modern world view evolved when the Greeks coined the term Arabia, and later when Islam in the 7th Century made Arabic the conquered regions' mandated language. The Jews, although some had to convert and did when they became dispersed via exiles, substantially did not convert and retained their ancient traits as a variant group since their original emergence. They are defined as a stiff-neck people in the Hebrew Bible and thus also an important source of reference of the ancient realm of this region.

Thereby, who are the pre-Islamic Arabs, when and how did they emerge as an identifiable group, and what attributes apply; is the quest of this enquiry. It will begin with the tracing of a name, focused on the historical term 'Arab'—but not limited to this name, and thereby trace wherefrom it emerged.

The Chinese, Indians and the Greeks belong to the same human species, yet these are distinctly separate ethnic groupings. The same context of such a demarcation applies with the Arab and Hebrew groups in this inquiry; namely, the quest of an identifiable group rather than a generic people which we all equally subscribe to.

The historical imprints portray today's Islamized Arabs as a relatively new group despite the name alignment with Arabia; such is based primarily on the historical records of names. The Hebrew is also a relatively new group when compared with the ancient Egyptians and Canaanites that preceded them. Abraham appeared some 1,200 years after the first pyramid emerged; the Indians supplied the red ochre for its ancient colored engravings which have since faded; the circumcision ritual predated Abraham.

The ancient groups do not render the new Arab assembly as equally ancient; such is in like measure as today's Jews do not display the ancient Egyptian and Canaanite traits that have dissolved away. Yet, the Arabs display very ancient traits, if not by their writings than their oral language. This may be due to a more isolated history whereby they were never exiled from Arabia as were the Jews, or that they accumulated traits from older groups that became Arabized. There are no ancient writings that mention Arabs by name, because this name is a recent application. Other imprints than the term Arab must be examined.

Egypt was not Arab.

The Arab people first invaded Egypt shortly after the religion of Islam emerged in the 7th Century, when most of the region of Arabia became conquered and made substantially Islamic. Egypt was not an Arab nation prior to the 7th Century and had different languages and traits. [41] Canaan, which was controlled by Egypt as a vassal state prior to the Hebrew rule, was also not of an Arab people. [42]

The Hebrew who had extensive interactions with ancient Egypt, via Abraham, Joseph, Jacob and Moses, give no accounting of Arab interactions. While Egypt's ancient relics dating 3,400 years ago mention the names Hebrews and Israel, no mention of Arabs appear; as well there are no explicit graphic items that align with a group as in parallel with the Hebrews. Here then is a variance, that the Hebrew group has survived, along with their belief, language and ancient writings; and that their historical imprints are ancient, explicit and substantial. This is not the case of the people called as Arabs; no imprints are available by the Arab name, a nation, city, king or a war 3,000 years ago. It is an anomaly for an ancient group of the region. Again, other imprints than the term Arab must be examined.

A Historical Conundrum.

A major issue is that while today's Arabs claim an ancient connection with Abraham, including a genealogical one, and an interaction with the ancient Canaanites and Philistines, there is a lacking of its validating by any historical imprints. The Canaanites, including the Jebusites and the original foreign Philistines who were foreign invaders in this region, all converted to the Hebrew belief under King David's reign some 200 years prior to the Assyrian invasion of the 8th Century that felled the northern state of Israel. All of the inhabitants were exiled by the Assyrians and are now deemed untraceable; thus the 'Lost Tribes of Israel' includes the remaining Canaanites and Philistines as Hebrew converts. Now, only the southern state of Judea remained.

Judea Becomes Palestine.

Ten centuries later, the Romans who destroyed Jerusalem in a war changed the name of Judea to Palestine. This says that today's Jews, having stemmed and formed as a Hebrew group in Canaan, are the only historical Canaanite residues. Two thousand years later, Palestine again became as the Modern State of Israel in 1948. It is the basis of the Arab-Israel conflict, and its premise based on today's Arabs accounted as stemming from an Abrahamic and Ishmaelite genealogy. It is a large conundrum; both premises are not equally validated by the historical accounting.

The historical imprints say the ancient Ishmaelite group has dissolved away with no residual traces anymore, even though both the Arabs and Hebrews claim to have lived together at one time in Canaan. Were the Arabs in ancient Canaan, and did they interact with the original Philistines, a name appearing in some 250 occasions in the Hebrew Bible? There is untapped cadence here that merits its historical exploring; it is also a controversial and emotive history and will thus be focused on the historical imprints. A foremost factor here is, because the ancient groups became Islamasized as Arabs in the 7th Century AD/CE, only the previous component groups can be potentially connected with Ishmael.

Ishmael's Imprints.

There are no recorded interactions of the Hebrews with Arabs in Abraham's time; yet there are between the Hebrews and Ishmael; the Ishmaelite thread were offspring of a Hebrew father Abraham and an Egyptian mother Hagar. Aside from the belief structure of Islam that emerged in the 7th Century, there are no historical records of any alignments with Hagar and Abraham with Arabs.

While there is no historical proof of Abraham, yet there are a number of circumstantial imprints, including the ancient Hebrew language and writings that no other people used, and a vast array of narratives that appear credible and authentic of their period. The written records and their archaeological validation are the basis of this historical conundrum of unequal records in two different claims of lineage.

First Arab Name.

The term 'Arab' is introduced in the Hebrew Bible in the Book of Nehemiah, dated as 450 BCE. There is no previous record of this name as a group of Arab people, ethnic race, belief structure, language or cities prior to this entry, nor any record of prior interactions of the Hebrews with the Arabs. There is a claim of a 8th century name of similar but not the same name that is subject to disputation and dealt separately; however this does not alter the basic premise no record of Arab exists even in King Solomon's time, which is prior to the 8th Century. That the Arab assembly has never been displaced from Arabia says they should have a more evidenced historical record than the Jews, yet this is not the case. It is one of many anomalies.

The issue of ancient imprints becomes more controversial when the people called as Arabs are connected with Abraham and Ishmael, two names that were introduced in the Hebrew writings and is also claimed as related with the pre-Islamic Arab peoples. A comparative historical analysis is thereby essential in tracing such a linkage.

Canaan is the land which became Israel, then renamed as Judea (from Judah), then as Palestine by the Romans in 135 CE. Thereafter, for

2,000 years, Palestine was the name referred to the Jews; yet it became the name used by an Arab group for the first time in the 20th Century. It asks whether there are any historically verifiable connections of Arabs with the ancient Philistines, Canaanites or Egyptians; and how extensive is the Arab connection with Palestine compared with the Jews. While the allocation of Arab Palestinians have become an inference that the Arabs are the ancient people of Canaan from time immemorial, what does history say of such a held premise becomes incumbent.

3,400 Year Hebrews.

Unlike the names 'Hebrew' and 'Israel' that appear in the ancient Egyptian Amarna Letters and the Merneptah Israel Stele, set in the reign of the ancient Egyptian King Merneptah (1213 to 1203 BC) and dated as 3,400 and 3,200 years respectively, there is no record of an Arab people as an identifiable group in this period, or when the original Philistines invaded this region some 4,000 years ago, or when Abraham appeared in Babylon (Ur), Canaan and Egypt. Aside from the absence of a name there are no imprints of a group of people mentioned in any Egyptian relics that can relate to a group displaying a pre-Arab connection with Abraham or the Hebrews; an anomaly considering a claim of older heritage than the Hebrews. Did the Arabs subsist by another name?

Arab is a term that emerged much later by the Greeks, thereby other historical alternatives must also be traced to determine the origins that evolved as an Arab people. A safe tracing backward can begin prior to the Roman era of the 20th Century when Arabs are positively mentioned at this time; they were embedded in the Roman legions in the Roman war with the Jews that destroyed Jerusalem in 70 AD/CE.

Judea Became Palestine.

The historical factors can positively affirm that Rome did not apply the name Palestine, a term anglicized from Philistine, to the Arabs in 135 CE. It is an event six centuries before Islam emerged and a positive factor of the Romans and Greeks directing this name at the Jews' ancient enemies, thus evidencing an ancient interaction of the Jews with the Philistines as held 2,000 years ago. Additionally, unlike the Hebrew writings and relics depicting Hebrew inscriptions 3,000

352

years old from Canaan, we have no such recorded writings of an ancient people from any source prior to the Book of Nehemiah dated as 450 BCE, that connects any group with Abraham or the Hebrew belief. These are negative factors of Arabs being present in ancient Canaan.

The Arab name is also referred to similar sounding names as possible alignments, namely one from the 8th Century BCE. Thereby, the issue of other forms of evidences via different but similar sounding names than Arab should also be traced, because the term Arab is relatively not old. The Arab group is logically older than the name coined by the Greeks in 300 BCE; the issue is how much older. All forms of imprints must be considered, including different names, archaeological relics and the archives of other ancient nations that possessed writings.

The term Palestine, Palestinians or Arabs do not feature as ruling figures of Judea prior to Rome changing its name to Palestine. There was no official Arab Palestine state at any time. The Babylonians who invaded Israel in the 6th Century BCE, one of the oldest recorded nations, do not align with Arabs at this time. Here, the Book of Esther records the chief antagonist of the Jews was a figure called as Haman, from the Amelekite dynasty and not an Arab; this people stemmed from one of Esau's seed which has long ago vanished from history.

Islam invaded Palestine which was called as Judea in the 7th Century. The new Islamic peoples of the Middle East called as Arabs were thus not of Judea or Palestine prior to the 7th Century; the Christians ruled Palestine after the Romans. Prior to Islam's invasion, there is no record of any Arabs governing this land; both the Gospel and Quran writings also subscribe to Israel and Jerusalem as the 'land of the Jews', as do the Roman, Greek and Persian archives. Thereby, the tracing of an ancient Arab peoples' origin prior to the 7th Century must shift to other regions of Arabia than Judea and Palestine, and back to Canaan to the time of Abraham and Ishmael via alternative pathways.

Canaan Became Israel.

The land once called as Canaan is recorded as a vassal state of Egypt, ruled by a group of kingdoms. The Hebrews entered this land some 4,000 years ago from Babylon (Mesopotamia; Iraq) with the figure of Abraham. Canaan became the land of Israel under the reign of King

David in circa 1002 BCE. Thereafter, Israel produced an array of Hebrew Kings, Prophets, a vast array of Hebrew books and encountered wars with many nations. A Temple monument in Jerusalem was destroyed by Babylon in the 6th Century BCE and again by the Romans in 70 AD/CE. These events did not incorporate Arabs as the ruling entity; these wars were fought against the Jews in Judea by forces that were not Arab. It says there were no prominent Arab and Jew interactions at this phase of history.

Such historical details of Israel's history are seen in other nations' archives, including of ancient Assyria, Persia and the Greek and Roman Empires. The same is recorded in the Hebrew writings and the Gospels, and by a vast display of archaeological relics. King David was evidenced as a 3,000 year historical figure in the 'House of David' relic of the Tel Dan discovery, and coins and Hebrew writings have also been un-earthed mentioning Israel and with Hebrew markings by Archaeologists extending to 1,000 BCE. [43]

The Dead Sea Scrolls discovery in 1947 fully affirmed Israel as incepting in the land of Canaan more than 3,000 years ago and less than 4,000 years. It posited Israel's territory under King David as overlapping some sectors east of the river Jordan and included Gaza, Hebron, Nazareth and Bethlehem as irrefutably part of Judea. Gaza was invaded by the Philistines and held as Philistia; it was conquered back to Israel by King David. Thereafter the Philistines became successfully incorporated into David's armed forces, abandoning their war with the Jews and becoming Hebrew citizens. It is an important juncture; the Philistines were not Hebrew or Arab but a Greek aligned people previous to their inclusion with Israel.

The original non-Hebrew Canaanites were also not originally Hebrew or Arab but an Egyptian aligned group. Their enjoining with the Hebrew monotheism that rejected divine emperors will re-surface as a historical disdain when the Greeks conquer Arabia, resulting in wars and Jerusalem's name changed to Aelia Capitolina and instigating Rome to change Judea's name to Palestine. Such wars of religious discordance were not seen with the Arabs.

The Scrolls is a parcel of writings with portions dated from 408 BCE, affirming Israel's ancient biblical history, with some of its portions dated to 600 BCE (The Psalms Scroll 11Q5). [44]

The Scrolls include a vast listing of ancient nations, kings, empires, geographical locations and ancient names that are authentic of their periods; its writings align almost exactly with today's Hebrew Bible and includes the first mention of the term Arab in the Book of Nehemiah, dated as 450 BCE. The Scrolls verify that the Jews preserved their history and scriptures from ancient times.

Abraham's Genealogy

The Hebrew writings that introduced this figurehead and a belief thread remain the only validation of Abraham; yet a substantial accumulation of circumstantial evidences render its credibility. The Hebrew writing is impressive; it is perhaps the most validated ancient writings possessed by humanity, with some 75% being well substantiated (King David onward), and by an estimated one million relics world-wide.

The five Hebrew Books of the Torah remain the oldest alphabetical works that constitute a multi-page continuing narrative story, as differing from inscription snippets or burial epitaphs. This writing is also upheld by many other scriptures and numerously used as a yardstick by historians by virtue of its minutiae detailing and extensive genealogy that spans almost 3,000 years of ancient history.

There is an absence of any connectivity between Arabs and Abraham via the Hebrew writings, with the term Arab appearing after the 5th Century; save that such a claim vests only with the later emergence of Islam in the 7th Century as a belief structure that also harbors a similar monotheistic faith and its scriptural connectivity with Abraham.

The Book of Nehemiah that mentions an Arab figure does not make its reference to a connection with Ismail or Abraham that can account for a relationship, a highly unusual situation considering the claim appears of a direct and contemporaneous connection made in the Islamic Scriptures. To cater to such an absence of records, there have been attempts to trace DNA alliances, which appear anomalous again by the absence of any corresponding historical and archaeological validating.

That all peoples are generic to a region is not the issue here; an identifiable ethnically distinguishable group with similar traits and attributes is the issue, including beliefs, cultures, languages, writings, name marks, genealogy and histories.

A Silent History.

Historically, there is a total vacancy of any distinct, implicit or graphically recorded archives from any source that illustrates an ancient connectivity of Arabs with the Philistines, Abraham and Ishmael. Chiefly, since the time of Abraham, there is no record of a people or group identifiable by the term Arab prior to 450 BCE; nor did the Arabs follow Abraham's monotheist belief till the advent of Islam, a period of over 2,500 years.

Thereby, the underlying imprints require further exploration of wider and secondary connectivity. While the absence of any imprints cannot positively conclude the non-existence of any people, equally, it renders the issue in a negative historical conclusion. Chiefly, the Arab history suffers an absence of records relative to all ancient peoples.

The absence of Arabic writings is a significant factor, sufficient to question, but not negate, an ancient claim, at least in regard of an identifiable and distinct group. Like speech, writing is an inherent human trait that evidences the historical imprints of different groupings. Almost every known ancient group of humanity possesses writings in some form, ranging from stone etching to cuneiform and alphabets.

The Inca writing system called quipu is estimated as 4,600 years (Archaeology About Org.); The oldest Asian writing, Proto-Cuneiform, dates to around 3000 BC (clay texts found at Jemdet Nasr); the oldest African writing is the "Proto Saharan" at 5,000 BCE (Taneter.org); writings from Mesopotamia date back slightly more than 5,000 years (Phys.org; world's oldest calendar); Chinese characters are believed to have been developed on similar ancient periods independently.

Professor Gershon Galil of the department of biblical studies at the University of Haifa has deciphered an inscription dating from the 10th century BCE (the period of King David's reign), and has shown that this is a Hebrew inscription (Phys.org).

Where are the Arabs?

The Arabic writing emerged as a full-fledged scripture (The Quran) in the 7th Century and minute inscriptions from the 3rd Century. A Saudi-French archaeological team has claimed the oldest known inscription in the Arabic alphabet at a site located near Najran in Saudi Arabia (according to a report in Arab News). The Nabataean script, itself relatively new, was developed from Aramaic during the 2nd century BCE [45] and is therefore considered the direct precursor of the Arabic script; it contains components of Aramaic, Hebrew, Greek and Latin. It says Arabic is a relatively new writing, one that does not yet display archival ancient connectivity with Canaan or Abraham at this juncture.

Thereby, the indirect connections, which are used by various historians and theologians in the place of direct connectivity, should be referred to. Namely, were the Arabs called differently before, and if so, what historical marks can be evidenced that align another group with the Arab people; especially, whether the Arabs are mentioned by another name by other ancient nation's writings.

Egypt and Israel.

The Hebrews, the Canaanites, the Philistines and the ancient Egyptians were closely interacted. The Egyptian writings referred to the Jews as Hebrews and Israel 3,400 years ago. Here, some question these names as similar sounding but perhaps not necessarily as concluded (E.g. *Yisra'el; Yi?rā'ēl*), while the majority of historians have accepted these ancient relics as connected with Israel. The names of a host of towns such as Urusalem, Ashkelon and Gaza; and the mention of a 'war with Israel' and its dating being in close approximation of the Exodus dating of the Hebrew Bible narratives are positive factors which have made the Egyptian relics compelling. The Canaanites, with whom the Hebrews belonged as one of this land's people, do not mention any group by the term Arab or of one that upheld the monotheistic faith of Abraham in any known recordings. The Assyrians who invaded Israel in the 8th Century BCE, and claimed as a possible reference to Arabs, mentions many groupings but also do not mention Arabs as an Abraham family group; instead the Arivi, if it is accepted as Arab, is mentioned as an invasive group outside of Canaan. Here, the Greeks who introduced the term Arab had yet not entered Arabia.

Thereby, while the Exodus transfer mode from Egypt to Canaan remains un-proven, the Hebrew interactions with ancient Egypt are confirmed by the Amarna letters. This says there was an exodus of a people from Egypt to Canaan, whereby a new sovereign nation emerged which name was changed to Israel; it says the Exodus (transfer of a people) did happen, only its mode of transfer being questionable or unknown.

Additionally, the Hebrew writings display a credible description of ancient Egypt that aligns well with the Merneptah and Egypt Steles that mentions a war with Israel. Here, the names of Egypt's Kings, diets, towns and highway routes to Canaan listed in the Hebrew narratives are positive and credible indicators. Hagar is an authentic ancient Egyptian name; Hagar and Abraham produced a son called as Ishmael; also authentic names of this place and time, and can satisfy the Paleontology criteria.

Ishmael was not Arab.

Ishmael is a Hebrew name introduced in the Hebrew bible (Gen.16:11). Abraham was bestowed with a gift of the Pharaoh's daughter Hagar, a common ancient custom in the proposal of a peace accord. Ishmael was thus half Hebrew via Abraham, and half Egyptian via his mother Hagar. Ishmael's name was secured by Abraham; it is a Hebrew name imposed on the lad by his father. Rabbi Ishmael was the High Priest of the first century Jerusalem Temple, denoting its ancient historical Hebrew connection with Abraham who lived in Canaan, the land that became the homeland of the Jews. [46]

Thus Ishmael cannot be historically referenced as Arab by its name application, and because Ancient Egypt was not an Arab people prior to the 7th Century emergence of Islam, a religion that occurred outside of Egypt. Thereby, other paths than the name Ishmael require examination.

The Coptic Christians are the closer related inhabitants to ancient Egypt; the ancient Egyptians did not speak or write Arabic, thereby the language path also gives no connectivity. Arabic is a new writing, with its first imprints in circa 4[th/ 6th] century CE and being an admix of other languages, then as the Quran in the 7th century CE. [47]

The ancient Egyptians and the Hebrew both used the name of Peleshet in 1100 BCE (The 20th. Dynasty of Egypt under Ramsey III), which evolved as the Anglicized Palestine, referring it to foreign invaders from across the seas; such again gives cross-reference credibility of the Hebrew writings via the Hebrew-Egyptian offspring of Ishmael.

Non-Arab Arabians.

Although the term Arabia appears to align all groups in the region as Arabs, such is not the case. Many groups of Arabia are not Arab. The ancient lands known as Cush was changed to Arabia in the 4th Century BCE by the Greeks from which Arab was also derived; it is an indicator when this name became a widespread usage, signifying a relatively new group emerging.

Thereafter, all the various nations and groups of Arabia became classed as Arabs with Islam's conquering rule in the 7th century; almost all its inhabitants were made to speak Arabic, including those Jews, Phoenicians, Copts and Christians that came under Arab ruled lands. Prior to Islam emerging, the nations of Arabia were not called as Arabs; today's Jordan was called as Moab, land of the Moabites mentioned in the Hebrew Bible. Almost all such Arabian groups and nations predate the advent of the Arab invasion, many retaining their ancient languages, such as the Jews, the Copts and the Kurds that were not Arab peoples; the Copts speak the ancient Egyptian language; Aramaic is still retained by some groups; and the Jews the ancient Hebrew. The Jews encountered many groups during their exiles incurred by conquering empires.

Assyria and Babylon.

The Northern state of Israel was invaded in the 8th Century BCE and all its inhabitants exiled and dispersed by Assyria; these became absorbed in the Ten Lost Tribes of Israel. The next phase of exile for the Jews concerned the invasion by Babylon (Mesopotamia/Iraq) in 586 BCE by Nebuchadnezzar. [48]

Now, the term Arab and Arabia have yet not emerged, yet the historical imprints begin to shed a quickening of the pace. The Persians and the Greeks have yet not entered this region.

Persian Empire.

Fifty years after Nebuchadnezzar destroyed the Jerusalem Temple, Babylon fell to the Persian Empire under King Cyrus the Great in 539 BCE. While the Book of Esther that is set in the Persian-ruled region of Babylon does not mention an Arab group, this name does appear for the first time after the Persian king granted the exiled Jews permission to return to their land and to re-build their Temple that was destroyed by Babylon:

• "Thus says Cyrus, king of Persia: 'All the kingdoms of the earth the Lord, the God of heaven, has given to me, and he has also charged me to build him a house in Jerusalem, which is in Judah. Whoever, therefore, among you belongs to any part of his people, let him go up, and may his God be with him! Let everyone who has survived, in whatever place he may have dwelt, be assisted by the people of that place with silver, gold, and goods, together with free will offerings for the house of God in Jerusalem." (Ezra 1:2; The Cyrus the Great Cylinder, The first known Charter of Rights of Nations, 539 BCE. Edited by Shapour Ghasemi)

First Jewish-Arab Interaction.

The Jews who returned from their Babylonian exile to rebuild their Temple confronted three groups that settled in destroyed Jerusalem. One of these was unimpressed with Israel's return, a newly formed group that entrenched themselves here when the Jews were in their Babylon exile. An entry in the Hebrew Scriptures dated 450 BCE marks the first recording of the term Arab:

• "But when Sanballat the Horonite, and Tobiah the servant, the Ammonite, and Geshem the *Arab* heard it, they laughed us to scorn, and despised us, and said: 'What is this thing that ye do? Will ye rebel against the king?' Then answered I them, and said unto them: 'The God of heaven, He will prosper us; therefore we His servants will arise and build." (Book of Nehemiah, 2:19)

Significantly, this is the first time the term Arab is applied to an Arabian group, and by its correct name; there are serious issues in all other similar sounding names cited as older. Here, we see definitive traits of a land dispute, a parallel of its future history; such is not seen prior to this date. In this instance, its listing among other groups signifies those are different groups than that from the tribe of Gesham. This does not mean there were no Arabs prior to this listing, but the reverse; for how can a group be named as a distinct people if they did not have a past. However, it is plausible there were no Arabs in this date's very ancient times; namely, the Arabs emerged around this time as a historically identifiable group, because this name does not commonly appear as a group previously. Or else they had not yet featured as a significant force, displaying no nation, cities, wars or monuments.

It is a name listed as Gesham the Arab, denoting one of many, namely from one such group among other groups as the Horonites and Ammonites that are not Arabs; its inference is this Arab group was not a large one at this time because all the groups mentioned are now under the Persian rule, as opposed an indication of an Arab king or nation applying. It is also of a people distinct and varied from the others by its marked disdain toward the Jews and a strong obsession of usurping their land that would enable them a nationhood that yet never existed. This is a significant foretelling entry; clearly the Jews were returning to their land and a rejection by an Arab is evidenced with this knowledge at hand. It foretells a future scenario of the 20th Century under the British watch.

The Arabic writings did not exist at this time in the 5th Century BCE, also indicative of a newly emerging people. The disdain toward the returning Jews is aligned with the Arabs inclined with the Samaritans who also had a similar negative disposition with the Jews. The descriptions do not mention or allude to a past history with Abraham or Ishmael, but appears as a new land usurping premise, with a disdain that pre-dates Islam by 1,000 years. Now there is no alluding to a belief conflict and no alignment mentioned with Abraham or Ishmael. It too is a significant factor, appearing prior to the advent of Islam. There is no record of the term 'Arab' as a similarly connective identifiable ethnic group before the Hebrew introduction of this term, with no records of interaction of such a group in Canaan and Egypt, nor any record prior to this time of an Arab nation, city, king, war, archaeological relics or writings from any source that mentions an Arabian group as Arabs. Pivotally, there is no prior discordance or disputation of these two groups prior to the Nehemiah entry.

However, this is not about generic human ancestry sources but a particular definable group of people with an evidential thread; otherwise all Arabian peoples ultimately emerged from one source point. Instead, the Arabs became prominent after the Greek invasion and the felling of the Persian Empire under Alexander the Great. Here, groups of Arabs offered the people of Arabia security protection from the foreign Greek invaders for a price, and thereby gathered themselves into stronger and larger forces of warriors; it is the Greeks that recognized this group to give them their name and an enlarged prominence. Thereby, that the term 'Arab' does not appear prior to the Hebrew Book of Nehemiah, which is dated less than 2,600 years ago (450 BCE), requires again tracing the Arab peoples' historical origins

361

via other pathways than the Jews. Here, the Jews and Arab interaction has no recorded precedent.

Indirect Connectivity.

Depictions or errors of a connection with other ethnic groups have emerged via name associations, whereby the term 'Aribi' is accounted as Arab from an entry dated as 853 BCE. This is almost 500 years older than the book of Nehemiah (450 BCE), nearing the time 150 years after King Solomon reigned (970 to 931 BCE). Notably, this name does not appear in the Book of Kings that incorporates King Solomon's era. Numerous sources, including Islamic writers, site this time as the first imprint of Arabs; in a sense they are saying the Arabs began some 1,000 years after Abraham. In 853 BCE, in the Kurkh monument, an Assyrian scribe records the term 'Aribi' in the event of a battle; it has gained support as referring to 'Arab' by its close resemblance with 'Aribi':

• "63,000 infantry, 2000 cavalry, 4000 chariots and 1000 warriors on camels; the men on camels are led to the battle by Gindibu the *"Aribi"* [49]

The Aribi reference as Arab has become equated with the Bedouins, who constitute an ancient yet small isolated part of the total population of the Middle East (Encyl. Britannica); however, this group is not known as followers or connected with the Abrahamic belief structure. The groups that became accounted as Arabs evolved as a conglomeration of ancient groups each with separate traits, most of which been lost; Copts, Phoenicians and Arabs are thereby different groups with varied languages, beliefs and histories, with the term Arab accorded them by the Greeks. If the Greeks coined the term Arab in 300 BCE, most probably taken from the Book of Nehemiah when the Hebrew Bible was first translated (the Greek Septuagint of 300 BCE), then the term Aribi suffers a claimed linkage with Arab by the time factor; namely, Arivi is some 300 years prior to Arab. Ultimately, the Aribi connection seeks to align with Ishmael and Abraham, and is both proposed and disputed by scholars amidst their historical anomalies and disagreements:

• "The first actual use of the word Arab in history is to be found in an Assyrian inscription of 853 B.C., commemorating the defeat of a mutinous chieftain called Gindibu the Aribi during the reign of king

Shalmaneser III (858-824 B.C.). - ["The origin of the word Arab"; IsmailiNet]

• "Concerning the origin, the most widespread myth is that Arabs are Ishmaelites. The equation Arab = Ishmaelite is a myth, because Ishmael was not an Arab, nor the forefather of all Arabs. The earliest sources where the term *Arab* appeared the first time are the Hebrew Scriptures of the post-exilic period, namely, during the rebuilding of the Temple under the Persian Empire (Nehemyah 2:19 - 5th century b.c.e.)" - [Myths, Hypotheses and Facts Concerning the Origin of Peoples; Origin and Identity of the Arabs.]

• "Arabian literature has its own version of prehistoric times, but it is entirely legendary." (Encyclopedia Britannica, Vol. 2:176)

• "The truth is that the term "Arab" designates peoples of diverse ethnic origins who are united only by the Arabic language and culture. The seed of Ishmael represents only a very small component of the genetic pool of the Arabic people." (CBN)

• "The Assyrian sources make no mention of an ethnic framework called Ishmael; and there is no evidence that the nomads were called by this name." (Jewish World Libr)

Thereby, there is support and dispute of the 'Aribi' allocation to Arab. In 853 BCE the Assyrian army was a most powerful one; it conquered the northern state of Israel and exiled all its inhabitants who are now called as 'The Ten Lost Tribes of Israel'. These northern tribes included the Israelites and other groups that became incorporated into the Hebrew nation and as citizens of Israel 150 years earlier in King David's reign. The Hebrew writing lists all the ten Hebrew tribes, along with the Jebusites, the Philistines and a host of other such groups by names; the names Arabs and/or Aribi are not mentioned.

It is a significant deficiency considering the term Arab and/or Aribi is proposing an alignment with Ishmael and Abraham from a 1,000 years earlier, whereas the Hebrew writing is fastidious in illustrating the lineages of its prominent figureheads by names of their parents (son of; daughter of'). It is akin to accepting that Hebrew and Israel are aligned with Abraham without any mention of those names in its narratives. There does not appear a positive conclusion favoring Aribi as Arab. The chief deficiency is the absence of imprints appearing periodical, such as an Aribi or even an Arab king, nation, war or other such provisions normally associated with a group.

The Ten Lost Tribes, which were Hebrew, are believed to have strayed to a host of faraway lands including to Europe and India; one such tribe has now been identified in NW India as the tribe of Menashe and this was not an Arab group. The Assyrians, not known as a group connected with Ishmael, were later conquered by Babylon and dissimilated as a people. Thus there is a reasonable enquiry to track an indirect connectivity applying of any Arabs and Ishmael.

The Name Absence. The term Aribi is directed at a singular Akkadian or Assyrian source, mentioned with a similar sounding term as Arab in 853 BCE. Its chief deficiency is not a variance of a name's phonetic sound and spelling, which can be legitimate in different languages and cultures. The major issue is the absence of a name appearing periodically, as is seen in the Hebrew writings and with all other nation's histories. The term Arab or Aribi does not appear before this time of 853 BCE, whether one accepts the date of 853 or 450 BCE. Here there are no dots to connect a historical thread, denoting an unusually vacant gap; these do not extend back to Abraham or Canaan.

On its positive side, the Aribi name is vested in the site of close proximity to Israel, even though as an adversary in an invasion from another unrelated nation. However, no Arab or Aribi names appear as a nation, king, wars, monuments or writings from any source, indicating an absence of Arabs as an identifiable ethnic group with a substantial historical record in the 9th Century or prior. In contrast, the term Arab appears numerously after its 450 BCE listing in the Hebrew Bible, also occurring periodically thereafter by other nations. The term Arab is used by the Greeks who first coined the term 'Arab' as a worldly spread, indicating this name's prominence emerged after the Greeks entered Arabia and that it was taken from the Hebrew Bible rather than the earlier Akkadian or Assyrian Aribi. The Greeks were the first to translate the Hebrew Bible to another language in 300 BCE (The Septuagint Bible). We have no Arab name usage by the Greeks prior to the Book of Nahemiah:

• "The term Arab is a Greek word, not an Akkadian or Assyrian one. The form in the Quran is taken either from Greek or Syriac sources." - (Islam, Alfred Guillaume, 1956, p 26-27, 61-62).

Solomon Older than Aribi.

The Assyrian nation incurred wars with the Jews since the 8th century BCE. In King Solomon's reign of 950 BCE, just 100 years prior, the term Arab or Aribi is not used among a host of nations' names appearing, such as the Phoenicians, Egyptians, Medianites and a listing of other smaller groups. This absence subsists of both the names Arab and Aribi from Abraham to the Assyrian war of 853 BCE, a period of some 1,200 years. It is one of the striking anomalies of this history, indicating Aribi is not an ancient name aligned with Abraham by the absence of implicit historical imprints. Thereby the 853 BCE Assyrian listing of Aribi is yet not older than the reign of King Solomon.

Contrastingly, there is positive evidence of Hebrew interaction with the ancient Egyptians that aligns with the estimated period of Abraham and the Hebrews. Thus in this juncture of history, and based on the Assyrian 853 BCE dating, there are no imprints of the term Arab or Aribi as a historically identifiable ethnic group in Solomon's time (930 BCE) or prior. The 853 BCE inscriptions incur disputes and deficiencies, but are held by others; it remains debatable by the lack of lineage imprints with Ishmael prior to 450 BCE, and most impacting, the absence of the monotheistic belief provision. Thereby, connectivity of Aribi with Ishmael, though proposed by some sectors, remains in contrast to other ancient groups of this region, as indeterminable and thereby questionable.

Who Are Ishmaelites?

The tracing of Ishmael and his descendents is a contentious history with an absence of clear and graphic Historical imprints. Introduced in the Book of Genesis, Ishmael's lineage disappeared from the historical record 3,000 years ago, then re-emerged 1,500 years later with the advent of Islam. The Jews and the Arab interactions are first recorded at the end of the Jews' seventy year exilic period after the Persian conquest of Babylon. The Book of Nehemiah's context relates to the Jews' request to the Persian king for permission to return to Jerusalem and re-build their temple, with its positive granting by the King Cyrus; it is also the basis of the earlier Book of Esther.

Here, the Jews' returning to their homeland encounters discordance with one of the groups mentioned as 'Gindibu the *Arab*'. The term Arab in this Hebrew entry is not disputable; it is explicit and correctly spelled and appears numerously hereafter; there is no gap of imprints anymore. This interaction also appears credible by the view that while the Jews were exiled in Babylon and their land unprotected, a new group sought to usurp this land, a generic syndrome in human history and a particular one seen between the Jews and the Arabs. Such is also described in the writings of Flavius Josephus, indicating its preferred understanding instead of the 'Gindibu the *Aribi*' source of the 8th Century. Notably, this entry of 450 BCE mentions the distinctive and correct name (Arab); yet no archives at this time refer to Ishmael's lineage of 'twelve princes' aligned with Gindibu or a 'great nation' as described in the Book of Genesis. It is surprising that the importance of an alignment with Abraham and Ishmael would not be referred to in this Hebrew writing, or the failure of any of these two people acknowledging a connection via the same parentage. It is cited by some sectors as a derivative to Abraham, yet it is not indicative of a biological adversity by the text.

However, the text is clear there was a historical animosity subsisting with the Arab peoples and the Jews in 450 BCE, or more than a thousand years prior to the emergence of the Islamic faith, yet it was not a theological one in 450 BCE. It says such discordance did not initiate with the Islamic Scriptures, but its reverse proposal more applies; such a view can make a historical discordance easier to resolve than the emotive one based on a religious belief.

Here there are also views the Arabs were already aware of Abraham and the Hebrew figures prior to the emergence of Islam, as were numerous other groups aware, such as the Medianites, Moabites, Phoenicians and Egyptians. It is less than plausible such would not be the case in this region at this time, due to the enormous adversities between the monotheist Jews and the nations. The pre-Islamic Arabs did know of Abraham prior to Islam emerging:

• "The sacrifice of his (Abraham's) first-born of whose separation he could not bear neither could he see him surrounded in foes." - [Pre-Islamic poet Umayyah Ibn Abi As-Salt, The Treasury of Literature, 437; Al-Kashf Wa Al-Bayan, Vol. 11, p32). Equally, such is contradicted by a theological view that is denoting a theologically based revelation with no prior knowledge of Abraham by the prophet of Islam:

• "Muhammad was not informed about the family of Abraham." (Encyclopedia of Islam; I: 184; pages 544-546)

The Theological Factor. It continues to be the most impacting feature in this history. Thereby, another pathway emerges about Ishmael based on the Hebrew Bible texts that introduced this important figurehead. Genesis marks the first introduction of Ishmael:

• "And as for Ishmael, I have heard thee; behold, I have blessed him, and will make him fruitful, and will multiply him exceedingly; twelve princes shall he beget, and I will make him a great nation." - (Gen. 17/20).

Here, who are referred to by 'twelve princes' and 'a great nation' are the significantly impacting factors. While many hold this refers to a thread that culminates with the Arab people, the Hebrew texts and historical criteria display incongruence and conundrums; they may also point elsewhere when a measure of respectful indulgence is considered of this text. Chiefly, there are no historical or theological connections uncovered between Ishmael and the pre-Islamic Arabs till the advent of Islam, a period more than 2,600 years.

The Hebrew writings that introduced Ishmael remain the only source that can be examined; this name appears again in the advent of Christianity 2,000 years later and this too only by its embracing the Hebrew bible. The next phase of the mention of Ishmael is 2,600 years later with the advent of Islam in the 7th century. It is a massive historical period of absence of this name; the same period is also absent of the monotheist belief.

The Egyptian Connection.

Ishmael was the son of a Hebrew father, Abraham; and an Egyptian mother, Hagar; their child was anointed with a Hebrew name given by Abraham:

• "And Hagar bore Abram a son; and Abram called the name of his son, whom Hagar bore, Ishmael. - (Gen. 16: 15).

The text is saying Hagar and Abraham's first son Ishmael was not Arab because both of his parents were not Arab, and that their son was given a Hebrew name. What happened thereafter opens other considerations. As Hagar was the Pharaoh's daughter, a princess, it renders her son Ishmael as the grandson of the Pharaoh, a royal blood line status in the Egyptian lineage. Hagar preserved her son's royal status by this act, separating Ishmael's descendents from a non-Egyptian genealogy:

• "And his mother took him a wife out of the land of Egypt" (Gen. 21:21).

Thereby, Ishmael's children would be Egyptian who married other Egyptians; namely, Ishmael's lineage would be Egyptian, not Arab and not Hebrew because the ancient Egyptians were not Arab or Hebrew. This factor does not change by later inter-marriages between their derived generations; there was fluidity in the non-monotheist assembly of the region, also seen with Abraham's genealogy. Moses inter-married; Moses' genealogy remained un-changed.

Abraham also remarried after the death of Sarah and after his separation from Hagar who begat Ishmael; thereby Genesis lists other genealogies stemming from other wives who did not inherit an Egyptian line as with Ishmael.

One Great Nation.

Genesis 17:20 also refers to Ishmael who will be the father of 12 princes and a (one) great nation. In Abraham's time, no other nation in the region can equally qualify as 'a great nation' as did Egypt. And now ancient Egypt was not Arab; nor was Ishmael via both his parents. Now there is no mention of an Arab group or other followers of the Abrahamic faith, whether accounted by the Assyrian or the Nehemiah dating. Significantly, the genealogy of Ishmael was not monotheistic as that of Abraham or of the Hebrew belief. The only connection of Ishmael with Islam is thereby the emergence of Islam some 2,600 years later, and accounted solely by theological belief; namely via revelation, yet not a historical pre-disposition of Abraham's faith.

Here there is an additional impact; that the Ishmaelite group is connected with the Midianites, also a group that is inter-mingled with Egypt. Jetro was a priest of Median and the father-in-law of Moses; he was also one of the chief counselors of the Egyptian Pharaoh. That the Ishmaelite and the Medianites became inherited as an Egyptian group is rendered by the text in the story of Joseph and his brethren. The Ishmaelite and the Midianites appear as one people or intertwined; namely they are both aligned as Egyptian:

• "And they sat down to eat bread; and they lifted up their eyes and looked, and, behold, a caravan of Ishmaelite came from Gilead, with their camels bearing spicery and balm and ladanum, going to carry it down to Egypt." And:

• "And there passed by Midianites, merchantmen; and they drew and lifted up Joseph out of the pit, and sold Joseph to the Ishmaelites for twenty shekels of silver. And they brought Joseph into Egypt." (Gen. 37:25-29).

Moses married Zipporah, the daughter of Jetro, also a Medianite (Ex. 2: 21), aligning with the Egyptian connection; as do several historical appraisals report:

• "The Midianites traditionally have been identified as Ishmaelite, in part because of an unclear passage in Genesis (37:28) that refers to the traders to whom Joseph was sold by his brothers as both Midianites and Ishmaelite. In addition, the story of Gideon in Judges contains a verse (8:24) that includes an apparent interpolation identifying the Midianites as Ishmaelite." - (Encyl. Britannica).

According to Genesis:

• 'And his mother took him a wife out of the land of Egypt' (Gen. 21:21).

That Hagar married Ishmael to an Egyptian woman selected by the Pharaoh's daughter, it explains how and why his sons became Egyptian princes, as is recorded of 12 princes, because Hagar was not Arab, and as an Egyptian princess she selected an Egyptian wife for her son Ishmael. Thereby, Hagar was prudently establishing a royal status for her son to be accounted as Egyptian; such is a plausible premise that acquires both status and security, while its denial would be surprising and less plausible. This says the 12 princes became Egyptian and varied from the later Arab assembly.

The reconciliation between the step brothers Ishmael and Isaac upon Abraham's death says the brothers lived different lives in different places, namely in Canaan and Egypt. Ishmael's father Abraham remained as a respected figure with the Pharaoh. The two step brothers reconciled upon the death of Abraham (Gen. 25:9). The terms 'twelve princes' and 'a great nation' have been pivotal as the identification of Ishmael's lineage; yet the term Arab or Aribi and the Abrahamic belief are absent; and the name of Egypt is clear and graphic, denoting an incongruence between the text and the held theological belief factors that exclude the Egyptian connection. Additionally, the lineage of Ishmael disappears from history and is not heard of again after some generations; no nations, wars, kings and cities emerged of Ishmael's descendents. The text refers only to princes, indicative again that the 'great nation' better refers to Egypt. There was no great Arab or Islamic nation, or any other 'Great Nation' at this time. Egypt was the mighty power and alone subscribing to 'Great'.

The Hebrew text setting is vested in the period around 4,000 years ago, while Egypt became Arab 2,600 years later in the 7TH Century AD/CE under the Islamic invasion; thus it better inclines Ishmael's lineage with an ancient non-Arab Egyptian connection that did not survive, although the 12 princes emerged as assured in the text. The term 'twelve princes' avoids the term 'king'; again pointing to the Pharaoh of a great nation.

Thereby, though controversial and varied from the widespread held position, Ishmael could have plausibly relinquished his Abraham connection and gradually dissolved away within the Egyptian Empire's dynasty which also fell away. Such a view favors the premise that Ishmael's descendents gradually lost their monotheistic belief. Ishmael's descendents did not form a monotheistic religion; the continuance of monotheism was upheld by the Jews. The Arab people also did not hold a monotheistic belief till the advent of Islam in the 7th Century; it is not indicative of an Abrahamic connection.

The Akkadian Connection.

Like the Assyrian connection, the Akkadian premise is another instance that seeks to align the Arabic language and writing with an older nation, and thereby to connect the Arabs as an ancient group that emerged over 4,000 years ago (2334-2154 BC), instead of one that became as Arab after the term Arabia emerged in 300 BCE. Yet these claims are again impacted by the same issue of an absence of imprints that should appear periodically, in its lead-up and follow-up history. Chiefly, the Akkadians spoke an Afroasiatic language and fell 4,000 years ago by the Sumerians, while the first Arabic written language appeared in full form in the 7th Century AD/CE, more than 4,500 years apart; there is nothing in-between to indicate an Akkadian connection save for some Arabic words that are seen as similar to the Akkadian language. We later learn the Arabic is an ad-mix of many languages, both ancient Aramaic and the pre-Islamic groups of Arabia, and the later Greek and Latin (European) that invaded in 300 BCE.

While the Arabic language does harbor ancient oral imprints older than its 7th Century writing, this better aligns with its absorption of many ancient languages more so than accounting for an absence of writing for 4,000 years. When the Jews were exiled in the 6th Century BCE to Babylon there is no reporting of Arabs at that time, yet the Hebrew Book of Nehemiah does mention the term Arab in the following century under the Persian Empire. There are thus discordances between the historical evidence and the premises held by different groups:

• The oldest known history of the Arabic language dates back to the 8th Century B.C. It wasn't until nearly 12 centuries later - in 4 A.D. - that a truly unique form of Arabic arose. Historians theorize that these Arabic roots initially sprung up in East Africa, particularly in the regions now known as Somalia and Ethiopia. - (Foreign Translations Org)

• The earliest inscriptions of Arabic in the (northern) Arabic script date CE 512-568.The Aramaic alphabet was introduced to the Arab people through traders from the Mediterranean Empire, and the Arab people began using the script during the Christian period in the Middle East (Bateson, Mary Catherine (2003). *Arabic Language Handbook*. Washington DC: Georgetown University Press. p. 54.)

• Arabic is related to two Semitic languages still used in the Middle East: chiefly Hebrew in its ancient liturgical and modern (nineteenth- and twentieth-century) revival forms, but also Amharic, the official language of Ethiopia. - (Enclopedia/com)

The Shem Connection.

It is also claimed that the word 'Shem' in Genesis, listing one of Noah's sons, refers to Arabs (Ismaili.Net). However, the Shem lineage culminates in the Hebrew thread, and the Hebrews were not Arab.

It becomes difficult to see how an ancient group of Arabs existed for 4,000 years in the region that produced the ancient world's most copious archives of writings and remain the only one without writings till the 7TH Century AD/CE. Historically, it appears the Shem connectivity is derived from the later emergence of Islam in the 7TH Century when it aligned itself with Abraham's monotheism. Yet this is not the case before this time when the Arab people did not observe a monotheistic belief since the time of Ishmael, a period of 2,600 years. Such can be referenced with Europe which absorbed the Hebrew Bible in the 4TH Century, yet it does not conclude that the Europeans stemmed from Abraham historically or genealogically, other than by the commonality of a later belief provision. The validated dating of the Arab people's historical emergence as a definitive group is controversial, contradictive and subjective prior to the Nehemiah dating of 450 BCE.

While all theological groups display an inherent inclination with their held beliefs, the historical requirements also persist in claiming equal consideration. We have the Hebrew writings as the only source that introduced Ishmael and Abraham from which the nations know of these two figures. The Hebrews retained their monotheist belief for 4,000 years via an un-broken thread of writings and amidst many interacting nations, often under difficult conditions. The genecology of Ishmael did not follow the monotheistic belief path, while Islam did become a monotheistic faith. This enquiry found that a sincere and powerful belief in Abraham and monotheism is apparent in the Islamic faith; and that there are questionable historical connections of Arabs with Ishmael prior to Islam's emergence in the 7th century. Such is a prevailing in all faiths, especially so in their inception periods.

The connection of the pre-Islamic Arabs with Abraham is substantially accepted world-wide, including by most of the Jewish scholars and by Israel; its controversy is an absence of historical validation. The issue will remain subjective and dependent on individual assessment.

The negative phase of the reporting of Arab history in the modern world is aligned with the accepting of Arabs as Palestinians. It is one that emerged recently in the 1960's and is false beyond dispute, although it too is also accepted by a worldly multitude.

A small sector, which includes prominent figures of the times, including respected Presidential candidates like Mr. Newt Gingrich, fully dismisses the Arabs as a Palestinian people; so does history. Its acceptance by the world at large and the strong upholding of this deception by the Arab communities has caused chaos and mayhem. It casts a negative impression of the Arab's portrayal of their upheld history.

25. What Does Archaeology Say?

Of Palestinian Territory. There have not been any relics affirming a previous Palestinian state anytime in history; there is an abundance of relics affirming the territory of Israel. Archaeology says the premise of Israel as illegally occupying Palestinian lands as politically created in the Mid-20th Century and has no historical veracity.

While a Palestinian State never existed, Palestine was never a sovereign state of the Arabs, nor was Jerusalem a capital of any nation. Contrastingly, some one Million relics and references unearthed in the Arabian region dating up to a 3,400 year period affirm the Jews as the original inhabitants of Canaan, Israel, Samaria and Judea - the earlier historical names accorded to Palestine. Since Rome applied the name Palestine on Judea 2,000 years ago, the Jews maintained a continuous, un-broken habitation in Palestine. No other group can make such a claim.

Thereby, the nativity and territory factors, including of the modern State of Israel and the disputed region called as West Bank in 1950, lie exclusively with Israel. Here, the greatest affirmation of archaeology remains the discovery of the Dead Sea Scrolls, a parcel of scrolls dating from the 6th Century BCE to the 3rd Century AD/CE. It is irrefutable proof the charges on Israel is false.

26. What Does Theology Say?

Israel existed as a sovereign nation more than 3,000 years ago. The ancient Hebrew and Christian Scriptures, and the Dead Sea Scrolls align with the archaeological relics unearthed. The name "Israel" first appears in the Hebrew Bible as the name given by God to the patriarch Jacob, whose name was changed to Israel:

• "And he said unto him: 'What is thy name?' And he said: 'Jacob.' And he said: 'Thy name shall be called no more Jacob, but Israel." (Gen. 32:28).

The names Israel and the Hebrew of scriptures are also affirmed in the ancient Egyptian Merneptah Stele and the Amarna Letters. This land's name is numerously mentioned in the Hebrew Bible as 'The land of Israel' and its early references with the Philistines who were not an Arab people but foreign invaders from the other side of the seas (Europe):

• "Not a blacksmith could be found in the whole land of Israel, because the Philistines had said, "Otherwise the Hebrews will make swords or spears!" (1 Samuel 13:19)

The Gospel also affirms the name of this land as Israel before it was changed to Judea and Palestine:

• "Verily I say to you, ye shall not have gone over the cities of *Israel*." [Matt.10:23]

The Islamic Scriptures and many of its scholars and theologians also affirm the Jews as this land's owners:

• "You will find very clearly that the traditional commentators from the eighth and ninth century onwards have included honest and noble Islamic figures who uniformly interpreted the Koran to say explicitly that *Eretz Yisrael* has been given by God to the Jewish people as a perpetual covenant. There is no Islamic counterclaim to the Land anywhere in the traditional corpus of commentary." - British-based Imam Sheikh Muhammad Al-Hussaini.

The historical record displays the antitheses of the worldly multitude's charges that are promoted by Britain and the Arab states; these were collaborations and promotions resultant when vast oil deposits were discovered in Arabia in 1920.

Israel has never occupied another peoples' land in all her 4,000 year recorded history, despite being dispersed throughout the nations via invasions and exiles. The Scrolls aligned with the Hebrew Scriptures that uniquely command the Jews not to take another peoples' land, not even a cubit of a country immediately bordering Israel, as with Seir to the south of Beersheba, also called as Edom. The precisely limited Mosaic boundary line is the strongest assurance to anyone making such claims upon Israel concerning any lands west of the River Jordan:

• "And the LORD said unto Moses prior to the Israelites returning to Canaan from Egypt: 'Ye are to pass through the border of your brethren the children of Esau, that dwell in Seir; take ye good heed unto yourselves therefore; contend not with them; for I will not give you of their land, no, not so much as for the sole of the foot to tread on; because I have given Mount Seir unto Esau for a possession." - (Duet. 2/4 & 2/9).

• 27. What Does History Say?

It is historically validated Jerusalem was the Capital of the sovereign homeland of the Jews established by King David in 1002 BCE, and that Islam invaded this city in the 7TH Century with no prior historical alignment with Jerusalem. A mosque was constructed on the Jewish temple site, and its dome gold-plated in the 20th Century with the fostering by Hajj al-Husseini as a denial and rejection of the Jews' homeland. In the 20th Century, Britain corrupted the Balfour Mandate and divided Palestine and created Jordan on 80% of Palestine.

Chaos and Mayhem.

It is a global syndrome now extended across the nations, yet it is not a surprising outcome. The inculcated flaunting of history and theology has consequences. When Christian State Representatives violate their own scriptures and history, when Britain *calls Jerusalem not part of Israel, when a Roman Pope calls Arabs as Palestinians* - and these are denied and rejected by an array of Islam's most prominent theologians and historians - chaos and mayhem is its assured consequences. Mostly, it has placed poor baggage on otherwise Godly inclined Christians and Muslims seeking the pursuit of truth.

One can say, the refugees that have extended across the nations have an ominous alignment with history's least credible refugees in Palestine. Those that were blessed with more lands and facilities than any other became the refugees of those who charged the world's most afflicted refugees with a false charge.

The 4,000 year Hebrew town names were illegally changed to 'West Bank' by Jordan in 1950, and soon thereafter the Arabs who entered

Palestine usurped the name Palestinians. Perhaps the honesty of Islamic scholars, not the worldly multitude, shall make the truth to set us free; these are historical archives:

• "The al-Aqsa Mosque was built on top of Solomon's Temple." - Eleventh century historian Muhammad Ibn Ahmad al-Maqdisi and fourteenth century Iranian religious scholar Hamdallah al-Mustawfi. [50]

• "Its identity with the site of Solomon's Temple is beyond dispute. This too is the spot, according to the universal belief, on which David built there an alter unto the Lord, and offered burnt sacrifices and peace offerings" - ("A Brief Guide to the Al-Haram Al Sharif Jerusalem"; published by the Supreme Moslem Council; Jerusalem, 1924. Historical sketch, Page 4).

• "O my people, enter the Holy Land which G-d has prescribed for you, and turn not back in your traces, to turn about losers." - [Surat Al-Mai'dah, The Noble Qur'an 5:21]

• "Allah Gave the Land of Israel to the Jews. I say to those who distort their Lord's book, the Koran: From where did you bring the name Palestine, you liars, you accursed, when Allah has already named it "The Holy Land" and bequeathed it to the Children of Israel until the Day of Judgment (Sura 5 Verse 21), and that Jews are the inheritors of Israel (Sura 26 Verse 59)." - (Sheikh Ahmad Adwan, Jordanian Muslim scholar.) [51]:

• The Qur'an expressly recognizes that Jerusalem plays the same role for Jews that Mecca has for Muslims. True Muslims must admit that there is no real link between al-Mi'raj and sovereign rights over Jerusalem. This was originally done by the late mufti of Jerusalem, Amin al-Husseini, who during World War Two collaborated with Adolf Hitler" - (Professor Abdul Hadi Palazzi)

• "Al-Aksa is not ours, and though the word comes from the word 'extreme,' it does not refer to the far mosque on the Temple Mount, but rather to a mosque that is the "further" of two mosques in Mecca." - (Renowned scholar of Arabic and Islamic studies Youssef Ziedan.)

• "Beit Hamikdash is a Hebrew term, hence, in my opinion, the al-Aksa mosque isn't legitimate. Al-Kuds, the temple, is an ancient Hebrew word, and Muslims adopted the word. You're annexing the city, annexing the word, and claiming that it is holy to you. But from where exactly? Can you tell a Jew that Jerusalem is not his? The religious aspect in the Arab-Israeli conflict is intentionally political" - (Youssef Ziedan, one of the most important researchers on religions in Egyptian academia)

• "According to our faith, Allah promised Israel to the Jewish people, and they are the sole official inheritors of that land. Therefore, the war of Muslims and Arabs against the Jews must stop, and they must let the Jews live in peace on their land." - (Sheikh Ahmad Adwan)

• Rabbi Aaron of Karlin wrote that the Land of Israel is like the Sabbath. The Land does not cease to be holy because some people violate its rules. - (Quoted by Rabbi Michael Skobac.)

• 28. JEWISH PALESTINE.

The following is part of the U.S. Congressional Record of 1922 by the members of Congress in favor of re-establishing Palestine as the historical land of the Jews. It says the name Palestine applied to the land of the Jews in alignment with the Hebrew Bible, the Dead Sea Scrolls, the land's archaeology and the region's theology:

• "Palestine of today, the land we now know as Palestine was peopled by the Jews from the dawn of history until the Roman era. It is the ancestral homeland of the Jewish people. They were driven from it by force by the relentless Roman military machine and for centuries prevented from returning. At different periods various alien people succeeded them, but the Jewish race had left an indelible impress upon the land. Every name, every landmark, every monument, and every trace of whatever civilization remaining there is still Jewish. And it has ever since remained a hope, a longing, as expressed in their prayers for these nearly 2,000 years. No other people have ever claimed Palestine as their national home." - Mr. Appleby, representative of New Jersey's 3rd Congressional district in the United States House of Representatives; 1922.

• 29. In Summary.

This thread has traced all source points of a 4,000 year history, theology, archaeology and the modern world's politics. Presented were Canaan, Israel, Judea, Palestine, The Philistines, Crete, Ancient

Egypt, Assyria, Babylon, Persia, The Greek Empire, The Roman Empire, The Vatican, Britain, America, Islamic and Christian Scholars, Islamic and Christian Scriptures, The Hebrew Bible, the UN and opinions and archives of prominent writers and figureheads from diverse and manifold sectors.

The multitude that promote an inversion of the term Palestine and Palestinian, intentionally or by sincere error, are not in concert of its historical or theological veracity, and do not appear as practicing and advocating truths that are based on humanity's history. Such deceptions do not assist Muslims, Christians, Jews, Arabs, Hindus, Buddhists, Atheists and all other institutions in our worldly community; instead they are made as victims by the legitimizing of a manipulated history that will impact all regions of humanity by extension and subsequence. This is already made manifest globally in the modern world.

This assessment is not vested in the offending of other groups or beliefs; rather, it is inclined with the negation of falsehoods that hold a theological doctrine negating an ancient nation's right to exist, despite that Israel was re-established legally via the UN.

30. A Solution.

The world's foremost figures and minds have endeavored to resolve the Middle East conflict; there is thereby a reason why all have failed and the conflict has instead extended globally. The history of this conflict says it cannot end in the absence of two deceptions being corrected as a minimum:

1. **The Historical Names Deception**s. That the terms 'Palestine' and its derivative 'Palestinian'; and the term 'West Bank' are covert genocide provisions that emulate the Roman Empire's deeds, one enacted again in the 20th Century. These name titles must be urgently and determinedly transferred as exclusive references to the Land of Israel, with the original Hebrew names of its towns restored. The new names are both un-historical and illegal implementations that constitute a heritage denial.

Jesus of Nazareth was not a Palestinian or an inhabitant of the West Bank; nor was King David or the Hebrew Patriarchs and Matriarchs who are laid to rest in Hebron.

No people should be compromised with the return of Israel; that they never existed as identifiable groups 4,000 years ago should only increase their belief; it was merited by choice not by choice-less genealogy. Usurping names does not turn falsehood into truth, nor can it change history.

2. **The Mathematical Accounting Deceptions.** That Jordan was the 2-state proclaimed by Britain via two treaties enacted in 1917 and 1948. A 3-state presented as a 2-state in the same landmass constitutes a genocide agenda that targets the minutest country in the region.

31. An Epiphany.

Give Israel what is of Israel.

A turn-around of restoring two deceptions appears unlikely with the accumulation of a worldly multitude and numerous organizations that have become vested in continuing an array of miss-information and miss-representation. Equally, it does not appear this conflict can diminish via any other means that do not include these two factors. The array of deceptions conducted at the UN aligns with a doctrine that insures Israel will hitherto always be charged as illegally occupying Israel. Thereby, the absence of a worldly epiphany to correct such grave miss-adventures renders an existential situation for Israel and an extension of the same issues extending globally. It has already begun. The history of this region affirms a syndrome of extension elsewhere by its precedence; its global impacts cannot be made as the onus of Israel.

The incumbent epiphany cannot come from the west, which has failed both the Jews and the Arabs with its 'Leave them fighting' stratagem, corrupting its own treaties and creating states with no conditions of rule for its own gains - not for the benefit of the people of this region.

It is the peoples of Islam which must see that a Roman Pope calling Arabs as Palestinians is such a falsehood that it negates the Gospels and surely not a truth. Muslims must not emulate this - verily your Holy Quran also told you which land is accounted as the 'Land of the Jews'. All scriptures have tests to see how we turn.

• "Why is it that on June 4th 1967 I was a Jordanian and overnight I became a Palestinian? The teaching of the destruction of Israel was a definite part of the curriculum, but we considered ourselves Jordanian until the Jews returned to Jerusalem. Then all of the sudden we were Palestinians - they removed the star from the Jordanian flag and all at once we had a Palestinian flag. When I finally realized the lies and myths I was taught it is my duty as a righteous person to speak out." - Walid Shoebat, a former PLO member.

"There is so much deceit…"

- Joan Peters, "From Time Immemorial: The Origins of the Arab-Jewish Conflict Over Palestine."

History Says:

Israel has never occupied another people's land in all her 4,000 year recorded history; Israel is the world's most accused country of illegally occupying another peoples' land.

What do you think will resolve this conflict for the benefit of all the other inhabitants of this region?

The End

Ethnic Cleansing of Jews from the Arab World

"WHEN I SEE A JEW BEFORE ME, I KILL HIM. IF EVERY ARAB DID THIS, IT WOULD BE THE END OF THE JEWS."

	# of Jews in 1948	Today
Algeria	140,000	100
Egypt	75,000	100
Iraq	150,000	35
Lebanon	20,000	100
Libya	38,000	0
Morocco	265,000	5,500
Syria	30,000	100
Tunisia	105,000	1,500
Yemen	55,000	200

AN ENTIRE HISTORY ERASED

Arab Jews lived as 2nd class citizens in the Arab world for centuries until the mid 20th century, when systematic policies of ethnic cleansing began.

MASS MURDER — STRIPPED OF CITIZENSHIP — CONFISCATION OF PROPERTY — SYNAGOGUES DESTROYED

Number of Jews in the Arab World: 878,000 (1948); 7,635 (Today)

... and now they say the Jewish State does not have a right to exist ...

When will this hatred end?

[1] Turn-Speak: Identity, origins & conflict in Israel; Zola Levitt Interview.

[2] The Amarna Letters. Letters from the Babylonian king, Kadashman-Enlil I, anchor in the time-frame of Akhenaten's reign to the mid-14th century BC. Here was also found the first mention of a Near Eastern group known as the Habiru, alluding to the battles waged by the Hebrews under Joshua: "They have seized the land of Rubute, the land of the king has fallen away to the Habiru..." [Language: Akkadian Cuneiform; Clay Tablets]

The Merneptah Stele - also known as The Israel Stele is an inscription by the Ancient Egyptian King Merneptah (reign: 1213 to 1203 BC). The writing provides the first evidence of the Hebrew tribes as active in the land and their interaction with the Pharaoh of Egypt and his armies engaged in a war. The last lines deal with a separate campaign in Canaan, then part of Egypt's imperial possessions, and include the first documented instance of the name Israel; Askelon, Urusalem; Canaan & Gaza: "Israel is laid waste and his seed is not.." -

[Discovered by Flinders Petriein in 1896 at Thebes; Housed at Egyptian Museum in Cairo/Merneptah Stele; Bible History/Archaeology/Israel/el-amarna-letters / [Language: Ancient Egyptian hieroglyphs]

[3] 1 Samuel 13:19:'Not a blacksmith could be found in the whole land of Israel.' / Book of Matthew, 2:20: 'Arise, and take the young child and his mother, and go into the land of Israel'.

[4] [Balfour Declaration, Faisal-Weizmann Agreement, W.W.2 Jewish Palestinian Brigade, US Presidents, Jewish National Institutions, Israeli Media]

[5] [Images: WorldEconimic Forum 2001; Davos, 2003; Palestinian Chief Negotiator Dr Saeb Erekat in London; 2014; NY 2014/ Creative Commons Attribution-ShareAlike 3.0 License.]

[6] The first known mention is at the temple at Medinat Habu which refers to the Peleset among those who fought with Egypt in Ramesses III's reign; Anceitn Recirds of Egypt: The first through the Seventeenth Dynasties, by James Henry Breasted, page 24.

[7] 'Therefore, the equation Arab = Ishmaelite is a myth, because Ishmael was not an Arab, nor the forefather of all Arabs' - (Origin and Identity of the Arabs; Myths, Hypotheses and Facts)

[8] From the Roman 'Palaestina' /Emp Hadrian/135 CE / The On-line Encyclopedia of the Roman Provinces. University of South Dakota. Archived from the original on 2009-08-11/Thomas S. McCall, Th.D. Palestine vs. Israel as the Name of the Holy Land, Zola Levitt Ministries.

[9] The History of the Words "Palestine" and "Palestinians"; Joseph E. Katz, Middle Eastern Political and Religious History Analyst, Brooklyn, New York.

[10] "They (the Philistines) met with a severe defeat, however, early in the reign of David (2 Samuel 5:20), he succeeded in reducing them to a state of vassalage (2 Samuel 8:1). In the year of the fall of Samaria (721 B.C.) they became vassals of Sargon. After the time of the Assyrians the Philistines cease to be mentioned by this name. In the ebb and flow of warring nations over this land it is more than probable that they were gradually absorbed and lost their identity. - [The Catholic Encyl.). / The Philistine cities lost their independence to Assyria, and revolts in following years were all crushed. [Myers 1997,

p. 313.] / The theory of the "Lost Ten Tribes" calls for (1) all inhabitants of the Northern Kingdom of Hoshea to be deported by Shalmaneser and Sargon, 722-718 B.C [Hearyhim, Weebly, Armstrongism] / They (the Canaanites) were indeed assimilated into the Israelite nation. When the Assyrians overran the Kingdom of Israel, they did not leave any Canaanite aside, as they had all become Israelites by that time. Therefore, the only people that can trace back a lineage to the ancient Canaanites are the Jews. The Canaanites did not exist any longer after the 8th century b.c.e. and they were not annihilated but assimilated into the Jewish people. - [The True Identity of the So-called Palestinians, imninalu] / The Bible describes the Philistines as remaining "subdued" during David's reign [Philistine; New World Encyl.]/ Josephus, Antiquities, Book 11, Ch.1] & [Esdras 13:39]

[11] FLAVIAN PROPAGANDA.

Vespasian gave financial rewards to ancient writers. The ancient historians of the period such as Tacitus, Suetonius, Josephus and Pliny the Elder speak suspiciously well of Vespasian while condemning the emperors that came before him. Tacitus admits that his status was elevated by Vespasian, Josephus identifies Vespasian as a patron and saviour, and Pliny dedicated his Natural Histories to Vespasian, Titus. Those that spoke against Vespasian were punished. A number of stoic philosophers were accused of corrupting students with inappropriate teachings and were expelled from Rome. Helvidius Priscus [70-79 AD/CE], a pro-republic philosopher, was executed for his teachings. - [Suetonius, The Lives of Twelve Caesars, Life of Vespasian; Tacitus, Histories I.1; Pliny the Elder, Natural Histories, preface]

Vespasian approved the histories written under his reign, thus ensuring biases against him were removed. - Josephus, Against Apion 9.

[12] Josephus Wars, Book V, Ch 13, 4.

[13] U.S. Presidents and Israel; Jewish Virtual Libr.

[14] In 1940, the Jews of Palestine were permitted to enlist in Jewish companies attached to the East Kent Regiment (the "Buffs"). These companies were formed into three infantry battalions of a newly-established "Palestine Regiment." The battalions were moved to Cyrenaica and Egypt, but there, too, as in Palestine, they continued to be engaged primarily in guard duties. The Jewish soldiers demanded

to participate in the fighting and the right to display the Jewish flag. Jewish Defense Organizations: The Jewish Brigade Group; Jewish Virtual Library.

[15] (James Parkes, Who's Land? A History of the Peoples of Palestine; Harmondsworth, Middlesex, Great Britain: Penguin Books, 1970, pp. 31, 26.)

[16] FLAVIAN PROPAGANDA. Vespasian gave financial rewards to ancient writers. The ancient historians of the period such as Tacitus, Suetonius, Josephus and Pliny the Elder speak suspiciously well of Vespasian while condemning the emperors that came before him. Tacitus admits that his status was elevated by Vespasian, Josephus identifies Vespasian as a patron and saviour, and Pliny dedicated his Natural Histories to Vespasian, Titus. Those that spoke against Vespasian were punished. A number of stoic philosophers were accused of corrupting students with inappropriate teachings and were expelled from Rome. Helvidius Priscus [70-79 AD/CE], a pro-republic philosopher, was executed for his teachings. - [Suetonius, The Lives of Twelve Caesars, Life of Vespasian; Tacitus, Histories I.1; Pliny the Elder, Natural Histories, preface]

[17] 'Londonistan: How Britain is Creating a Terror State Within', by Melanie Phillips, 2006

[18] Edict of Expulsion. In 1290, King Edward I issued an edict expelling all Jews from England. The expulsion edict remained in force for the rest of the Middle Ages. The edict was not an isolated incident, but the culmination of over 200 years of increased persecution [Wikipedia].

[19] Britain was one of the two most important military commands in the empire. Dio reports that Hadrian dispatched "his best generals" to crush the Jewish revolt. The "first of these" Generals (and the only one Dio names) was Julius Severus, who was dispatched from Britain, where he was governor and commanded the Roman troops. - [Cassius Dio, Roman History 69.13.2].

[20] "The Hashemite Kingdom of Jordan illegally occupied the West Bank [Judea and Samaria), while Egypt occupied Gaza." - (THE HATE AND HYPOCRISY OF THE BDS MOVEMENT; by Joseph Puder; Think-Israel Org.); Francisco [West Bank]

[21] In the Second Century CE, the Roman Emperor Hadrian determined to wipe out the identity of Israel-Judah-Judea. Therefore, he took the name Palastina and imposed it on all the Land of Israel. - (Tzemach Institute for Biblical Studies)

[22] "The Jerusalem Temple was destroyed in 587/586 BCE, when the Babylonians captured the city, torched it and exiled the Judean leadership to Babylon" - (The Destruction of the Temple; Tamara Ashkenazi; Bible Odyssey Org.)

[23] Israel developed into a united kingdom under the leadership of King David (c.1000-960 BCE) who consolidated the various tribes under his single rule (having taken over from Israel's first king, Saul, who ruled circa 1020 BCE). David chose the Canaanite city of Jerusalem as his capital and is said to have had the Ark of the Covenant moved there. - (by Joshua J. Mark, Ancient History Encyl.)

[24] 'There were no mosques in Jerusalem in 632CE when the Prophet Mohammed died... Jerusalem was [then] a Christian city' - by Dr. Manfred R. Lehmann. / 'In the year 637 the armies of Islam lead by the Caliph Omar conquered the city of Jerusalem, the centre of the Christian world and a magnet for Christian pilgrims.' - (Eye Witness to History Org; The Crusaders Capture Jerusalem.)

[25] Jerusalem was a Christian city within the Byzantine Empire. Jerusalem was captured by Khalif Omar only in 638, six years after Mohammed's death. Throughout all this time there were only churches in Jerusalem, and a church stood on the Temple Mount, called the Church of Saint Mary of Justinian, built in the Byzantine architectural style. by Dr. Manfred R. Lehmann, DR. MANFRED R. LEHMANN was a writer for the Algemeiner Journal.

[26] Muslim Period; American University

[27] Muslim Period; American University.

[28] "Jerusalem Blessed, Jerusalem Cursed" by Thomas A. Idinopulos. Ivan R. Dee: Chicago; 1991; pg: 23-24

[29] 'Les Sept Vies de Yasser Arafat' by French Biographers Christophe Boltanski and Jihan El-Tahri; Romanian Intelligence Official Ian Pacepa disclosed that the KGB invented Jerusalem birthplace.

[30] King David. An inscription dating from the 10th century BCE (the period of King David's reign) has been deciphered, showing that

it is a Hebrew inscription. The discovery makes this the earliest known Hebrew writing, according to one scholar. Professor Gershon Galil of the Department of Biblical Studies at the University of Haifa has deciphered an inscription on a pottery shard discovered in the Elah valley dating from the 10th century BCE (the period of King David's reign), and has shown that this is a Hebrew inscription. The discovery makes this the earliest known Hebrew writing. It indicates that the Kingdom of Israel already existed in the 10th century BCE and that at least some of the biblical texts were written hundreds of years before the dates presented in current research."- ["Most ancient Hebrew biblical inscription deciphered"; ScienceDaily.]

[31] Hussein-McMahon Correspondence.

[32] - (WW1 Document Archive - Letters between Hussein Ibn Ali and Sir Henry Mcmahon; Library BYU Education/Index php. /'who are Palestinians?' Memri)

[33] ONE MILLION BIBLICAL & HISTORICAL ARTEFACTS. Israel Relics Collection: National archaeological centre to store and showcase country's rich collection of some two million ancient artifacts, including world's largest collection of Dead Sea Scrolls. [Israel Antiquities Authority, Associated Press, Ynet/0, 7340, L-4500754, 00] / Israel Relics Display: The Israel Antiquities Authorities estimates that there are one million archaeological artifacts on display in Israel at present. - [Israel National News/ aspx/132808].

[34] (Marjorie M. Whiteman, Digest of International Law, vol. 1, US State Department, pp 650-652).

[35] Briton Recruits. Dio reports that Hadrian dispatched "his best generals" to crush the Jewish revolt. The "first of these" Generals (and the only one Dio names) was Julius Severus, who was dispatched from Britain, where he was governor and commanded the Roman troops. Britain was one of the two most important military commands in the empire. - [Cassius Dio, Roman History 69.13.2]

[36] "As I lived in Palestine, everyone I knew could trace their heritage back to the original country their great grandparents came from. Everyone knew their origin was not from the Canaanites, but ironically, this is the kind of stuff our education in the Middle East included. The fact is that today's Palestinians are immigrants from the surrounding nations! I grew up well knowing the history and origins of today's Palestinians as being from Yemen, Saudi Arabia, Morocco,

Christians from Greece, Muslim Sherkas from Russia, Muslims from Bosnia, and the Jordanians next door. My grandfather used to tell us that his village Beit Sahur (The Shepherds Fields) in Bethlehem County was empty before his father settled in the area with six other families". - Walid Shoebat, an "ex-Palestinian" Arab." and terrorism expert on several television appearances including on CNN, The BBC, Fox News and CNN] // "There has never been a land known as Palestine governed by Palestinians. Palestinians are Arabs, indistinguishable from Jordanians (another recent invention), Syrians, Iraqis, etc. - [Joseph Farah, "Myths of the Middle East"]

[37] ONE MILLION BIBLICAL & HISTORICAL ARTEFACTS. Israel Relics Collection: National archaeological centre to store and showcase country's rich collection of some two million ancient artifacts, including world's largest collection of Dead Sea Scrolls. [Israel Antiquities Authority, Associated Press, Ynet/0, 7340, L-4500754, 00] / Israel Relics Display: The Israel Antiquities Authorities estimates that there are one million archaeological artifacts on display in Israel at present. - [Israel National News/ aspx/132808]

[38] Titus, son of Emperor Vespasian and who destroyed the Jerusalem Temple, charges Arabian and Roman soldiers as barbarians when corpses are disemboweled for gold - Josephus Wars, Book V, Ch 13, 4.

[39] "The al-Aqsa Mosque was built on top of Solomon's Temple." - Eleventh century historian Muhammad Ibn Ahmad al-Maqdisi and fourteenth century Iranian religious scholar Hamdallah al-Mustawfi ["Allah Gave the Land of Israel to the Jews", JerusalemOnLine].

[40] "During the last few centuries, the world, Christians included, has fallen into a bad habit. We have bought into some early Roman propaganda. We have used the name Palestine, which Roman Emperor Hadrian placed on the country of Israel in 135 A.D., for so long that it has become common usage. There is a propaganda war going on now with regard to the term "Palestine." It is specifically employed to avoid the use of the name Israel, and must be considered an anti-Israel term. In all Arab maps published in Jordan, Egypt, etc., the area west of the Jordan River is called Palestine, without any reference to Israel. Palestine is the term now used by those who want to deny the legitimate existence of Israel as a genuine nation among the family of nations." - [Dr. Thomas McCall, the Senior Theologian of Levitt Ministry, quoting Zola Levitt]

387

[41] An absence of Arab records and imprints in ancient Egypt is the primary deficiency / "The Copts are the proper representatives of the Ancient Egyptians", which is neither Greek, Negro nor Arab" - Count Volney, 18th century / In the early 20th century, Flinders Petrie, a Professor of Egyptology at the University of London, described a Nubian queen, Aohmes Nefertari, who was the "divine ancestress of the XVIIIth dynasty" as having "had an aquiline nose, long and thin, and was of a type not in the least prognathous." - Petrie, Flinders (1939). The Making of Egypt. New York: The Sheldon Press. pp. 105, 155. / "The Moslem population of Egypt (about 90%) are Arab settlers from the Arab Peninsula (Saudi Arabia.) The Christian population (about 10%) is the true Egyptians, referred to as Copts, and the descendants of the ancient Egyptians." - 'WHO ARE THESE MODERN DAY EGYPTIANS?' By Moustafa Gadalla, Egyptian-American independent Egyptologist, who was born in Cairo, Egypt in 1944. / "Prior to the Arab conquest of Egypt in the 7th century AD, the Egyptians spoke Coptic, a later phase of ancient Egyptian. Following the Arab conquest, there was a prolonged period of time when both Coptic and Arabic were spoken in Egypt" - By Irene Thompson, About World Languages. / Many nations invaded Egypt, including the Greeks, Romans, Christianity and Islam; some Arab scholars uphold Egyptian lineage, some Europeans even point to Aryan and African sources. /

[42] Canaanites were NOT Arabs. Today the ancient Canaanites are represented by two nations: the Phoenicians are Lebanese, while the Yevusites, Hivvites, Amorites and other mountain tribes are now Jews. Lebanon is erroneously considered an "Arab" country, since the Lebanese themselves do not agree with such classification. - [Concerning the Origin of Peoples, Origin and Identity of the Arabs; Myths, Hypotheses and Facts.]

[43] "An unnamed king boasts of his victories over the king of Israel and his ally the king of the "House of David" (bytdwd), the first time the name David had been found outside of the Bible" - Finkelstein 2007, p.14. // "A breakthrough in the research of the Hebrew Scriptures has shed new light on the period in which the Bible was written. Prof. Gershon Galil of the Department of Biblical Studies has deciphered an inscription dating from the 10th century BCE (the period of King David's reign). The discovery makes this the earliest known Hebrew writing. The significance of this breakthrough relates to the fact that at least some of the biblical scriptures were composed

388

hundreds of years before the dates presented today in research and that the Kingdom of Israel already existed at that time." - Phys.org/News 182101034.

[44] DEAD SEA SCROLLS. 8th century BCE: "The Digital Library: Introduction" Leon Levy/ Dead Sea Scrolls Digital Library. Dated as 408 BCE to 318 CE and from around 600 BCE. - Wikipedia.

[45] Ancient Scripts Org.

[46] "Rabbi Ishmael ben Elisha Kohen Gadol", lit. "Rabbi Ishmael ben (son of) Elisha [the] Kohen Gadol (High priest)"; sometimes in short Ishmael ha-Kohen, lit. "Ishmael the Priest") was one of the prominent leaders of the first generation of the Tannaim. [Wikipeda] // Rabbi Ishmael, the High Priest [Sacred-texts jud/pol17]

[47] Scholars believe that the earliest extant example of Arabic script is a royal funerary inscription of the Nabataeans dating from AD 328. Others believe that this epigraph shows characteristics of Arabic but is essentially Aramaic and that the earliest extant example of Arabic is a trilingual inscription in Greek, Syriac, and Arabic dating from AD512. [Encyl. Britannica]

[48] Dunn, James G.; Rogerston, John William (2003).Eerdmans Commentary on the Bible. Wm. B. Eerdmans Publishing. p. 545.

[49] This is the first known reference to the Arabs as a distinct group. [History of the Arabs, History World]

[50] The Mounting Problem of Temple Denial, Daily Alert Org.

[51] Muslim Scholar: "Allah Gave Israel to the Jews". [Front Page Magazine, February 8, 2014].

Thank You!

Shhhh! Studios

Out Now!

**What 'REALY' Happened
In the First Century?**

Made in the USA
Middletown, DE
12 November 2023

42539241R00216